# Марк Яковлевич Блох

**Марк Яковлевич Блох** — известный ученый-лингвист, доктор филологических наук, профессор.

Заведует кафедрой грамматики и истории английского языка Московского государственного педагогического университета. Ведет исследовательскую работу в области теории английского языка, общего, типологического и германского языкознания, теории перевода, лингводидактики.

В рамках выдвинутых проф. М.Я.Блохом научных направлений успешно работают его многочисленные ученики—кандидаты и доктора филологических наук.

# М.Я.Блох

# Теоретическая грамматика английского языка

Издание третье, исправленное

*Рекомендовано
Министерством образования
Российской Федерации
в качестве учебника
для студентов институтов
и факультетов иностранных языков*

Москва
«Высшая школа»
2000

UDK 802.0
ББК 81.2 Англ
Б 70

Рецензент:

кафедра грамматики и истории английского языка Московского государственного лингвистического университета (зав. кафедрой проф. Т.С. Сорокина)

ISBN 5-06-003669-3

# FOREWORD

The present theoretical outline of English grammar, 3rd edition, is intended as a manual for the departments of English in universities and teacher training colleges. Its purpose is to introduce the students into the problems of up-to-date grammatical study of English on a systemic basis, sustained by demonstrations of applying modern analytical techniques to various grammatical phenomena of living English speech.

The given description of the grammatical structure of English, naturally, is not to be regarded as exhaustive in any point of detail. The author's immediate aims were to supply the students with such information as will enable them to form judgements of their own on questions of diverse grammatical intricacies (the practical mastery of the elements of English grammar is supposed to have been gained by the students at the earlier stages of tuition); to bring forth in the students a steady habit of trying to see into the deeper implications underlying the outward appearances of lingual correlations bearing on grammar; to teach them to independently improve their linguistic qualifications through reading and critically appraising the available works on grammatical language study; to foster their competence in facing academic controversies concerning problems of grammar.

The emphasis laid on cultivating an active element in the student's approach to language and its grammar explains why the book gives prominence both to the technicalities of grammatical observations and to the general methodology of linguistic knowledge: the due application of the latter will lend the necessary demonstrative force to any serious consideration of the many special points of grammatical analysis. In this connection, the author has tried, throughout the whole of the book, to point out the progressive character of the development of modern grammatical theory. Indeed, one is to clearly understand that in the course of disputes and continued research in manifold particular fields, the grammatical section of the science of language arrives at an ever more adequate presentation of the structure of language in its integral description.

This kind of outlining the foundations of the discipline in question is especially important at the present stage of the developing linguistic knowledge — the knowledge which has found itself in the midst of the radical advance of science characteristic of the last decades of the XX century.

In preparing the third edition of the book the author has been guided by the experience gained from its academic use since the first publication in 1983 and second publication in 1994. During this time a number of new ideas have been put forward both in general and English linguistics that should be presented to the students. It especially concerns the theory of units of language and levels of language and the linguistic study of continual text. The main additions and revisions made by the author mostly deal with these important fields of description.

Materials illustrating the analysed elements of English grammar have been mostly collected from the literary works of British and American authors. Some of the cited examples have been subjected to slight alterations aimed at giving the necessary prominence to the lingual phenomena under study. Source references for limited stretches of text are not supplied except in cases of special relevance (such as implications of individual style or involvement in contextual background).

The author pays tribute to his friends and colleagues — teachers of the Moscow State Pedagogical University for encouragement and help they extended during the years of his work on the subject matter of the book.

The author wishes to express his gratitude to the staff of the Department of Grammar and History of English of the Moscow State Linguistic University, and in particular to the Head of the Department Prof. T.S. Sorokina, for the careful review of the book.

The author's sincere thanks are due to Prof. O.V. Alexandrova, Prof. N.A. Kobrina, Prof. A.T. Krivonosov, Prof. E.S. Kubryakova, Prof. F.A. Litvin, Prof. M.M. Makovsky, Prof. F.I. Mauler, Prof. S.M. Mezenin, Prof. L.L. Nyelubin, Prof. V.Y. Plotkin, Prof. G.G. Pocheptsov, Prof. S.G. Ter-Minasova, Prof. N.N. Semenyuk, Prof. Z.Y. Turayeva and all other specialists who shared with him their opinions and criticisms touching upon the matters presented. Their expert suggestions have been very helpful in bringing the text to its final shape.

*M. Blokh*

CHAPTER I

# GRAMMAR IN THE SYSTEMIC CONCEPTION OF LANGUAGE

§ 1. Language is a means of forming and storing ideas as reflections of reality and exchanging them in the process of human intercourse. Language is social by nature; it is inseparably connected with the people who are its creators and users; it grows and develops together with the development of society.

Language incorporates the three constituent parts ("sides"), each being inherent in it by virtue of its social nature. These parts are the phonological system, the lexical system, the grammatical system. Only the unity of these three elements forms a language; without any one of them there is no human language in the above sense.

The phonological system is the subfoundation of language; it determines the material (phonetical) appearance of its significative units. The lexical system is the whole set of naming means of language, that is, words and stable word-groups. The grammatical system is the whole set of regularities determining the combination of naming means in the formation of utterances as the embodiment of thinking process.

Each of the three constituent parts of language is studied by a particular linguistic discipline. These disciplines, presenting a series of approaches to their particular objects of analysis, give the corresponding "descriptions" of language consisting in ordered expositions of the constituent parts in question. Thus, the phonological description of language is effected by the science of phonology; the lexical description of language is effected by the science of lexicology; the grammatical description of language is effected by the science of grammar.

Any linguistic description may have a practical or theoretical purpose. A practical description is aimed at providing the student with a manual of practical mastery of the corresponding part of language (within the limits determined by various factors of educational destination and scientific possibilities). Since the practice of lingual intercourse, however, can only be realized by employing language as a unity of all its constituent parts, practical linguistic manuals more often than not comprise the three types of description presented in a complex. As for theoretical linguistic descriptions, they pursue analytical aims and therefore present the studied parts of language in relative isolation, so as to gain insights into their inner structure and expose the intrinsic mechanisms of their functioning. Hence, the aim of theoretical grammar of a language is to present a theoretical description of its grammatical system, i.e. to scientifically analyse and define its grammatical categories and study the mechanisms of grammatical formation of utterances out of words in the process of speech making.

§ 2. In earlier periods of the development of linguistic knowledge, grammatical scholars believed that the only purpose of grammar was to give strict rules of writing and speaking correctly. The rigid regulations for the correct ways of expression, for want of the profound understanding of the social nature of language, were often based on purely subjective and arbitrary judgments of individual grammar compilers. The result of this "prescriptive" approach was that alongside quite essential and useful information, non-existent "rules" were formulated that stood in sheer contradiction with the existing language usage, i.e. lingual reality. Traces of this arbitrary prescriptive approach to the grammatical teaching may easily be found even in to-date's school practice.

To refer to some of the numerous examples of this kind, let us consider the well-known rule of the English article stating that the noun which denotes an object "already known" by the listener should be used with the definite article. Observe, however, English sentences taken from the works of distinguished authors directly contradicting this "rule".

"I've just read *a* book of yours about Spain and I wanted to ask you about it." – "It's not *a* very good book, I'm afraid" (S. Maugham). I feel a good deal of hesitation about telling you this story of my own. You see it is not *a* story like other stories I have been telling you: it is *a* true story (J.K. Jerome).

Or let us take the rule forbidding the use of the continuous tense-forms with the verb *be* as a link, as well as with verbs of perception. Here are examples to the contrary:

My holiday at Crome *isn't being* a disappointment (A. Huxley). For the first time, Bobby felt, he *was* really *seeing* the man (A. Christie).

The given examples of English articles and verb-forms, though not agreeing with the above "prescriptions", contain no grammar mistakes in them.

The said traditional view of the purpose of grammar has lately been re-stated by some modern trends in linguistics. In particular, scholars belonging to these trends pay much attention to artificially constructing and analysing incorrect utterances with the aim of a better formulation of the rules for the construction of correct ones. But their examples and deductions, too, are often at variance with real facts of lingual usage.

Worthy of note are the following two artificial utterances suggested as far back as 1956:

*Colourless green ideas sleep furiously. Furiously sleep ideas green colourless.*

According to the idea of their creator, the prominent American scholar N. Chomsky, the first of the utterances, although nonsensical logically, was to be classed as grammatically correct, while the second one, consisting of the same words placed in the reverse order, had to be analysed as a disconnected, "ungrammatical" enumeration, a "non-sentence". Thus, the examples, by way of contrast, were intensely demonstrative (so believed the scholar) of the fact that grammar as a whole amounted to a set of non-semantic rules of sentence formation.

However, a couple of years later this assessment of the lingual value of the given utterances was disputed in an experimental investigation with informants – natural speakers of English, who could not come to a unanimous conclusion about the correctness or incorrectness of both of them. In particular, some of the informants classed the second utterance as "sounding like poetry".

To understand the contradictions between the bluntly formulated "rules" and reality, as well as to evaluate properly the results of informant tests like the one mentioned above, we must bear in mind that the true grammatical rules or regularities cannot be separated from the expression of meanings; on the contrary, they are themselves meaningful. Namely, they are connected with the most general and abstract parts of content inherent in the elements of language. These parts of content, together with the formal means through which they are expressed, are treated by grammarians in terms of "grammatical categories". Such are, for instance, the categories of number or mood in morphology, the categories of communicative purpose or emphasis in syntax, etc. Since the grammatical forms and regularities are meaningful, it becomes clear that the rules of grammar must be stated semantically, or, more specifically, they must be worded functionally. For example, it would be fallacious to state without any further comment that the inverted word order in the

English declarative sentence is grammatically incorrect. Word order as an element of grammatical form is laden with its own meaningful functions. It can express, in particular, the difference between the central idea of the utterance and the marginal idea, between emotive and unemotive modes of speech, between different types of style. Thus, if the inverted word order in a given sentence does express these functions, then its use should be considered as quite correct. *E.g.:*

In the centre of the room, under the chandelier, as became a host, stood *the head of the family, old Jolyon himself* (J. Galsworthy).

The word arrangement in the utterance expresses a narrative description, with the central informative element placed in the strongest semantic position in narration, i.e. at the end. Compare the same sort of arrangement accompanying a plainer presentation of subject matter:

Inside on a wooden bunk lay *a young Indian woman* (E. Hemingway).

Compare, further, the following:

And ever *did his Soul tempt* him with evil, and whisper of terrible things. Yet *did it not prevail* against him, so great was the power of his love (O. Wilde). (Here the inverted word order is employed to render intense emphasis in a legend-stylised narration.) One thing and one thing only *could she* do for him (R. Kipling). (Inversion in this case is used to express emotional intensification of the central idea.)

Examples of this and similar kinds will be found in plenty in modern English literary texts of good style repute.

§ 3. The nature of grammar as a constituent part of language is better understood in the light of explicitly discriminating the two planes of language, namely, the plane of content and the plane of expression.

The plane of content comprises the purely semantic elements contained in language, while the plane of expression comprises the material (formal) units of language taken by themselves, apart from the meanings rendered by them. The two planes are inseparably connected, so that no meaning can be realised without some material means of expression. Grammatical elements of language present a unity of content and expression (or, in somewhat more familiar terms, a unity of form and meaning). In this the grammatical elements are similar to the lingual lexical elements, though the quality of grammatical meanings, as we have stated above, is different in principle from the quality of lexical meanings.

On the other hand, the correspondence between the planes of content and expression is very complex, and it is peculiar to each language. This complexity is clearly illustrated by the phenomena of polysemy, homonymy, and synonymy.

In cases of polysemy and homonymy, two or more units of the plane of content correspond to one unit of the plane of expression. For instance, the verbal form of the present indefinite (one unit in the plane of expression) polysemantically renders the grammatical meanings of habitual action, action at the present moment, action taken as a general truth (several units in the plane of content). *E.g.:*

I get up at half past six in the morning. I do see your point clearly now. As a rational being, I hate war.

The morphemic material element -s / -es (in pronunciation [-s, -z, -ɪz]), i.e. one unit in the plane of expression (in so far as the functional semantics of the elements is common to all of them indiscriminately), homonymically renders the grammatical meanings of the third person singular of the verbal present tense, the plural of the noun, the possessive form of the noun, i.e. several units of the plane of content. *E.g.:*

John trusts his friends. We have new desks in our classroom. The chief's order came as a surprise.

In cases of synonymy, conversely, two or more units of the plane of expression correspond to one unit of the plane of content. For instance, the forms of the verbal future indefinite, future continuous, and present continuous (several units in the plane of expression) can in certain contexts synonymically render the meaning of a future action (one unit in the plane of content). *E.g.:*

Will you come to the party, too? Will you be coming to the party, too? Are you coming to the party, too?

Taking into consideration the discrimination between the two planes, we may say that the purpose of grammar as a linguistic discipline is, in the long run, to disclose and formulate the regularities of the correspondence between the plane of content and the plane of expression in the formation of utterances out of the stocks of words as part of the process of speech production.

§ 4. Modern linguistics lays a special stress on the systemic character of language and all its constituent parts. It accentuates the idea that language is a system of signs (meaningful units) which are closely interconnected and interdependent. Units of immediate interdependencies (such as classes and subclasses of words, various subtypes of syntactic construction, etc.) form different microsystems (subsystems) within the framework of the global macrosystem (supersystem) of the whole of language.

Each system is a structured set of elements related to one another by a common function. The common function of all the lingual signs is to give expression to human thoughts.

The systemic nature of grammar is probably more evident than that of any other sphere of language, since grammar is responsible for the very organization of the informative content of utterances [Блох, 1986, 11]. Due to this fact, even the earliest grammatical treatises, within the cognitive limits of their times, disclosed some systemic features of the described material. But the scientifically sustained and consistent principles of systemic approach to language and its grammar were essentially developed in the linguistics of the twentieth century, namely, after the publication of the works by the Russian scholar Beaudoin de Courtenay and the Swiss scholar Ferdinand de Saussure. These two great men demonstrated the difference between lingual synchrony (coexistence of lingual elements) and diachrony (different time-periods in the development of lingual elements as well as language as a whole) and defined language as a synchronic system of meaningful elements at any stage of its historical evolution.

On the basis of discriminating synchrony and diachrony, the difference between language proper and speech proper can be strictly defined, which is of crucial importance for the identification of the object of linguistic science.

Language in the narrow sense of the word is a system of means of expression, while speech in the same narrow sense should be understood as the manifestation of the system of language in the process of intercourse.

The system of language includes, on the one hand, the body of material units – sounds, morphemes, words, word-groups; on the other hand, the regularities or "rules" of the use of these units. Speech comprises both the act of producing utterances, and the utterances themselves, i.e. the text. Language and speech are inseparable, they form together an organic unity. As for grammar (the grammatical system), being an integral part of the lingual macrosystem it dynamically connects language with speech, because it categorially determines the lingual process of utterance production.

Thus, we have broad philosophical concept of language which is analysed by linguistics into two different aspects – the system of signs (language proper) and the use of signs (speech proper). The generalizing term "language" is also preserved in linguistics, showing the unity of these two aspects [Блох, 1986, 18].

The sign (meaningful unit) in the system of language has only a potential meaning. In speech, the potential meaning of the lingual sign is "actualized", i.e. made situationally significant as part of the grammatically organized text.

Lingual units stand to one another in two fundamental types of relations: *syntagmatic* and *paradigmatic*.

*Syntagmatic* relations are immediate linear relations between units in a segmental sequence (string). *E.g.*:

The spaceship was launched without the help of a booster rocket.

In this sentence syntagmatically connected are the words and word-groups "the spaceship", "was launched", "the spaceship was launched", "was launched without the help", "the help of a rocket", "a booster rocket".

Morphemes within the words are also connected syntagmatically. *E.g.*: space/ship; launch/ed; with/out; boost/er.

Phonemes are connected syntagmatically within morphemes and words, as well as at various juncture points (*cf.* the processes of assimilation and dissimilation).

The combination of two words or word-groups one of which is modified by the other forms a unit which is referred to as a syntactic "syntagma". There are four main types of notional syntagmas: *predicative* (the combination of a subject and a predicate), *objective* (the combination of a verb and its object), *attributive* (the combination of a noun and its attribute), *adverbial* (the combination of a modified notional word, such as a verb, adjective, or adverb, with its adverbial modifier).

Since syntagmatic relations are actually observed in utterances, they are described by the Latin formula as relations "in praesentia" ("in the presence").

The other type of relations, opposed to syntagmatic and called *"paradigmatic"*, are such as exist between elements of the system outside the strings where they co-occur. These intra-systemic relations and dependencies find their expression in the fact that each lingual unit is included in a set or series of connections based on different formal and functional properties.

In the sphere of phonology such series are built up by the correlations of phonemes on the basis of vocality or consonantism, voicedness or devoicedness, the factor of nazalization, the factor of length, etc. In the sphere of the vocabulary these series are founded on the correlations of synonymy and antonymy, on various topical connections, on different word-building dependencies. In the domain of grammar, series of related forms realize grammatical numbers and cases, persons and tenses, gradations of modalities, sets of sentence patterns of various functional nature, etc.

Unlike syntagmatic relations, paradigmatic relations cannot be directly observed in utterances, that is why they are referred to as relations "in absentia" ("in the absence").

Paradigmatic relations coexist with syntagmatic relations in such a way that some sort of syntagmatic connection is necessary for the realization of any paradigmatic series. This is especially evident in a classical grammatical paradigm which presents a productive series of forms each consisting of a syntagmatic connection of two elements: one common for the whole of the series (stem), the other specific for every individual form in the series (grammatical feature – inflexion, suffix, auxiliary word). Grammatical paradigms express various grammatical categories.

The minimal paradigm consists of two form-stages. This kind of paradigm we see, for instance, in the expression of the category of number: *boy – boys*. A more complex paradigm can be divided into component paradigmatic series, i.e. into the corresponding sub-paradigms (*cf.* numerous paradigmatic series constituting the system of the finite verb). In other words, with paradigms, the same as with any other systemically organized material, macro- and micro-series are to be discriminated.

§ 5. Units of language are divided into *segmental* and *supra-segmental*. Segmental units consist of phonemes, they form phonemic strings of various status (syllables, morphemes, words, etc.). Supra-segmental units do not exist by themselves, but are realized together with segmental units and express different modificational meanings (functions) which are reflected on the strings of segmental units. To the supra-segmental units belong intonations (intonation contours), accents, pauses, patterns of word-order.

The segmental units of language form a hierarchy of levels. This hierarchy is of a kind that units of any higher level are analysable into (i.e. are formed of) units of the immediately lower level. Thus, morphemes are decomposed into phonemes, words are decomposed into morphemes, phrases are decomposed into words, etc.

But this hierarchical relation is by no means reduced to the mechanical composition of larger units from smaller ones; units of each level are characterized by their own, specific functional features which provide for the very recognition of the corresponding levels of language.

The lowest level of lingual segments is *phonemic*: it is formed by phonemes as the material elements of the higher-level segments. The phoneme has no meaning, its function is purely differential: it differentiates morphemes and words as material bodies. Since the phoneme has no meaning, it is not a sign.

Phonemes are combined into syllables. The syllable, a rhythmic segmental group of phonemes, is not a sign, either; it has a purely formal significance. Due to this fact, it could hardly stand to reason to recognize in language a separate syllabic level; rather, the syllables should be considered in the light of the intra-level combinability properties of phonemes.

Phonemes are represented by letters in writing. Since the letter has a representative status, it is a sign, though different in principle from the level-forming signs of language.

Units of all the higher levels of language are meaningful; they may be called "signemes" as opposed to "cortemes" (from Lat. *cortex* "bark, crust, shell"), i.e. non-meaningful units of different status, such as phonemes (and letters as phoneme representatives), syllables, and some others.

The level located above the phonemic one is the *morphemic* level. The morpheme is the elementary meaningful part of the word. It is built up by phonemes, so that the shortest morphemes include only one phoneme. *E.g.*: ros-y [-ɪ]; a-fire [ə-]; come-s [-z].

The morpheme expresses abstract, "significative" meanings which are used as constituents for the formation of more concrete, "nominative" meanings of words.

The third level in the segmental lingual hierarchy is the level of words, or *lexemic* level.

The word (lexeme), as different from the morpheme, is a directly naming (nominative) unit of language: it names things and their relations. Since words are built up by morphemes, the shortest words consist of one explicit morpheme only. *Cf.*: man; will; but; I; etc.

The next higher unit is the phrase (word-group), it is located at the *phrasemic* level. To level-forming phrase types belong combinations of two or more notional words. These combinations, like separate words, have a nominative function, but they represent the referent of nomination as a complicated phenomenon, be it a concrete thing, an action, a quality, or a whole situation. *Cf.,* respectively: a picturesque village; to start with a jerk; extremely difficult; the unexpected arrival of the chief.

This kind of nomination can be called "polynomination", as different from "mononomination" effected by separate words.

Notional phrases may be of a stable type and of a free type. The stable phrases (phraseological units) form the phraseological part of the lexicon, and are studied by the phraseological division of lexicology. Free phrases are built up in the process of speech on the existing productive models, and are studied in the lower division of syntax. The grammatical description of phrases is sometimes called "minor syntax", in distinction to "major syntax" studying the sentence and its textual connections.

In order to better understand the nature of phrases as level-forming units we must take into consideration their status in the larger lingual units built up by them. These larger units are sentences. It is within the sentence that any phrase performs its level-determined function (being used as a notional part of the sentence). On the other hand, any notional word, not only a phrase, can be used in the role of a separate part of the sentence, such as subject, object, predicate, etc. We infer from this that in more exact terms the units located above the words in the segmental lingual hierarchy are notional parts of the sentence. These can be formed by phrases (word-groups), or by separate notional words. Since the function of these parts is *denotative* (they not only name, but also indicate, or *denote,* objects and phenomena involved in the situation expressed by the sentence), they may be called "*denotemes*" (in the previous editions of the book they were referred to as "nomemes"). The level at which denotemes are identified is then the *denotemic* level of language. In this connection, the phrasemic level should be presented as the upper sublevel of the denotemic level. The demonstrated approach marks the necessary development of the theory of levels of language emphasizing the strictly hierarchical principle of inter-level derivational relations of lingual units (see above).

Above the denotemic level, the level of sentences is located, or the *proposemic* level.

The peculiar character of the sentence ("proposeme") as a signemic unit of language consists in the fact that, naming a certain situation, or situational event, it expresses predication, i.e. shows the relation of the denoted event to reality. Namely, it shows whether this event is real or unreal, desirable or obligatory, stated as a truth or asked about, etc. In this sense, as different from the word and the phrase, the sentence is a predicative unit. *Cf.*: to receive – to receive a letter – Early in June I received a letter from Peter Melrose.

The sentence is produced by the speaker in the process of speech as a concrete, situationally bound utterance. At the same time it enters the system of language by its syntactic pattern which, as all the other lingual unit-types, has both syntagmatic and paradigmatic characteristics.

But the sentence is not the highest unit of language in the hierarchy of levels. Above the proposemic level there is still another one whose units are formed by separate sentences united into topical groupings. These sentence-groups each distinguished by its micro-topic as part of a continual text are tentatively called "super-sentential constructions". For the sake of unified terminology, the level at which they are identified can be called "supra-proposemic".

In the printed text, the supra-sentential construction very often coincides with the paragraph (as in the example above).

The supra-sentential construction is a combination of separate sentences forming a textual unity. Such combinations are subject to regular lingual patterning making them into syntactic elements. The syntactic process by which sentences are connected into textual unities is analysed under the heading of "cumulation". Cumulation, the same as formation of composite sentences, can be both syndetic and asyndetic. *Cf.*:

He went on with his interrupted breakfast. Lisette did not speak and there was silence between them. *But* his appetite satisfied, his mood changed; he began to feel sorry for himself rather than angry with her, and with a strange ignorance of woman's heart he thought to arouse Lisette's remorse by exhibiting himself as an object of pity (S. Maugham).

In the printed text, the supra-sentential construction very often coincides with the paragraph (as in the example above). However, the constitutive unit of the level in question, obeying the universal derivational regularity of segmental lingual hierarchy, should be reducible to one sentence only, the same as the sentence is reducible to one denoteme (sentence-part), the same as the nomeme is re-ducible to one lexeme (word), etc. This regularity considered, we come to the conclusion that the generalized unit that is located above the sentence and is distinguished by its topical (micro-topical) function is not necessarily represented by a group of sentences, i.e. by a super-sentential construction; in general terms, this unit is formed either by a group of sentences (a super-sentential construction shown above), or by one separate sentence which is placed in a semantically (topically) significant position in speech. In oral speech it is delimited by a long pause combined with the corresponding "concluding" tone of voice. We have called this generalized unit the "dicteme" (from Lat. *dico* "I speak") [Блох, 1986, 48]. In written (printed) text it is often represented by a sentence-paragraph, i.e. by a paragraph formed by a single independent sentence.

Thus, from the point of view of its constitutive units, the supra-sentential level may be called the *dictemic level*, the *dicteme* being defined as an elementary topical segmental unit of the continual text.

We have surveyed six levels of language, each identified by its own, functional type of segmental units. If now we carefully observe the functional status of the level-forming segments, we can distinguish between them more self-sufficient and less self-sufficient types, the latter being defined only in relation to the functions of other level units. Indeed, the phonemic, lexemic and proposemic levels are most strictly and exhaustively identified from the functional point of view: the function of the phoneme is differential, the function of the word is nominative, the function of the sentence is predicative. As different from these, morphemes are identified only as significative components of words, denotemes present notional parts of sentences, and dictemes mark the transition from the sentence to the text.

Furthermore, bearing in mind that the phonemic level forms the subfoundation of language, i.e. the non-meaningful matter of meaningful expressive means, the two notions of grammatical description shall be pointed out as central even within the framework of the structural hierarchy of language: these are, first, the notion of the word and, second, the notion of the sentence. The first is analysed by morphology, which is the grammatical teaching of the word; the second is analysed by syntax, which is the grammatical teaching of the sentence.

## CHAPTER II
## MORPHEMIC STRUCTURE OF THE WORD

§ 1. The morphological system of language reveals its properties through the morphemic structure of words. It follows from this that morphology as part of grammatical theory faces the two segmental units: the morpheme and the word. But, as we have already pointed out, the morpheme is not identified otherwise than part of the word; the functions of the morpheme are effected only as the corresponding constituent functions of the word as a whole.

For instance, the form of the verbal past tense is built up by means of the dental grammatical suffix: train-*ed* [-d]; publish-*ed* [-t]; meditat-*ed* [-ıd].

However, the past tense as a definite type of grammatical meaning is expressed not by the dental morpheme in isolation, but by the verb (i.e. word) taken in the corresponding form (realized by its morphemic composition); the dental suffix is immediately related to the stem of the verb and together with the stem constitutes the temporal correlation in the paradigmatic system of verbal categories.

Thus, in studying the morpheme we actually study the word in the necessary details of its composition and functions.

§ 2. It is very difficult to give a rigorous and at the same time universal definition to the word, i.e. such a definition as would unambiguously apply to all the different word-units of the lexicon. This difficulty is explained by the fact that the word is an extremely complex and many-sided phenomenon. Within the framework of different linguistic trends and theories the word is defined as the minimal potential sentence, the minimal free linguistic form, the elementary component of the sentence, the articulate sound-symbol, the grammatically arranged combination of sound with meaning, the meaningfully integral and immediately identifiable lingual unit, the uninterrupted string of morphemes, etc., etc. None of these definitions, which can be divided into formal, functional, and mixed, has the power to precisely cover all the lexical segments of language without a residue remaining outside the field of definition.

The said difficulties compel some linguists to refrain from accepting the word as the basic element of language. In particular, American scholars – representatives of Descriptive Linguistics founded by L. Bloomfield – recognized not the word and the sentence, but the phoneme and the morpheme as the basic categories of linguistic description, because these units are the easiest to be isolated in the continual text due to their "physically" minimal, elementary segmental character: the phoneme being the minimal formal segment of language, the morpheme, the minimal meaningful segment. Accordingly, only two segmental levels were originally identified in language by Descriptive scholars: the phonemic level and the morphemic level; later, a third one was added to these – the level of "constructions", i.e. the level of morphemic combinations.

In fact, if we take such notional words as, say, *water*, *pass*, *yellow* and the like, as well their simple derivatives, *e.g. watery*, *passer*, *yellowness*, we shall easily see their definite nominative function and unambiguous segmental delimitation, making them beyond all doubt into "separate words of language". But if we compare with the given one-stem words the corresponding composite formations, such as *waterman*, *password*, *yellowback*, we shall immediately note that the identification of the latter as separate words is greatly complicated by the fact that they themselves are decomposable into separat words. One could point out that the peculiar property distinguishii composite words from phrases is their linear indivisibility, i.e. the impossibility for them to be divided by a third word. But this would-be rigorous criterion is quite irrelevant for analytical word-forms, *e.g.*: has met – has never met; is coming – is not by any circumstances coming.

As for the criterion according to which the word is identified as a minimal sign capable of functioning alone (the word understood as the "smallest free form", or interpreted as the "potential minimal sentence"), it is irrelevant for the bulk of functional words which cannot be used "independently" even in elliptical responses (to say nothing of the fact that the very notion of ellipsis is essentially the opposite of self-dependence).

In spite of the shown difficulties, however, there remains the unquestionable fact that each speaker has at his disposal a ready stock of naming units (more precisely, units standing to one another in nominative correlation) by which he can build up an infinite number of utterances reflecting the ever changing situations of reality.

This circumstance urges us to seek the identification of the word as a lingual unit-type on other lines than the "strictly operational definition". In fact, we do find the clarification of the problem in taking into consideration the difference between the two sets of lingual phenomena: on the one hand, "polar" phenomena; on the other hand, "intermediary" phenomena.

Within a complex system of interrelated elements, polar phenomena are the most clearly identifiable, they stand to one another in an utterly unambiguous opposition. Intermediary phenomena are located in the system in between the polar phenomena, making up a gradation of transitions or the so-called "continuum". By some of their properties intermediary phenomena are similar or near to one of the corresponding poles, while by other properties they are similar to the other, opposing pole. Either of the two poles together with the intermediary elements connected with it on the principle of gradation, forms a "field". The polar elements of this field constitute its "centre", the non-polar elements, respectively, its "periphery".

The analysis of the intermediary phenomena from the point of view of their relation to the polar phenomena reveal their own status in the system. At the same time this kind of analysis helps evaluate the definitions of the polar phenomena between which a continuum is established.

In this connection, the notional one-stem word and the morpheme should be described as the opposing polar phenomena among the meaningful segments of language; it is these elements that can be defined by their formal and functional features most precisely and unambiguously. As for functional words, they occupy intermediary positions between these poles, and their very intermediary status is gradational. In particular, the variability of their status is expressed in the fact that some of them can be used in an isolated response position (for instance, words of affirmation and negation, interrogative words, demonstrative words, etc.), while others cannot (such as prepositions or conjunctions).

The nature of the element of any system is revealed in the character of its function. The function of words is realized in their nominative correlation with one another. On the basis of this correlation a number of functional words are distinguished by the "negative delimitation" (i.e. delimitation as a residue after the identification of the co-positional textual elements),[*] e.g.: the/people; to/speak; by/way/of.

The "negative delimitation" immediately connects these functional words with the directly nominative, notional words in the system. Thus, the correlation in question (which is to be implied by the conventional term "nominative function") unites functional words

---

[*] See: *Смирницкий А.И.* К вопросу о слове (проблема «отдельности слова»). // Вопросы теории и истории языка. М., 1955.

with notional words, or "half-words" (word-morphemes) with "full words". On the other hand, nominative correlation reduces the morpheme as a type of segmental signeme to the role of an element in the composition of the word.

As we see, if the elementary character (indivisibility) of the morpheme (as a significative unit) is established in the structure of words, the elementary character of the word (as a nominative unit) is realized in the system of lexicon.

Summing up what has been said in this paragraph, we may point out some of the properties of the morpheme and the word which are fundamental from the point of view of their systemic status and therefore require detailed investigations and descriptions.

The morpheme is a meaningful segmental component of the word; the morpheme is formed by phonemes; as a meaningful component of the word it is elementary (i.e. indivisible into smaller segments as regards its significative function).

The word is a nominative unit of language; it is formed by morphemes; it enters the lexicon of language as its elementary component (i.e. a component indivisible into smaller segments as regards its nominative function); together with other nominative units the word is used for the formation of the sentence – a unit of information in the communication process.

§ 3. In traditional grammar the study of the morphemic structure of the word was conducted in the light of the two basic criteria: positional criterion (the location of the marginal morphemes in relation to the central ones) and semantic or functional criterion (the correlative contribution of the morphemes to the general meaning of the word). The combination of these two criteria in an integral description has led to the rational classification of morphemes that is widely used both in research linguistic work and in practical lingual tuition.

In accord with the traditional classification, morphemes on the upper level are divided into root-morphemes (roots) and affixal morphemes (affixes). The roots express the concrete, "material" part of the meaning of the word, while the affixes express the specificational part of the meaning of the word, the specifications being of lexico-semantic and grammatico-semantic character.

The roots of notional words are classical lexical morphemes.

The affixal morphemes include prefixes, suffixes, and inflexions (in the tradition of the English school, grammatical inflexions are commonly referred to as "suffixes"). Of these, prefixes and lexical

21

suffixes have word-building functions, together with the root they form the stem of the word; inflexions (grammatical suffixes) express different morphological categories.

The root, according to the positional content of the term (i.e. the border-area between prefixes and suffixes), is obligatory for any word, while affixes are not obligatory. Therefore one and the same morphemic segment of functional (i.e. non-notional) status, depending on various morphemic environments, can in principle be used now as an affix (mostly, a prefix), now as a root. *Cf.:*

*out* – a root-word (preposition, adverb, verbal postposition, adjective, noun, verb);

*throughout* – a composite word, in which *-out* serves as one of the roots (the categorial status of the meaning of both morphemes is the same);

*outing* – a two-morpheme word, in which *out-* is a root, and *-ing* is a suffix;

*outlook, outline, outrage, out-talk,* etc. – words, in which *out-* serves as a prefix;

*look-out, knock-out, shut-out, time-out,* etc. – words (nouns), in which *-out* serves as a suffix.

The morphemic composition of modern English words has a wide range of varieties; in the lexicon of everyday speech the preferable morphemic types of stems are root stems (one-root stems or two-root stems) and one-affix stems. With grammatically changeable words, these stems take one grammatical suffix (two "open" grammatical suffixes are used only with some plural nouns in the possessive case, *cf.:* the children's toys, the oxen's yokes).

Thus, the abstract complete morphemic model of the common English word is the following: prefix + root + lexical suffix + grammatical suffix.

The syntagmatic connections of the morphemes within the model form two types of hierarchical structure. The first is characterized by the original prefixal stem (*e.g.* prefabricated), the second is characterized by the original suffixal stem (*e.g.* inheritors). If we use the symbols *St* for stem, *R* for root, *Pr* for prefix, *L* for lexical suffix, *Gr* for grammatical suffix, and, besides, employ three graphical symbols of hierarchical grouping – braces, brackets, and parentheses, then the two morphemic word-structures can be presented as follows:

$$W_1 = \{[Pr + (R + L)] + Gr\};$$
$$W_2 = \{[(Pr + R) + L] + Gr\}$$

§ 4. Further insights into the correlation between the formal and functional aspects of morphemes within the composition of the word may be gained in the light of the so-called *"allo-emic" theory* put forward by Descriptive Linguistics and broadly used in the current linguistic research.

In accord with this theory, lingual units are described by means of two types of terms: *allo*-terms and *eme*-terms. Eme-terms denote the generalized invariant units of language characterized by a certain functional status: phonemes, morphemes. Allo-terms denote the concrete manifestations, or variants of the generalized units dependent on the regular co-location with other elements of language: allophones, allomorphs. A set of iso-functional allo-units identified in the text on the basis of their co-occurrence with other lingual units (distribution) is considered as the corresponding eme-unit with its fixed systemic status.

The allo-emic identification of lingual elements is achieved by means of the so-called "distributional analysis". The immediate aim of the distributional analysis is to fix and study the units of language in relation to their textual environments, i.e. the adjoining elements in the text.

The environment of a unit may be either "right" or "left", *e.g.*: un-pardon-able.

In this word the left environment of the root is the negative prefix *un-*, the right environment of the root is the qualitative suffix *-able.* Respectively, the root *-pardon-* is the right environment for the prefix, and the left environment for the suffix.

The distribution of a unit may be defined as the total of all its environments; in other words, the distribution of a unit is its environment in generalized terms of classes or categories.

In the distributional analysis at the morphemic level, phonemic distribution of morphemes and morphemic distribution of morphemes are discriminated. The study is conducted in two stages.

At the first stage, the analysed text (i.e. the collected lingual materials, or "corpus") is divided into recurrent segments consisting of phonemes. These segments are called "morphs", i.e. morphemic units distributionally uncharacterized, *e.g.*: the/boat/s/were/gain/ing/ speed.

At the second stage, the environmental features of the morphs are established and the corresponding identifications are effected.

Three main types of distribution are discriminated in the distributional analysis, namely, *contrastive* distribution, *non-contrastive* distribution, and *complementary* distribution.

Contrastive and non-contrastive distributions concern identical environments of different morphs. The morphs are said to be in contrastive distribution if their meanings (functions) are different. Such morphs constitute different morphemes. *Cf.* the suffixes -*(e)d* and -*ing* in the verb-forms *returned*, *returning*. The morphs are said to be in non-contrastive distribution (or free alternation) if their meaning (function) is the same. Such morphs constitute "free alternants", or "free variants" of the same morpheme. *Cf.* the suffixes -*(e)d* and -*t* in the verb-forms *learned*, *learnt*.

As different from the above, complementary distribution concerns different environments of formally different morphs which are united by the same meaning (function). If two or more morphs have the same meaning and the difference in their form is explained by different environments, these morphs are said to be in complementary distribution and considered the allomorphs of the same morpheme. *Cf.* the allomorphs of the plural morpheme /-s/, /-z/, /-ɪz/ which stand in phonemic complementary distribution; the plural allomorph -*en* in *oxen, children*, which stands in morphemic complementary distribution with the other allomorphs of the plural morpheme.

As we see, for analytical purposes the notion of complementary distribution is the most important, because it helps establish the identity of outwardly altogether different elements of language, in particular, its grammatical elements.

§ 5. As a result of the application of distributional analysis to the morphemic level, different types of morphemes have been discriminated which can be called the "distributional morpheme types". It must be stressed that the distributional classification of morphemes cannot abolish or in any way depreciate the traditional morpheme types. Rather, it supplements the traditional classification, showing some essential features of morphemes on the principles of environmental study.

We shall survey the distributional morpheme types arranging them in pairs of immediate correlation.

On the basis of the *degree of self-dependence*, "free" morphemes and "bound" morphemes are distinguished. Bound morphemes cannot form words by themselves, they are identified only as component segmental parts of words. As different from this, free morphemes can build up words by themselves, i.e. can be used "freely".

For instance, in the word *handful* the root *hand* is a free morpheme, while the suffix *-ful* is a bound morpheme.

There are very few productive bound morphemes in the morphological system of English. Being extremely narrow, the list of them is complicated by the relations of homonymy. These morphemes are the following:

1) the segments -(*e*)*s* [-z, -s, -ɪz]: the plural of nouns, the possessive case of nouns, the third person singular present of verbs;

2) the segments -(*e*)*d* [-d, -t, -ɪd]: the past and past participle of verbs;

3) the segments *-ing*: the gerund and present participle;

4) the segments *-er*, *-est*: the comparative and superlative degrees of adjectives and adverbs.

The auxiliary word-morphemes of various standings should be interpreted in this connection as "semi-bound" morphemes, since, being used as separate elements of speech strings, they form categorial unities with their notional stem-words.

On the basis of *formal presentation*, "overt" morphemes and "covert" morphemes are distinguished. Overt morphemes are genuine, explicit morphemes building up words; the covert morpheme is identified as a contrastive absence of morpheme expressing a certain function. The notion of covert morpheme coincides with the notion of zero morpheme in the oppositional description of grammatical categories (see further).

For instance, the word-form *clocks* consists of two overt morphemes: one lexical (root) and one grammatical expressing the plural. The outwardly one-morpheme word-form *clock*, since it expresses the singular, is also considered as consisting of two morphemes, i.e. of the overt root and the covert (implicit) grammatical suffix of the singular. The usual symbol for the covert morpheme employed by linguists is the sign of the empty set: ∅.

On the basis of *segmental relation*, "segmental" morphemes and "supra-segmental" morphemes are distinguished. Interpreted as suprasegmental morphemes in distributional terms are intonation contours, accents, pauses.

The said elements of language, as we have stated elsewhere, should beyond dispute be considered signemic units of language, since they are functionally bound. They form the secondary line of speech, accompanying its primary phonemic line (phonemic complexes). On the other hand, from what has been stated about the morpheme proper, it is not difficult to see that the morphemic interpretation of supra-segmental units can hardly stand to reason. Indeed, these units are functionally connected not with morphemes, but with larger elements of guage: words, word-groups, sentences, supra-sentential constructions.

On the basis of *grammatical alternation*, "additive" morphemes and "replacive" morphemes are distinguished. Interpreted as additive morphemes are outer grammatical suffixes, since, as a rule, they are opposed to the absence of morphemes in grammatical alternation. *Cf.* look + *ed*, small + *er*, etc. In distinction to these, the root phonemes of grammatical interchange are considered as replacive morphemes, since they replace one another in the paradigmatic forms. *Cf.* dr-i-ve – dr-o-ve – dr-i-ven; m-a-n – m-e-n; etc.

It should be remembered that the phonemic interchange is utterly unproductive in English as in all the Indo-European languages. If it were productive, it might rationally be interpreted as a sort of replacive "infixation" (correlated with "exfixation" of the additive type). As it stands, however, this type of grammatical means can be understood as a kind of suppletivity (i.e. partial suppletivity).

On the basis of *linear characteristic*, "continuous" (or "linear") morphemes and "discontinuous" morphemes are distinguished.

By the discontinuous morpheme, opposed to the common, i.e. uninterruptedly expressed, continuous morpheme, a two-element grammatical unit is meant which is identified in the analytical grammatical form comprising an auxiliary word and a grammatical suffix. These two elements, as it were, embed the notional stem; hence, they are symbolically represented as follows:

be ... ing – for the continuous verb forms (*e.g.* is going);
have ... en – for the perfect verb forms (*e.g.* has gone);
be ... en – for the passive verb forms (*e.g.* is taken).

It is easy to see that the notion of morpheme applied to the analytical form of the word violates the principle of the identification of morpheme as an elementary meaningful segment: the analytical "framing" consists of two meaningful segments, i.e. of two different morphemes. On the other hand, the general notion "discontinuous constituent", "discontinuous unit" is quite rational and can be helpfully used in linguistic description in its proper place.

CHAPTER III

## CATEGORIAL STRUCTURE OF THE WORD

§ 1. Notional words, first of all verbs and nouns, possess some morphemic features expressing grammatical (morphological) meanings. These features determine the grammatical form of the word.

Grammatical meanings are very abstract, very general. Therefore the grammatical form is not confined to an individual word, but unites a whole class of words, so that each word of the class expresses the corresponding grammatical meaning together with its individual, concrete semantics.

For instance, the meaning of the substantive plural is rendered by the regular plural suffix -(e)s, and in some cases by other, more specific means, such as phonemic interchange and a few lexeme-bound suffixes. Due to the generalized character of the plural, we say that different groups of nouns "take" this form with strictly defined variations in the mode of expression, the variations being of more systemic (phonological conditioning) and less systemic (etymological conditioning) nature. Cf.: faces, branches, matches, judges; books, rockets, boats, chiefs, proofs; dogs, beads, films, stones, hens; lives, wives, thieves, leaves; girls, stars, toys, heroes, pianos, cantos; oxen, children, brethren, kine; swine, sheep, deer; cod, trout, salmon, men, women, feet, teeth, geese, mice, lice; formulae, antennae; data, errata, strata, addenda, memoranda; radii, genii, nuclei, alumni; crises, bases, analyses, axes; phenomena, criteria.

As we see, the grammatical form presents a division of the word on the principle of expressing a certain grammatical meaning.

§ 2. The most general notions reflecting the most general properties of phenomena are referred to in logic as "categorial notions", or "categories". The most general meanings rendered by language and expressed by systemic correlations of word-forms are interpreted in linguistics as categorial grammatical meanings. The forms themselves are identified within definite paradigmatic series.

The categorial meaning (e.g. the grammatical number) unites the individual meanings of the correlated paradigmatic forms (e.g. singular – plural) and is exposed through them; hence, the meaning of the grammatical category and the meaning of the grammatical form are related to each other on the principle of the logical relation between the categorial and generic notions.

As for the grammatical category itself, it presents the same as the grammatical "form", a unity of form (i.e. material factor) and meaning (i.e. ideal factor) and constitutes a certain signemic system.

More specifically, the grammatical category is a system of expressing a generalized grammatical meaning by means of paradigmatic correlation of grammatical forms.

The ordered set of grammatical forms expressing a categorial function constitutes a paradigm.

The paradigmatic correlations of grammatical forms in a category are exposed by the so-called "grammatical oppositions".

The opposition (in the linguistic sense) may be defined as a generalized correlation of lingual forms by means of which a certain function is expressed. The correlated elements (members) of the opposition must possess two types of features: common features and differential features. Common features serve as the basis of contrast, while differential features immediately express the function in question.

The oppositional theory was originally formulated as a phonological theory. Three main qualitative types of oppositions were established in phonology: "privative", "gradual", and "equipollent". By the number of members contrasted, oppositions were divided into binary (two members) and more than binary (ternary, quaternary, etc.).

The most important type of opposition is the binary privative opposition; the other types of oppositions are reducible to the binary privative opposition.

The binary privative opposition is formed by a contrastive pair of members in which one member is characterized by the presence of a certain differential feature ("mark"), while the other member is characterized by the absence of this feature. The member in which the feature is present is called the "marked", or "strong", or "positive" member, and is commonly designated by the symbol + (plus); the member in which the feature is absent is called the "unmarked", or "weak", or "negative" member, and is commonly designated by the symbol – (minus).

For instance, the voiced and devoiced consonants form a privative opposition [b, d, g – p, t, k]. The differential feature of the opposition is "voice". This feature is present in the voiced consonants, so their set forms the marked member of the opposition. The devoiced consonants, lacking the feature, form the unmarked member of the opposition. To stress the marking quality of "voice" for the opposition in questions, the devoiced consonants may be referred to as "non-voiced".

The gradual opposition is formed by a contrastive group of members which are distinguished not by the presence or absence of a feature, but by the degree of it.

For instance, the front vowels [i: – ɪ – e – æ] form a quarternary gradual opposition, since they are differentiated by the degree of their openness (their length, as is known, is also relevant, as well as some other individualizing properties, but these factors do not spoil the gradual opposition as such).

The equipollent opposition is formed by a contrastive pair or group in which the members are distinguished by different positive features.

For instance, the phonemes [m] and [b], both bilabial consonants, form an equipollent opposition, [m] being sonorous nazalized, [b] being plosive.

We have noted above that any opposition can be reformulated in privative terms. Indeed, any positive feature distinguishing an oppositionally characterized lingual element is absent in the oppositionally correlated element, so that considered from the point of view of this feature alone, the opposition, by definition, becomes privative. This reformulation is especially helpful on an advanced stage of oppositional study of a given microsystem, because it enables us to characterize the elements of the system by the corresponding strings ("bundles") of values of their oppositional featuring ("bundles of differential features"), each feature being represented by the values + or – .

For instance, [p] is distinguished from [b] as voiceless (voice – ), from [t] as bilabial (labialization +), from [m] as non-nazalized (nazalization – ), etc. The descriptive advantages of this kind of characterization are self-evident.

Unlike phonemes which are monolateral lingual elements, words as units of morphology are bilateral; therefore morphological oppositions must reflect both the plane of expression (form) and the plane of content (meaning).

The most important type of opposition in morphology, the same as in phonology, is the binary privative opposition.

The privative morphological opposition is based on a morphological differential feature which is present in its strong (marked) member and absent in its weak (unmarked) member. In another kind of wording, this differential feature may be said to mark one of the members of the opposition positively (the strong member), and the other one negatively (the weak member). The featuring in question serves as the immediate means of· expressing a grammatical meaning.

For instance, the expression of the verbal present and past tenses is based on a privative opposition the differential feature of which is the dental suffix -(e)d. This suffix, rendering the meaning of the past tense, marks the past form of the verb positively (*we worked*), and the present form negatively (*we work*).

The meanings differentiated by the oppositions of signemic units (signemic oppositions) are referred to as "semantic features", or "semes".

For instance, the nounal form *cats* expresses the seme of plurality, as opposed to the form *cat* which expresses, by contrast, the seme of singularity. The two forms constitute a privative opposition in which the plural is the marked member. In order to stress the negative marking of the singular, it can be referred to as "non-plural".

It should be noted that the designation of the weak members of privative morphological oppositions by the "non-" terms is significant not only from the point of view of the plane of expression, but also from the point of view of the plane of content. It is connected with the fact that the meaning of the weak member of the privative opposition is more general and abstract as compared with the meaning of the strong member, which is, respectively, more particular and concrete. Due to this difference in meaning, the weak member is used in a wider range of contexts than the strong member. For instance, the present tense form of the verb, as different from the past tense, is used to render meanings much broader than those directly implied by the corresponding time-plane as such. *Cf.*:

The sun *rises* in the East. To err *is* human. They *don't speak* French in this part of the country. Etc.

Equipollent oppositions in the system of English morphology constitute a minor type and are mostly confined to formal relations only. An example of such an opposition can be seen in the correlation of the person forms of the verb *be*: *am – are – is*.

Gradual oppositions in morphology are not generally recognized; in principle, they can be identified as a minor type at the semantic level only. An example of the gradual morphological opposition can be seen in the category of comparison: *strong – stronger – strongest.*

A grammatical category must be expressed by at least one opposition of forms. These forms are ordered in a paradigm in grammatical descriptions.

Both equipollent and gradual oppositions in morphology, the same as in phonology, can be reduced to privative oppositions within the framework of an oppositional presentation of some categorial system as a whole. Thus, a word-form, like a phoneme, can be represented by a bundle of values of differential features, graphically exposing its categorial structure. For instance, the verb-form *listens* is marked negatively as the present tense (tense – ), negatively as the indicative mood (mood – ), negatively as the passive voice (voice – ), positively as the third person (person +), etc. This principle of presentation, making a morphological description more compact, at the same time has the advantage of precision and helps penetrate deeper into the inner mechanisms of grammatical categories.

§ 3. In various contextual conditions, one member of an opposition can be used in the position of the other, counter-member. This phenomenon should be treated under the heading of "oppositional reduction" or "oppositional substitution". The first version of the term ("reduction") points out the fact that the opposition in this case is contracted, losing its formal distinctive force. The second version of the term ("substitution") shows the very process by which the opposition is reduced, namely, the use of one member instead of the other.

By way of example, let us consider the following case of the singular noun-subject: *Man* conquers nature.

The noun *man* in the quoted sentence is used in the singular, but it is quite clear that it stands not for an individual person, but for people in general, for the idea of "mankind". In other words, the noun is used generically, it implies the class of denoted objects as a whole. Thus, in the oppositional light, here the weak member of the categorial opposition of number has replaced the strong member.

Consider another example: Tonight we *start* for London.

The verb in this sentence takes the form of the present, while its meaning in the context is the future. It means that the opposition "present – future" has been reduced, the weak member (present) replacing the strong one (future).

The oppositional reduction shown in the two cited cases is stylistically indifferent, the demonstrated use of the forms does not transgress the expressive conventions of ordinary speech. This kind of

31

oppositional reduction is referred to as "neutralization" of oppositions. The position of neutralization is, as a rule, filled in by the
weak member of the opposition due to its more general semantics.

Alongside the neutralizing reduction of oppositions there exists
another kind of reduction, by which one of the members of the opposition is placed in contextual conditions uncommon for it; in other
words, the said reductional use of the form is stylistically marked.
*E.g.*: That man *is* constantly *complaining* of something.

The form of the verbal present continuous in the cited sentence
stands in sharp contradiction with its regular grammatical meaning
"action in progress at the present time". The contradiction is, of
course, purposeful: by exaggeration, it intensifies the implied disapproval of the man's behaviour.

This kind of oppositional reduction should be considered under
the heading of "transposition". Transposition is based on the contrast
between the members of the opposition, it may be defined as a
contrastive use of the counter-member of the opposition. As a rule
(but not exclusively) transpositionally employed is the strong member
of the opposition, which is explained by its comparatively limited
regular functions.

§ 4. The means employed for building up member-forms of
categorial oppositions are traditionally divided into *synthetical* and
*analytical*; accordingly, the grammatical forms themselves are classed
into synthetical and analytical, too.

Synthetical grammatical forms are realized by the inner morphemic composition of the word, while analytical grammatical forms
are built up by a combination of at least two words, one of which
is a grammatical auxiliary (word-morpheme), and the other, a word
of "substantial" meaning.

Synthetical grammatical forms are based on inner inflexion, outer
inflexion, and suppletivity; hence, the forms are referred to as inner-
inflexional, outer-inflexional, and suppletive.

Inner inflexion, or phonemic (vowel) interchange, is not productive in modern Indo-European languages, but it is peculiarly employed in some of their basic, most ancient lexemic elements. By
this feature, the whole family of Indo-European languages is identified in linguistics as typologically "inflexional".

Inner inflexion (grammatical "infixation", see above) is used in
English in irregular verbs (the bulk of them belong to the Germanic
strong verbs) for the formation of the past indefinite and past participle; besides, it is used in a few nouns for the formation of the

plural. Since the corresponding oppositions of forms are based on phonemic interchange, the initial paradigmatic form of each lexeme in question should also be considered as inflexional. *Cf.*: take – took – taken, drive – drove – driven, keep – kept – kept, etc.; man – men, brother – brethren, etc.

Suppletivity, like inner inflexion, is not productive as a purely morphological type of form. It is based on the correlation of different roots as a means of paradigmatic differentiation. In other words, it consists in the grammatical interchange of word roots, and this, as we pointed out in the foregoing chapter, unites it in principle with inner inflexion (or, rather, makes the latter into a specific variety of the former).

Suppletivity is used in the forms of the verbs *be* and *go*, in the irregular forms of the degrees of comparison, in some forms of personal pronouns. *Cf.*: be – am – are – is – was – were; go – went; good – better; bad – worse; much – more; little – less; I – me; we – us; she – her.

In a broader morphological interpretation, suppletivity can be recognized in paradigmatic correlations of some modal verbs, some indefinite pronouns, as well as certain nouns of peculiar categorial properties (lexemic suppletivity – see Ch. IV, § 8). *Cf.*: can – be able; must – have (to), be obliged (to); may – be allowed (to); one – some; man – people; news – items of news; information – pieces of information; etc.

The shown unproductive synthetical means of English morphology are outbalanced by the productive means of affixation (outer inflexion), which amount to grammatical suffixation (grammatical prefixation could only be observed in the Old English verbal system).

In the previous chapter we enumerated the few grammatical suffixes possessed by the English language. These are used to build up the number and case forms of the noun; the person-number, tense, participial and gerundial forms of the verb; the comparison forms of the adjective and adverb. In the oppositional correlations of all these forms, the initial paradigmatic form of each opposition is distinguished by a zero suffix. *Cf.*: boy+∅ – boys;  go+∅ – goes; work+∅ – worked; small+∅ – smaller; etc.

Taking this into account, and considering also the fact that each grammatical form paradigmatically correlates with at least one other grammatical form on the basis of the category expressed (*e.g.* the form of the singular with the form of the plural), we come to the conclusion that the total number of synthetical forms in English morphology, though certainly not very large, at the same time is not so small as it is commonly believed. Scarce in English are not the synthetical forms as such, but the actual affixal segments on which the paradigmatic differentiation of forms is based.

As for analytical forms which are so typical of modern English that they have long made this language into the "canonized" representative of lingual analytism, they deserve some special comment on their substance.

The traditional view of the analytical morphological form recognizes two lexemic parts in it, stating that it presents a combination of an auxiliary word with a basic word. However, there is a tendency with some linguists to recognize as analytical not all such grammatically significant combinations, but only those of them that are "grammatically idiomatic", i.e. whose relevant grammatical meaning is not immediately dependent on the meanings of their component elements taken apart. Considered in this light, the form of the verbal perfect where the auxiliary *have* has utterly lost its original meaning of possession, is interpreted as the most standard and indisputable analytical form in English morphology. Its opposite is seen in the analytical degrees of comparison which, according to the cited interpretation, come very near to free combinations of words by their lack of "idiomatism" in the above sense [Смирницкий, 1959, 68 ff.; Бархударов, 1975, 67 ff.].*

The scientific achievement of the study of "idiomatic" analytism in different languages is essential and indisputable. On the other hand, the demand that "grammatical idiomatism" should be regarded as the basis of "grammatical analytism" seems, logically, too strong. The analytical means underlying the forms in question consist in the discontinuity of the corresponding lexemic constituents. Proceeding from this fundamental principle, it can hardly stand to reason to exclude "unidiomatic" grammatical combinations (i.e. combinations of oppositional-categorial significance) from the system of analytical expression as such. Rather, they should be regarded as an integral part of this system, in which, the provision granted, a gradation of idiomatism is to be recognized. In this case, alongside the classical analytical forms of verbal perfect or continuous, such analytical forms should also be discriminated as the analytical infinitive (*go – to go*), the analytical verbal person (verb plus personal pronoun), the ana-

---

* *Cf.* Аналитические конструкции в языках различных типов: Сб. ст./Отв. ред. Жирмунский В.М. и Суник О.П. М. – Л., 1965.

lytical degrees of comparison of both positive and negative varieties (*more important – less important*), as well as some other, still more unconventional form-types.

Moreover, alongside the standard analytical forms characterized by the unequal ranks of their components (auxiliary element – basic element), as a marginal analytical form-type grammatical repetition should be recognized, which is used to express specific categorial semantics of processual intensity with the verb, of indefinitely high degree of quality with the adjective and the adverb, of indefinitely large quantity with the noun. *Cf.*:

He *knocked* and *knocked* and *knocked* without reply (Gr. Greene). Oh, I feel I've got such *boundless, boundless* love to give to somebody (K. Mansfield). Two white-haired severe women were in charge of *shelves* and *shelves* of knitting materials of every description (A. Christie).

§ 5. The grammatical categories which are realized by the described types of forms organized in functional paradigmatic oppositions, can either be innate for a given class of words, or only be expressed on the surface of it, serving as a sign of correlation with some other class.

For instance, the category of number is organically connected with the functional nature of the noun: it directly exposes the number of the referent substance, *e.g. one ship – several ships*. The category of number in the verb, however, by no means gives a natural meaningful characteristic to the denoted process: the process is devoid of numerical features such as are expressed by the grammatical number. Indeed, what is rendered by the verbal number is not a quantitative characterization of the process, but a numerical featuring of the subject-referent. *Cf.*:

The *girl* is smiling. – The *girls* are smiling. The *ship* is in the harbour. – The *ships* are in the harbour.

Thus, from the point of view of referent relation, grammatical categories should be divided into "immanent" categories, i.e. categories innate for a given lexemic class, and "reflective" categories, i.e. categories of a secondary, derivative semantic value. Categorial forms based on subordinative grammatical agreement (such as the verbal person, the verbal number) are reflective, while categorial forms stipulating grammatical agreement in lexemes of a contiguous word-class (such as the substantive-pronominal person, the substantive number) are immanent. Immanent are also such categories and their forms as are confined within a word-class, i.e. do not transgress its borders; to these belong the tense of the verb, the comparison of the adjective and adverb, etc.

Another essential division of grammatical categories is based on the changeability factor of the exposed feature. Namely, the feature of the referent expressed by the category can be either constant (unchangeable, "derivational"), or variable (changeable, "demutative").

An example of constant feature category can be seen in the category of gender, which divides the class of English nouns into non-human names, human male names, human female names, and human common gender names. This division is represented by the system of the third person pronouns serving as gender-indices (see further). *Cf.*:

*It* (non-human): mountain, city, forest, cat, bee, etc.
*He* (male human): man, father, husband, uncle, etc.
*She* (female human): woman, lady, mother, girl, etc.
*He* or *she* (common human): person, parent, child, cousin, etc.

Variable feature categories can be exemplified by the substantive number (singular – plural) or the degrees of comparison (positive – comparative – superlative).

Constant feature categories reflect the static classifications of phenomena, while variable feature categories expose various connections between phenomena. Some marginal categorial forms may acquire intermediary status, being located in-between the corresponding categorial poles. For instance, the nouns singularia tantum and pluralia tantum present a case of hybrid variable-constant formations, since their variable feature of number has become "rigid", or "lexicalized". *Cf.*: news, advice, progress; people, police; bellows, tongs; colours, letters; etc.

In distinction to these, the gender word-building pairs should be considered as a clear example of hybrid constant-variable formations, since their constant feature of gender has acquired some changeability properties, i.e. has become to a certain extent "grammaticalized". *Cf.*: actor – actress, author – authoress, lion – lioness, etc.

§ 6. In the light of the exposed characteristics of the categories, we may specify the status of grammatical paradigms of changeable forms.

Grammatical change has been interpreted in traditional terms of declension and conjugation. By declension the nominal change is im-

36

plied (first of all, the case system), while by conjugation the verbal change is implied (the verbal forms of person, number, tense, etc.). However, the division of categories into immanent and reflective invites a division of forms on a somewhat more consistent basis.

Since the immanent feature is expressed by essentially independent grammatical forms, and the reflective feature, correspondingly, by essentially dependent grammatical forms, all the forms of the first order (immanent) should be classed as "declensional", while all the forms of the second order (reflective) should be classed as "conjugational".

In accord with this principle, the noun in such synthetical languages as Russian or Latin is declined by the forms of gender, number, and case, while the adjective is conjugated by the same forms. As for the English verb, it is conjugated by the reflective forms of person and number, but declined by the immanent forms of tense, aspect, voice, and mood.

CHAPTER IV

## GRAMMATICAL CLASSES OF WORDS

§ 1. The words of language, depending on various formal and semantic features, are divided into grammatically relevant sets or classes. The traditional grammatical classes of words are called "parts of speech". Since the word is distinguished not only by grammatical, but also by semantico-lexemic properties, some scholars refer to parts of speech as "lexico-grammatical" series of words, or as "lexico-grammatical categories" [Смирницкий, 1957, 33; 1959, 100].

It should be noted that the term "part of speech" is purely traditional and conventional, it cannot be taken as in any way defining or explanatory. This name was introduced in the grammatical teaching of Ancient Greece, where the concept of the sentence was not yet explicitly identified in distinction to the general idea of speech, and where, consequently, no strict differentiation was drawn between the word as a vocabulary unit and the word as a functional element of the sentence.

In modern linguistics, parts of speech are discriminated on the basis of the three criteria: "semantic", "formal", and "functional". The *semantic* criterion presupposes the evaluation of the generalized meaning, which is characteristic of all the subsets of words constituting a given part of speech. This meaning is understood as the "categorial meaning of the part of speech". The *formal* criterion provides for the exposition of the specific inflexional and derivational (word-building) features of all the lexemic subsets of a part of speech. The *functional* criterion concerns the syntactic role of words in the sentence typical of a part of speech. The said three factors of categorial characterization of words are conventionally referred to as, respectively, "meaning", "form", and "function".

§ 2. In accord with the described criteria, words on the upper level of classification are divided into notional and functional, which reflects their division in the earlier grammatical tradition into changeable and unchangeable.

To the notional parts of speech of the English language belong the noun, the adjective, the numeral, the pronoun, the verb, the adverb.

The *features of the noun* within the identificational triad "meaning – form – function" are, correspondingly, the following: 1) the categorial meaning of substance ("thingness"); 2) the changeable forms of number and case; the specific suffixal forms of derivation (prefixes in English do not discriminate parts of speech as such); 3) the substantive functions in the sentence (subject, object, substantival predicative); prepositional connections; modification by an adjective.

The *features of the adjective*: 1) the categorial meaning of property (qualitative and relative); 2) the forms of the degrees of comparison (for qualitative adjectives); the specific suffixal forms of derivation; 3) adjectival functions in the sentence (attribute to a noun, adjectival predicative).

The *features of the numeral*: 1) the categorial meaning of number (cardinal and ordinal); 2) the narrow set of simple numerals; the specific forms of composition for compound numerals; the specific suffixal forms of derivation for ordinal numerals; 3) the functions of numerical attribute and numerical substantive.

The *features of the pronoun*: 1) the categorial meaning of indication (deixis); 2) the narrow sets of various status with the corresponding formal properties of categorial changeability and word-building; 3) the substantival and adjectival functions for different sets.

The *features of the verb*: 1) the categorial meaning of process (presented in the two upper series of forms, respectively, as finite process and non-finite process); 2) the forms of the verbal categories of person, number, tense, aspect, voice, mood; the opposition of the finite and non-finite forms; 3) the function of the finite predicate for the finite verb; the mixed verbal – other than verbal functions for the non-finite verb.

The *features of the adverb*: 1) the categorial meaning of the secondary property, i.e. the property of process or another property; 2) the forms of the degrees of comparison for qualitative adverbs; the specific suffixal forms of derivation; 3) the functions of various adverbial modifiers.

We have surveyed the identifying properties of the notional parts of speech that unite the words of complete nominative meaning characterized by self-dependent functions in the sentence.

Contrasted against the notional parts of speech are words of incomplete nominative meaning and non-self-dependent, mediatory functions in the sentence. These are functional parts of speech.

On the principle of "generalized form" only unchangeable words are traditionally treated under the heading of functional parts of speech. As for their individual forms as such, they are simply presented by the list, since the number of these words is limited, so that they needn't be identified on any general, operational scheme.

To the basic functional series of words in English belong the article, the preposition, the conjunction, the particle, the modal word, the interjection.

The *article* expresses the specific limitation of the substantive functions.

The *preposition* expresses the dependencies and interdependencies of substantive referents.

The *conjunction* expresses connections of phenomena.

The *particle* unites the functional words of specifying and limiting meaning. To this series, alongside other specifying words, should be referred verbal postpositions as functional modifiers of verbs, etc.

The *modal word*, occupying in the sentence a more pronounced or less pronounced detached position, expresses the attitude of the speaker to the reflected situation and its parts. Here belong the functional words of probability (*probably, perhaps,* etc.), of qualitative evaluation (*fortunately, unfortunately, luckily,* etc.), and also of affirmation and negation.

The *interjection*, occupying a detached position in the sentence, is a signal of emotions.

§ 3. Each part of speech after its identification is further subdivided into subseries in accord with various particular semantico-functional and formal features of the constituent words. This subdivision is sometimes called "subcategorization" of parts of speech.

Thus, nouns are subcategorized into proper and common, animate and inanimate, countable and uncountable, concrete and abstract, etc. *Cf.*:

Mary, Robinson, London, the Mississippi, Lake Erie – girl, person, city, river, lake;

man, scholar, leopard, butterfly – earth, field, rose, machine;

coin/coins, floor/floors, kind/kinds – news, growth, water, furniture;

stone, grain, mist, leaf – honesty, love, slavery, darkness.

Verbs are subcategorized into fully predicative and partially predicative, transitive and intransitive, actional and statal, purely nominative and evaluative, etc. *Cf.*:

walk, sail, prepare, shine, blow – can, may, shall, be, become;

take, put, speak, listen, see, give – live, float, stay, ache, ripen, rain;

write, play, strike, boil, receive, ride – exist, sleep, rest, thrive, revel, suffer;

roll, tire, begin, ensnare, build, tremble – consider, approve, mind, desire, hate, incline.

Adjectives are subcategorized into qualitative and relative, of constant feature and temporary feature (the latter are referred to as "statives" and identified by some scholars as a separate part of speech under the heading of "category of state"), factual and evaluative, etc. *Cf.*:

long, red, lovely, noble, comfortable – wooden, rural, daily, subterranean, orthographical;

healthy, sickly, joyful, grievous, wry, blazing – well, ill, glad, sorry, awry, ablaze;

tall, heavy, smooth, mental, native – kind, brave, wonderful, wise, stupid.

The adverb, the numeral, the pronoun are also subject to the corresponding subcategorizations.

§ 4. We have drawn a general outline of the division of the lexicon into part of speech classes developed by modern linguists on the lines of traditional morphology.

It is known that the distribution of words between different parts of speech may to a certain extent differ with different authors. This fact gives cause to some linguists for calling in question the rational character of the part of speech classification as a whole, gives them cause for accusing it of being subjective or "prescientific" in essence. Such nihilistic criticism, however, should be rejected as utterly ungrounded.

Indeed, considering the part of speech classification on its merits, one must clearly realize that what is above all important about it is the fundamental principles of word-class identification, and not occasional enlargements or diminutions of the established groups, or redistributions of individual words due to re-considerations of their subcategorial features. The very idea of subcategorization as the obligatory second stage of the undertaken classification testifies to the objective nature of this kind of analysis.

For instance, prepositions and conjunctions can be combined into one united series of "connectives", since the function of both is just to connect notional components of the sentence. In this case, on the second stage of classification, the enlarged word-class of connectives will be subdivided into two main subclasses, namely, prepositional connectives and conjunctional connectives. Likewise, the articles can be included as a subset into the more general set of particles-specifiers. As is known, nouns and adjectives, as well as numerals, are treated in due contexts of description under one common class-term "names": originally, in the Ancient Greek grammatical teaching they were not differentiated because they had the same forms of morphological change (declension). On the other hand, in various descriptions of English grammar such narrow lexemic sets as the two words *yes* and *no*, the pronominal determiners of nouns, even the one anticipating pronoun *it* are given a separate class-item status – though in no way challenging or distorting the functional character of the treated units.

It should be remembered that modern principles of part of speech identification have been formulated as a result of painstaking research conducted on the vast materials of numerous languages. The three celebrated names are especially notable for the elaboration of these criteria, namely, V.V. Vinogradov in connection with his study of Russian grammar, A.I. Smirnitsky and B.A. Ilyish in connection with their study of English grammar.

§ 5. Alongside the three-criteria principle of dividing the words into grammatical (lexico-grammatical) classes modern linguistics has developed another, narrower principle of word-class identification based on syntactic featuring of words only.

The fact is that the three-criteria principle faces a special difficulty in determining the part of speech status of such lexemes as have morphological characteristics of notional words, but are essentially distinguished from notional words by their playing the role of grammatical mediators in phrases and sentences. Here belong, for instance, modal verbs together with their equivalents – suppletive fillers, auxiliary verbs, aspective verbs, intensifying adverbs, determiner pronouns. This difficulty, consisting in the intersection of heterogeneous properties in the established word-classes, can evidently be overcome by recognizing only one criterion of the three as decisive.

Worthy of note is that in the original Ancient Greek grammatical teaching which put forward the first outline of the part of speech theory, the division of words into grammatical classes was also based on one determining criterion only, namely, on the formal-morphological featuring. It means that any given word under analysis was turned into a classified lexeme on the principle of its relation to grammatical change. In conditions of the primary acquisition of linguistic knowledge, and in connection with the study of a highly inflexional language this characteristic proved quite efficient.

Still, at the present stage of the development of linguistic science, syntactic characterization of words that has been made possible after the exposition of their fundamental morphological properties, is far more important and universal from the point of view of the general classificational requirements.

This characterization is more important, because it shows the distribution of words between different sets in accord with their functional specialization. The role of morphology by this presentation is not underrated, rather it is further clarified from the point of view of exposing connections between the categorial composition of the word and its sentence-forming relevance.

This characterization is more universal, because it is not specially destined for the inflexional aspect of language and hence is equally applicable to languages of various morphological types.

On the material of Russian, the principles of syntactic approach to the classification of word stock were outlined in the works of A.M. Peshkovsky. The principles of syntactic (syntactico-distributional) classification of English words were worked out by L. Bloomfield and his followers Z. Harris and especially Ch. Fries.

§ 6. The syntactico-distributional classification of words is based on the study of their combinability by means of substitution testing. The testing results in developing the standard model of four main "positions" of notional words in the English sentence: those of the noun (N), verb (V), adjective (A), adverb (D). Pronouns are included into the corresponding positional classes as their substitutes. Words standing outside the "positions" in the sentence are treated as function words of various syntactic values.

Here is how Ch. Fries presents his scheme of English word-classes [Fries].

For his materials he chooses tape-recorded spontaneous conversations comprising about 250,000 word entries (50 hours of talk). The words isolated from this corpus are tested on the three typical sentences (that are isolated from the records, too), and used as substitution test-frames:

*Frame A.* The concert was good (always).
*Frame B.* The clerk remembered the tax (suddenly).
*Frame C.* The team went there.

The parenthesised positions are optional from the point of view of the structural completion of sentences.

As a result of successive substitution tests on the cited "frames" the following lists of positional words ("form-words", or "parts of speech") are established:

*Class 1.* (A) concert, coffee, taste, container, difference, etc. (B) clerk, husband, supervisor, etc.; tax, food, coffee, etc. (C) team, husband, woman, etc.

*Class 2.* (A) was, seemed, became, etc. (B) remembered, wanted, saw, suggested, etc. (C) went, came, ran,... lived, worked, etc.

*Class 3.* (A) good, large, necessary, foreign, new, empty, etc.

*Class 4.* (A) there, here, always, then, sometimes, etc. (B) clearly, sufficiently, especially, repeatedly, soon, etc. (C) there, back, out, etc.; rapidly, eagerly, confidently, etc.

All these words can fill in the positions of the frames without affecting their general structural meaning (such as "thing and its quality at a given time" – the first frame; "actor – action – thing acted upon – characteristic of the action" – the second frame; "actor – action – direction of the action" – the third frame). Repeated interchanges in the substitutions of the primarily identified positional (i.e. notional) words in different collocations determine their morphological characteristics, i.e. characteristics referring them to various subclasses of the identified lexemic classes.

Functional words (function words) are exposed in the cited process of testing as being unable to fill in the positions of the frames without destroying their structural meaning. These words form limited groups totalling 154 units.

The identified groups of functional words can be distributed among the three main sets. The words of the first set are used as specifiers of notional words. Here belong determiners of nouns, modal verbs serving as specifiers of notional verbs, functional modifiers and intensifiers of adjectives and adverbs. The words of the second set play the role of interpositional elements, determining the relations of notional words to one another. Here belong prepositions and conjunctions. The words of the third set refer to the sentence as a whole. Such are question-words (*what, how,* etc.), inducement-words (*lets, please,* etc.), attention-getting words, words of affirmation and negation, sentence introducers (*it, there*) and some others.

§ 7. Comparing the syntactico-distributional classification of words with the traditional part of speech division of words, one cannot but see the similarity of the general schemes of the two: the opposition of notional and functional words, the four absolutely cardinal classes of notional words (since numerals and pronouns have no positional functions of their own and serve as pro-nounal and pro-adjectival elements), the interpretation of functional words as syntactic mediators and their formal representation by the list.

However, under these unquestionable traits of similarity are distinctly revealed essential features of difference, the proper evaluation of which allows us to make some important generalizations about the structure of the lexemic system of language.

§ 8. One of the major truths as regards the linguistic mechanism arising from the comparison of the two classifications is the explicit and unconditional division of the lexicon into the notional and functional parts. The open character of the notional part of the lexicon and the closed character of the functional part of it (not excluding the intermediary field between the two) receives the strict status of a formal grammatical feature.

The unity of notional lexemes finds its essential demonstration in an inter-class system of derivation that can be presented as a formal four-stage series permeating the lexicon and reflected in regular phrase correlations. *Cf.*:

a recognizing note – a notable recognition – to note recognizingly – to recognize notably; silent disapproval – disapproving silence – to disapprove silently – to silence disapprovingly; etc.

This series can symbolically be designated by the formula St (n.v.a.d.) where St represents the morphemic stem of the series, while the small letters in parentheses stand for the derivational features of the notional word-classes (parts of speech). Each stage of the series can in principle be filled in by a number of lexemes of the same stem with possible hierarchical relations between them. The primary presentation of the series, however, may be realized in a four-unit version as follows:

strength – to strengthen – strong – strongly
peace – to appease – peaceful – peacefully
nation – to nationalize – national – nationally
friend – to befriend – friendly – friendly, etc.

This derivational series that unites the notional word-classes can be named the "lexical paradigm of nomination". The general order of classes in the series evidently corresponds to the logic of mental perception of reality, by which a person discriminates, first, objects and their actions, then the properties of the former and the latter. Still, as the actual initial form of a particular nomination paradigm within the general paradigmatic scheme of nomination can prove a lexeme of any word-class, we are enabled to speak about the concrete "derivational perspective" of this or that series, i.e. to identify nomination paradigms with a nounal (N→), verbal (V→), adjectival (A→), and adverbial (D→) derivational perspectives. Cf.:

N→power – to empower – powerful – powerfully
V→to suppose – supposition – supposed – supposedly
A→clear – clarity – to clarify – clearly
D→out – outing – to out – outer

The nomination paradigm with the identical form of the stem for all the four stages is not represented on the whole of the lexicon; in this sense it is possible to speak of lexemes with a complete paradigm of nomination and lexemes with an incomplete paradigm of nomination. Some words may even stand apart from this paradigm, i.e. be nominatively isolated (here belong, for instance, some simple adverbs).

On the other hand, the universal character of the nomination paradigm is sustained by suppletive completion, both lexemic and phrasemic. Cf.:

an end – to end – final – finally
good – goodness – well – to better

evidence – evident – evidently – to make evident
wise – wisely – wisdom – to grow wise, etc.

The role of suppletivity within the framework of the lexical paradigm of nomination (hence, within the lexicon as a whole) is extremely important, indeed. It is this type of suppletivity, i.e. lexemic suppletivity, that serves as an essential factor of the open character of the notional lexicon of language.

§ 9. Functional words re-interpreted by syntactic approach also reveal some important traits that remained undiscovered in earlier descriptions.

The essence of their paradigmatic status in the light of syntactic interpretation consists in the fact that the lists of functional words may be regarded as paradigmatic series themselves – which, in their turn, are grammatical constituents of higher paradigmatic series at the level of phrases and especially sentences.

As a matter of fact, functional words, considered by their role in the structure of the sentence, are proved to be exposers of various syntactic categories, i.e. they render structural meanings referring to phrases and sentences in constructional forms similar to derivational (word-building) and relational (grammatical) morphemes in the composition of separate words. *Cf.*:

The words were obscure, *but* she understood the uneasiness that produced them. →The words were obscure, *weren't* they? *How then* could she understand the uneasiness that produced them? →*Or* perhaps the words were *not too* obscure, after all? *Or*, conversely, she *didn't* understand the uneasiness that produced them? →*But* the words were obscure. *How* obscure they were! *Still* she *did* understand the uneasiness that produced them. *Etc.*

This role of functional words which are identified not by their morphemic composition, but by their semantico-syntactic features in reference to the embedding constructions, is exposed on a broad linguistic basis within the framework of the theory of paradigmatic syntax (see further).

§ 10. Pronouns considered in the light of the syntactic principles receive a special systemic status that characteristically stamps the general presentation of the structure of the lexicon as a whole.

Pronouns are traditionally recognized on the basis of indicatory (deictic) and substitutional semantic functions. The two types of meanings form a unity, in which the deictic semantics is primary. As a matter of fact, indication is the semantic foundation of substitution.

As for the syntactic principle of the word stock division, while recognizing the deictic aspect of pronouns, it lays a special stress on their substitutive features. Indeed, it is the substitutional function that immediately isolates all the heterogeneous groups of pronouns into a special set of the lexicon.

The generalizing substitutional function of pronouns makes them into syntactic representatives of all the notional classes of words, so that a pronominal positional part of the sentence serves as a categorial projection of the corresponding notional subclass identified as the filler set of the position in question. It should be clearly understood that even personal pronouns of the first and second persons play the cited representative role, which is unambiguously exposed by examples with direct addresses and appositions. *Cf.*:

*I, Little Foot*, go away making noises and tramplings. Are *you* happy, *Lil?*

Included into the system of pronouns are pronominal adverbs and verb-substitutes, in due accord with their substitutional functions. Besides, notional words of broad meaning are identified as forming an intermediary layer between the pronouns and notional words proper. Broad meaning words adjoin the pronouns by their substitutional function. *Cf.*:

I wish at her age she'd learn to sit quiet and not *do things*. Flora's suggestion is *making* sense. I will *therefore* briefly set down the circumstances which led to my being connected with the *affair*. Etc.

As a result of these generalizations, the lexical paradigm of nomination receives a complete substitutive representation. *Cf.*: one, it, they... – do, make, act... – such, similar, same... – thus, so, there...

Symbolically the correlation of the nominal and pronominal paradigmatic schemes is stated as follows:

N – V – A – D – Npro – Vpro – Apro – Dpro.

§ 11. As a result of the undertaken analysis we have obtained a foundation for dividing the whole of the lexicon on the upper level of classification into three unequal parts.

The first part of the lexicon forming an open set includes an indefinitely large number of notional words which have a complete nominative function. In accord with the said function, these words can be referred to as "names": nouns as substance names, verbs as process names, adjectives as primary property names and adverbs as secondary property names. The whole notional set is represented by the four-stage derivational paradigm of nomination.

The second part of the lexicon forming a closed set includes substitutes of names (pro-names). Here belong pronouns, and also broad-meaning notional words which constitute various marginal subsets.

The third part of the lexicon also forming a closed set includes specifiers of names. These are function-categorial words of various servo-status.

Substitutes of names (pro-names) and specifiers of names, while standing with the names in nominative correlation as elements of the lexicon, at the same time serve as connecting links between the names within the lexicon and their actual uses in the sentences of living speech.

<h3 style="text-align:center">C H A P T E R  V</h3>

<h2 style="text-align:center">NOUN: GENERAL</h2>

§ 1. The noun as a part of speech has the categorial meaning of "substance" or "thingness". It follows from this that the noun is the main nominative part of speech, effecting nomination of the fullest value within the framework of the notional division of the lexicon.

The noun has the power, by way of nomination, to isolate different properties of substances (i.e. direct and oblique qualities, and also actions and states as processual characteristics of substantive phenomena) and present them as corresponding self-dependent substances. *E.g.*:

Her words were unexpectedly *bitter.* – We were struck by the unexpected *bitterness* of her words. At that time he was *down* in his career, but we knew well that very soon he would be *up* again. – His career had its *ups* and *downs*. The cable arrived when John was *preoccupied* with the arrangements for the party. – The arrival of the cable interrupted his *preoccupation* with the arrangements for the party.

This natural and practically unlimited substantivization force establishes the noun as the central nominative lexemic unit of language.

§ 2. The categorial functional properties of the noun are determined by its semantic properties.

The most characteristic substantive function of the noun is that of the subject in the sentence, since the referent of the subject is the person or thing immediately named. The function of the object in the sentence is also typical of the noun as the substance word. Other syntactic functions, i.e. attributive, adverbial, and even predicative, although performed by the noun with equal ease, are not immediately characteristic of its substantive quality as such. It should be noted that, while performing these non-substantive functions, the noun essentially differs from the other parts of speech used in similar sentence positions. This may be clearly shown by transformations shifting the noun from various non-subject syntactic positions into subject syntactic positions of the same general semantic value, which is impossible with other parts of speech. *E.g.*:

Mary is a *flower-girl.* →*The flower-girl* (you are speaking of) is Mary. He lives in *Glasgow.* →*Glasgow* is his place of residence. This happened *three years* ago. →*Three years* have elapsed since it happened.

Apart from the cited sentence-part functions, the noun is characterized by some special types of combinability.

In particular, typical of the noun is the prepositional combinability with another noun, a verb, an adjective, an adverb. *E.g.*: an entrance to the house; to turn round the corner; red in the face; far from its destination.

The casal (possessive) combinability characterizes the noun alongside its prepositional combinability with another noun. *E.g.*: the speech of the President – the President's speech; the cover of the book – the book's cover.

English nouns can also easily combine with one another by sheer contact, unmediated by any special lexemic or morphemic means. In the contact group the noun in pre-position plays the role of a semantic qualifier to the noun in post-position. *E.g.*: a cannon ball; a log cabin; a sports event; film festivals.

The lexico-grammatical status of such combinations has presented a big problem for many scholars, who were uncertain as to the linguistic heading under which to treat them: either as one separate word, or a word-group.* In the history of linguistics the controversy

---

* See: *Смирницкий А.И.* Лексикология английского языка. М., 1956, § 133; *Жигадло В.Н., Иванова И.П., Иофик Л.Л.,* § 255.

about the lexico-grammatical status of the constructions in question has received the half-facetious name "The cannon ball problem".

Taking into account the results of the comprehensive analysis undertaken in this field up to now, we may define the combination as a specific word-group with intermediary features. Crucial for this decision is the isolability test (separation shift of the qualifying noun) which is performed for the contact noun combinations by an easy, productive type of transformation. *Cf.*: a cannon ball → a ball for cannon; the court regulation → the regulation of the court; progress report → report about progress; the funds distribution → the distribution of the funds.

The corresponding compound nouns (formed from substantive stems), as a rule, cannot undergo the isolability test with an equal ease. The transformations with the nounal compounds are in fact reduced to sheer explanations of their etymological motivation. The comparatively closer connection between the stems in compound nouns is reflected by the spelling (contact or hyphenated presentation). *E.g.*: fireplace →place where fire is made; starlight → light coming from stars; story-teller →teller (writer, composer) of stories; theatre-goer → a person who goes to (frequents) theatres.

Contact noun attributes forming a string of several words are very characteristic of professional language. *E.g.*:

A number of *Space Shuttle trajectory optimization problems* were simulated in the development of the algorithm, including three ascent problems and a re-entry problem (From a scientific paper on spacecraft). The accuracy of *offshore tanker unloading operations* is becoming more important as the cost of petroleum products increases (From a scientific paper on control systems).

§ 3. As a part of speech, the noun is also characterized by a set of formal features determining its specific status in the lexical paradigm of nomination. It has its word-building distinctions, including typical suffixes, compound stem models, conversion patterns. It discriminates the grammatical categories of gender, number, case, article determination, which will be analysed below.

The cited formal features taken together are relevant for the division of nouns into several subclasses, which are identified by means of explicit classificational criteria. The most general and rigorously delimited subclasses of nouns are grouped into four oppositional pairs.

50

The first nounal subclass opposition differentiates *proper* and *common* nouns. The foundation of this division is "type of nomination". The second subclass opposition differentiates *animate* and *inanimate* nouns on the basis of "form of existence". The third subclass opposition differentiates *human* and *non-human* nouns on the basis of "personal quality". The fourth subclass opposition differentiates *countable* and *uncountable* nouns on the basis of "quantitative structure".

Somewhat less explicitly and rigorously distinguished is the division of English nouns into *concrete* and *abstract*.

The order in which the subclasses are presented is chosen by convention, not by categorially relevant features: each subclass correlation is reflected in the whole of the noun system; this means that the given set of eight subclasses cannot be structured hierarchically in any linguistically consistent sense (some sort of hierarchical relations can be observed only between animate – inanimate and human – non-human groupings). Consider the following examples:

There were three *Marys* in our company. The *cattle* have been driven out into the pastures.

The noun *Mary* used in the first of the above sentences is at one and the same time "proper" (first subclass division), "animate" (second subclass division), "human" (third subclass division), "countable" (fourth subclass division). The noun *cattle* used in the second sentence is at one and the same time "common" (first subclass division), "animate" (second subclass division), "non-human" (third subclass division), "uncountable" (fourth subclass division).

The subclass differentiation of nouns constitutes a foundation for their selectional syntagmatic combinability both among themselves and with other parts of speech. In the selectional aspect of combinability, the subclass features form the corresponding selectional bases.

In particular, the inanimate selectional base of combinability can be pointed out between the noun subject and the verb predicate in the following sentence: The sandstone was crumbling. (Not: *The horse was crumbling.)

The animate selectional base is revealed between the noun subject and the verb in the following sentence: The poor creature was laming. (Not: *The tree was laming.)

The human selectional base underlies the connection between the nouns in the following combination: John's love of music (not: *the cat's love of music).

The phenomenon of subclass selection is intensely analysed as part of current linguistic research work.

## CHAPTER VI
## NOUN: GENDER

§ 1. There is a peculiarly regular contradiction between the presentation of gender in English by theoretical treatises and practical manuals. Whereas theoretical treatises define the gender subcategorization of English nouns as purely lexical or "semantic", practical manuals of English grammar do invariably include the description of the English gender in their subject matter of immediate instruction.

In particular, a whole ten pages of A.I. Smirnitsky's theoretical "Morphology of English" are devoted to proving the non-existence of gender in English either in the grammatical, or even in the strictly lexico-grammatical sense [Смирницкий, 1959, 139-148]. On the other hand, the well-known practical "English grammar" by M.A. Ganshina and N.M. Vasilevskaya, after denying the existence of grammatical gender in English by way of an introduction to the topic, still presents a pretty comprehensive description of the would-be non-existent gender distinctions of the English noun as a part of speech [Ganshina, Vasilevskaya, 40 ff.].

That the gender division of nouns in English is expressed not as variable forms of words, but as nounal classification (which is not in the least different from the expression of substantive gender in other languages, including Russian), admits of no argument. However, the question remains, whether this classification has any serious grammatical relevance. Closer observation of the corresponding lingual data cannot but show that the English gender does have such a relevance.

§ 2. The category of gender is expressed in English by the obligatory correlation of nouns with the personal pronouns of the third person. These serve as specific gender classifiers of nouns, being potentially reflected on each entry of the noun in speech.

The category of gender is strictly oppositional. It is formed by two oppositions related to each other on a hierarchical basis.

One opposition functions in the whole set of nouns, dividing them into person (human) nouns and non-person (non-human) nouns. The other opposition functions in the subset of person nouns only, dividing them into masculine nouns and feminine nouns. Thus, the first, general opposition can be referred to as the upper opposition in the category of gender, while the second, partial opposition can be referred to as the lower opposition in this category.

As a result of the double oppositional correlation, a specific system of three genders arises, which is somewhat misleadingly represented by the traditional terminology: the *neuter* (i.e. non-person) gender, the *masculine* (i.e. masculine person) gender, the *feminine* (i.e. feminine person) gender.

The strong member of the upper opposition is the human subclass of nouns, its sememic mark being "person", or "personality". The weak member of the opposition comprises both inanimate and animate non-person nouns. Here belong such nouns as *tree, mountain, love,* etc.; *cat, swallow, ant,* etc.; *society, crowd, association,* etc.; *bull* and *cow, cock* and *hen, horse* and *mare,* etc.

In cases of oppositional reduction, non-person nouns and their substitute (*it*) are naturally used in the position of neutralization. *E.g.:*

Suddenly *something* moved in the darkness ahead of us. Could *it* be a man, in this desolate place, at this time of night? The *object* of her maternal affection was nowhere to be found. *It* had disappeared, leaving the mother and nurse desperate.

The strong member of the lower opposition is the feminine subclass of person nouns, its sememic mark being "female sex". Here belong such nouns as *woman, girl, mother, bride,* etc. The masculine subclass of person nouns comprising such words as *man, boy, father, bridegroom,* etc. makes up the weak member of the opposition.

The oppositional structure of the category of gender can be shown schematically on the following diagramme (see Fig. 1).

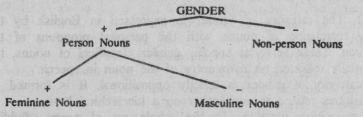

GENDER

+ Person Nouns    — Non-person Nouns

+ Feminine Nouns    — Masculine Nouns

Fig. 1

A great many person nouns in English are capable of expressing both feminine and masculine person genders by way of the pronominal correlation in question. These are referred to as nouns of the "common gender". Here belong such words as *person, parent, friend, cousin, doctor, president,* etc. *E.g.*:

*The President* of our Medical Society isn't going to be happy about the suggested way of cure. In general *she* insists on quite another kind of treatment in cases like that.

The capability of expressing both genders makes the gender distinctions in the nouns of the common gender into a variable category. On the other hand, when there is no special need to indicate the sex of the person referents of these nouns, they are used neutrally as masculine, i.e. they correlate with the masculine third person pronoun.

In the plural, all the gender distinctions are neutralized in the immediate explicit expression, though they are rendered obliquely through the correlation with the singular.

§ 3. Alongside the demonstrated grammatical (or lexico-grammatical, for that matter) gender distinctions, English nouns can show the sex of their referents lexically, either by means of being combined with certain notional words used as sex indicators, or else by suffixal derivation. *Cf.*: boy-friend, girl-friend; man-producer, woman-producer; washer-man, washer-woman; landlord, landlady; bull-calf, cow-calf; cock-sparrow, hen-sparrow; he-bear, she-bear; master, mistress; actor, actress; executor, executrix; lion, lioness; sultan, sultana; etc.

One might think that this kind of the expression of sex runs contrary to the presented gender system of nouns, since the sex distinctions inherent in the cited pairs of words refer not only to human beings (persons), but also to all the other animate beings. On closer observation, however, we see that this is not at all so. In fact, the referents of such nouns as *jenny-ass*, or *pea-hen*, or the like will in the common use quite naturally be represented as *it*, the same as the referents of the corresponding masculine nouns *jack-ass*, *pea-cock*, and the like. This kind of representation is different in principle from the corresponding representation of such nounal pairs as *woman – man, sister – brother*, etc.

On the other hand, when the pronominal relation of the non-person animate nouns is turned, respectively, into *he* and *she*, we can speak of a grammatical personifying transposition, very typical of

English. This kind of transposition affects not only animate nouns, but also a wide range of inanimate nouns, being regulated in everyday language by cultural-historical traditions. Compare the reference of *she* with the names of countries, vehicles, weaker animals, etc.; the reference of *he* with the names of stronger animals, the names of phenomena suggesting crude strength and fierceness, etc.

§ 4. As we see, the category of gender in English is inherently semantic, i.e. meaningful in so far as it reflects the actual features of the named objects. But the semantic nature of the category does not in the least make it into "non-grammatical", which follows from the whole content of what has been said in the present work.

In Russian, German, and many other languages characterized by the gender division of nouns, the gender has purely formal features that may even "run contrary" to semantics. Suffice it to compare such Russian words as *стакан – он, чашка – она, блюдце – оно*, as well as their German correspondences *das Glas – es, die Tasse – sie, der Teller – er*, etc. But this phenomenon is rather an exception than the rule in terms of grammatical categories in general.

Moreover, alongside the "formal" gender, there exists in Russian, German and other "formal gender" languages a meaningful gender, featuring, within the respective idiomatic systems, the natural sex distinctions of the noun referents.

In particular, the Russian gender differs idiomatically from the English gender in so far as it divides the nouns by the higher opposition not into "person – non-person" ("human – non-human"), but into "animate – inanimate", discriminating within the former (the animate nounal set) between masculine, feminine, and a limited number of neuter nouns. Thus, the Russian category of gender essentially divides the nouns into the inanimate set having no meaningful gender, and the animate set having a meaningful gender. In distinction to this, the English category of gender is only meaningful, and as such it is represented in the nounal system as a whole.

CHAPTER VII

NOUN: NUMBER

§ 1. The category of number is expressed by the opposition of the plural form of the noun to the singular form of the noun. The strong member of this binary opposition is the plural, its productive formal mark being the suffix -(e)s [-z, -s, -ız] as presented in the forms *dog – dogs, clock – clocks, box – boxes*. The productive formal mark correlates with the absence of the number suffix in the singular form of the noun. The semantic content of the unmarked form, as has been shown above, enables the grammarians to speak of the zero-suffix of the singular in English.

The other, non-productive ways of expressing the number opposition are vowel interchange in several relict forms (*man – men, woman – women, tooth – teeth,* etc.), the archaic suffix *-(e)n* supported by phonemic interchange in a couple of other relict forms (*ox – oxen, child – children, cow – kine, brother – brethren*), the correlation of individual singular and plural suffixes in a limited number of borrowed nouns (*formula – formulae, phenomenon – phenomena, alumnus – alumni,* etc.). In some cases the plural form of the noun is homonymous with the singular form (*sheep, deer, fish,* etc.).

§ 2. The semantic nature of the difference between singular and plural may present some difficulties of interpretation.

On the surface of semantic relations, the meaning of the singular will be understood as simply "one", as opposed to the meaning of the plural "many" in the sense of "more than one". This is apparently obvious for such correlations as *book – books, lake – lakes* and the like. However, alongside these semantically unequivocal correlations, there exist plurals and singulars that cannot be fully accounted for by the above ready-made approach. This becomes clear when we take for comparison such forms as *tear* (one drop falling from the eye) and *tears* (treacles on the cheeks as tokens of grief or joy), *potato* (one item of the vegetables) and *potatoes* (food), *paper* (material) and *papers* (notes or documents), *sky* (the vault of heaven) and *skies* (the same sky taken as a direct or figurative background), etc. As a result of the comparison we conclude that the broader sememic mark of the plural, or "plurality" in the grammatical sense, should be described as the potentially dismembering reflection of the structure of the referent, while the sememic mark of the singular will be understood as the non-dismembering reflection of the structure of the referent, i.e. the presentation of the referent in its indivisible entireness.

It is sometimes stated that the plural form indiscriminately presents both multiplicity of separate objects ("discrete" plural, *e.g. three houses*) and multiplicity of units of measure for an indivisible object ("plural of measure", *e.g. three hours*) [Ilyish, 36 ff.]. However, the difference here lies not in the content of the plural as such, but in the quality of the objects themselves. Actually, the singulars of the respective nouns differ from one another exactly on the same lines as the plurals do (cf. one house – one hour).

On the other hand, there are semantic varieties of the plural forms that differ from one another in their plural quality as such. Some distinctions of this kind were shown above. Some further distinctions may be seen in a variety of other cases. Here belong, for example, cases where the plural form expresses a definite set of objects (eyes of the face, wheels of the vehicle, etc.), various types of the referent (wines, tees, steels), intensity of the presentation of the idea (years and years, thousands upon thousands), picturesqueness (sands, waters, snows). The extreme point of this semantic scale is marked by the lexicalization of the plural form, i.e. by its serving as a means of rendering not specificational, but purely notional difference in meaning. Cf. colours as a "flag", attentions as "wooing", pains as "effort", quarters as "abode", etc.

The scope of the semantic differences of the plural forms might pose before the observer a question whether the category of number is a variable grammatical category at all.

The answer to the question, though, does not leave space for any uncertainty: the category of number is one of the regular variable categories in the grammatical system of the English language. The variability of the category is simply given in its form, i.e. in the forms of the bulk of English nouns which do distinguish it by means of the described binary paradigm. As for the differences in meaning, these arise from the interaction between the underlying oppositional sememic marks of the category and the more concrete lexical differences in the semantics of individual words.

§ 3. The most general quantitative characteristics of individual words constitute the lexico-grammatical base for dividing the nounal vocabulary as a whole into countable nouns and uncountable nouns. The constant categorial feature "quantitative structure" (see Ch. V, § 3) is directly connected with the variable feature "number", since uncountable nouns are treated grammatically as either singular or plural. Namely, the singular uncountable nouns are modified by the non-discrete quantifiers much or little, and they take the finite verb in the singular, while the plural uncountable nouns take the finite verb in the plural.

The two subclasses of uncountable nouns are usually referred to, respectively, as singularia tantum (only singular) and pluralia tantum (only plural). In terms of oppositions we may say that in the formation of the two subclasses of uncountable nouns the number opposition is "constantly" (lexically) reduced either to the weak member (singularia tantum) or to the strong member (pluralia tantum).

Since the grammatical form of the uncountable nouns of the singularia tantum subclass is not excluded from the category of number, it stands to reason to speak of it as the "absolute" singular, as different from the "correlative" or "common" singular of the countable nouns. The absolute singular excludes the use of the modifying numeral *one*, as well as the indefinite article.

The absolute singular is characteristic of the names of abstract notions (*peace, love, joy, courage, friendship*, etc.), the names of the branches of professional activity (*chemistry, architecture, mathematics, linguistics*, etc.), the names of mass materials (*water, snow, steel, hair*, etc.), the names of collective inanimate objects (*foliage, fruit, furniture, machinery*, etc.). Some of these words can be used in the form of the common singular with the common plural counterpart, but in this case they come to mean either different sorts of materials, or separate concrete manifestations of the qualities denoted by abstract nouns, or concrete objects exhibiting the respective qualities. *Cf.*:

*Joy* is absolutely necessary for normal human life. – It was *a joy* to see her among us. Helmets for motor-cycling are nowadays made of plastics instead of *steel*. – Using different modifications of the described method, super-strong *steels* are produced for various purposes. Etc.

The lexicalizing effect of the correlative number forms (both singular and plural) in such cases is evident, since the categorial component of the referential meaning in each of them is changed from uncountability to countability. Thus, the oppositional reduction is here nullified in a peculiarly lexicalizing way, and the full oppositional force of the category of number is rehabilitated.

Common number with uncountable singular nouns can also be expressed by means of combining them with words showing discreteness, such as *bit, piece, item, sort. Cf.*:

The last two *items of news* were quite sensational. Now I'd like to add one more *bit of information*. You might as well dispense with one or two *pieces of furniture* in the hall.

58

This kind of rendering the grammatical meaning of common number with uncountable nouns is, in due situational conditions, so regular that it can be regarded as special suppletivity in the categorial system of number (see Ch. III, § 4).

On the other hand, the absolute singular, by way of functional oppositional reduction, can be used with countable nouns. In such cases the nouns are taken to express either the corresponding abstract ideas, or else, the meaning of some mass material correlated with its countable referent. *Cf.*:

*Waltz* is a lovely dance. There was dead *desert* all around them. The refugees needed *shelter*. Have we got *chicken* for the second course?

Under this heading (namely, the first of the above two subpoints) comes also the generic use of the singular. *Cf.*:

*Man's* immortality lies in his deeds. Wild *elephant* in the Jungle can be very dangerous.

In the sphere of the plural, likewise, we must recognize the common plural form as the regular feature of countability, and the absolute plural form peculiar to the uncountable subclass of pluralia tantum nouns. The absolute plural, as different from the common plural, cannot directly combine with numerals, and only occasionally does it combine with discrete quantifiers (*many, few*, etc.).

The absolute plural is characteristic of the uncountable nouns which denote objects consisting of two halves (*trousers, scissors, tongs, spectacles*, etc.), the nouns expressing some sort of collective meaning, i.e. rendering the idea of indefinite plurality, both concrete and abstract (*supplies, outskirts, clothes, parings; tidings, earnings, contents, politics; police, cattle, poultry*, etc.), the nouns denoting some diseases as well as some abnormal states of the body and mind (*measles, rickets, mumps, creeps, hysterics*, etc.). As is seen from the examples, from the point of view of number as such, the absolute plural forms can be divided into set absolute plural (objects of two halves) and non-set absolute plural (the rest).

The set plural can also be distinguished among the common plural forms, namely, with nouns denoting fixed sets of objects, such as *eyes* of the face, *legs* of the body, *legs* of the table, *wheels* of the vehicle, *funnels* of the steamboat, *windows* of the room, etc.

The necessity of expressing definite numbers in cases of uncountable pluralia tantum nouns, as well as in cases of countable nouns denoting objects in fixed sets, has brought about different suppletive combinations specific to the plural form of the noun, which exist alongside the suppletive combinations specific to the singular form of the noun shown above. Here belong collocations with such words as *pair, set, group, bunch* and some others. *Cf.*: a pair of pincers; three pairs of bathing trunks; a few groups of police; two sets of dice; several cases of measles; etc.

The absolute plural, by way of functional oppositional reduction, can be represented in countable nouns having the form of the singular, in uncountable nouns having the form of the plural, and also in countable nouns having the form of the plural.

The first type of reduction, consisting in the use of the absolute plural with countable nouns in the singular form, concerns collective nouns, which are thereby changed into "nouns of multitude". *Cf.*:

*The family* were gathered round the table. *The government* are unanimous in disapproving the move of the opposition.

This form of the absolute plural may be called "multitude plural".

The second type of the described oppositional reduction, consisting in the use of the absolute plural with uncountable nouns in the plural form, concerns cases of stylistical marking of nouns. Thus, the oppositional reduction results in expressive transposition. *Cf.*: the sands of the desert; the snows of the Arctic; the waters of the ocean; the fruits of the toil; etc.

This variety of the absolute plural may be called "descriptive uncountable plural".

The third type of oppositional reduction concerns common countable nouns used in repetition groups. The acquired implication is indefinitely large quantity intensely presented. The nouns in repetition groups may themselves be used either in the plural ("featured" form) or in the singular ("unfeatured" form). *Cf.*:

There were *trees and trees* all around us. I lit *cigarette after cigarette*.

This variety of the absolute plural may be called "repetition plural". It can be considered as a peculiar analytical form in the marginal sphere of the category of number (see Ch. III, § 4).

## CHAPTER VIII

## NOUN: CASE

§ 1. Case is the immanent morphological category of the noun manifested in the forms of noun declension and showing the relations of the nounal referent to other objects and phenomena. Thus, the case form of the noun, or contractedly its "case" (in the narrow sense of the word), is a morphological-declensional form.

This category is expressed in English by the opposition of the form in -'s [-z, -s, -ız], usually called the "possessive" case, or more traditionally, the "genitive" case (to which term we will stick in the following presentation*), to the unfeatured form of the noun, usually called the "common" case. The apostrophized -s serves to distinguish in writing the singular noun in the genitive case from the plural noun in the common case. E.g.: the man's duty, the President's decision, Max's letter; the boy's ball, the clerk's promotion, the Empress's jewels.

The genitive of the bulk of plural nouns remains phonetically unexpressed: the few exceptions concern only some of the irregular plurals. Thereby the apostrophe as the graphic sign of the genitive acquires the force of a sort of grammatical hieroglyph. Cf.: the carpenters' tools, the mates' skates, the actresses' dresses.

Functionally, the forms of the English nouns designated as "case forms" relate to one another in an extremely peculiar way. The peculiarity is that the common form is absolutely indefinite from the semantic point of view, whereas the genitive form in its productive uses is restricted to the functions which have a parallel expression by prepositional constructions. Thus, the common form, as appears from the presentation, is also capable of rendering the genitive semantics (namely, in contact and prepositional collocation), which makes the whole of the genitive case into a kind of subsidiary element in the grammatical system of the English noun. This feature stamps the English noun declension as something utterly different from every conceivable declension in principle. In fact, the inflexional oblique case forms as normally and imperatively expressing the immediate syntactic parts of the ordinary sentence in "noun-declen-

---

\* The traditional term "genitive case" seems preferable on the ground that not all the meanings of the genitive case are "possessive".

sional" languages do not exist in English at all. Suffice it to compare a German sentence taken at random with its English rendering:

Erhebung der Anklage gegen die Witwe Capet scheint wünschenswert aus Rücksicht auf die Stimmung der Stadt Paris (L. Feuchtwanger). *Eng.*: (The bringing of) the accusation against the Widow Capet appears desirable, taking into consideration the mood of the City of Paris.

As we see, the five entries of nounal oblique cases in the German utterance (rendered through article inflexion), of which two are genitives, all correspond to one and the same indiscriminate common case form of nouns in the English version of the text. By way of further comparison, we may also observe the Russian translation of the same sentence with its four genitive entries: Выдвижение обвинения против вдовы Капет кажется желательным, если учесть настроение города Парижа.

Under the described circumstances of fact, there is no wonder that in the course of linguistic investigation the category of case in English has become one of the vexed problems of theoretical discussion.

§ 2. Four special views advanced at various times by different scholars should be considered as successive stages in the analysis of this problem.

The first view may be called the "theory of positional cases". This theory is directly connected with the old grammatical tradition, and its traces can be seen in many contemporary text-books for school in the English-speaking countries. Linguistic formulations of the theory, with various individual variations (the number of cases recognized, the terms used, the reasoning cited), may be found in the works of J.C. Nesfield, M. Deutschbein, M. Bryant and other scholars.

In accord with the theory of positional cases, the unchangeable forms of the noun are differentiated as different cases by virtue of the functional positions occupied by the noun in the sentence. Thus, the English noun, on the analogy of classical Latin grammar, would distinguish, besides the inflexional genitive case, also the non-inflexional, i.e. purely positional cases: nominative, vocative, dative, and accusative. The uninflexional cases of the noun are taken to be supported by the parallel inflexional cases of the personal pronouns. The would-be cases in question can be exemplified as follows.*

The nominative case (subject to a verb): *Rain* falls. The vocative case (address): Are you coming, my *friend*? The dative case (indirect object to a verb): I gave *John* a penny. The accusative case (direct object, and also object to a preposition): The man killed a *rat*. The earth is moistened by *rain*.

In the light of all that has been stated in this book in connection with the general notions of morphology, the fallacy of the positional case theory is quite obvious. The cardinal blunder of this view is, that it substitutes the functional characteristics of the part of the sentence for the morphological features of the word class, since the case form, by definition, is the variable morphological form of the noun. In reality, the case forms as such serve as means of expressing the functions of the noun in the sentence, and not vice versa. Thus, what the described view does do on the positive lines is that, within the confused conceptions of form and meaning, it still rightly illustrates the fact that the functional meanings rendered by cases can be expressed in language by other grammatical means, in particular, by word-order.

The second view may be called the "theory of prepositional cases". Like the theory of positional cases, it is also connected with the old school grammar teaching, and was advanced as a logical supplement to the positional view of the case.

In accord with the prepositional theory, combinations of nouns with prepositions in certain object and attributive collocations should be understood as morphological case forms. To these belong first of all the "dative" case (*to* + Noun, *for* + Noun) and the "genitive" case (*of* + Noun). These prepositions, according to G. Curme, are "inflexional prepositions", i.e. grammatical elements equivalent to case-forms. The would-be prepositional cases are generally taken (by the scholars who recognize them) as coexisting with positional cases, together with the classical inflexional genitive completing the case system of the English noun.

---

* The examples are taken from the book: *Nesfield J.C.* Manual of English Grammar and Composition. Ldn., 1942, p. 24.

The prepositional theory, though somewhat better grounded than the positional theory, nevertheless can hardly pass a serious linguistic trial. As is well known from noun-declensional languages, all their prepositions, and not only some of them, do require definite cases of nouns (prepositional case-government); this fact, together with a mere semantic observation of the role of prepositions in the phrase, shows that any preposition by virtue of its functional nature stands in essentially the same general grammatical relations to nouns. It should follow from this that not only the *of-*, *to-*, and *for-*phrases, but also all the other prepositional phrases in English must be regarded as "analytical cases." As a result of such an approach illogical redundancy in terminology would arise: each prepositional phrase would bear then another, additional name of "prepositional case", the total number of the said "cases" running into dozens upon dozens without any gain either to theory or practice [Ilyish, 42].

The third view of the English noun case recognizes a limited inflexional system of two cases in English, one of them featured and the other one unfeatured. This view may be called the "limited case theory".

The limited case theory is at present most broadly accepted among linguists both in this country and abroad. It was formulated by such scholars as H. Sweet, O. Jespersen, and has since been radically developed by A.I. Smirnitsky, L.S. Barkhudarov and others.

The limited case theory in its modern presentation is based on the explicit oppositional approach to the recognition of grammatical categories. In the system of the English case the functional mark is defined, which differentiates the two case forms: the possessive or genitive form as the strong member of the categorial opposition and the common, or "non-genitive" form as the weak member of the categorial opposition. The opposition is shown as being effected in full with animate nouns, though a restricted use with inanimate nouns is also taken into account. The detailed functions of the genitive are specified with the help of semantic transformational correlations [Бархударов, 1975, 89 ff.].

§ 3. We have considered the three theories which, if at basically different angles, proceed from the assumption that the English noun does distinguish the grammatical case in its functional structure. However, another view of the problem of the English noun cases has been put forward which sharply counters the theories hitherto observed. This view approaches the English noun as having completely lost the category of case in the course of its historical development. All the nounal cases, including the much spoken of genitive, are considered as extinct, and the lingual unit that is named the "genitive case" by force of tradition, would be in reality a combination of a noun with a postposition (i.e. a relational postpositional word with preposition-like functions). This view, advanced in an explicit form by G.N. Vorontsova [Воронцова, 168 ff.] may be called the "theory of the possessive postposition" ("postpositional theory"). *Cf.*: [Ilyish, 44 ff.; Бархударов, Штелинг, 42 ff.].

Of the various reasons substantiating the postpositional theory the following two should be considered as the main ones.

First, the postpositional element -'s is but loosely connected with the noun, which finds the clearest expression in its use not only with single nouns, but also with whole word-groups of various status. Compare some examples cited by G.N. Vorontsova in her work: somebody else's daughter; another stage-struck girl's stage finish; the man who had hauled him out to dinner's head.

Second, there is an indisputable parallelism of functions between the possessive postpositional constructions and the prepositional constructions, resulting in the optional use of the former. This can be shown by transformational reshuffles of the above examples: ... → the daughter of somebody else; ... → the stage finish of another stage-struck girl; ... → the head of the man who had hauled him out to dinner.

One cannot but acknowledge the rational character of the cited reasoning. Its strong point consists in the fact that it is based on a careful observation of the lingual data. For all that, however, the theory of the possessive postposition fails to take into due account the consistent insight into the nature of the noun form in -'s achieved by the limited case theory. The latter has demonstrated beyond any doubt that the noun form in -'s is systemically, i.e. on a strictly structural-functional basis, contrasted against the unfeatured form of the noun, which does make the whole correlation of the nounal forms into a grammatical category of case-like order, however specific it might be.

As the basic arguments for the recognition of the noun form in -'s in the capacity of grammatical case, besides the oppositional nature of the general functional correlation of the featured and unfeatured forms of the noun, we will name the following two.

First, the broader phrasal uses of the postpositional -'s like those shown on the above examples, display a clearly expressed stylistic colouring; they are, as linguists put it, stylistically marked, which fact proves their transpositional nature. In this connection we may formulate the following regularity: the more self-dependent the construction covered by the case-sign -'s, the stronger the stylistic mark (colouring) of the resulting genitive phrase. This functional analysis is corroborated by the statistical observation of the forms in question in the living English texts. According to the data obtained by B.S. Khaimovich and B.I. Rogovskaya, the -'s sign is attached to individual nouns in as many as 96 per cent of its total textual occurrences [Khaimovich, Rogovskaya, 64]. Thus, the immediate casal relations are realized by individual nouns, the phrasal, as well as some non-nounal uses of the -'s sign, being on the whole of a secondary grammatical order.

Second, the -'s sign from the point of view of its segmental status in language differs from ordinary functional words. It is morpheme-like by its phonetical properties; it is strictly postpositional unlike the prepositions; it is semantically by far a more bound element than a preposition, which, among other things, has hitherto prevented it from being entered into dictionaries as a separate word.

As for the fact that the "possessive postpositional construction" is correlated with a parallel prepositional construction, it only shows the functional peculiarity of the form, but cannot disprove its case-like nature, since cases of nouns in general render much the same functional semantics as prepositional phrases (reflecting a wide range of situational relations of noun referents).

§ 4. The solution of the problem, then, is to be sought on the ground of a critical synthesis of the positive statements of the two theories: the limited case theory and the possessive postposition theory.

A two-case declension of nouns should be recognized in English, with its common case as a "direct" case, and its genitive case as the only oblique case. But, unlike the case system in ordinary noun-declensional languages based on inflexional word change, the case system in English is founded on a particle expression. The particle nature of -'s is evident from the fact that it is added in post-position both to individual nouns and to nounal word-groups of various status, rendering the same essential semantics of appurtenance in the broad sense of the term. Thus, within the expression of the genitive in English, two subtypes are to be recognized: the first (principal) is the word genitive; the second (of a minor order) is the phrase genitive. Both of them are not inflexional, but particle case-forms.

The described particle expression of case may to a certain extent be likened to the particle expression of the subjunctive mood in Russian [Иртеньева, 40]. As is known, the Russian subjunctive particle *бы* not only can be distanced from the verb it refers to, but it can also relate to a lexical unit of non-verb-like nature without losing its basic subjunctive-functional quality. *Cf.*: Если *бы* не он. Мне *бы* такая возможность. Как *бы* не так.

From the functional point of view the English genitive case, on the whole, may be regarded as subsidiary to the syntactic system of prepositional phrases. However, it still displays some differential points in its functional meaning, which, though neutralized in isolated use, are revealed in broader syntagmatic collocations with prepositional phrases.

One of such differential points may be defined as "animate appurtenance" against "inanimate appurtenance" rendered by a prepositional phrase in contrastive use. *Cf.*:

The *people's* voices drowned in the roar of the started engines. The *tiger's* leap proved quicker than the click of the rifle.

Another differential point expressed in cases of textual co-occurrence of the units compared consists in the subjective use of the genitive noun (subject of action) against the objective use of the prepositional noun (object of action). *Cf.*: My Lord's choice of the butler; the partisans' rescue of the prisoners; the treaty's denunciation of mutual threats.

Furthermore, the genitive is used in combination with the *of*-phrase on a complementary basis expressing the functional semantics which may roughly be called "appurtenance rank gradation": a difference in construction (i.e. the use of the genitive against the use of the *of*-phrase) signals a difference in correlated ranks of semantic domination. *Cf.*: the country's strain of wartime (lower rank: the strain of wartime; higher rank: the country's strain); the sight of Satispy's face (higher rank: the sight of the face; lower rank: Satispy's face).

It is certainly these and other differential points and complementary uses that sustain the particle genitive as part of the systemic expression of nounal relations in spite of the disintegration of the inflexional case in the course of historical development of English.

§ 5. Within the general functional semantics of appurtenance, the English genitive expresses a wide range of relational meanings specified in the regular interaction of the semantics of the subordinating and subordinated elements in the genitive phrase. Summarizing the results of extensive investigations in this field, the following basic semantic types of the genitive can be pointed out.

First, the form which can be called the "genitive of possessor" (*Lat.* "genetivus possessori"). Its constructional meaning will be defined as "inorganic" possession, i.e. possessional relation (in the broad sense) of the genitive referent to the object denoted by the head-noun. *E.g.*: Christine's living-room; the assistant manager's desk; Dad's earnings; Kate and Jerry's grandparents; the Steel Corporation's hired slaves.

The diagnostic test for the genitive of possessor is its transformation into a construction that explicitly expresses the idea of possession (belonging) inherent in the form. *Cf.*: Christine's living-room → the living-room belongs to Christine; the Steel Corporation's hired slaves → the Steel Corporation possesses hired slaves.*

Second, the form which can be called the "genitive of integer" (*Lat.* "genetivus integri"). Its constructional meaning will be defined as "organic possession", i.e. a broad possessional relation of a whole to its part. *E.g.*: Jane's busy hands; Patrick's voice; the patient's health; the hotel's lobby.

Diagnostic test: ... → the busy hands as part of Jane's person; ... → the health as part of the patient's state; ... → the lobby as a component part of the hotel, etc.

A subtype of the integer genitive expresses a qualification received by the genitive referent through the head-word. *E.g.*: Mr. Dodson's vanity; the computer's reliability.

This subtype of the genitive can be called the "genitive of received qualification" (*Lat.* "genetivus qualificationis receptae").

Third, the "genitive of agent" (*Lat.* "genetivus agentis"). The more traditional name of this genitive is "subjective" (*Lat.* "genetivus subjectivus"). The latter term seems inadequate because of its unjustified narrow application: nearly all the genitive types stand in subjective relation to the referents of the head-nouns. The general meaning of the genitive of agent is explained in its name: this form renders an activity or some broader processual relation with the referent of the genitive as its subject. *E.g.*: the great man's arrival; Pe-

---

* We avoid the use of the verb *have* in diagnostic constructions, because *have* itself, due to its polysemantism, wants diagnostic contextual specifications.

ter's insistence; the councillor's attitude; Campbell Clark's gaze; the hotel's competitive position.

Diagnostic test: ... → the great man arrives; ... → Peter insists; ... → the hotel occupies a competitive position, etc.

A subtype of the agent genitive expresses the author, or, more broadly considered, the producer of the referent of the head-noun. Hence, it receives the name of the "genitive of author" (*Lat.* "genetivus auctori"). *E.g.*: Beethoven's sonatas; John Galsworthy's "A Man of Property"; the committee's progress report.

Diagnostic test: ... → Beethoven composed (is the author of) the sonatas; ... → the committee has compiled (is the compiler of) the progress report, etc.

Fourth, the "genitive of patient" (*Lat.* "genetivus patientis"). This type of genitive, in contrast to the above, expresses the recipient of the action or process denoted by the head-noun. *E.g.*: the champion's sensational defeat; Erick's final expulsion; the meeting's chairman; the St Gregory's proprietor; the city's business leaders; the Titanic's tragedy.

Diagnostic test: ... → the champion is defeated (i.e. his opponent defeated him); ... → Erick is expelled; ... → the meeting is chaired by its chairman; ... → the St Gregory is owned by its proprietor, etc.

Fifth, the "genitive of destination" (*Lat.* "genetivus destinationis"). This form denotes the destination, or function of the referent of the head-noun. *E.g.*: women's footwear; children's verses; a fishers' tent.

Diagnostic test: ... → footwear for women; ... → a tent for fishers, etc.

Sixth, the "genitive of dispensed qualification" (*Lat.* "genetivus qualificationis dispensatae"). The meaning of this genitive type, as different from the subtype "genitive of received qualification", is some characteristic or qualification, not received, but given by the genitive noun to the referent of the head-noun. *E.g.*: a girl's voice; a book-keeper's statistics; Curtis O'Keefe's kind (of hotels – *M.B.*).

Diagnostic test: ... → a voice characteristic of a girl; ... → statistics peculiar to a book-keeper's report; ... → the kind (of hotels) characteristic of those owned by Curtis O'Keefe.

Under the heading of this general type comes a verv important subtype of the genitive which expresses a comparison. The comparison, as different from a general qualification, is supposed to be of a vivid, descriptive nature. The subtype is called the "genitive of comparison" (*Lat.* "genetivus comparationis"). This term has been used

69

to cover the whole class. *E.g.*: the cock's self-confidence of the man; his perky sparrow's smile.

Diagnostic test: ... → the self-confidence like that of a cock; ... → the smile making the man resemble a perky sparrow.

Seventh, the "genitive of adverbial" (*Lat.* "genetivus adverbii"). The form denotes adverbial factors relating to the referent of the head-noun, mostly the time and place of the event. Strictly speaking, this genitive may be considered as another subtype of the genitive of dispensed qualification. Due to its adverbial meaning, this type of genitive can be used with adverbialized substantives. *E.g.*: the evening's newspaper; yesterday's encounter; Moscow's talks.

Diagnostic test: ... → the newspaper issued in the evening; ... → the encounter which took place yesterday; ... → the talks that were held in Moscow.

Eighth, the "genitive of quantity" (*Lat.* "genetivus quantitatis"). This type of genitive denotes the measure or quantity relating to the referent of the head-noun. For the most part, the quantitative meaning expressed concerns units of distance measure, time measure, weight measure. *E.g.*: three miles' distance; an hour's delay; two months' time; a hundred tons' load.

Diagnostic test: ... → a distance the measure of which is three miles; ... → a time lasting two months; ... → a load weighing a hundred tons.

The given survey of the semantic types of the genitive is by no means exhaustive in any analytical sense. The identified types are open both to subtype specifications, and inter-type generalizations (for instance, on the principle of the differentiation between subject – object relations), and the very set of primary types may be expanded.

However, what does emerge out of the survey is the evidence of ҁ wide functional range of the English particle genitive, making it into a helpful and flexible, if subsidiary, means of expressing relational semantics in the sphere of the noun.

§ 6. We have considered theoretical aspects of the problem of case of the English noun, and have also observed the relevant lingual data instrumental in substantiating the suggested interpretations. As a result of the analysis, we have come to the conclusion that the inflexional case of nouns in English has ceased to exist. In its place a new, peculiar two-case system has developed based on the particle expression of the genitive falling into two segmental types: the word-genitive and the phrase-genitive.

The undertaken study of the case in the domain of the noun, as the next step, calls upon the observer to re-formulate the accepted interpretation of the form-types of the English personal pronouns.

The personal pronouns are commonly interpreted as having a case system of their own, differing in principle from the case system of the noun. The two cases traditionally recognized here are the nominative case (*I, you, he*, etc.) and the objective case (*me, you, him*, etc.). To these forms the two series of forms of the possessive pronouns are added – respectively, the conjoint series (*my, your, his*, etc.) and the absolute series (*mine, yours, his*, etc.). A question now arises, if it is rational at all to recognize the type of case in the words of substitutional nature which is absolutely incompatible with the type of case in the correlated notional words?

Attempts have been made in linguistics to transfer the accepted view of pronominal cases to the unchangeable forms of the nouns (by way of the logical procedure of back substitution), thereby supporting the positional theory of case (M. Bryant). In the light of the present study, however, it is clear that these attempts lack an adequate linguistic foundation.

As a matter of fact, the categories of the substitute have to reflect the categories of the antecedent, not vice versa. As an example we may refer to the category of gender (see Ch. VI): the English gender is expressed through the correlation of nouns with their pronominal substitutes by no other means than the reflection of the corresponding semantics of the antecedent in the substitute. But the proclaimed correlation between the case forms of the noun and the would-be case forms of the personal pronouns is of quite another nature: the nominative "case" of the pronoun has no antecedent case in the noun; nor has the objective "case" of the pronoun any antecedent case in the noun. On the other hand, the only oblique case of the English noun, the genitive, does have its substitutive reflection in the pronoun, though not in the case form, but in the lexical form of possession (possessive pronouns). And this latter relation of the antecedent to its substitute gives us a clue to the whole problem of pronominal "case": the inevitable conclusion is that there is at present no case in the English personal pronouns; the personal pronominal system of cases has completely disintegrated, and in its place the four individual word-types of pronouns have appeared: the nominative form, the objective form, and the possessive form in its two versions, conjoint and absolute.

An analysis of the pronouns based on more formal considerations can only corroborate the suggested approach proceeding from the principle of functional evaluation. In fact, what is traditionally accepted as case-forms of the pronouns are not the regular forms of productive morphological change implied by the very idea of case declension, but individual forms sustained by suppletivity and given to the speaker as a ready-made set. The set is naturally completed by the possessive forms of pronouns, so that actually we are faced with a lexical paradigmatic series of four subsets of personal pronouns, to which the relative *who* is also added: *I – me – my – mine, you – you – your – yours*, ... *who – whom – whose – whose*. Whichever of the former case correlations are still traceable in this system (as, for example, in the subseries *he – him – his*), they exist as mere relics, i.e. as a putrified evidence of the old productive system that has long ceased to function in the morphology of English.

Thus, what should finally be meant by the suggested terminological name "particle case" in English, is that the former system of the English inflexional declension has completely and irrevocably disintegrated, both in the sphere of nouns and their substitute pronouns; in its place a new, limited case system has arisen based on a particle oppositional feature and subsidiary to the prepositional expression of the syntactic relations of the noun.

CHAPTER IX

NOUN: ARTICLE DETERMINATION

§ 1. Article is a determining unit of specific nature accompanying the noun in communicative collocation. Its special character is clearly seen against the background of determining words of half-notional semantics. Whereas the function of the determiners such as *this, any, some* is to explicitly interpret the referent of the noun in relation to other objects or phenomena of a like kind, the semantic purpose of the article is to specify the nounal referent, as it were, altogether unostentatiously, to define it in the most general way, without any explicitly expressed contrasts.

This becomes obvious when we take the simplest examples ready at hand. *Cf.*:

Will you give me *this* pen, Willy? (I.e. the pen that I am pointing out, not one of your choice.) – Will you give me *the* pen, please? (I.e. simply the pen from the desk, you understand which.) *Any* blade will do, I only want it for scratching out the wrong word from the type-script. (I.e. any blade of the stock, however blunt it may be.) – Have you got something sharp? I need a penknife or *a* blade. (I.e. simply a blade, if not a knife, without additional implications.) *Some* woman called in your absence, she didn't give her name. (I.e. a woman strange to me.) – *A* woman called while you were out, she left a message. (I.e. simply a woman, without a further connotation.)

Another peculiarity of the article, as different from the determiners in question, is that, in the absence of a determiner, the use of the article with the noun is quite obligatory, in so far as the cases of non-use of the article are subject to no less definite rules than the use of it.

Taking into consideration these peculiar features of the article, the linguist is called upon to make a sound statement about its segmental status in the system of morphology. Namely, his task is to decide whether the article is a purely auxiliary element of a special grammatical form of the noun which functions as a component of a definite morphological category, or it is a separate word, i.e. a lexical unit in the determiner word set, if of a more abstract meaning than other determiners.

The problem is a vexed one; it has inspired intensive research activity in the field, as well as animated discussion with various pros and cons affirmed, refuted and re-affirmed.[*] In the course of these investigations, however, many positive facts about articles have been established, which at present enables an observer, proceeding from the systemic principle in its paradigmatic interpretation, to expose the status of the article with an attempt at demonstrative conviction.

To arrive at a definite decision, we propose to consider the properties of the English articles at four successive stages, beginning with their semantic evaluation as such, then adding to the obtained data a situational estimation of their uses, thereafter analysing their categorial features in the light of the oppositional theory, and finally concluding the investigation by a paradigmatic generalization.

§ 2. A mere semantic observation of the articles in English, i.e. the definite article *the* and the indefinite article *a/an*, at once discloses not two but three meaningful characterizations of the nounal referent achieved by their correlative functioning, namely: one ren-

---

[*] Different aspects of the discussion about the English article are very well shown by B.A. Ilyish in the cited book (p. 49 ff.).

dered by the definite article, one rendered by the indefinite article, and one rendered by the absence (or non-use) of the article. Let us examine them separately.

The definite article expresses the identification or individualization of the referent of the noun: the use of this article shows that the object denoted is taken in its concrete, individual quality. This meaning can be brought to explicit exposition by a substitution test. The test consists in replacing the article used in a construction by a demonstrative word, e.g. a demonstrative determiner, without causing a principal change in the general implication of the construction. Of course, such an "equivalent" substitution should be understood in fact as nothing else but analogy: the difference in meaning between a determiner and an article admits of no argument, and we pointed it out in the above passages. Still, the replacements of words as a special diagnostic procedure, which is applied with the necessary reservations and according to a planned scheme of research, is quite permissible. In our case it undoubtedly shows a direct relationship in the meanings of the determiner and the article, the relationship in which the determiner is semantically the more explicit element of the two. Cf.:

But look at *the* apple-tree! → But look at *this* apple-tree! *The* town lay still in the Indian summer sun. → *That* town lay still in the Indian summer sun. *The* water is horribly hot. → *This* water is horribly hot. It's *the* girls who are to blame. → It's *those* girls who are to blame.

The justification of the applied substitution, as well as its explanatory character, may be proved by a counter-test, namely, by the change of the definite article into the indefinite article, or by omitting the article altogether. The replacement either produces a radical, i.e. "non-equivalent" shift in the meaning of the construction, or else results in a grammatically unacceptable construction. Cf.: ... → Look at *an* apple-tree! → *Look at apple-tree! ... → *A water is horribly hot. → *Water is horribly hot.

The indefinite article, as different from the definite article, is commonly interpreted as referring the object denoted by the noun to a certain class of similar objects; in other words, the indefinite article expresses a classifying generalization of the nounal referent, or takes it in a relatively general sense. To prove its relatively generalizing functional meaning, we may use the diagnostic insertions of specifying-classifying phrases into the construction in question; we may also employ the transformation of implicit comparative constructions with the indefinite article into the corresponding explicit comparative constructions. *Cf.*:

We passed *a* water-mill. → We passed *a certain* water-mill. It is *a* very young country, isn't it? → It is *a* very young *kind of* country, isn't it? What *an* arrangement! → What *sort of* arrangement! This child is *a* positive nightmare. → This child is positively *like a* nightmare.

The procedure of a classifying contrast employed in practical textbooks exposes the generalizing nature of the indefinite article most clearly in many cases of its use. *E.g.*:

*A* door opened in the wall. → *A* door (not *a* window) opened in the wall. We saw *a* flower under the bush. → We saw *a* flower (not *a* strawberry) under the bush.

As for the various uses of nouns without an article, from the semantic point of view they all should be divided into two types. In the first place, there are uses where the articles are deliberately omitted out of stylistical considerations. We see such uses, for instance, in telegraphic speech, in titles and headlines, in various notices. *E.g.*:

*Telegram* received *room* reserved for *week-end*. (The text of a telegram.) *Conference* adjourned until further notice. (The text of an announcement.) *Big red bus* rushes food to *strikers*. (The title of a newspaper article.)

The purposeful elliptical omission of the article in cases like that is quite obvious, and the omitted articles may easily be restored in the constructions in the simplest "back-directed" refilling procedures. *Cf.*:

... → *The telegram* is received, *a room* is reserved for *the week-end*. ... → *The conference* is adjourned until further notice. ... → *A big red bus* rushes food to *the strikers*.

Alongside free elliptical constructions, there are cases of the semantically unspecified non-use of the article in various combinations of fixed type, such as prepositional phrases (*on fire, at hand, in debt*, etc.), fixed verbal collocations (*take place, make use, cast anchor*, etc.), descriptive coordinative groups and repetition groups (*man and wife, dog and gun, day by day*, etc.), and the like. These cases of traditionally fixed absence of the article are quite similar to the cases of traditionally fixed uses of both indefinite and definite articles (*cf.*: *in a hurry, at a loss, have a look, give a start*, etc.; *in the main, out of the question, on the look-out*, etc.).

Outside the elliptical constructions and fixed uses, however, we know a really semantic absence of the article with the noun. It is this semantic absence of the article that stands in immediate meaningful correlation with the definite and indefinite articles as such.

As is widely acknowledged, the meaningful non-uses of the article are not homogeneous; nevertheless, they admit of a very explicit classification founded on the countability characteristics of the noun. Why countability characteristics? For the two reasons. The first reason is inherent in the nature of the noun itself: the abstract generalization reflected through the meaningful non-use of the article is connected with the suppression of the idea of the number in the noun. The second reason is inherent in the nature of the article: the indefinite article which plays the crucial role in the semantic correlation in question reveals the meaning of oneness within its semantic base, having originated from the indefinite pronoun *one*, and that is why the abstract use of the noun naturally goes with the absence of the article.

The essential points of the said classification are three in number.

*First*. The meaningful absence of the article before the countable noun in the singular signifies that the noun is taken in an abstract sense, expressing the most general idea of the object denoted. This meaning, which may be called the meaning of "absolute generalization", can be demonstrated by inserting in the tested construction a chosen generalizing modifier (such as *in general, in the abstract, in the broadest sense*). *Cf.*:

*Law* (in general) begins with the beginning of human society. *Steam-engine* (in general) introduced for locomotion a couple of centuries ago has now become obsolete.

*Second*. The absence of the article before the uncountable noun corresponds to the two kinds of generalization: both relative and absolute. To decide which of the two meanings is realized in any particular case, the described tests should be carried out alternately. *Cf.*:

John laughed with *great bitterness* (that sort of bitterness – relative generalization). The subject of *health* (in general – absolute generalization) was carefully avoided by everybody. *Coffee* (a kind of beverage served at the table – relative generalization) or *tea*, please? *Coffee* (in general – absolute generalization) stimulates the function of the heart.

*Third*. The absence of the article before the countable noun in the plural, likewise, corresponds to both kinds of generalization, and the exposition of the meaning in each case can be achieved by the same semantic tests. *Cf.*:

*Stars, planets* and *comets* (these kinds of objects: relative generalization) are different *celestial bodies* (not terrestrial bodies: relative generalization). *Wars* (in general: absolute generalization) should be eliminated as means of deciding international disputes.

To distinguish the demonstrated semantic functions of the non-uses of the article by definition, we may say that the absence of the article with uncountable nouns, as well as with countable nouns in the plural, renders the meaning of "uncharacterized generalization", as different from the meaning of "absolute generalization", achieved by the absence of the article with countable nouns in the singular.

So much for the semantic evaluation of the articles as the first stage of our study.

§ 3. Passing to the situational assessment of the article uses, we must point out that the basic principle of their differentiation here is not a direct consideration of their meanings, but disclosing the informational characteristics that the article conveys to its noun in concrete contextual conditions. Examined from this angle, the definite article serves as an indicator of the type of nounal information which is presented as the "facts already known", i.e. as the starting point of the communication. In contrast to this, the indefinite article or the meaningful absence of the article introduces the central communicative nounal part of the sentence, i.e. the part rendering the immediate informative data to be conveyed from the speaker to the listener. In the situational study of syntax (see Ch. XXII) the starting point of the communication is called its "theme", while the central informative part is called its "rheme".

In accord with the said situational functions, the typical syntactic position of the noun modified by the definite article is the "thematic" subject, while the typical syntactic position of the noun modified by the indefinite article or by the meaningful absence of the article is the "rhematic" predicative. *Cf.*:

*The day* (subject) was drawing to a close, *the busy noises of the city* (subject) were dying down. How to handle the situation was *a big question* (predicative). The sky was *pure gold* (predicative) above the setting sun.

It should be noted that in many other cases of syntactic use, i.e. non-subjective or non-predicative, the articles reflect the same situational functions. This can be probed by reducing the constructions in question on re-arrangement lines to the logically "canonized" link-type constructions. *Cf.*:

If you would care to verify *the incident* (object), pray do so. → If you would care *the incident* (subject) to be verified, pray have it verified. I am going to make *a rather strange request* (object) to you. → What I am going to make is *a rather strange request* (predicative) to you. You are talking *nonsense* (object), lad. → What you are talking, lad, is *nonsense* (predicative).

Another essential contextual-situational characteristic of the articles is their immediate connection with the two types of attributes to the noun. The first type is a "limiting" attribute, which requires the definite article before the noun; the second type is a "descriptive" attribute, which requires the indefinite article or the meaningful absence of the article before the noun. *Cf.*:

The events *chronicled in this narrative* took place some four years ago. (A limiting attribute) She was a person of *strong will and iron self-control*. (A descriptive attribute) He listened to her story with *grave and kindly* attention. (A descriptive attribute)

The role of descriptive attributes in the situational aspect of articles is particularly worthy of note in the constructions of syntactic "convergencies", i.e. chained attributive-repetitional phrases modifying the same referent from different angles. *Cf.*:

My longing for *a house, a fine and beautiful house, such a house I could never hope to have*, flowered into life again.

§ 4. We have now come to the third stage of the undertaken analysis of the English articles, namely to their consideration in the light of the oppositional theory. The oppositional examination of any grammatically relevant set of lingual objects is of especial importance from the point of view of the systemic conception of language, since oppositions constitute the basis of the structure of grammatical paradigms.

Bearing in mind the facts established at the two previous stages of observation, it is easy to see that oppositionally, the article determination of the noun should be divided into two binary correlations connected with each other hierarchically.

The opposition of the higher level operates in the whole system of articles. It contrasts the definite article with the noun against the two other forms of article determination of the noun, i.e. the indefinite article and the meaningful absence of the article. In this opposition the definite article should be interpreted as the strong member by virtue of its identifying and individualizing function, while the other forms of article determination should be interpreted as the weak member, i.e. the member that leaves the feature in question ("identification") unmarked.

The opposition of the lower level operates within the article subsystem that forms the weak member of the upper opposition. This opposition contrasts the two types of generalization, i.e. the relative generalization distinguishing its strong member (the indefinite article plus the meaningful absence of the article as its analogue with uncountable nouns and nouns in the plural) and the absolute, or "abstract" generalization distinguishing the weak member of the opposition (the meaningful absence of the article).

The described oppositional system can be shown on the following diagram (see Fig. 2).

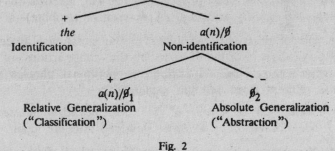

ARTICLE DETERMINATION

| + | − |
| the | $a(n)/\emptyset$ |
| Identification | Non-identification |

| + | − |
| $a(n)/\emptyset_1$ | $\emptyset_2$ |
| Relative Generalization | Absolute Generalization |
| ("Classification") | ("Abstraction") |

Fig. 2

It is the oppositional description of the English articles that involves the interpretation of the article non-use as the zero form of the article, since the opposition of the positive exponent of the feature to the negative exponent of the feature (i.e. its absence) realizes an important part of the integral article determination semantics. As

79

for the heterogeneity of functions displayed by the absence of the article, it by no means can be taken as a ground for denying the relevance or expediency of introducing the notion of zero in the article system. As a matter of fact, each of the two essential meanings of this dialectically complex form is clearly revealed in its special oppositional correlation and, consequently, corresponds to the really existing lingual facts irrespective of the name given to the form by the observer.

The best way of demonstrating the actual oppositional value of the articles on the immediate textual material is to contrast them in syntactically equivalent conditions in pairs. *Cf.* the examples given below.

Identical nounal positions for the pair "the definite article – the indefinite article": *The train* hooted (that train). – *A train* hooted (some train).

Correlative nounal positions for the pair "the definite article – the absence of the article": I'm afraid *the oxygen* is out (our supply of oxygen). – *Oxygen* is necessary for life (oxygen in general, life in general).

Correlative nounal positions for the pair "the indefinite article – the absence of the article": Be careful, there is *a puddle* under your feet (a kind of puddle). – Be careful, there is *mud* on the ground (as different from clean space).

Finally, correlative nounal positions for the easily neutralized pair "the zero article of relative generalization – the zero article of absolute generalization": *New information* should be gathered on this subject (some information). – *Scientific information* should be gathered systematically in all fields of human knowledge (information in general).

On the basis of the oppositional definition of the article it becomes possible to explicate the semantic function of the article determination of nouns for cases where the inherent value of the article is contrasted against the contrary semantic value of the noun or the nounal collocation.

In particular, the indefinite article may occasionally be used with a nounal collocation of normally individualizing meaning, *e.g.*:

Rodney Harrington laughed out loud as he caught *a last glimpse of Allison Mackenzie and Norman Page* in his rear-vision mirror (Gr. Metalious). After all, you've got *a best side* and *a worst side of yourself* and it's no good showing the worst side and harping on it (A. Christie).

Conversely, the definite article may occasionally be used with a nounal collocation of normally descriptive meaning, *e.g.*:

Ethel still went in the evenings to bathe in *the silent pool* (S. Maugham).

The indefinite article may occasionally be used with a unique referent noun, *e.g.*:

Ted Latimer from beyond her murmured: "The sun here isn't *a real sun*" (A. Christie).

The zero article may occasionally be used with an ordinary concrete noun the semantic nature of which stands, as it were, in sharp contradiction to the idea of uncountable generalization, *e.g.*:

The glasses had a habit of slipping down her button nose which did not have enough *bridge* to hold them up (S.M. Disney). He went up a well-kept drive to a modern house with a square roof and a good deal of *window* (A. Christie).

In all these and similar cases, by virtue of being correlated with semantic elements of contrary nature, the inherent categorial meanings of the articles appear, as it were, in their original, pure quality. Having no environmental support, the articles become intensely self-dependent in the expression of their categorial semantics, and, against the alien contextual background, traces of transposition can be seen in their use.

§ 5. Having established the functional value of articles in oppositional assessment, we can now, in broader systemic contraposition, probe the correlation of the meanings of articles with the meanings of functional determiners. As a result of this observation, within the system of the determiners two separate subsets can be defined, one of which is centred around the definite article with its individualizing semantics (*this – these, that – those, my, our, your, his, her, its, their*), and the other one around the indefinite article with its generalizing semantics (*another, some, any, every, no*). The type of the division is such as to show the integration of the article meanings into the total semantic volume of the determiners. In other words, the observation inevitably leads us to the conclusion that the article determination of the noun as a specific grammatical category remains valid also in such cases when the noun is modified not by the article itself, but by a semi-notional determiner. This is clearly seen in equivalency confrontations such as the following:

But unhappily *the wife* wasn't listening. – But unhappily *his wife* wasn't listening.

*The whispering voices* caught the attention of the guards. – *Those whispering voices* caught their attention.

What could *a woman* do in a situation like that? – What could *any woman* do in that sort of situation?

At least I saw *interest* in her eyes. – At least I saw *some interest* in her eyes.

*Not a word* had been pronounced about the terms of the document. – *No word* had been pronounced about those terms.

The demonstration of the organic connection between the articles and semi-notional determiners, in its turn, makes it possible to disclose the true function of the grammatical use of articles with proper nouns. *E.g.*:

"This," said Froelich, "is *the James Walker* who wrote 'The Last of the Old Lords'" (M. Bradbury). *Cf*.: This is *the same James Walker*.

I came out to Iraq with *a Mrs. Kelsey* (A. Christie). *Cf*.: The woman was *a certain Mrs. Kelsey*.

It was like seeing *a Vesuvius* at the height of its eruption. *Cf*.: The sight looked to us like *another Vesuvius*.

"I prophesy *a wet August*," said Old Moore Abinger (M. Dickens). *Cf*.: Next August will be a wet month, unlike *some other Augusts* in retrospect.

In the exemplified grammatical uses transpositional features are revealed similar to those the article acquires when used with a noun characterized by a contrary semantic base. On the other hand, the analysis of these cases clearly stamps the traditional proper name combinations with embedded articles, both of the onomastic set (*Alexander the Great*, etc.) and the toponymic set (*The Hague*, etc.) as lexicalized collocations that only come into contact with the periphery of grammar.

§ 6. The essential grammatical features of the articles exposed in the above considerations and tests leave no room for misinterpretation at the final, generalizing stage of analysis.

The data obtained show that the English noun, besides the variable categories of number and case, distinguishes also the category of determination expressed by the article paradigm of three grammatical forms: the definite, the indefinite, the zero. The paradigm is generalized for the whole system of the common nouns, being transpositionally outstretched also into the system of proper nouns. Various cases of asymmetry in the realization of this paradigm (such as the article determination of certain nouns of the types singularia tantum and pluralia tantum), similar to, and in connection with the expression of the category of number, are balanced by suppletive collocations. Cf.: ∅ progress – a kind of progress, some progress – the progress; ∅ news – an item of news – the news, etc.

The semi-notional determiners used with nouns in the absence of articles, expose the essential article meanings as in-built in their semantic structure.

Thus, the status of the combination of the article with the noun should be defined as basically analytical, the article construction as such being localized by its segmental properties between the free syntactic combination of words (the upper bordering level) and the combination of a grammatical affix with a notional stem in the morphological composition of an indivisible word (the lower bordering level). The article itself is a special type of grammatical auxiliary.

### CHAPTER X

### VERB: GENERAL

§ 1. Grammatically the verb is the most complex part of speech. This is due to the central role it performs in the expression of the predicative functions of the sentence, i.e. the functions establishing the connection between the situation (situational event) named in the utterance and reality. The complexity of the verb is inherent not only in the intricate structure of its grammatical categories, but also in its various subclass divisions, as well as in its falling into two sets of forms profoundly different from each other: the finite set and the non-finite set.

The complicated character of the grammatical and lexico-grammatical structure of the verb has given rise to much dispute and controversy. However, the application of the principles of systemic linguistic analysis to the study of this interesting sphere of language helps overcome many essential difficulties in its theoretical description, and also a number of terminological disagreements among the scholars. This refers in particular to the fundamental relations between the categories of tense and aspect, which have aroused of late very heated disputes.

§ 2. The general categorial meaning of the verb is process presented dynamically, i.e. developing in time. This general processual meaning is embedded in the semantics of all the verbs, including those that denote states, forms of existence, types of attitude, evaluations, etc., rather than actions. Cf.:

Edgar's room *led* out of the wall without a door. She *had* herself a liking for richness and excess. It *was* all over the morning papers. That's what I'*m* afraid of. I *do love* you, really I *do.*

And this holds true not only about the finite verb, but also about the non-finite verb. The processual semantic character of the verbal lexeme even in the non-finite form is proved by the fact that in all its forms it is modified by the adverb and, with the transitive verb, it takes a direct object. Cf.:

Mr. Brown received *the visitor instantly*, which was unusual. – Mr. Brown's receiving *the visitor instantly* was unusual. – It was unusual for Mr. Brown to receive *the visitor instantly.* But: An *instant* reception *of the visitor* was unusual for Mr. Brown.

The processual categorial meaning of the notional verb determines its characteristic combination with a noun expressing both the doer of the action (its subject) and, in cases of the objective verb, the recipient of the action (its object); it also determines its combination with an adverb as the modifier of the action.

In the sentence the finite verb invariably performs the function of the verb-predicate, expressing the processual categorial features of predication, i.e. time, aspect, voice, and mood.

The non-finite verb performs different functions according to its intermediary nature (those of the syntactic subject, object, adverbial modifier, attribute), but its non-processual functions are always actualized in close combination with its processual semantic features. This is especially evident in demonstrative correlations of the "sentence – phrase" type. Cf.:

His rejecting the proposal surprised us. – That *he had rejected the proposal* surprised us. *Taking this into consideration*, her attitude can be understood. – If *one takes this into consideration*, her attitude can be understood.

In other words, the non-finite forms of the verb in self-dependent use (i.e. if they are used not as parts of the analytical verb-forms) perform a potentially predicative function, constituting secondary predicative centres in the sentence. In each case of such use they refer to some subject which is expressed either explicitly or implicitly. *Cf.*:

Roddy cared enough about his mother *to want to make amends* for Arabella. → Roddy *wanted to make amends...* → Roddy *will make amends... Changing* gear, the taxi turned the sharp corner. → The taxi *changed* gear and turned the corner. *Acting* as mate is often more difficult than *acting* as captain. → One acts as mate; one acts as captain.

§ 3. From the point of view of their outward structure, verbs are characterized by specific forms of word-building, as well as by the formal features expressing the corresponding grammatical categories.

The verb stems may be simple, sound-replacive, stress-replacive, expanded, composite, and phrasal.

The original simple verb stems are not numerous. *Cf.* such verbs as *go, take, read*, etc. But conversion (zero-suffixation) as means of derivation, especially conversion of the "noun – verb" type, greatly enlarges the simple stem set of verbs, since it is one of the most productive ways of forming verb lexemes in modern English. *Cf.*: a cloud – to cloud; a house – to house; a man – to man; a park – to park, etc.

The sound-replacive type of derivation and the stress-replacive type of derivation are unproductive. *Cf.*: food – to feed, blood – to bleed; 'import – to im'port, 'transport – to trans'port.

The typical suffixes expanding the stem of the verb are: *-ate* (*cultivate*), *-en* (*broaden*), *-ify* (*clarify*), *-ize* (*normalize*). The verb-deriving prefixes of the inter-class type are: *be-* (*belittle, befriend, bemoan*) and *en-/em-* (*engulf, embed*). Some other characteristic verbal prefixes are: *re-* (*remake*), *under-* (*undergo*), *over-* (*overestimate*), *sub-* (*submerge*), *mis-* (*misunderstand*), *un-* (*undo*), etc.

The composite (compound) verb stems correspond to the composite non-verb stems from which they are etymologically derived. Here belong the compounds of the conversion type (*blackmail n. – blackmail v.*) and of the reduction type (*proof-reader n. – proof-read v.*).

The phrasal verb stems occupy an intermediary position between analytical forms of the verb and syntactic word combinations. Among such stems two specific constructions should be mentioned. The first is a combination of the head-verb *have, give, take,* and occasionally some others with a noun; the combination has as its equivalent an ordinary verb. *Cf.*: to have a smoke – to smoke; to give a smile – to smile; to take a stroll – to stroll.

The second is a combination of . head-verb with a verbal postposition that has a specificational value. *Cf.*: stand up, go on, give in, be off, get along, etc.

§ 4. The grammatical categories which find formal expression in the outward structure of the verb and which will be analysed further are, first, the category of finitude dividing the verb into finite and non-finite forms (the corresponding contracted names are "finites" and "verbids";[*] this category has a lexico-grammatical force); second, the categories of person, number, tense, aspect, voice, and mood, whose complete set is revealed in every word-form of the notional finite verb.

Each of the identified categories constitutes a whole system of its own presenting its manifold problems to the scholar. However, the comparative analysis of the categorial properties of all the forms of the verb, including the properties of verbids, shows the unquestionable unity of the class, in spite of some inter-class features of verbids.

Among the various forms of the verb the infinitive occupies a unique position. Its status is that of the principal representative of the verb-lexeme as a whole. This head-form status of the infinitive is determined by the two factors. The first factor consists in the verbal-nominative nature of the infinitive, i.e. in its function of giving the most general dynamic name to the process which is denoted by all the other forms of the verb-lexeme in a more specifie way, conditioned by their respective semantico-grammatical specializations. The second factor determining the representative status of the infinitive consists in the infinitive serving as the actual derivative base for all the other regular forms of the verb.

§ 5. The class of verbs falls into a number of subclasses distinguished by different semantic and lexico-grammatical features.

---

[*] The term "verbids" for the non-finite forms of the verb was introduced by O. Jespersen. Its merit lies in the fact that, unlike the more traditional term "verbals", it is devoid of dubious connotations as well as homonymic correlations.

On the upper level of division two unequal sets are identified: the set of verbs of *full nominative* value (notional verbs), and the set of verbs of *partial nominative* value (semi-notional and functional verbs). The first set is derivationally open, it includes the bulk of the verbal lexicon. The second set is derivationally closed, it includes limited subsets of verbs characterized by individual relational properties.

§ 6. Semi-notional and functional verbs serve as markers of predication in the proper sense, since they show the connection between the nominative content of the sentence and reality in a strictly specialized way. These "predicators" include auxiliary verbs, modal verbs, semi-notional verbid introducer verbs, and link-verbs.

Auxiliary verbs constitute grammatical elements of the categorial forms of the verb. These are the verbs *be, have, do, shall, will, should, would, may, might.*

Modal verbs are used with the infinitive as predicative markers expressing relational meanings of the subject attitude type, i.e. ability, obligation, permission, advisability, etc. By way of extension of meaning, they also express relational probability, serving as probability predicators. These two types of functional semantics can be tested by means of correlating pure modal verb collocations with the corresponding two sets of stative collocations of equivalent functions: on the one hand, the groups *be obliged, be permitted,* etc.; on the other hand, the groups *be likely, be probable,* etc. *Cf.*:

Tom *may* stay for the teleview if he will.→Tom *is permitted* to stay. The storm *may* come any minute, you had better leave the deck. → The storm *is likely* to come any minute.

The modal verbs *can, may, must, shall, will, ought, need, used (to), dare* are defective in forms, and are suppletively supplemented by stative groups similar to those shown above (cf. Ch. III, § 4). The supplementation is effected both for the lacking finite forms and the lacking non-finite forms. *Cf.*:

The boys *can* prepare the play-ground themselves.→The boys *will be able* to prepare the play-ground themselves.→The boys' *being able* to prepare the play-ground themselves.

The verbs *be* and *have* in the modal meanings "be planned", "be obliged" and the like are considered by many modern grammarians as modal verbs and by right are included in the general modal verb list.

Semi-notional verbid introducer verbs are distributed among the verbal sets of discriminatory relational semantics (*seem, happen, turn out,* etc.), of subject-action relational semantics (*try, fail, manage,* etc.), of phasal semantics (*begin, continue, stop,* etc.). The predicator verbs should be strictly distinguished from their grammatical homonyms in the subclasses of notional verbs. As a matter of fact, there is a fundamental grammatical difference between the verbal constituents in such sentences as, say, "They *began* to fight" and "They *began* the fight". Whereas the verb in the first sentence is a semi-notional predicator, the verb in the second sentence is a notional transitive verb normally related to its direct object. The phasal predicator *begin* (the first sentence) is grammatically inseparable from the infinitive of the notional verb *fight*, the two lexemes making one verbal-part unit in the sentence. The transitive verb *begin* (the second sentence), on the contrary, is self-dependent in the lexico-grammatical sense, it forms the predicate of the sentence by itself and as such can be used in the passive voice, the whole construction of the sentence in this case being presented as the regular passive counterpart of its active version. *Cf.*:

They *began* the fight. –→ The fight *was begun* (by them).
They *began* to fight. → (*)* *To fight was begun* (by them).

Link-verbs introduce the nominal part of the predicate (the predicative) which is commonly expressed by a noun, an adjective, or a phrase of a similar semantico-grammatical character. It should be noted that link-verbs, although they are named so, are not devoid of meaningful content. Performing their function of connecting ("linking") the subject and the predicative of the sentence, they express the actual semantics of this connection, i.e. expose the relational aspect of the characteristics ascribed by the predicative to the subject.

The linking predicator function in the purest form is effected by the verb *be*; therefore *be* as a link-verb can be referred to as the "pure link-verb". It is clear from the above that even this pure link-verb has its own relational semantics, which can be identified as "linking predicative ascription". All the link-verbs other than the pure link *be* express some specification of this general predicative-linking semantics, so that they should be referred to as "specifying" link-verbs. The common specifying link-verbs fall into two main groups:

_____
* The transformation is unacceptable.

those that express perceptions and those that express non-perceptional, or "factual" link-verb connection. The main perceptional link-verbs are *seem, appear, look feel, taste*; the main factual link-verbs are *become, get, grow, remain, keep.*

As is to be seen from the comparison of the specifying link-verbs with the verbid introducer predicators described above, the respective functions of these two verbal subsets are cognate, though not altogether identical. The difference lies in the fact that the specifying link-verbs combine the pure linking function with the predicator function. Furthermore, separate functions of the two types of predicators are evident from the fact that specifying link-verbs, the same as the pure link, can be used in the text in combination with verbid introducer predicators. *E.g.*:

The letter *seemed to have remained* unnoticed. I *began to feel* better. You *shouldn't try to look* cleverer than you are.

*Cf.* the use of verbid introducer predicators with the pure link-verb:

The news *has proved to be* true. The girl's look *ceased to be* friendly. The address shown to us *seemed to be* just the one we needed.

Besides the link-verbs proper hitherto presented, there are some notional verbs in language that have the power to perform the function of link-verbs without losing their lexical nominative value. In other words, they perform two functions simultaneously, combining the role of a full notional verb with that of a link-verb. *Cf.*:

Fred *lay* awake all through the night. Robbie *ran in* out of breath. The moon *rose* red.

Notional link-verb function is mostly performed by intransitive verbs of motion and position. Due to the double syntactic character of the notional link-verb, the whole predicate formed by it is referred to as a "double predicate" (see Ch. XXIX).

§ 7. Notional verbs undergo the three main grammatically relevant categorizations. The first is based on the relation of the subject of the verb to the process denoted by the verb. The second is based on the aspective characteristics of the process denoted by the verb, i.e. on the inner properties of the process as reflected in the verbal meaning. The third is based on the combining power of the verb in relation to other notional words in the utterance.

§ 8. On the basis of the subject-process relation, all the notional verbs can be divided into actional and statal.

Actional verbs express the action performed by the subject, i.e. they present the subject as an active doer (in the broadest sense of the word). To this subclass belong such verbs as *do, act, perform, make, go, read, learn, discover*, etc. Statal verbs, unlike their subclass counterparts, denote the state of their subject. That is, they either give the subject the characteristic of the inactive recipient of some outward activity, or else express the mode of its existence. To this subclass belong such verbs as *be, live, survive, worry, suffer, rejoice, stand, see, know*, etc.

Alongside the two verbal sets, a third one could be distinguished which is made up of verbs expressing neither actions, nor states, but "processes". As representatives of the "purely processual" subclass one might point out the verbs *thaw, ripen, deteriorate, consider, neglect, support, display*, and the like. On closer observation, however, it becomes clear that the units of this medial subclass are subject to the same division into actional and statal sets as were established at the primary stage of classification. For instance, the "purely processual" verb *thaw* referring to an inactive substance should be defined, more precisely, as "processual-statal", whereas the "processual" verb *consider* relating to an active doer should be looked upon, more precisely, as "processual-actional". This can be shown by transformational tests:

The snow *is thawing.* → The snow is *in the state of thawing.*

The designer *is considering* another possibility. → The action of the designer is that he *is considering* another possibility.

Thus, the primary binary division of the verbs upon the basis of the subject-process relation is sustained.

Similar criteria apply to some more specific subsets of verbs permitting the binary actional-statal distribution. Among these of a special significance are the verbal sets of mental processes and sensual processes. Within the first of them we recognize the correlation between the verbs of mental perception and mental activity. *E.g.:* know – think; understand – construe; notice – note; admire – assess; forget – reject; etc.

Within the second set we recognize the correlation between the verbs of physical perception as such and physical perceptional activity. *E.g.:* see – look; hear – listen; feel (inactive) – feel (active) – touch; taste (inactive) – taste (active); smell (inactive) – smell (active); etc.

The initial member of each correlation pair given above presents a case of a statal verb, while the succeeding member, respectively, of an actional verb. *Cf.* the corresponding transformational tests:

The explorers knew only one answer to the dilemma.→The mental state of the explorers was such that they knew only one answer to the dilemma.

I am thinking about the future of the village. → My mental activity consists in thinking about the future of the village. Etc.

The grammatical relevance of the classification in question, apart from its reflecting the syntactically generalized relation of the subject of the verb to the process denoted by it, is disclosed in the difference between the two subclasses in their aspectual behaviour. While the actional verbs take the form of the continuous aspect quite freely, i.e. according to the general rules of its use, the statal verbs, in the same contextual conditions, are mainly used in the indefinite form. The continuous with statal verbs, which can be characterized as a more or less occasional occurrence, will normally express some sort of intensity or emphasis (see further).

§ 9. Aspective verbal semantics exposes the inner character of the process denoted by the verb. It represents the process as durative (continual), iterative (repeated), terminate (concluded), interminate (not concluded), instantaneous (momentary), ingressive (starting), overcompleted (developed to the extent of superfluity), undercompleted (not developed to its full extent), and the like.

Some of these aspectual meanings are inherent in the basic semantics of certain subsets of English verbs. Compare, for instance, verbs of ingression (*begin, start, resume, set out, get down*), verbs of instantaneity (*burst, click, knock, bang, jump, drop*), verbs of termination (*terminate, finish, end, conclude, close, solve, resolve, sum up, stop*), verbs of duration (*continue, prolong, last, linger, live, exist*). The aspectual meanings of overcompletion, undercompletion, repetition, and the like can be rendered by means of lexical derivation, in particular, prefixation (*oversimplify, outdo, underestimate, reconsider*). Such aspectual meanings as ingression, duration, termination, and iteration are regularly expressed by aspective verbal collocations, in particular, by combinations of aspective predicators with verbids (*begin, start, continue, finish, used to, would,* etc., plus the corresponding verbid component).

In terms of the most general subclass division related to the grammatical structure of language, two aspective subclasses of verbs should be recognized in English. These will comprise numerous minor aspective groups of the types shown above as their microcomponent sets.

The basis of this division is constituted by the relation of the verbal semantics to the idea of a processual limit, i.e., some border point beyond which the process expressed by the verb or implied in its semantics is discontinued or simply does not exist. For instance, the verb *arrive* expresses an action which evidently can only develop up to the point of arriving; on reaching this limit, the action ceases. The verb *start* denotes a transition from some preliminary state to some kind of subsequent activity, thereby implying a border point between the two. As different from these cases, the verb *move* expresses a process that in itself is alien to any idea of a limit, either terminal or initial.

The verbs of the first order, presenting a process as potentially limited, can be called "limitive". In the published courses of English grammar where they are mentioned, these verbs are called "terminative",[*] but the latter term seems inadequate. As a matter of fact, the word suggests the idea of a completed action, i.e. of a limit attained, not only the implication of a potential limit existing as such. To the subclass of limitive belong such verbs as *arrive, come, leave, find, start, stop, conclude, aim, drop, catch*, etc. Here also belong phrasal verbs with limitive postpositions, *e.g. stand up, sit down, get out, be off*, etc.

The verbs of the second order presenting a process as not limited by any border point, should be called, correspondingly, "unlimitive" (in the existing grammar books they are called either "non-terminative" or else "durative", or "cursive"). To this subclass belong such verbs as *move, continue, live, sleep, work, behave, hope, stand*, etc.

Alongside the two aspective subclasses of verbs, some authors recognize also a third subclass, namely, verbs of double aspective nature (of "double", or "mixed" lexical character). These, according to the said authors, are capable of expressing either a "terminative" or "non-terminative" ("durative") meaning depending on the context.

However, applying the principle of oppositions, these cases can be interpreted as natural and easy reductions (mostly neutralizations) of the lexical aspective opposition. *Cf.*:

---

[*] See the cited books on English grammar by M.A. Ganshina and N.M. Vasilevskaya, B.A. Ilyish, B.S. Khaimovich and B.I. Rogovskaya.

Mary and Robert *walked* through the park pausing at variegated flower-beds. (Unlimitive use, basic function). In the scorching heat, the party *walked* the whole way to the ravine bareheaded. (Limitive use, neutralization). He *turned* the corner and found himself among a busy crowd of people. (Limitive use, basic function). It took not only endless scientific effort, but also an enormous courage to prove that the earth *turns* round the sun. (Unlimitive use, neutralization).

Observing the given examples, we must admit that the demarcation line between the two aspective verbal subclasses is not rigidly fixed, the actual differentiation between them being in fact rather loose. Still, the opposition between limitive and unlimitive verbal sets does exist in English, however indefinitely determined it may be. Moreover, the described subclass division has an unquestionable grammatical relevance, which is expressed, among other things, in its peculiar correlation with the categorial aspective forms of the verbs (indefinite, continuous, perfect); this correlation is to be treated further (see Ch. XV).

§ 10. From the given description of the aspective subclass division of English verbs, it is evident that the English lexical aspect differs radically from the Russian aspect. In terms of semantic properties, the English lexical aspect expresses a *potentially* limited or unlimited process, whereas the Russian aspect expresses the *actual* conclusion (the perfective, or terminative aspect) or non-conclusion (the imperfective, or non-terminative aspect) of the process in question. In terms of systemic properties, the two English lexical aspect varieties, unlike their Russian absolutely rigid counterparts, are but loosely distinguished and easily reducible.

In accord with these characteristics, both the English limitive verbs and unlimitive verbs may correspond alternately either to the Russian perfective verbs or imperfective verbs, depending on the contextual uses.

For instance, the limitive verb *arrive* expressing an instantaneous action that took place in the past will be translated by its perfective Russian equivalent:

The exploratory party *arrived* at the foot of the mountain. *Russ.*: Экспедиция *прибыла* к подножию горы.

But if the same verb expresses a habitual, interminately repeated action, the imperfective Russian equivalent is to be chosen for its translation:

In those years trains seldom *arrived* on time. *Russ.*: В те годы поезда редко *приходили* вовремя.

93

*Cf.* the two possible versions of the Russian translation of the following sentence:

The liner *takes off* tomorrow at ten. *Russ.*: Самолет *вылетит* завтра в десять (the flight in question is looked upon as an individual occurrence). Самолет *вылетает* завтра в десять (the flight is considered as part of the traffic schedule, or some other kind of general plan).

Conversely, the English unlimitive verb *gaze* when expressing a continual action will be translated into Russian by its imperfective equivalent:

The children *gazed* at the animals holding their breaths. Russ.: Дети *глядели* на животных, затаив дыхание.

But when the same verb renders the idea of an aspectually limited, e.g. started action, its perfective Russian equivalent should be used in the translation:

The boy turned his head and *gazed* at the horseman with wide-open eyes. *Russ.*: Мальчик повернул голову и *уставился* на всадника широко открытыми глазами.

Naturally, the unlimitive English verbs in strictly unlimitive contextual use correspond, by definition, only to the imperfective verbs in Russian.

§ 11. The inner qualities of any signemic lingual unit are manifested not only in its immediate informative significance in an utterance, but also in its combinability with other units, in particular with units of the same segmental order. These syntagmatic properties are of especial importance for verbs, which is due to the unique role performed by the verb in the sentence. As a matter of fact, the finite verb, being the centre of predication, organizes all the other sentence constituents. Thus, the organizational function of the verb, immediately exposed in its syntagmatic combinability, is inseparable from (and dependent on) its semantic value. The morphological relevance of the combining power of the verb is seen from the fact that directly dependent on this power are the categorial voice distinctions.

The combining power of words in relation to other words in syntactically subordinate positions (the positions of "adjuncts" – see Ch. XX) is called their syntactic "valency". The valency of a word is said to be "realized" when the word in question is actually combined in an utterance with its corresponding valency partner, i.e. its valency adjunct. If, on the other hand, the word is used without its valency adjunct, the valency conditioning the position of this adjunct (or "directed" to it) is said to be "not realized".

The syntactic valency falls into two cardinal types: *obligatory* and *optional*.

The *obligatory valency* is such as must necessarily be realized for the sake of the grammatical completion of the syntactic construction. For instance, the subject and the direct object are obligatory parts of the sentence, and, from the point of view of sentence structure, they are obligatory valency partners of the verb. Consequently, we say that the subjective and the direct objective valencies of the verb are obligatory. *E.g.*: *We* saw a *house* in the distance.

This sentence presents a case of a complete English syntactic construction. If we eliminate its subject or object, the remaining part of the construction will be structurally incomplete, i.e. it will be structurally "gaping". *Cf.*: *We saw in the distance. *Saw a house in the distance.

The *optional valency*, as different from the obligatory valency, is such as is not necessarily realized in grammatically complete constructions: this type of valency may or may not be realized depending on the concrete information to be conveyed by the utterance. Most of the adverbial modifiers are optional parts of the sentence, so in terms of valency we say that the adverbial valency of the verb is mostly optional. For instance, the adverbial part in the above sentence may be freely eliminated without causing the remainder of the sentence to be structurally incomplete: We saw a house (*in the distance*).

Link-verbs, although their classical representatives are only half-notional, should also be included into the general valency characterization of verbs. This is due to their syntactically essential position in the sentence. The predicative valency of the link-verbs proper is obligatory. *Cf.*:

The reporters seemed *pleased* with the results of the press conference. That young scapegrace made *a good husband*, after all.

The obligatory adjuncts of the verb, with the exception of the subject (whose connection with the verb cannot be likened to the other valency partners), may be called its "complements"; the optional adjuncts of the verb, its "supplements". The distinction between the two valency types of adjuncts is highly essential, since not all the objects or predicatives are obligatory, while, conversely, not all the adverbial modifiers are optional. Thus, we may have both objective complements and objective supplements; both predicative complements and predicative supplements; both adverbial supplements and adverbial complements.

Namely, the object of addressee, i.e. a person or thing for whom or which the action is performed, may sometimes be optional, as in the following example: We did it *for you.*

The predicative to a notional link-verb is mostly optional, as in the example: The night came *dark and stormy.*

The adverbials of place, time, and manner (quality) may sometimes be obligatory, as in the examples below:

Mr. Torrence was staying *in the Astoria Hotel.* The described events took place *at the beginning of the century.* The patient is doing *fine.*

Thus, according as they have or have not the power to take complements, the notional verbs should be classed as "complementive" or "uncomplementive", with further subcategorizations on the semantico-syntagmatic principles.

In connection with this upper division, the notions of verbal transitivity and objectivity should be considered.

Verbal transitivity, as one of the specific qualities of the general "completivity", is the ability of the verb to take a direct object, i.e. an object which is immediately affected by the denoted process. The direct object is joined to the verb "directly", without a preposition. Verbal objectivity is the ability of the verb to take any object, be it direct, or oblique (prepositional), or that of addressee. Transitive verbs are opposed to intransitive verbs; objective verbs are opposed to non-objective verbs (the latter are commonly called "subjective" verbs, but the term contradicts the underlying syntactic notion, since all the English finite verbs refer to their textual subjects).

As is known, the general division of verbs into transitive and intransitive is morphologically more relevant for Russian than English, because the verbal passive form is confined in Russian to transitive verbs only. The general division of verbs into objective and non-objective, being of relatively minor significance for the morphology of Russian, is highly relevant for English morphology, since in English all the three fundamental types of objects can be made into the subjects of the corresponding passive constructions.

On the other hand, the term "transitive" is freely used in English grammatical treatises in relation to all the objective verbs, not only to those that take a direct object. This use is due to the close association of the notion of transitivity not only with the type of verbal object as such, but also with the ability of the verb to be used in the passive voice. We do not propose to call for the terminological corrective in this domain; rather, we wish to draw the attention of the reader to the accepted linguistic usage in order to avoid unfortunate misunderstandings based on the differences in terminology.

Uncomplementive verbs fall into two unequal subclasses of "personal" and "impersonal" verbs.

The personal uncomplementive verbs, i.e. uncomplementive verbs normally referring to the real subject of the denoted process (which subject may be either an actual human being, or a non-human being, or else an inanimate substance or an abstract notion), form a large set of lexemes of various semantic properties. Here are some of them: *work, start, pause, hesitate, act, function, materialize, laugh, cough, grow, scatter,* etc.

The subclass of impersonal verbs is small and strictly limited. Here belong verbs mostly expressing natural phenomena of the self-processual type, i.e. natural processes going on without a reference to a real subject. *Cf.: rain, snow, freeze, drizzle, thaw,* etc.

Complementive verbs, as follows from the above, are divided into the predicative, objective and adverbial sets.

The predicative complementive verbs, i.e. link-verbs, have been discussed as part of the predicator verbs. The main link-verb subsets are, first, the pure link *be*; second, the specifying links *become, grow, seem, appear, look, taste,* etc.; third, the notional links.

The objective complementive verbs are divided into several important subclasses, depending on the kinds of complements they combine with. At the upper level of division they fall into monocomplementive verbs (taking one object-complement) and bicomplementive verbs (taking two complements).

The monocomplementive objective verbs fall into five main subclasses. The first subclass is the possession objective verb *have* forming different semantic varieties of constructions. This verb is normally not passivized. The second subclass includes direct objective verbs, *e.g. take, grasp, forget, enjoy, like.* The third subclass is formed by the prepositional objective verbs, *e.g. look at, point to, send for, approve of, think about.* The fourth subclass includes non-passivized direct objective verbs, *e.g. cost, weigh, fail, become, suit.*

The fifth subclass includes non-passivized prepositional objective verbs, *e.g. belong to, relate to, merge with, confer with, abound in.*

The bicomplementive objective verbs fall into five main subclasses. The first subclass is formed by addressee-direct objective verbs, i.e. verbs taking a direct object and an addressee object, *e.g. a) give, bring, pay, hand, show* (the addressee object with these verbs may be both non-prepositional and prepositional); b) *explain, introduce, mention, say, devote* (the addressee object with these verbs is only prepositional). The second subclass includes double direct objective verbs, i.e. verbs taking two direct objects, *e.g. teach, ask, excuse, forgive, envy, fine.* The third subclass includes double prepositional objective verbs, i.e. verbs taking two prepositional objects, *e.g. argue, consult, cooperate, agree.* The fourth subclass is formed by addressee prepositional objective verbs, i.e. verbs taking a prepositional object and an addressee object, *e.g. remind of, tell about, apologize for, write of, pay for.* The fifth subclass includes adverbial objective verbs, i.e. verbs taking an object and an adverbial modifier (of place or of time), *e.g. put, place, lay, bring, send, keep.*

Adverbial complementive verbs include two main subclasses. The first is formed by verbs taking an adverbial complement of place or of time, *e.g. be, live, stay, go, ride, arrive.* The second is formed by verbs taking an adverbial complement of manner, *e.g. act, do, keep, behave, get on.*

§ 12. Observing the syntagmatic subclasses of verbs, we see that the same verb lexeme, or lexico-phonemic unit (phonetical word), can enter more than one of the outlined classification sets. This phenomenon of the "subclass migration" of verbs is not confined to cognate lexemic subsets of the larger subclasses, but, as is widely known, affects the principal distinctions between the English complementive and uncomplementive verbs, between the English objective and non-objective verbs. Suffice it to give a couple of examples taken at random:

Who *runs* faster, John or Nick? (*run* – uncomplementive). The man *ran* after the bus. (*run* – adverbial complementive, non-objective). I *ran* my eyes over the uneven lines. (*run* – adverbial objective, transitive). And *is* the fellow still *running* the show? (*run* – monocomplementive, transitive).

The railings *felt* cold. (*feel* – link-verb, predicative complementive). We *felt* fine after the swim. (*feel* – adverbial complementive, nor-objective). You shouldn't *feel* your own pulse like that. (*feel* – monocomplementive, transitive).

The problem arises how to interpret these different subclass entries – as cases of grammatical or lexico-grammatical homonymy, or some kind of functional variation, or merely variation in usage. The problem is vexed, since each of the interpretations has its strong points.

To reach a convincing decision, one should take into consideration the actual differences between various cases of the "subclass migration" in question. Namely, one must carefully analyse the comparative characteristics of the corresponding subclasses as such, as well as the regularity factor for an individual lexeme subclass occurrence.

In the domain of notional subclasses proper, with regular interclass occurrences of the analysed lexemes, probably the most plausible solution will be to interpret the "migration forms" as cases of specific syntactic variation, i.e. to consider the different subclass entries of migrating units as syntactic variants of the same lexemes [Почепцов, 1976, 87 ff.]. In the light of this interpretation, the very formula of "lexemic subclass migration" will be vindicated and substantiated.

On the other hand, for more cardinally differing lexemic sets, as, for instance, functional versus notional, the syntactic variation principle is hardly acceptable. This kind of differentiation should be analysed as lexico-grammatical homonymy, since it underlies the expression of categorially different grammatical functions.

## CHAPTER XI

### NON-FINITE VERBS (VERBIDS)

§ 1. Verbids are the forms of the verb intermediary in many of their lexico-grammatical features between the verb and the non-processual parts of speech. The mixed features of these forms are revealed in the principal spheres of the part-of-speech characterization, i.e. in their meaning, structural marking, combinability, and syntactic functions.

The processual meaning is exposed by them in a substantive or adjectival-adverbial interpretation: they render processes as peculiar kinds of substances and properties. They are formed by special morphemic elements which do not express either grammatical time or mood (the most specific finite verb categories). They can be combined with verbs like non-processual lexemes (performing non-verbal functions in the sentence), and they can be combined with non-processual lexemes like verbs (performing verbal functions in the sentence).

From these characteristics, one might call in question the very justification of including the verbids in the system of the verb. As a matter of fact, one can ask oneself whether it wouldn't stand to reason to consider the verbids as a special lexemic class, a separate part of speech, rather than an inherent component of the class of verbs.

On closer consideration, however, we can't but see that such an approach would be utterly ungrounded. The verbids do betray intermediary features. Still, their fundamental grammatical meaning is processual (though modified in accord with the nature of the interclass reference of each verbid). Their essential syntactic functions, directed by this relational semantics, unquestionably reveal the property which may be called, in a manner of explanation, "verbality", and the statement of which is corroborated by the peculiar combinability character of verbid collocations, namely, by the ability of verbids to take adjuncts expressing the immediate recepients, attendants, and addressees of the process inherently conveyed by each verbid denotation.

One might likewise ask oneself, granted the verbids are part of the system of the verb, whether they do not constitute within this system a special subsystem of purely lexemic nature, i.e. form some sort of a specific verbal subclass. This counter-approach, though, would evidently be devoid of any substantiality, since a subclass of a lexemic class, by definition, should share the essential categorial structure, as well as primary syntactic functions with other subclasses, and in case of verbids the situation is altogether different. In fact, it is every verb stem (except a few defective verbs) that by means of morphemic change takes both finite and non-finite forms, the functions of the two sets being strictly differentiated: while the finite forms serve in the sentence only one syntactic function, namely, that of the finite predicate, the non-finite forms serve various syntactic functions other than that of the finite predicate.

The strict, unintersecting division of functions (the functions themselves being of a fundamental nature in terms of the grammatical structure of language as a whole) clearly shows that the opposition between the finite and non-finite forms of the verb creates a special grammatical category. The differential feature of the opposi-

100

tion is constituted by the expression of verbal time and mood: while the time-mood grammatical signification characterizes the finite verb in a way that it underlies its finite predicative function, the verbid has no immediate means of expressing time-mood categorial semantics and therefore presents the weak member of the opposition. The category expressed by this opposition can be called the category of "finitude" [Strang, 143; Бархударов, 1975, 106]. The syntactic content of the category of finitude is the expression of predication (more precisely, the expression of verbal predication).

As is known, the verbids, unable to express the predicative meanings of time and mood, still do express the so-called "secondary" or "potential" predication, forming syntactic complexes directly related to certain types of subordinate clauses. *Cf.*:

Have you ever had *anything caught in your head*? – – Have you ever had anything *that was caught in your head*? He said it half under his breath *for the others not to hear it*. – – He said it half under his breath, *so that the others couldn't hear it.*

The verbid complexes *anything caught in your head*, or *for the others not to hear it*, or the like, while expressing secondary predication, are not self-dependent in a predicative sense. They normally exist only as part of sentences built up by genuine, primary predicative constructions that have a finite verb as their core. And it is through the reference to the finite verb-predicate that these complexes set up the situations denoted by them in the corresponding time and mood perspective.

In other words, we may say that the opposition of the finite verbs and the verbids is based on the expression of the functions of full predication and semi-predication. While the finite verbs express predication in its genuine and complete form, the function of the verbids is to express semi-predication, building up semi-predicative complexes within different sentence constructions.

The English verbids include four forms distinctly differing from one another within the general verbid system: the infinitive, the gerund, the present participle, and the past participle. In compliance with this difference, the verbid semi-predicative complexes are distinguished by the corresponding differential properties both in form and in syntactic-contextual function.

§ 2. *The infinitive* is the non-finite form of the verb which combines the properties of the verb with those of the noun, serving as the verbal name of a process. By virtue of its general process-naming function, the infinitive should be considered as the head-form of the whole paradigm of the verb. In this quality it can be likened to the nominative case of the noun in languages having a normally developed noun declension, as, for instance, Russian. It is not by chance that A.A. Shakhmatov called the infinitive the "verbal nominative". With the English infinitive, its role of the verbal paradigmatic head-form is supported by the fact that, as has been stated before, it represents the actual derivation base for all the forms of regular verbs.

The infinitive is used in three fundamentally different types of functions: first, as a notional, self-positional syntactic part of the sentence; second, as the notional constituent of a complex verbal predicate built up around a predicator verb; third, as the notional constituent of a finite conjugation form of the verb. The first use is grammatically "free", the second is grammatically "half-free", the third is grammatically "bound".

The dual verbal-nominal meaning of the infinitive is expressed in full measure in its free, independent use. It is in this use that the infinitive denotes the corresponding process in an abstract, substance-like presentation. This can easily be tested by question-transformations. *Cf.*:

Do you really mean *to go away* and *leave* me here alone? → *What* do you really mean? It made her proud sometimes *to toy* with the idea. → *What* made her proud sometimes?

The combinability of the infinitive also reflects its dual semantic nature, in accord with which we distinguish between its verb-type and noun-type connections. The verb-type combinability of the infinitive is displayed in its combining, first, with nouns expressing the object of the action; second, with nouns expressing the subject of the action; third, with modifying adverbs; fourth, with predicator verbs of semi-functional nature forming a verbal predicate; fifth, with auxiliary finite verbs (word-morphemes) in the analytical forms of the verb. The noun-type combinability of the infinitive is displayed in its combining, first, with finite notional verbs as the object of the action; second, with finite notional verbs as the subject of the action.

The self-positional infinitive, in due syntactic arrangements, performs the functions of all types of notional sentence-parts, i.e. the subject, the object, the predicative, the attribute, the adverbial modifier. *Cf.*:

*To meet* the head of the administration and not *to speak* to him about your predicament was unwise, to say the least of it. (Infinitive subject position). The chief arranged *to receive* the foreign delegation in the afternoon. (Infinitive object position). The parents' wish had always been *to see* their eldest son the continuator of their joint scientific work. (Infinitive predicative position). Here again we are faced with a plot *to overthrow* the legitimately elected government of the republic. (Infinitive attributive position). Helen was far too worried *to listen* to the remonstrances. (Infinitive adverbial position).

If the infinitive in free use has its own subject, different from that of the governing construction, it is introduced by the preposition-particle *for*. The whole infinitive construction of this type is traditionally called the "for-to infinitive phrase". *Cf.*:

*For that shy-looking young man to have stated his purpose so boldly* – incredible!

The prepositional introduction of the inner subject in the English infinitive phrase is analogous to the prepositional-casal introduction of the same in the Russian infinitive phrase (i.e. either with the help of the genitive-governing preposition *для*, or with the help of the dative case of the noun). *Cf.: Для нас очень важно понять* природу подобных соответствий.

With some transitive verbs (of physical perceptions, mental activity, declaration, compulsion, permission, etc.) the infinitive is used in the semi-predicative constructions of the complex object and complex subject, the latter being the passive counterparts of the former. *Cf.*:

We have never heard *Charlie play his violin.* → *Charlie* has never been heard *to play his violin.* The members of the committee expected *him to speak against the suggested resolution.* → *He* was expected by the members of the committee *to speak against the suggested resolution.*

Due to the intersecting character of joining with the governing predicative construction, the subject of the infinitive in such complexes, naturally, has no introductory preposition-particle.

The English infinitive exists in two presentation forms. One of them, characteristic of the free uses of the infinitive, is distinguished by the pre-positional marker *to*. This form is called traditionally the "to-infinitive", or in more recent linguistic works, the "marked infinitive". The other form, characteristic of the bound uses of the infinitive, does not employ the marker *to*, thereby presenting the infinitive in the shape of the pure verb stem, which in modern interpretation is understood as the zero-suffixed form. This form is called traditionally the "bare infinitive", or in more recent linguistic works, respectively, the "unmarked infinitive".

The infinitive marker *to* is a word-morpheme, i.e. a special formal particle analogous, mutatis mutandis, to other auxiliary elements in the English grammatical structure. Its only function is to build up and identify the infinitive form as such. As is the case with the other analytical markers, the particle *to* can be used in an isolated position to represent the whole corresponding construction syntagmatically zeroed in the text. *Cf.*:

You are welcome to acquaint yourself with any of the documents if you want *to*.

Like other analytical markers, it can also be separated from its notional, i.e. infinitive part by a word or a phrase, usually of adverbial nature, forming the so-called "split infinitive". *Cf.*:

My task is not to accuse or acquit; my task it *to* thoroughly *investigate*, *to* clearly *define*, and *to* consistently *systematize* the facts.

Thus, the marked infinitive presents just another case of an analytical grammatical form. The use or non-use of the infinitive marker depends on the verbal environment of the infinitive. Namely, the unmarked infinitive is used, besides the various analytical forms, with modal verbs (except the modals *ought* and *used*), with verbs of physical perceptions, with the verbs *let, bid, make, help* (with the latter – optionally), with the verb *know* in the sense of "experience", with a few verbal phrases of modal nature (*had better, would rather, would have*, etc.), with the relative-inducive *why*. All these uses are detailed in practical grammar books.

The infinitive is a categorially changeable form. It distinguishes the three grammatical categories sharing them with the finite verb, namely, the aspective category of development (continuous in opposition), the aspective category of retrospective coordination (perfect in opposition), the category of voice (passive in opposition). Consequently, the categorial paradigm of the infinitive of the objective verb includes eight forms: the indefinite active, the continuous active, the perfect active, the perfect continuous active; the indefinite passive, the continuous passive, the perfect passive, the perfect continuous passive. *E.g.*: to take – to be taking – to have taken – to have been taking; to be taken – to be being taken – to have been taken – to have been being taken.

The infinitive paradigm of the non-objective verb, correspondingly, includes four forms. *E.g.*: to go – to be going – to have gone – to have been going.

The continuous and perfect continuous passive can only be used occasionally, with a strong stylistic colouring. But they underlie the corresponding finite verb forms. It is the indefinite infinitive that constitutes the head-form of the verbal paradigm.

§ 3. *The gerund* is the non-finite form of the verb which, like the infinitive, combines the properties of the verb with those of the noun. Similar to the infinitive, the gerund serves as the verbal name of a process, but its substantive quality is more strongy pronounced than that of the infinitive. Namely, as different from the infinitive, and similar to the noun, the gerund can be modified by a noun in the possessive case or its pronominal equivalents (expressing the subject of the verbal process), and it can be used with prepositions.

Since the gerund, like the infinitive, is an abstract name of the process denoted by the verbal lexeme, a question might arise, why the infinitive, and not the gerund is taken as the head-form of the verbal lexeme as a whole, its accepted representative in the lexicon.

As a matter of fact, the gerund cannot perform the function of the paradigmatic verbal head-form for a number of reasons. In the first place, it is more detached from the finite verb than the infinitive semantically, tending to be a far more substantival unit categorially. Then, as different from the infinitive, it does not join in the conjugation of the finite verb. Unlike the infinitive, it is a suffixal form, which makes it less generalized than the infinitive in terms of the formal properties of the verbal lexeme (although it is more abstract in the purely semantic sense). Finally, it is less definite than the infinitive from the lexico-grammatical point of view, being subject to easy neutralizations in its opposition with the verbal noun in -*ing*, as well as with the present participle. Hence, the gerund is no rival of the infinitive in the paradigmatic head-form function.

The general combinability of the gerund, like that of the infinitive, is dual, sharing some features with the verb, and some features with the noun. The verb-type combinability of the gerund is displayed in its combining, first, with nouns expressing the object of the action; second, with modifying adverbs; third, with certain semi-functional predicator verbs, but other than modal. Of the noun-type is the combinability of the gerund, first, with finite notional verbs as the object of the action; second, with finite notional verbs as the prepositional adjunct of various functions; third, with finite notional verbs as the subject of the action; fourth, with nouns as the prepositional adjunct of various functions.

The gerund, in the corresponding positional patterns, performs the functions of all the types of notional sentence-parts, i.e. the subject, the object, the predicative, the attribute, the adverbial modifier. *Cf.*:

*Repeating* your accusations over and over again doesn't make them more convincing. (Gerund subject position). No wonder he delayed *breaking* the news to Uncle Jim. (Gerund direct object position). She could not give her mind to *pressing* wild flowers in Pauline's botany book. (Gerund addressee object position). Joe felt annoyed at *being shied* by his room-mates. (Gerund prepositional object position). You know what luck is? Luck is *believing* you're lucky. (Gerund predicative position). Fancy the pleasant prospect of *listening* to all the gossip they've in store for you! (Gerund attributive position). He could not push against the furniture without *bringing* the whole lot down. (Gerund adverbial of manner position).

One of the specific gerund patterns is its combination with the noun in the possessive case or its possessive pronominal equivalent expressing the subject of the action. This gerundial construction is used in cases when the subject of the gerundial process differs from the subject of the governing sentence-situation, i.e. when the gerundial sentence-part has its own, separate subject. *E.g.*:

*Powell's being rude* like that was disgusting. How can she know about *the Mortons' being connected* with this unaccountable affair? Will he ever excuse *our having interfered*?

The possessive with the gerund displays one of the distinctive categorial properties of the gerund as such, establishing it in the English lexemic system as the form of the verb with nounal characteristics. As a matter of fact, from the point of view of the inner semantic relations, this combination is of a verbal type, while from the point of view of the formal categorial features, this combination is of a nounal type. It can be clearly demonstrated by the appropriate transformations, i.e. verb-related and noun-related re-constructions. *Cf.*:

I can't stand *his criticizing* artistic works that are beyond his competence. (T-verbal → He is criticizing artistic works. T-nounal → His criticism of artistic works.)

Besides combining with the possessive noun-subject, the verbal *ing*-form can also combine with the noun-subject in the common case or its objective pronominal equivalent. *E.g.*:

I read in yesterday's paper about *the hostages having been released*.

This gerundial use as presenting very peculiar features of categorial mediality will be discussed after the treatment of the participle.

The formal sign of the gerund is wholly homonymous with that of the present participle: it is the suffix *-ing* added to its grammatically (categorially) leading element.

Like the infinitive, the gerund is a categorially changeable (variable, demutative) form; it distinguishes the two grammatical categories, sharing them with the finite verb and the present participle, namely, the aspective category of retrospective coordination (perfect in opposition), and the category of voice (passive in opposition). Consequently, the categorial paradigm of the gerund of the objective verb includes four forms: the simple active, the perfect active; the simple passive, the perfect passive. *E.g.*: taking – having taken – being taken – having been taken.

The gerundial paradigm of the non-objective verb, correspondingly, includes two forms. *E.g.*: going – having gone.

The perfect forms of the gerund are used, as a rule, only in semantically strong positions, laying special emphasis on the meaningful categorial content of the form.

§ 4. *The present participle* is the non-finite form of the verb which combines the properties of the verb with those of the adjective and adverb, serving as the qualifying-processual name. In its outer form the present participle is wholly homonymous with the gerund, ending in the suffix *-ing* and distinguishing the same grammatical categories of retrospective coordination and voice.

Like all the verbids, the present participle has no categorial time distinctions, and the attribute "present" in its conventional name is not immediately explanatory; it is used in this book from force of tradition. Still, both terms "present participle" and "past participle" are not altogether devoid of elucidative signification, if not in the categorial sense, then in the derivational-etymological sense, and are none the worse in their quality than their doublet-substitutes "participle I" and "participle II".

The present participle has its own place in the general paradigm of the verb, different from that of the past participle, being distinguished by the corresponding set of characterization features.

Since it possesses some traits both of adjective and adverb, the present participle is not only dual, but triple by its lexico-grammatical properties, which is displayed in its combinability, as well as in its syntactic functions.

The verb-type combinability of the present participle is revealed, first, in its being combined, in various uses, with nouns expressing the object of the action; second, with nouns expressing the subject of the action (in semi-predicative complexes); third, with modifying adverbs; fourth, with auxiliary finite verbs (word-morphemes) in the analytical forms of the verb. The adjective-type combinability of the present participle is revealed in its association with the modified nouns, as well as with some modifying adverbs, such as adverbs of degree. The adverb-type combinability of the present participle is revealed in its association with the modified verbs.

The self-positional present participle, in the proper syntactic arrangements, performs the functions of the predicative (occasional use, and not with the pure link *be*), the attribute, the adverbial modifier of various types. *Cf.*:

The questions became more and more *irritating* (Present participle predicative position). She had thrust the crucifix on to the *surviving* baby (Present participle attributive front-position). Norman stood on the pavement like a man *watching* his loved one go aboard an ocean liner (Present participle attributive back-position). He was no longer the cocky, pugnacious boy, always *squaring up* for a fight (Present participle attributive back-position, detached). She went up the steps, *swinging* her hips and *tossing* her fur with bravado (Present participle manner adverbial back-position). And *having read* in the papers about truth drugs, of course Gladys would believe it absolutely (Present participle cause adverbial front-position).

The present participle, similar to the infinitive, can build up semi-predicative complexes of objective and subjective types. The two groups of complexes, i.e. infinitival and present participial, may exist in parallel (e.g. when used with some verbs of physical perceptions), the difference between them lying in the aspective presentation of the process. *Cf.*:

Nobody noticed *the scouts approach the enemy trench.* – Nobody noticed *the scouts approaching the enemy trench with slow, cautious, expertly calculated movements.* Suddenly *a telephone* was heard *to buzz*, breaking the spell. – *The telephone* was heard *vainly buzzing* in the study.

A peculiar use of the present participle is seen in the absolute participial constructions of various types, forming complexes of detached semi-predication. Cf.:

*The messenger waiting in the hall*, we had only a couple of minutes to make a decision. The dean sat at his desk, *with an electric fire glowing warmly behind the fender at the opposite wall.*

These complexes of descriptive and narrative stylistic nature seem to be gaining ground in present-day English.

§ 5. *The past participle* is the non-finite form of the verb which combines the properties of the verb with those of the adjective, serving as the qualifying-processual name. The past participle is a single form, having no paradigm of its own. By way of the paradigmatic correlation with the present participle, it conveys implicitly the categorial meaning of the perfect and the passive. As different from the present participle, it has no distinct combinability features or syntactic function features specially characteristic of the adverb. Thus, the main self-positional functions of the past participle in the sentence are those of the attribute and the predicative. Cf.:

Moyra's *softened* look gave him a new hope (Past participle attributive front-position). The cleverly *chosen* timing of the attack determined the outcome of the battle (Past participle attributive front-position). It is a face *devastated* by passion (Past participle attributive back-position). His was a victory *gained* against all rules and predictions (Past participle attributive back-position). *Looked upon* in this light, the wording of the will didn't appear so odious (Past participle attributive detached position). The light is bright and inconveniently *placed* for reading (Past participle predicative position).

The past participle is included in the structural formation of the present participle (perfect, passive), which, together with the other differential properties, vindicates the treatment of this form as a separate verbid.

In the attributive use, the past participial meanings of the perfect and the passive are expressed in dynamic correlation with the aspective lexico-grammatical character of the verb. As a result of this correlation, the attributive past participle of limitive verbs in a neutral context expresses priority, while the past participle of unlimitive verbs expresses simultaneity. *E.g.*:

A tree *broken* by the storm blocked the narrow passage between the cliffs and the water. (Priority in the passive; the implication is "a tree that had been broken by the storm"). I saw that the picture *admired* by the general public hardly had a fair chance with the judges. (Simultaneity in the passive; the implication is "the picture which was being admired by the public").

Like the present participle, the past participle is capable of making up semi-predicative constructions of complex object, complex subject, as well as of absolute complex.

The past participial complex object is specifically characteristic with verbs of wish and oblique causality (*have, get*). *Cf.*:

I want *the document prepared* for signing by 4 p.m. Will you have *my coat brushed up*, please?

Compare the use of the past participial complex object and the complex subject as its passive transform with a perception verb:

We could hear *a shot or two fired* from a field mortar. → *A shot or two* could be heard *fired* from a field mortar.

The complex subject of this type, whose participle is included in the double predicate of the sentence, is used but occasionally. A more common type of the participial complex subject can be seen with notional links of motion and position. *Cf.*:

*We* sank down and for a while *lay* there *stretched out and exhausted*.

The absolute past participial complex as a rule expresses priority in the correlation of two events. *Cf.*:

*The preliminary talks completed*, it became possible to concentrate on the central point of the agenda.

The past participles of non-objective verbs are rarely used in independent sentence-part positions; they are mostly included in phraseological or cliché combinations like *faded photographs, fallen leaves, a retired officer, a withered flower, dream come true*, etc. In these and similar cases the idea of pure quality rather than that of processual quality is expressed, the modifying participles showing the features of adjectivization.

As is known, the past participle is traditionally interpreted as being capable of adverbial-related use (like the present participle), notably in detached syntactical positions, after the introductory subordinative conjunctions. *Cf.*:

*Called up* by the conservative minority, the convention failed to pass a satisfactory resolution. Though *welcomed* heartily by his host, Frederick felt at once that something was wrong.

Approached from the paradigmatic point of view in the constructional sense, this interpretation is to be re-considered. As a matter of fact, past participial constructions of the type in question display clear cases of syntactic compression. The true categorial nature of the participial forms employed by them is exposed by the corresponding transformational correlations ("back transformations") as being not of adverbial, but of definitely adjectival relation. *Cf.*:

... → The convention, *which was called up* by the conservative minority, failed to pass a satisfactory resolution. ... → Though *he was welcomed* heartily by his host, Frederick felt at once that something was wrong.

*Cf.* a more radical diagnostic transformational change of the latter construction:

... → Frederick, *who was welcomed* heartily by his host, nevertheless felt at once that something was wrong.

As is seen from the analysis, the adjectival relation of the past participle in the quoted examples is proved by the near-predicative function of the participle in the derived transforms, be it even within the composition of the finite passive verb form. The adverbial uses of the present participle react to similar tests in a different way. *Cf.*:

*Passing* on to the library, he found Mabel entertaining her guests. → *As he passed* on to the library, he found Mabel entertaining her guests.

The adverbial force of the present participle in constructions like that is shown simply, as resulting from the absence of obligatory mediation of *be* between the participle and its subject (in the derivationally underlying units).

As an additional proof of our point, we may take an adjectival construction for a similar diagnostic testing. *Cf.*:

Though *red* in the face, the boy kept denying his guilt. → Though *he was red* in the face, the boy kept denying his guilt.

As we see, the word *red*, being used in the diagnostic concessive clause of complete composition, does not change its adjectival quality for an adverbial quality. *Being red in the face* would again present another categorial case. *Being*, as a present participial form, is in the observed syntactic conditions neither solely adjectival-related, nor solely adverbial-related; it is by nature adjectival-adverbial, the whole composite unity in question automatically belonging to the same categorial class, i.e. the class of present participial constructions of different subtypes.

§ 6. The consideration of the English verbids in their mutual comparison, supported and supplemented by comparing them with their non-verbal counterparts, puts forward some points of structure and function worthy of special notice.

In this connection, the infinitive-gerund correlation should first be brought under observation.

Both forms are substance-processual, and the natural question that one has to ask about them is, whether the two do not repeat each other by their informative destination and employment. This question was partly answered in the paragraph devoted to the general outline of the gerund. Observations of the actual uses of the gerund and the infinitive in texts do show the clear-cut semantic difference between the forms, which consists in the gerund being, on the one hand, of a more substantive nature than the infinitive, i.e. of a nature nearer to the thingness-signification type; on the other hand, of a more abstract nature in the logical sense proper. Hence, the forms do not repeat, but complement each other, being both of them inalienable components of the English verbal system.

The difference between the forms in question may be demonstrated by the following examples:

*Seeing* and *talking* to people made him tired. (As characteristic of a period of his life; as a general feature of his disposition) – – It made him tired *to see* and *talk* to so many people. (All at a time, on that particular occasion); *Spending* an afternoon in the company of that gentle soul was always a wonderful pleasure. (Repeated action, general characteristic) – – *To spend* an afternoon on the grass – lovely! (A response utterance of enthusiastic agreement); Who doesn't like *singing*? (In a general reference) – – Who doesn't like to sing? (In reference to the subject).

Comparing examples like these, we easily notice the more dynamic, more actional character of the infinitive as well as of the whole collocations built up around it, and the less dynamic character of the corresponding gerundial collocations. Furthermore, beyond the boundaries of the verb, but within the boundaries of the same inter-class paradigmatic derivation (see above, Ch. IV, § 8), we find the cognate verbal noun which is devoid of processual dynamics altogether, though it denotes, from a different angle, the same referential process, situation, event. *Cf.*:

For them *to have arrived* so early! Such a surprise! – – *Their having arrived* so early was indeed a great surprise. – – *Their early arrival* was a great surprise, really.

The triple correlation, being of an indisputably systemic nature and covering a vast proportion of the lexicon, enables us to interpret it in terms of a special lexico-grammatical category of processual representation. The ti ee stages of this category represent the referential processual entity of the lexemic series, respectively, as dynamic (the infinitive and its phrase), semi-dynamic (the gerund and its phrase), and static (the verbal noun and its phrase). The category of processual representation underlies the predicative differences between various situation-naming constructions in the sphere of syntactic nominalization (see further, Ch. XXV).

Another category specifically identified within the framework of substantival verbids and relevant for syntactic analysis is the category of modal representation. This category, pointed out by L.S. Barkhudarov [Бархударов, 1975, 151 – 152], marks the infinitive in contrast to the gerund, and it is revealed in the infinitive having a modal force, in particular, in its attributive uses, but also elsewhere. *Cf.*:

This is a kind of peace *to be desired* by all. (A kind of peace that should be desired). Is there any hope for us *to meet* this great violinist in our town? (A hope that we may meet this violinist). It was arranged for the mountaineers *to have a rest* in tents before climbing the peak. (It was arranged so that they could have a rest in tents).

When speaking about the functional difference between lingual forms, we must bear in mind that this difference might become subject to neutralization in various systemic or contextual conditions. But however vast the corresponding field of neutralization might be, the rational basis of correlations of the forms in question still lies in their difference, not in neutralizing equivalence. Indeed, the difference is linguistically so valuable that one well-established occurrence of a differential correlation of meaningful forms outweighs by its significance dozens of their textual neutralizations. Why so? For the simple reason that language is a means of forming and exchanging ideas – that is, ideas differing from one another, not coinciding with one another. And this simple truth should thoroughly be taken into consideration when tackling certain cases of infinitive-gerund equivalence in syntactic constructions – as, for instance, the freely alternating gerunds and infinitives with some phasal predicators (*begin, start, continue, cease,* etc.). The functional equivalence of the infinitive and the gerund in the composition of the phasal predicate by no means can be held as testifying to their functional equivalence in other spheres of expression.

As for the preferable or exclusive use of the gerund with a set of transitive verbs (*e.g. avoid, delay, deny, forgive, mind, postpone*) and especially prepositional-complementive verbs and word-groups (*e.g. accuse of, agree to, depend on, prevent from, think of, succeed in, thank for; be aware of, be busy in, be indignant at, be sure of*), we clearly see here the tendency of mutual differentiation and complementation of the substantive verbid forms based on the demonstrated category of processual representation. In fact, it is the gerund, not the infinitive, that denotes the processual referent of the lexeme not in a dynamic, but in a half-dynamic representation, which is more appropriate to be associated with a substantive-related part of the sentence.

§ 7. Within the gerund-participle correlation, the central point of our analysis will be the very lexico-grammatical identification of the two verbid forms in *-ing* in their reference to each other. Do they constitute two different verbids, or do they present one and the same form with a somewhat broader range of functions than either of the two taken separately?

The ground for raising this problem is quite substantial, since the outer structure of the two elements of the verbal system is absolutely identical: they are outwardly the same when viewed in isolation. It is not by chance that in the American linguistic tradition which can be traced back to the school of Descriptive Linguistics the two forms are recognized as one integral V-*ing*.

In treating the *ing*-forms as constituting one integral verbid entity, opposed, on the one hand, to the infinitive (V-*to*), on the other hand, to the past participle (V-*en*), appeal is naturally made to the alternating use of the possessive and the common-objective nounal element in the role of the subject of the *ing*-form (mostly observed in various object positions of the sentence). *Cf.*:

I felt annoyed at *his failing* to see my point at once. ↔ I felt annoyed at *him failing* to see my point at once. He was not, however, averse to *Elaine Fortescue's entertaining* the hypothesis. ↔ He was not, however, averse to *Elaine Fortescue entertaining* the hypothesis.

This use presents a case known in linguistics as "half-gerund". So, in terms of the general *ing*-form problem, we have to choose between the two possible interpretations of the half-gerund: either as an actually intermediary form with double features, whose linguistic semi-status is truly reflected in its conventional name, or as an element of a non-existent categorial specification, i.e. just another variant of the same indiscriminate V-*ing*.

In this connection, the reasoning of those who support the idea of the integral V-*ing* form can roughly be presented thus: if the two uses of V-*ing* are functionally identical, and if the "half-gerund" V-*ing* occurs with approximately the same frequency as the "full-gerund" V-*ing*, both forms presenting an ordinary feature of an ordinary English text, then there is no point in discriminating the "participle" V-*ing* and the "gerund" V-*ing*.

In compliance with the general principle of approach to any set of elements forming a categorial or functional continuum, let us first consider the correlation between the polar elements of the continuum, i.e. the correlation between the pure present participle and the pure gerund, setting aside the half-gerund for a further discussion.

The comparative evaluations of the actually different uses of the *ing*-forms cannot fail to show their distinct categorial differentiation: one range of uses is definitely noun-related, definitely of process-substance signification; the other range of uses is definitely adjective-adverb-related, definitely of process-quality signification. This differentiation can easily be illustrated by specialized gerund-testing and participle-testing, as well as by careful textual observations of the forms.

The gerund-testing, partly employed while giving a general outline of the gerund, includes the noun-substitution procedure backed by the question-procedure. *Cf*.:

My chance of *getting*, or *achieving*, anything that I long for will always be gravely reduced by the interminable existence of that block. → My chance of *what*? → My chance of *success*.

He insisted on *giving* us some coconuts. → *What* did he insist on? → He insisted on *our acceptance* of the gift.

All his relatives somehow disapproved of his *writing* poetry. →
*What* did all his relatives disapprove *of*? → His relatives disapproved
of *his poetical work*.

The other no less convincing evidence of the nounal featuring of
the form in question is its natural occurrence in coordinative connections with the noun. *Cf.*:

I didn't stop to think of an answer; it came immediately off my
tongue without any *pause* or *planning*. Your husband isn't ill, no.
What he does need is *relaxation* and simply *cheering* a bit, if you
know what I mean. He carried out rigorously all the precepts concerning *food, bathing, meditation* and so on of the orthodox Hindu.

The participle-testing, for its part, includes the adjective-adverb
substitution procedure backed by the corresponding question-procedure, as well as some other analogies. *Cf.*:

He was in a *terrifying* condition. → In *what kind* of condition
was he? → He was in an *awful* condition. (Adjective substitution
procedure). *Pursuing* this course of free association, I suddenly remembered a dinner date I once had with a distinguished colleague.
→ *When* did I suddenly remember a dinner date? → *Then* I suddenly remembered a dinner date. (Adverb-substitution procedure).
She sits up *gasping* and *staring* wild-eyed about her. → *How* does
she sit up? → She sits up *so*. (Adverb-substitution procedure).

The participle also enters into easy coordinative and parallel associations with qualitative and stative adjectives. *Cf.*:

That was a *false*, but *convincing* show of affection. The ears are
*large, protruding*, with the heavy lobes of the sensualist. On the
great bed are two figures, a *sleeping* woman, and a young man
*awake*.

Very important in this respect will be analogies between the present participle qualitative function and the past participle qualitative
function, since the separate categorial standing of the past participle
remains unchallenged. *Cf.*:

an *unmailed* letter – a *coming* letter; the *fallen* monarchy – the
*falling* monarchy; *thinned* hair – *thinning* hair.

Of especial significance for the differential verbid identification
purposes are the two different types of conversion the compared
forms are subject to, namely, the nounal conversion of the gerund
and, correspondingly, the adjectival conversion of the participle.

Compare the gerund-noun conversional pairs:

your *airing* the room – – to take *an airing* before going to bed; his *breeding* his son to the profession – – a person of unimpeachable *breeding*; their *calling* him a liar – – the youth's choice of a *calling* in life.

Compare the participle-adjective conversional pairs:

animals *living* in the jungle – – *living* languages; a man never *daring* an open argument – – a *daring* inventor; a car *passing* by – – a *passing* passion.

Having recourse to the evidence of the analogy type, as a counter-thesis against the attempted demonstration, one might point out cases of categorial ambiguity, where the category of the qualifying element remains open to either interpretation, such as the *typing instructor*, the *boiling kettle*, or the like. However, cases like these present a trivial homonymy which, being resolved, can itself be taken as evidence in favour of, not against, the two *ing*-forms differing from each other on the categorial lines. *Cf.*:

the *typing* instructor → the instructor of *typing*; the instructor who is typing; the *boiling* kettle → the kettle for *boiling*; the kettle that is boiling

At this point, the analysis of the cases presenting the clear-cut gerund versus present participle difference can be considered as fulfilled. The two *ing*-forms in question are shown as possessing categorially differential properties establishing them as two different verbids in the system of the English verb.

And this casts a light on the categorial nature of the half-gerund, since it is essentially based on the positional verbid neutralization. As a matter of fact, let us examine the following examples:

You may count on *my doing* all that is necessary on such occasions. – – You may count on *me doing* all that is necessary on such occasions.

The possessive subject of the *ing*-form in the first of the two sentences is clearly disclosed as a structural adjunct of a nounal collocation. But the objective subject of the *ing*-form in the second sentence, by virtue of its morphological constitution, cannot be associated with a noun: this would contradict the established regularities of the categorial compatibility. The casal-type government (direct, or representative-pronominal) in the collocation being lost (or, more precisely, being non-existent), the *ing*-form of the collocation can only be understood as a participle. This interpretation is strongly supported by comparing half-gerund constructions with clear-cut participial constructions governed by perception verbs:

To think of *him turning* sides! – – To see *him turning* sides! I don't like *Mrs. Tomson complaining* of her loneliness. – – I can't listen to *Mrs. Tomson complaining* of her loneliness. Did you ever hear of *a girl playing* a trombone? – – Did you ever hear *a girl playing* a trombone?

On the other hand, the position of the participle in the collocation is syntactically peculiar, since semantic accent in such constructions is made on the fact or event described, i.e. on the situational content of it, with the processual substance as its core. This can be demonstrated by question-tests:

(The first half-gerund construction in the above series) ↔ To think of what in connection with him? (The second half-gerund construction) ↔ What don't you like about Mrs. Tomson? (The third half-gerund construction) ↔ Which accomplishment of a girl presents a surprise for the speaker?

Hence, the verbid under examination is rather to be interpreted as a transferred participle, or a gerundial participle, the latter term seeming to relevantly disclose the essence of the nature of this form; though the existing name "half-gerund" is as good as any other, provided the true character of the denoted element of the system is understood.

Our final remark in connection with the undertaken observation will be addressed to linguists who, while recognizing the categorial difference between the gerund and the present participle, will be inclined to analyse the half-gerund (the gerundial participle) on exactly the same basis as the full gerund, refusing to draw a demarcation line between the latter two forms and simply ascribing the occurrence of the common case subject in this construction to the limited use of the possessive case in modern English in general. As regards this interpretation, we should like to say that an appeal to the limited sphere of the English noun possessive in an attempt to prove the wholly gerundial character of the intermediary construction in question can hardly be considered of any serious consequence. True, a vast proportion of English nouns do not admit of the possessive case form, or, if they do, their possessive in the construction would create contextual ambiguity, or else some sort of stylistic ineptitude. *Cf.*:

The headlines bore a flaring announcement of the strike being called off by the Amalgamated Union. (No normal possessive with the noun *strike*); I can't fancy their daughter entering a University college. (Ambiguity in the oral possessive: *daughter's – daughters'*); They were surprised at the head of the family rejecting the services of the old servant. (Evading the undesirable shift of the possessive particle *-'s* from the head-noun to its adjunct); The notion of this woman who had had the world at her feet paying a man half a dollar to dance with her filled me with shame. (Semantic and stylistic incongruity of the clause possessive with the statement).

However, these facts are but facts in themselves, since they only present instances when a complete gerundial construction for this or that reason either cannot exist at all, or else should be avoided on diverse reasons of usage. So, the quoted instances of gerundial participle phrases are not more demonstrative of the thesis in question than, say, the attributive uses of nouns in the common form (*e.g. the inquisitor judgement, the Shakespeare Fund, a Thompson way of refusing*, etc.) would be demonstrative of the possessive case "tendency" to coincide with the bare stem of the noun: the absence of the possessive nounal form as such cannot be taken to testify that the "possessive case" may exist without its feature sign.

## CHAPTER XII

## FINITE VERB: INTRODUCTION

§ 1. The finite forms of the verb express the processual relations of substances and phenomena making up the situation reflected in the sentence. These forms are associated with one another in an extremely complex and intricate system. The peculiar aspect of the complexity of this system lies in the fact that, as we have stated before, the finite verb is directly connected with the structure of the sentence as a whole. Indeed, the finite verb, through the working of its categories, is immediately related to such sentence-constitutive factors as morphological forms of predication, communication purposes, subjective modality, subject-object relation, gradation of probabilities, and quite a few other factors of no lesser importance.

As has been mentioned elsewhere, the complicated character of the system in question has given rise to a lot of controversies about the structural formation of the finite verb categories, as well as the bases of their functional semantics. It would be not an exaggeration to say that each fundamental type of grammatical expression capable of being approached in terms of generalized categories in the domain of the finite verb has created a subject for a scholarly dispute. For instance, taking as an example the sphere of the categorial person and number of the verb, we are faced with the argument among grammarians about the existence or non-existence of the verbal-pronominal forms of these categories. In connection with the study of the verbal expression of time and aspect, the great controversy is going on as to the temporal or aspective nature of the verbal forms of the indefinite, continuous, perfect, and perfect-continuous series. Grammatical expression of the future tense in English is stated by some scholars as a matter-of-fact truth, while other linguists are eagerly negating any possibility of its existence as an element of grammar. The verbal voice invites its investigators to exchange mutually opposing views regarding both the content and the number of its forms. The problem of the subjunctive mood may justly be called one of the most vexed in the theory of grammar: the exposition of its structural properties, its inner divisions, as well as its correlation with the indicative mood vary literally from one linguistic author to another.

On the face of it, one might get an impression that the morphological study of the English finite verb has amounted to interminable aimless exchange of arguments, ceaseless advances of opposing "points of view", the actual aim of which has nothing to do with the practical application of linguistic theory to life. However, the fallacy of such an impression should be brought to light immediately and uncompromisingly.

As a matter of fact, it is the verb system that, of all the spheres of morphology, has come under the most intensive and fruitful analysis undertaken by contemporary linguistics. In the course of these studies the oppositional nature of the categorial structure of the verb was disclosed and explicitly formulated; the paradigmatic system of the expression of verbal functional semantics was described competently, though in varying technical terms, and the correlation of form and meaning in the composition of functionally relevant parts of this system was demonstrated explicitly on the copious material gathered.

Theoretical discussions have not ceased, nor subsided. On the contrary, they continue and develop, though on an ever more solid scientific foundation; and the cumulative descriptions of the English verb provide now an integral picture of its nature which the grammatical theory has never possessed before. Indeed, it is due to this advanced types of study that the structural and semantic patterning of verbal constructions successfully applied to teaching practices on all the stages of tuition has achieved so wide a scope.

§ 2. The following presentation of the categorial system of the English verb is based on oppositional criteria worked out in the course of grammatical studies of language by scholars of different countries. We do not propose to develop a description in which the many points of discussion would receive an exposition in terms of anything like detailed analysis. Our aim will rather be only to demonstrate some general principles of approach – such principles as would stimulate the student's desire to see into the inner meaningful workings of any grammatical construction which are more often than not hidden under the outer connections of its textual elements; such principles as would develop the student's ability to rely on his own resources when coming across concrete dubious cases of grammatical structure and use; such principles as, finally, would provide the student with a competence enabling him to bring his personal efforts of grammatical understanding to relevant correlation with the recognized theories, steering open-eyed among the differences of expert opinion.

The categorial spheres to be considered in this book are known from every topical description of English grammar. They include the systems of expressing verbal person, number, time, aspect, voice, and mood. But the identification and the distribution of the actual grammatical categories of the verb recognized in our survey will not necessarily coincide with the given enumeration, which will be exposed and defended with the presentation of each particular category that is to come under study.

CHAPTER XIII
## VERB: PERSON AND NUMBER

§ 1. The categories of person and number are closely connected with each other. Their ediate connection is conditioned by the two factors: first, by thei ituational semantics, referring the process denoted by the verb to the subject of the situation, i.e. to its central substance (which exists in inseparable unity of "quality" reflected in the personal denotation, and "quantity" reflected in the numerical denotation); second, by their direct and immediate relation to the syntactic unit expressing the subject as the functional part of the sentence.

Both categories are different in principle from the other categories of the finite verb, in so far as they do not convey any inherently "verbal" semantics, any constituents of meaning realized and confined strictly within the boundaries of the verbal lexeme. The nature of both of them is purely "reflective" (see Ch. III, § 5).

Indeed, the process itself, by its inner quality and logical status, cannot be "person-setting" in any consistent sense, the same as it cannot be either "singular" or "plural"; and this stands in contrast with the other properties of the process, such as its development in time, its being momentary or repeated, its being completed or incompleted, etc. Thus, both the personal and numerical semantics, though categorially expressed by the verb, cannot be characterized as process-relational, similar to the other aspects of the verbal categorial semantics. These aspects of semantics are to be understood only as substance-relational, reflected in the verb from the interpretation and grammatical featuring of the subject.

§ 2. Approached from the strictly morphemic angle, the analysis of the verbal person and number leads the grammarian to the statement of the following converging and diverging features of their forms.

The expression of the category of person is essentially confined to the singular form of the verb in the present tense of the indicative mood and, besides, is very singularly presented in the future tense. As for the past tense, the person is alien to it, except for a trace of personal distinction in the archaic conjugation.

In the present tense the expression of the category of person is divided into three peculiar subsystems.

The first subsystem includes the modal verbs that have no personal inflexions: *can, may, must, shall, will, ought, need, dare*. So, in the formal sense, the category of person is wholly neutralized with these verbs, or, in plainer words, it is left unexpressed.

The second subsystem is made up by the unique verbal lexeme *be*. The expression of person by this lexeme is the direct opposite to its expression by modal verbs: if the latter do not convey the indication of person in any morphemic sense at all, the verb *be* has three different suppletive personal forms, namely: *am* for the first person singular, *is* for the third person singular, and *are* as a feature marking the finite form negatively: neither the first, nor the third person singular. It cannot be taken for the specific positive mark of the second person for the simple reason that it coincides with the plural all-person (equal to none-person) marking.

The third subsystem presents just the regular, normal expression of person with the remaining multitude of the English verbs, with each morphemic variety of them. From the formal point of view, this subsystem occupies the medial position between the first two: if the verb *be* is at least two-personal, the normal personal type of the verb conjugation is one-personal. Indeed, the personal mark is confined here to the third person singular -(e)s [-z, -s, -ɪz], the other two persons (the first and the second) remaining unmarked, *e.g.* *comes – come, blows – blow, stops – stop, chooses – choose*.

As is known, alongside this universal system of three sets of personal verb forms, modern English possesses another system of person-conjugation characterizing elevated modes of speech (solemn addresses, sermons, poetry, etc.) and stamped with a flavour of archaism. The archaic person-conjugation has one extra feature in comparison with the common conjugation, namely, a special inflexion for the second person singular. The three described subsystems of the personal verb forms receive the following featuring:

The modal person-conjugation is distinguished by one morphemic mark, namely, the second person: *canst, may(e)st, wilt, shalt, shouldst, wouldst, ought(e)st, need(e)st, durst*.

The personal *be*-conjugation is complete in three explicitly marked forms, having a separate suppletive presentation for each separate person: *am, art, is*.

The archaic person-conjugation of the rest of the verbs, though richer than the common system of person forms, still occupies the medial position between the modal and *be*-conjugation. Two of the three of its forms, the third and second persons, are positively marked, while the first person remains unmarked, *e.g. comes* – *comest* – *come, blows* – *blowest* – *blow, stops* – *stoppest* – *stop, chooses* – *choosest* – *choose.*

As regards the future tense, the person finds here quite another mode of expression. The features distinguishing it from the present-tense person conjugation are, first, that it marks not the third, but the first person in distinction to the remaining two; and second, that it includes in its sphere also the plural. The very principle of the person featuring is again very peculiar in the future tense as compared with the present tense, consisting not in morphemic inflexion, nor even in the simple choice of person-identifying auxiliaries, but in the oppositional use of *shall – will* specifically marking the first person (expressing, respectively, voluntary and non-voluntary future), which is contrasted against the oppositional use of *will – shall* specifically marking the second and third persons together (expressing, respectively, mere future and modal future). These distinctions, which will be described at more length further on, are characteristic only of British English.

A trace of person distinction is presented in the past tense with the archaic form of the second person singular. The form is used but very occasionally, still it goes with the pronoun *thou*, being obligatory with it. Here is an example of its individualizing occurrence taken from E. Hemingway:

*Thyself* and *thy* horses. Until *thou hadst* horses *thou wert* with us. Now *thou art* another capitalist more.

Thus, the peculiarity of the archaic past tense person-conjugation is that its only marked form is not the third person as in the present tense, nor the first person as in the British future tense, but the second person. This is what might be called "little whims of grammar"!

§ 3. Passing on to the expression of grammatical number by the English finite verb, we are faced with the interesting fact that, from the formally morphemic point of view, it is hardly featured at all.

As a matter of fact, the more or less distinct morphemic featuring of the category of number can be seen only with the archaic forms of the unique *be*, both in the present tense and in the past tense. But even with this verb the featuring cannot be called quite explicit, since the opposition of the category consists in the unmarked plural form for all the persons being contrasted against the

124

marked singular form for each separate person, each singular person thereby being distinguished by its own, specific form. It means that the expressions of person and number by the archaic conjugation of *be* in terms of the lexeme as a whole are formally not strictly separated from each other, each singular mark conveying at once a double grammatical sense, both of person and number. *Cf.*: am – are; art – are; was (the first and the third persons, i.e. non-second person) – were; wast (second person) – were.

In the common conjugation of *be*, the blending of the person and number forms is more profound, since the suppletive *are*, the same as its past tense counterpart *were*, not being confined to the plural sphere, penetrate the singular sphere, namely, the expression of the second person (which actually becomes non-expression because of the formal coincidence).

As for the rest of the verbs, the blending of the morphemic expression of the two categories is complete, for the only explicit morphemic opposition in the integral categorial sphere of person and number is reduced with these verbs to the third person singular (present tense, indicative mood) being contrasted against the unmarked finite form of the verb.

§ 4. The treatment of the analysed categories on a formal basis, though fairly consistent in the technical sense, is, however, lacking an explicit functional appraisal. To fill the gap, we must take into due account not only the meaningful aspect of the described verbal forms in terms of their reference to the person-number forms of the subject, but also the functional content of the subject-substantival categories of person and number themselves.

The semantic core of the substantival (or pronominal, for that matter) category of person is understood nowadays in terms of deictic, or indicative signification.

The deictic function of lingual units, which has come under careful linguistic investigation of late, consists not in their expressing self-dependent and self-sufficient elements of meaning, but in pointing out entities of reality in their spatial and temporal relation to the participants of speech communication. In this light, the semantic content of the first person is the indication of the person who is speaking, but such an indication as is effected by no other individual than himself. This self-indicative role is performed lexically by the personal pronoun *I*. The semantic content of the second person is the indication of the individual who is listening to the first person speaking – but again such an indication as viewed and effected by the speaker. This listener-indicative function is performed by the personal pronoun *you*. Now, the semantic content of the third person is quite different from that of either the first or second person. Whereas the latter two express the immediate participants of the communication, the third person indicates all the other entities of reality, i.e. beings, things, and phenomena not immediately included in the communicative situation, though also as viewed by the speaker, at the moment of speech. This latter kind of indication may be effected in the two alternative ways. The first is a direct one, by using words of a full-meaning function, either proper, or common, with the corresponding specifications achieved with the help of indicators-determiners (articles and pronominal words of diverse linguistic standings). The second is an oblique one, by using the personal pronouns *he*, *she*, or *it*, depending on the gender properties of the referents. It is the second way, i.e. the personal pronominal indication of the third person referent, that immediately answers the essence of the grammatical category of person as such, i.e. the three-stage location of the referent in relation to the speaker: first, the speaker himself; second, his listener; third, the non-participant of the communication, be it a human non-participant or otherwise.

As we see, the category of person taken as a whole is, as it were, inherently linguistic, the significative purpose of it being confined to indications centering around the production of speech.

Let us now appraise the category of number represented in the forms of personal pronouns, i.e. the lexemic units of language specially destined to serve the speaker-listener lingual relation.

One does not have to make great exploratory efforts in order to realize that the grammatical number of the personal pronouns is extremely peculiar, in no wise resembling the number of ordinary substantive words. As a matter of fact, the number of a substantive normally expresses either the singularity or plurality of its referent ("one – more than one", or, in oppositional appraisal, "plural – non-plural"), the quality of the referents, as a rule, not being re-interpreted with the change of the number (the many exceptions to this rule lie beyond the purpose of our present discussion). For instance, when speaking about a few powder-compacts, I have in mind just several pieces of them of absolutely the same nature. Or when referring to a team of eleven football-players, I mean exactly so many members of this sporting group. With the personal pronouns, though, it is different, and the cardinal feature of the difference is the heterogeneity of the plural personal pronominal meaning.

Indeed, the first person plural does not indicate the plurality of the "ego", it cannot mean several *I*'s. What it denotes in fact, is the speaker plus some other person or persons belonging, from the point of view of the utterance content, to the same background. The second person plural is essentially different from the first person plural in so far as it does not necessarily express, but is only capable of expressing similar semantics. Thus, it denotes either more than one listener (and this is the ordinary, general meaning of the plural as such, not represented in the first person); or, similar to the first person, one actual listener plus some other person or persons belonging to the same background in the speaker's situational estimation; or, again specifically different from the first person, more than one actual listener plus some other person or persons of the corresponding interpretation. Turning to the third person plural, one might feel inclined to think that it would wholly coincide with the plural of an ordinary substantive name. On closer observation, however, we note a fundamental difference here also. Indeed, the plural of the third person is not the substantive plural proper, but the deictic, indicative, pronominal plural; it is expressed through the intermediary reference to the direct name of the denoted entity, and so may either be related to the singular *he*-pronoun, or the *she*-pronoun, or the *it*-pronoun, or to any possible combination of them according to the nature of the plural object of denotation.

The only inference that can be made from the given description is that in the personal pronouns the expression of the plural is very much blended with the expression of the person, and what is taken to be three persons in the singular and plural, essentially presents a set of six different forms of blended person-number nature, each distinguished by its own individuality. Therefore, in the strictly categorial light, we have here a system not of three, but of six persons.

Returning now to the analysed personal and numerical forms of the finite verb, the first conclusion to be drawn on the ground of the undertaken analysis is that their intermixed character, determined on the formal basis, answers in general the mixed character of the expression of person and number by the pronominal subject name of the predicative construction. The second conclusion to be drawn, however, is that the described formal person-number system of the finite verb is extremely and very singularly deficient. In fact, what in this connection the regular verb-form does express morphemically, is only the oppositional identification of the third person singular (to leave alone the particular British English mode of expressing the person in the future).

A question naturally arises: What is the actual relevance of this deficient system in terms of the English language? Can one point out any functional, rational significance of it, if taken by itself?

The answer to this question can evidently be only in the negative: in no wise. There cannot be any functional relevance in such a system, if taken by itself. But in language it does not exist by itself.

§ 5. As soon as we take into consideration the functional side of the analysed forms, we discover at once that these forms exist in unity with the personal-numerical forms of the subject. This unity is of such a nature that the universal and true indicator of person and number of the subject of the verb will be the subject itself, however trivial this statement may sound. Essentially, though, there is not a trace of triviality in the formula, bearing in mind, on the one hand, the substantive character of the expressed categorial meanings, and on the other, the analytical basis of the English grammatical structure. The combination of the English finite verb with the subject is obligatory not only in the general syntactic sense, but also in the categorial sense of expressing the subject-person of the process.

An objection to this thesis can be made on the ground that in the text the actual occurrence of the subject with the finite verb is not always observed. Moreover, the absence of the subject in constructions of living colloquial English is, in general, not an unusual feature. Observing textual materials, we may come across cases of subject-wanting predicative units used not only singly, as part of curt question-response exchange, but also in a continual chain of speech. Here is an example of a chain of this type taken from E. Hemingway:

"No one shot from cars," said Wilson coldly.

"I mean chase them from cars."

"*Wouldn't* ordinarily," Wilson said. "*Seemed* sporting enough to me though while we were doing it. *Taking* more chance driving that way across the plain full of holes and one thing and another than hunting on foot. Buffalo could have charged us each time we shot if he liked. *Gave* him every chance. *Wouldn't mention* it to any one though. It's illegal if that's what you mean."

However, examples like this cannot be taken for a disproof of the obligatory connection between the verb and its subject, because

128

the corresponding subject-nouns, possibly together with some other accompanying words, are zeroed on certain syntactico-stylistical principles (brevity of expression in familiar style, concentration on the main informative parts of the communication, individual speech habits, etc.). Thus, the distinct zero-representation of the subject does give expression to the verbal person-number category even in conditions of an outwardly gaping void in place of the subject in this or that concrete syntactic construction used in the text. Due to the said zero-representation, we can easily reconstruct the implied person indications in the cited passage: "I wouldn't ordinarily"; "It seemed sporting enough"; "It was taking more chance driving that way"; "We gave him every chance"; "I wouldn't mention it to any one".

Quite naturally, the non-use of the subject in an actual utterance may occasionally lead to a referential misunderstanding or lack of understanding, and such situations are reflected in literary works by writers – observers of human speech as well as of human nature. A vivid illustration of this type of speech informative deficiency can be seen in one of K. Mansfield's stories:

"*Fried or boiled*?" asked the bold voice.

*Fried or boiled*? Josephine and Constantia were quite bewildered for the moment. They could hardly take it in.

"*Fried or boiled* what, Kate?" asked Josephine, trying to begin to concentrate.

Kate gave a loud sniff. "Fish."

"Well, why didn't you say so immediately?" Josephine reproached her gently. "How could you expect us to understand, Kate? There are a great many things in this world, you know, which are fried or boiled."

The referential gap in Kate's utterance gave cause to her bewildered listener for a just reproach. But such lack of positive information in an utterance is not to be confused with the non-expression of a grammatical category. In this connection, the textual zeroing of the subject-pronoun may be likened to the textual zeroing of different constituents of classical analytical verb-forms, such as the continuous, the perfect, and others: no zeroing can deprive these forms of their grammatical, categorial status.

Now, it would be too strong to state that the combination of the subject-pronoun with the finite verb in English has become an analytical person-number form in the full sense of this notion. The English subject-pronoun, unlike the French conjoint subject-pronoun (*e.g.*

*Je* vous remercie – "*I* thank you"; but: mon mari et *moi* – "my husband and *I*"), still retains its self-positional syntactic character, and the personal pronominal words, without a change of their nominative form, are used in various notional functions in sentences, building up different positional sentence-parts both in the role of head-word and in the role of adjunct-word. What we do see in this combination is, probably, a very specific semi-analytical expression of a reflective grammatical category through an obligatory syntagmatic relation of the two lexemes: the lexeme-reflector of the category and the lexeme-originator of the category. This mode of grammatical expression can be called "junctional". Its opposite, i.e. the expression of the categorial content by means of a normal morphemic or word-morphemic procedure, can be, by way of contrast, tentatively called "native". Thus, from the point of view of the expression of a category either through the actual morphemic composition of a word, or through its being obligatorily referred to another word in a syntagmatic string, the corresponding grammatical forms will be classed into native and junctional. About the person-numerical forms of the finite verb in question we shall say that in the ordinary case of the third person singular present indicative, the person and number of the verb are expressed natively, while in most of the other paradigmatic locations they are expressed junctionally, through the obligatory reference of the verb-form to its subject.

This truth, not incapable of inviting an objection on the part of the learned, noteworthily has been exposed from time immemorial in practical grammar books, where the actual conjugation of the verb is commonly given in the form of pronoun-verb combinations: I read, you read, he reads, we read, you read, they read.

In point of fact, the English finite verb presented without its person-subject is grammatically almost meaningless. The presence of the two *you*'s in practical tables of examples like the one above, in our opinion, is also justified by the inner structure of language. Indeed, since *you* is part of the person-number system, and not only of the person system, it should be but natural to take it in the two different, though mutually complementing interpretations – one for each of the two series of pronouns in question, i.e. the singular series and the plural series. In the light of this approach, the archaic form *thou* plus the verb should be understood as a specific variant of the second person singular with its respective stylistic connotations.

130

§ 6. The exposition of the verbal categories of person and number presented here helps conveniently explain some special cases of the subject-verb categorial relations. The bulk of these cases have been treated by traditional grammar in terms of "agreement in sense", or "notional concord". We refer to the grammatical agreement of the verb not with the categorial form of the subject expressed morphemically, but with the actual personal-numerical interpretation of the denoted referent.

Here belong, in the first place, combinations of the finite verb with collective nouns. According as they are meant by the speaker either to reflect the plural composition of the subject, or, on the contrary, to render its integral, single-unit quality, the verb is used either in the plural, or in the singular. *E.g.*:

The government *were* definitely against the bill introduced by the opposing liberal party. - - The newly appointed government *has gathered* for its first session.

In the second place, we see here predicative constructions whose subject is made imperatively plural by a numeral attribute. Still, the corresponding verb-form is used to treat it both ways: either as an ordinary plural which fulfils its function in immediate keeping with its factual plural referent, or as an integrating name, whose plural grammatical form and constituent composition give only a measure to the subject-matter of denotation. *Cf.*:

Three years *have elapsed* since we saw him last. - - Three years *is* a long time to wait.

In the third place, under the considered hearding come constructions whose subject is expressed by a coordinative group of nouns, the verb being given an option of treating it either as a plural or as a singular. *E.g.*:

My heart and soul *belongs* to this small nation in its desperate struggle for survival. - - My emotional self and rational self *have been* at variance about the attitude adopted by Jane.

The same rule of "agreement in sense." is operative in relative clauses, where the finite verb directly reflects the categories of the nounal antecedent of the clause-introductory relative pronoun-subject. *Cf.*:

I who *am* practically unacquainted with the formal theory of games can hardly suggest an alternative solution. - - Your words show the courage and the truth that I have always felt *was* in your heart.

On the face of it, the cited examples might seem to testify to the analysed verbal categories being altogether self-sufficient, capable, as it were, even of "bossing" the subject as to its referential content. However, the inner regularities underlying the outer arrangement of grammatical connections are necessarily of a contrary nature: it is the subject that induces the verb, through its inflexion, however scanty it may be, to help express the substantival meaning not represented in the immediate substantival form. That this is so and not otherwise, can be seen on examples where the subject seeks the needed formal assistance from other quarters than the verbal, in particular, having recourse to determiners. *Cf.*:

*A* full *thirty miles was* covered in less than half an hour; the car could be safely relied on.

Thus, the role of the verb in such and like cases comes at most to that of a grammatical intermediary.

From the functional point of view, the direct opposite to the shown categorial connections is represented by instances of dialectal and colloquial person-number neutralization. *Cf.*:

"Ah! It's a pity *you* never *was trained* to use your reason, miss" (B. Shaw). "He's been in his room all day," the landlady said downstairs. "I guess *he don't feel* well" (E. Hemingway). "What are they going to do to me?" Johnny said. – "Nothing," I said. "*They ain't going* to do nothing to you" (W. Saroyan).

Such and similar oppositional neutralizations of the surviving verbal person-number indicators, on their part, clearly emphasize the significance of the junctional aspect of the two inter-connected categories reflected in the verbal lexeme from the substantival subject.

CHAPTER XIV

VERB: TENSE

§ 1. The immediate expression of grammatical time, or "tense" (*Lat.* tempus), is one of the typical functions of the finite verb. It is typical because the meaning of process, inherently embedded in the verbal lexeme, finds its complete realization only if presented in certain time conditions. That is why the expression or non-expression of grammatical time, together with the expression or non-expression of grammatical mood in person-form presentation, constitutes the basis of the verbal category of finitude, i.e. the basis of the division of all the forms of the verb into finite and non-finite.

When speaking of the expression of time by the verb, it is necessary to strictly distinguish between the general notion of time, the lexical denotation of time, and the grammatical time proper, or grammatical temporality.

The philosophical notion of time exposes it as the universal form of the continual consecutive change of phenomena. Time, as well as space are the basic forms of the existence of matter, they both are inalienable properties of reality and as such are absolutely independent of human perception. On the other hand, like other objective factors of the universe, time is reflected by man through his perceptions and intellect, and finds its expression in his language.

It is but natural that time as the universal form of consecutive change of things should be appraised by the individual in reference to the moment of his immediate perception of the outward reality. This moment of immediate perception, or "present moment", which is continually shifting in time, and the linguistic content of which is the "moment of speech", serves as the demarcation line between the past and the future. All the lexical expressions of time, according as they refer or do not refer to the denoted points or periods of time, directly or obliquely, to this moment, are divided into "present-oriented", or "absolutive" expressions of time, and "non-present-oriented", "non-absolutive" expressions of time.

The absolutive time denotation, in compliance with the experience gained by man in the course of his cognitive activity, distributes the intellective perception of time among three spheres: the sphere of the present, with the present moment included within its framework; the sphere of the past, which precedes the sphere of the present by way of retrospect; the sphere of the future, which follows the sphere of the present by way of prospect.

Thus, words and phrases like *now, last week, in our century, in the past, in the years to come, very soon, yesterday, in a couple of days*, giving a temporal characteristic to an event from the point of view of its orientation in reference to the present moment, are absolutive names of time.

The non-absolutive time denotation does not characterize an event in terms of orientation towards the present. This kind of denotation may be either "relative" or "factual".

The relative expression of time correlates two or more events showing some of them either as preceding the others, or following the others, or happening at one and the same time with them. Here belong such words and phrases as *after that, before that, at one and the same time with, some time later, at an interval of a day or two, at different times*, etc.

The factual expression of time either directly states the astronomical time of an event, or else conveys this meaning in terms of historical landmarks. Under this heading should be listed such words and phrases as *in the year 1066, during the time of the First World War, at the epoch of Napoleon, at the early period of civilization*, etc.

In the context of real speech the above types of time naming are used in combination with one another, so that the denoted event receives many-sided and very exact characterization regarding its temporal status.

Of all the temporal meanings conveyed by such detailing lexical denotation of time, the finite verb generalizes in its categorial forms only the most abstract significations, taking them as dynamic characteristics of the reflected process. The fundamental divisions both of absolutive time and of non-absolutive relative time find in the verb a specific presentation, idiomatically different from one language to another. The form of this presentation is dependent, the same as with the expression of other grammatical meanings, on the concrete semantic features chosen by a language as a basis for the functional differentiation within the verb lexeme. And it is the verbal expression of abstract, grammatical time that forms the necessary background for the adverbial contextual time denotation in an utterance; without the verbal background serving as a universal temporal "polarizer" and "leader", this marking of time would be utterly inadequate.

Indeed, what informative content should the following passage convey with all its lexical indications of time (*in the morning, in the afternoon, as usual, never, ever*), if it were deprived of the general indications of time achieved through the forms of the verb – the unit of the lexicon which the German grammarians very significantly call "Zeitwort" – the "time-word":

My own birthday passed without ceremony. I worked as usual *in the morning* and *in the afternoon* went for a walk in the solitary woods behind my house. I have *never* been able to discover what it is that gives these woods their mysterious attractiveness. They are like no woods I have *ever* known (S. Maugham).

In Modern English, the grammatical expression of verbal time, i.e. tense, is effected in two correlated stages. At the first stage, the process receives an absolutive time characteristic by means of opposing the past tense to the present tense. The marked member of this opposition is the past form. At the second stage, the process receives a non-absolutive relative time characteristic by means of opposing the forms of the future tense to the forms of no future marking. Since the two stages of the verbal time denotation are expressed separately, by their own oppositional forms, and, besides, have essentially different orientation characteristics (the first stage being absolutive, the second stage, relative), it stands to reason to recognize in the system of the English verb not one, but two temporal categories. Both of them answer the question: "What is the timing of the process?" But the first category, having the past tense as its strong member, expresses a direct retrospective evaluation of the time of the process, fixing the process either in the past or not in the past; the second category, whose strong member is the future tense, gives the timing of the process a prospective evaluation, fixing it either in the future (i.e. in the prospective posterior), or not in the future. As a result of the combined working of the two categories, the time of the event reflected in the utterance finds its adequate location in the temporal context, showing all the distinctive properties of the lingual presentation of time mentioned above.

According to the oppositional marking of the two temporal categories under analysis, we shall call the first of them the category of "primary time", and the second, the category of "prospective time", or, contractedly, "prospect".

§ 2. The category of primary time, as has just been stated, provides for the absolutive expression of the time of the process denoted by the verb, i.e. such an expression of it as gives its evaluation, in the long run, in reference to the moment of speech. The formal sign of the opposition constituting this category is, with regular verbs, the dental suffix -(e)d [-d, -t, -ɪd], and with irregular verbs, phonemic interchanges of more or less individual specifications. The suffix marks the verbal form of the past time (the past tense), leaving the opposite form unmarked. Thus, the opposition is to be rendered by the formula "the past tense – the present tense", the latter member representing the non-past tense, according to the accepted oppositional interpretation

The specific feature of the category of primary time is that it divides all the tense forms of the English verb into two temporal planes: the plane of the present and the plane of the past, which affects also the future forms. Very important in this respect is the structural nature of the expression of the category: the category of primary time is the only verbal category of immanent order which is expressed by inflexional forms. These inflexional forms of the past and present coexist in the same verb-entry of speech with the other, analytical modes of various categorial expression, including the future. Hence, the English verb acquires the two futures: on the one hand, the future of the present, i.e. as prospected from the present; on the other hand, the future of the past, i.e. as prospected from the past. The following example will be illustrative of the whole four-member correlation:

Jill *returns* from her driving class at five o'clock. – – At five Jill *returned* from her driving class. I know that Jill *will return* from her driving class at five o'clock. – – I knew that at five Jill *would return* from her driving class.

An additional reason for identifying the verbal past-present time system as a separate grammatical category is provided by the fact that this system is specifically marked by the *do*-forms of the indefinite aspect with their various, but inherently correlated functions. These forms, found in the interrogative constructions (*Does* he *believe* the whole story?), in the negative constructions (He *doesn't believe* the story), in the elliptical response constructions and elsewhere, are confined only to the category of primary time, i.e. the verbal past and present, not coming into contact with the expression of the future.

§ 3. The fact that the present tense is the unmarked member of the opposition explains a very wide range of its meanings exceeding by far the indication of the "moment of speech" chosen for the identification of primary temporality. Indeed, the present time may be understood as literally the moment of speaking, the zero-point of all subjective estimation of time made by the speaker. The meaning of the present with this connotation will be conveyed by such phrases as *at this very moment*, or *this instant*, or *exactly now*, or some other phrase like that. But an utterance like "now while I *am speaking*" breaks the notion of the zero time proper, since the speaking process is not a momentary, but a durative event. Furthermore, the present will still be the present if we relate it to such vast periods of time as *this month, this year, in our epoch, in the present millennium*, etc. The denoted stretch of time may be prolonged by a collocation like that beyond any definite limit. Still furthermore, in utterances of general truths as, for instance, "Two plus two *makes* four", or "The sun *is* a star", or "Handsome *is* that handsome *does*", the idea of time as such is almost suppressed, the implication of constancy, unchangeability of the truth at all times being made prominent. The present tense as the verbal form of generalized meaning covers all these denotations, showing the present time in relation to the process as inclusive of the moment of speech, incorporating this moment within its definite or indefinite stretch and opposed to the past time.

Thus, if we say, "Two plus two *makes* four", the linguistic implication of it is "always, and so at the moment of speech". If we say, "I *never take* his advice", we mean linguistically "at no time in terms of the current state of my attitude towards him, and so at the present moment". If we say, "*In our millennium* social formations *change* quicker than in the previous periods of man's history", the linguistic temporal content of it is "in our millennium, that is, in the millennium including the moment of speech". This meaning is the invariant of the present, developed from its categorial opposition to the past, and it penetrates the uses of the finite verb in all its forms, including the perfect, the future, the continuous.

Indeed, if the radio carries the news, "The two suspected terrorists *have been taken* into custody by the police", the implication of the moment of speech refers to the direct influence or after-effects of the event announced. Similarly, the statement "You *will be informed* about the decision later in the day" describes the event, which, although it has not yet happened, is prospected into the future from the present, i.e. the prospection itself incorporates the moment of speech. As for the present continuous, its relevance for the present moment is self-evident.

Thus, the analysed meaning of the verbal present arises as a result of its immediate contrast with the past form which shows the exclusion of the action from the plane of the present and so the action itself as capable of being perceived only in temporal retrospect. Again, this latter meaning of the disconnection from the present penetrates all the verbal forms of the past, including the perfect, the future, the continuous. Due to the marked character of the past verbal form, the said quality of its meaning does not require special demonstration.

Worthy of note, however, are utterances where the meaning of the past tense stands in contrast with the meaning of some adverbial phrase referring the event to the present moment. *Cf.:*

*Today* again I *spoke* to Mr. Jones on the matter, and again he *failed* to see the urgency of it.

The seeming linguistic paradox of such cases consists exactly in the fact that their two-type indications of time, one verbal-grammatical, and one adverbial-lexical, approach the same event from two opposite angles. But there is nothing irrational here. As a matter of fact, the utterances present instances of two-plane temporal evaluation of the event described: the verb-form shows the process as past and gone, i.e. physically disconnected from the present; as for the adverbial modifier, it presents the past event as a particular happening, belonging to a more general time situation which is stretched out up to the present moment inclusive, and possibly past the present moment into the future.

A case directly opposite to the one shown above is seen in the transpositional use of the present tense of the verb with the past adverbials, either included in the utterance as such, or else expressed in its contextual environment. *E.g.:*

*Then* he *turned* the corner, and what do you think *happens* next? He *faces* nobody else than Mr. Greggs accompanied by his private secretary!

The stylistic purpose of this transposition, known under the name of the "historic present" (*Lat.* praesens historicum) is to create a vivid picture of the event reflected in the utterance. This is achieved in strict accord with the functional meaning of the verbal present, sharply contrasted against the general background of the past plane of the utterance content.

§ 4. The combinations of the verbs *shall* and *will* with the infinitive have of late become subject of renewed discussion. The controversial point about them is whether these combinations really constitute, together with the forms of the past and present, the categorial expression of verbal tense, or are just modal phrases, whose expression of the future time does not differ in essence from the general future orientation of other combinations of modal verbs with the infinitive. The view that *shall* and *will* retain their modal meanings in all their uses was defended by such a recognized authority on English grammar of the older generation of the twentieth century linguists as O. Jespersen. In our times, quite a few scholars, among them the successors of Descriptive Linguistics, consider these verbs as part of the general set of modal verbs, "modal auxiliaries", expressing the meanings of capability, probability, permission, obligation, and the like.

A well-grounded objection against the inclusion of the construction *shall/will* + Infinitive in the tense system of the verb on the same basis as the forms of the present and past has been advanced by L. S. Barkhudarov [Бархударов, 1975, 126 ff.]. His objection consists in the demonstration of the double marking of this would-be tense form by one and the same category: the combinations in question can express at once both the future time and the past time (the form "future-in-the-past"), which hardly makes any sense in terms of a grammatical category. Indeed, the principle of the identification of any grammatical category demands that the forms of the category in normal use should be mutually exclusive. The category is constituted by the opposition of its forms, not by their co-position!

However, reconsidering the status of the construction *shall/will* + Infinitive in the light of oppositional approach, we see that far from comparing with the past-present verbal forms as the third member-form of the category of primary time it marks its own grammatical category, namely, that of prospective time (prospect). The meaningful contrast underlying the category of prospective time is between an after-action and a non-after-action. The after-action, or the "future", having its *shall/will*-feature, constitutes the marked member of the opposition.

The category of prospect is also temporal, in so far as it is immediately connected with the expression of processual time, like the category of primary time. But the semantic basis of the category of prospect is different in principle from that of the category of primary time: while the primary time is absolutive, i.e. present-oriented, the prospective time is purely relative; it means that the future form of the verb only shows that the denoted process is prospected as an after-action relative to some other action or state or event, the timing of which marks the zero-level for it. The two times are presented, as it were, in prospective coordination: one is shown as prospected for the future, the future being relative to the primary time, either present or past. As a result, the expression of the future receives the two mutually complementary manifestations: one manifestation for the present time-plane of the verb, the other manifestation for the past time-plane of the verb. In other words, the process of the verb is characterized by the category of prospect irrespective of its primary time characteristic, or rather, as an addition to this characteristic, and this is quite similar to all the other categories capable of entering the sphere of verbal time, e.g. the category of development (continuous in opposition), the category of retrospective coordination (perfect in opposition), the category of voice (passive in opposition): the respective forms of all these categories also have the past and present versions, to which, in due course, are added the future and non-future versions. Consider the following examples:

(1) I *was making* a road and all the coolies struck. (2) None of us doubted in the least that Aunt Emma *would* soon *be marvelling* again at Eustace's challenging success. (3) The next thing she wrote she sent to a magazine, and for many weeks worried about what *would happen* to it. (4) She did not protest, for she *had given* up the struggle. (5) Felix knew that they *would have settled* the dispute by the time he could be ready to have his say. (6) He *was being watched, shadowed, chased* by that despicable gang of hirelings. (7) But *would* little Johnny *be *being looked* after properly? The nurse was so young and inexperienced!

The oppositional content of the exemplified cases of finite verb-forms will, in the chosen order of sequence, be presented as follows: the past non-future continuous non-perfect non-passive (1); the past future continuous non-perfect non-passive (2); the past future non-continuous non-perfect non-passive (3); the past non-future non-continuous perfect non-passive (4); the past future non-continuous perfect non-passive (5); the past non-future continuous non-perfect passive (6); the past future continuous non-perfect passive (7) – the latter form, not in practical use.

As we have already stated before, the future tenses reject the *do*-forms of the indefinite aspect, which are confined to the expression of the present and past verbal times only. This fact serves as a supplementary ground for the identification of the expression of prospect as a separate grammatical category.

Of course, it would be an ill turn to grammar if one tried to introduce the above circumstantial terminology with all its pedantic strings of "non's" into the elementary teaching of language. The stringed categorial "non"-terms are apparently too redundant to be recommended for ordinary use even at an advanced level of linguistic training. What is achieved by this kind of terminology, however, is a comprehensive indication of the categorial status of verb-forms

140

under analysis in a compact, terse presentation. Thus, whenever a presentation like that is called for, the terms will be quite in their place.

§ 5. In analysing the English future tenses, the modal factor, naturally, should be thoroughly taken into consideration. A certain modal colouring of the meaning of the English future cannot be denied, especially in the verbal form of the first person. But then, as is widely known, the expression of the future in other languages is not disconnected from modal semantics either; and this is conditioned by the mere fact that the future action, as different from the present or past action, cannot be looked upon as a genuine feature of reality. Indeed, it is only foreseen, or anticipated, or planned, or desired, or otherwise prospected for the time to come. In this quality, the Russian future tense does not differ in principle from the verbal future of other languages, including English. Suffice it to give a couple of examples chosen at random:

Я *буду рассказывать* тебе интересные истории. *Расскажу* о страшных кометах, о битве воздушных кораблей, о гибели прекрасной страны по ту сторону гор. Тебе *не будет* скучно любить меня (А. Толстой). Немедленно на берег. *Найдешь* генерала Иолшина, *скажешь*: путь свободен. Пусть строит дорогу для артиллерии (Б. Васильев).

The future forms of the verbs in the first of the above Russian examples clearly express promise (i.e. a future action conveyed as a promise); those in the second example render a command.

Moreover, in the system of the Russian tenses there is a specialized modal form of analytical future expressing intention (the combination of the verb *стать* with the imperfective infinitive). *E.g.*: Что же вы теперь хотите делать? – Тебя это не касается, что я *стану делать*. Я план обдумываю (А. Толстой).

Within the framework of the universal meaningful features of the verbal future, the future of the English verb is highly specific in so far as its auxiliaries in their very immediate etymology are words of obligation and volition, and the survival of the respective connotations in them is backed by the inherent quality of the future as such. Still, on the whole, the English categorial future differs distinctly from the modal constructions with the same predicator verbs.

§ 6. In the clear-cut modal uses of the verbs *shall* and *will* the idea of the future either is not expressed at all, or else is only rendered by way of textual connotation, the central semantic accent being laid on the expression of obligation, necessity, inevitability, promise, intention, desire. These meanings may be easily seen both on the examples of ready phraseological citation, and in genuine everyday conversation exchanges. *Cf.*:

He who does not work neither *shall* he *eat* (phraseological citation). "I want a nice hot curry, do you hear?" – "All right, Mr. Crackenthorpe, you *shall have* it" (everyday speech). None are so deaf as those who *will not hear* (phraseological citation). Nobody's allowed to touch a thing – I *won't have* a woman near the place (everyday speech).

The modal nature of the *shall/will* + Infinitive combinations in the cited examples can be shown by means of equivalent substitutions:

... → He who does not work must not eat, either. ... → All right, Mr. Crackenthorpe, I promise to have it cooked. ... → None are so deaf as those who do not want to hear. ... → I intend not to allow a woman to come near the place.

Accounting for the modal meanings of the combinations under analysis, traditional grammar gives the following rules: *shall* + Infinitive with the first person, *will* + Infinitive with the second and third persons express pure future; the reverse combinations express modal meanings, the most typical of which are intention or desire for *I will* and promise or command on the part of the speaker for *you shall, he shall.* Both rules apply to refined British English. In American English *will* is described as expressing pure future with all the persons, *shall* as expressing modality.

However, the cited description, though distinguished by elegant simplicity, cannot be taken as fully agreeing with the existing lingual practice. The main feature of this description contradicted by practice is the British use of *will* with the first person without distinctly pronounced modal connotations (making due allowance for the general connection of the future tense with modality, of which we have spoken before). *Cf.*:

I *will call* for you and your young man at seven o'clock (J. Galsworthy). When we wake I *will take* him up and carry him back (R. Kipling). I *will let* you know on Wednesday what expenses have been necessary (A. Christie). If you wait there on Thursday evening between seven and eight I *will come* if I can (H.C. Merriman).

That the combinations of *will* with the infinitive in the above examples do express the future time, admits of no dispute. Furthermore, these combinations, seemingly, are charged with modal connotations in no higher degree than the corresponding combinations of *shall* with the infinitive. *Cf.*:

Haven't time; I *shall miss* my train (A. Bennett). I *shall be happy* to carry it to the House of Lords, if necessary (J. Galsworthy). You never know what may happen. I *shan't have* a minute's peace (M. Dickens).

Granted our semantic intuitions about the exemplified uses are true, the question then arises: what is the real difference, if any, between the two British first person expressions of the future, one with *shall*, the other one with *will*? Or are they actually just semantic doublets, i.e. units of complete synonymy, bound by the paradigmatic relation of free alternation?

A solution to this problem is to be found on the basis of syntactic distributional and transformational analysis backed by a consideration of the original meanings of both auxiliaries.

§ 7. Observing combinations with *will* in stylistically neutral collocations, as the first step of our study we note the adverbials of time used with this construction. The environmental expressions, as well as implications, of future time do testify that from this point of view there is no difference between *will* and *shall*, both of them equally conveying the idea of the future action expressed by the adjoining infinitive.

As our next step of inferences, noting the types of the infinitive-environmental semantics of *will* in contrast to the contextual background of *shall*, we state that the first person *will*-future expresses an action which is to be performed by the speaker for choice, of his own accord. But this meaning of free option does not at all imply that the speaker actually wishes to perform the action, or else that he is determined to perform it, possibly in defiance of some contrary force. The exposition of the action shows it as being not bound by any extraneous circumstances or by any special influence except the speaker's option; this is its exhaustive characteristic. In keeping with this, the form of the *will*-future in question may be tentatively called the "voluntary future".

On the other hand, comparing the environmental characteristics of *shall* with the corresponding environmental background of *will*, it is easy to see that, as different from *will*, the first person *shall* expresses a future process that will be realized without the will of the speaker, irrespective of his choice. In accordance with the exposed meaning, the *shall*-form of the first person future should be referred to as the "non-voluntary", i.e. as the weak member of the corresponding opposition.

Further observations of the relevant textual data show that some verbs constituting a typical environment of the non-voluntary *shall*-future (i.e. verbs inherently alien to the expression of voluntary actions) occur also with the voluntary *will*, but in a different meaning, namely, in the meaning of an active action the performance of which is freely chosen by the speaker. *Cf.*:

Your arrival cannot have been announced to his Majesty. I *will see* about it (B. Shaw).

In the given example the verb *see* has the active meaning of ensuring something, of intentionally arranging matters connected with something, etc.

Likewise, a number of verbs of the voluntary *will*-environmental features (i.e. verbs presupposing the actor's free will in performing the action) combine also with the non-voluntary *shall*, but in the meaning of an action that will take place irrespective of the will of the speaker. *Cf.*:

I'm very sorry, madam, but I'm going to faint. I *shall go off*, madam, if I don't have something (K. Mansfield).

Thus, the would-be same verbs are in fact either homonyms, or else lexico-semantic variants of the corresponding lexemes of the maximally differing characteristics.

At the final stage of our study the disclosed characteristics of the two first-person futures are checked on the lines of transformational analysis. The method will consist not in free structural manipulations with the analysed constructions, but in the textual search for the respective changes of the auxiliaries depending on the changes in the infinitival environments.

Applying these procedures to the texts, we note that when the construction of the voluntary *will*-future is expanded (complicated) by a syntactic part re-modelling the whole collocation into one expressing an involuntary action, the auxiliary *will* is automatically replaced by *shall*. In particular, it happens when the expanding elements convey the meaning of supposition or uncertainty. *Cf.*:

Give me a goddess's work to do; and I *will do* it (B. Shaw). →
I don't know what I *shall do* with Barbara (B. Shaw). Oh, very
well, very well: I *will write* another prescription (B. Shaw). → I
*shall* perhaps *write* to your mother (K. Mansfield).

Thus, we conclude that within the system of the English future
tense a peculiar minor category is expressed which affects only the
forms of the first person. The category is constituted by the opposition of the forms *will* + Infinitive and *shall* + Infinitive expressing,
respectively, the voluntary future and the non-voluntary future. Accordingly, this category may tentatively be called the "category of
futurity option".

The future in the second and third persons, formed by the indiscriminate auxiliary *will*, does not express this category, which is dependent on the semantics of the persons: normally it would be irrelevant to indicate in an obligatory way the aspect of futurity option
otherwise than with the first person, i.e. the person of self.

This category is neutralized in the contracted form -'*ll*, which is
of necessity indifferent to the expression of futurity option. As is
known, the traditional analysis of the contracted future states that -'*ll*
stands for *will*, not for *shall*. However, this view is not supported by
textual data. Indeed, bearing in mind the results of our study, it is
easy to demonstrate that the contracted forms of the future may be
traced both to *will* and to *shall*. Cf.:

I'*ll marry* you then, Archie, if you really want it (M. Dickens).
→ I *will marry* you. I'*ll have* to think about it (M. Dickens). → I
*shall have* to think about it.

From the evidence afforded by the historical studies of the language we know that the English contracted form of the future -'*ll*
has actually originated from the auxiliary *will*. So, in Modern English
an interesting process of redistribution of the future forms has taken
place, based apparently on the contamination *will* → -'*ll* ← *shall*.
As a result, the form -'*ll* in the first person expresses not the same
"pure" future as is expressed by the indiscriminate *will* in the second and third persons.

The described system of the British future is by far more complicated than the expression of the future tense in the other national
variants of English, in particular, in American English, where the
future form of the first person is functionally equal with the other
persons. In British English a possible tendency to a similar levelled
expression of the future is actively counteracted by the two structural

145

factors. The first is the existence of the two functionally differing contractions of the future auxiliaries in the negative form, i.e. *shan't* and *won't*, which imperatively support the survival of *shall* in the first person against the levelled positive (affirmative) contraction -*'ll*. The second is the use of the future tense in interrogative sentences, where with the first person only *shall* is normally used. Indeed, it is quite natural that a genuine question directed by the speaker to himself, i.e. a question showing doubt or speculation, is to be asked about an action of non-wilful, involuntary order, and not otherwise. *Cf.*:

What *shall* we *be shown* next? *Shall* I *be able* to master shorthand professionally? The question was, *should* I *see* Beatrice again before her departure?

The semantics of the first person futurity question is such that even the infinitives of essentially volition-governed actions are transferred here to the plane of non-volition, subordinating themselves to the general implication of doubt, hesitation, uncertainty. *Cf.*:

What *shall* I *answer* to an offer like that? How *shall* we *tackle* the matter if we are left to rely on our own judgment?

Thus, the vitality of the discriminate *shall/will* future, characteristic of careful English speech, is supported by logically vindicated intra-lingual factors. Moreover, the whole system of Modern British future with its mobile inter-action of the two auxiliaries is a product of recent language development, not a relict of the older periods of its history. It is this subtly regulated and still unfinished system that gave cause to H.W. Fowler for his significant statement: "... of the English of the English *shall* and *will* are the shibboleth."[*]

§ 8. Apart from *shall/will* + Infinitive construction, there is another construction in English which has a potent appeal for being analysed within the framework of the general problem of the future tense. This is the combination of the predicator *be going* with the infinitive. Indeed, the high frequency occurrence of this construction in contexts conveying the idea of an immediate future action cannot but draw a very close attention on the part of a linguistic observer.

The combination may denote a sheer intention (either the speaker's or some other person's) to perform the action expressed by

---

[*] *Fowler H.W.* A Dictionary of Modern English Usage. Ldn., 1941, p. 729.

the infinitive, thus entering into the vast set of "classical" modal constructions. *E.g.*:

I *am going to ask* you a few more questions about the mysterious disappearance of the document, Mr. Gregg. He looked across at my desk and I thought for a moment he *was going to give* me the treatment, too.

But these simple modal uses of *be going* are countered by cases where the direct meaning of intention rendered by the predicator stands in contradiction with its environmental implications and is subdued by them. *Cf.*:

You are trying to frighten me. But you *are not going to frighten* me any more (L. Hellman). I did not know how I *was going to get out* of the room. (D. du Maurier).

Moreover, the construction, despite its primary meaning of intention, presupposing a human subject, is not infrequently used with non-human subjects and even in impersonal sentences. *Cf.*:

She knew what she was doing, and she was sure it *was going to be* worth doing (W. Saroyan). There's *going to be* a contest over Ezra Grolley's estate (E. Gardner).

Because of these properties it would appear tempting to class the construction in question as a specific tense form, namely, the tense form of "immediate future", analogous to the French futur immédiat (*e.g.* Le spectacle *va commencer* – The show *is going to begin*).

Still, on closer consideration, we notice that the non-intention uses of the predicator *be going* are not indifferent stylistically. Far from being neutral, they more often than not display emotional colouring mixed with semantic connotations of oblique modality.

For instance, when the girl from the first of the above examples appreciates something as "going to be worth doing", she is expressing her assurance of its being so. When one labels the rain as "never going to stop", one clearly expresses one's annoyance at the bad state of the weather. When a future event is introduced by the formula "there to be going to be", as is the case in the second of the cited examples, the speaker clearly implies his foresight of it, or his anticipation of it, or, possibly, a warning to beware of it, or else some other modal connotation of a like nature. Thus, on the whole, the non-intention uses of the construction *be going* + Infinitive cannot be rationally divided into modal and non-modal, on the analogy of the construction *shall/will* + Infinitive. Its broader combinability is based on semantic transposition and can be likened to broader uses of the modal collocation *be about*, also of basically intention semantics.

§ 9. The oppositional basis of the category of prospective time is neutralized in certain uses, in keeping with the general regularities of oppositional reductions. The process of neutralization is connected with the shifting of the forms of primary time (present and past) from the sphere of absolute tenses into the sphere of relative tenses.

One of the typical cases of the neutralization in question consists in using a non-future temporal form to express a future action which is to take place according to some plan or arrangement. *Cf.*:

The government *meets* in emergency session today over the question of continued violations of the cease-fire. I hear your sister *is* soon *arriving* from Paris? Naturally I would like to know when he's *coming*. Etc.

This case of oppositional reduction is optional, the equivalent reconstruction of the correlated member of the opposition is nearly always possible (with the respective changes of connotations and style). *Cf.*:

... → The government *will meet* in emergency session. ... → Your sister *will* soon *arrive* from Paris? ... → When *will* he *be coming*?

Another type of neutralization of the prospective time opposition is observed in modal verbs and modal word combinations. The basic peculiarity of these units bearing on the expression of time is, that the prospective implication is inherently in-built in their semantics, which reflects not the action as such, but the attitude towards the action expressed by the infinitive. For that reason, the present verb-form of these units actually renders the idea of the future (and, respectively, the past verb-form, the idea of the future-in-the-past). *Cf.*:

There's no saying what *may happen* next. At any rate, the woman *was sure to come* later in the day. But you *have to present* the report before Sunday, there's no alternative.

Sometimes the explicit expression of the future is necessary even with modal collocations. To make up for the lacking categorial forms, special modal substitutes have been developed in language, some of which have received the status of suppletive units (see above, Ch. III). *Cf.*:

But do not make plans with David. You *will not be able* to carry them out. Things *will have to go* one way or the other.

Alongside the above and very different from them, there is still another typical case of neutralization of the analysed categorial opposition, which is strictly obligatory. It occurs in clauses of time and condition whose verb-predicate expresses a future action. *Cf.*:

If things *turn out* as has been arranged, the triumph will be all ours. I repeated my request to notify me at once whenever the messenger *arrived*.

The latter type of neutralization is syntactically conditioned. In point of fact, the neutralization consists here in the primary tenses shifting from the sphere of absolutive time into the sphere of relative time, since they become dependent not on their immediate orientation towards the moment of speech, but on the relation to another time level, namely, the time level presented in the governing clause of the corresponding complex sentence.

This kind of neutralizing relative use of absolutive tense forms occupies a restricted position in the integral tense system of English. In Russian, the syntactic relative use of tenses is, on the contrary, widely spread. In particular, this refers to the presentation of reported speech in the plane of the past, where the Russian present tense is changed into the tense of simultaneity, the past tense is changed into the tense of priority, and the future tense is changed into the tense of prospected posteriority. *Cf.*:

(1) Он *сказал*, что *изучает* немецкий язык. (2) Он *сказал*, что *изучал* немецкий язык. (3) Он *сказал*, что *будет изучать* немецкий язык.

In English, the primary tenses in similar syntactic conditions retain their absolutive nature and are used in keeping with their direct, unchangeable meanings. Compare the respective translations of the examples cited above:

(1) He *said* that he *was learning* German (then). (2) He *said* that he *had learned* German (before). (3) He *said* that he *would learn* German (in the time to come).

It does not follow from this that the rule of sequence of tenses in English complex sentences formulated by traditional grammar should be rejected as false. Sequence of tenses is an important feature of all narration, for, depending on the continual consecutive course of actual events in reality, they are presented in the text in definite successions ordered against a common general background. However, what should be stressed here is that the tense-shift involved in the translation of the present-plane direct information into the past-plane reported information is not a formal, but essentially a meaningful procedure.

CHAPTER XV

## VERB: ASPECT

§ 1. The aspective meaning of the verb, as different from its temporal meaning, reflects the inherent mode of the realization of the process irrespective of its timing.

As we have already seen, the aspective meaning can be in-built in the semantic structure of the verb, forming an invariable, derivative category. In English, the various lexical aspective meanings have been generalized by the verb in its subclass division into limitive and unlimitive sets. On the whole, this division is loose, the demarcation line between the sets is easily trespassed both ways. In spite of their want of rigour, however, the aspective verbal subclasses are grammatically relevant in so far as they are not indifferent to the choice of the aspective grammatical forms of the verb. In Russian, the aspective division of verbs into perfective and imperfective is, on the contrary, very strict. Although the Russian category of aspect is derivative, it presents one of the most typical features of the grammatical structure of the verb, governing its tense system both formally and semantically.

On the other hand, the aspective meaning can also be represented in variable grammatical categories. Aspective grammatical change is wholly alien to the Russian language, but it forms one of the basic features of the categorial structure of the English verb.

Two systems of verbal forms, in the past grammatical tradition analysed under the indiscriminate heading of the "temporal inflexion", i.e. synthetic inflexion proper and analytical composition as its equivalent, should be evaluated in this light: the continuous forms and the perfect forms.

The aspective or non-aspective identification of the forms in question will, in the long run, be dependent on whether or not they express the direct, immediate time of the action denoted by the verb, since a general connection between the aspective and temporal verbal semantics is indisputable.

The continuous verbal forms analysed on the principles of oppositional approach admit of only one interpretation, and that is aspective. The continuous forms are aspective because, reflecting the inherent character of the process named by the verb, they do not, and cannot, denote the timing of the process. The opposition constituting the corresponding category is effected between the continuous and the non-continuous, (indefinite) verbal forms. The categorial meaning discloses the nature of development of the verbal action, on which ground the suggested name for the category as a whole will be "development". As is the case with the other categories, its expression is combined with other categorial expressions in one and the same verb-form, involving also the category that features the perfect. Thus, to be consistent in our judgments, we must identify, within the framework of the manifestations of the category of development, not only the perfect continuous forms, but also the perfect indefinite forms (i.e. non-continuous).

The perfect, as different from the continuous, does reflect a kind of timing, though in a purely relative way. Namely, it coordinates two times, locating one of them in retrospect torwards the other. Should the grammatical meaning of the perfect have been exhausted by this function, it ought to have been placed into one and the same categorial system with the future, forming the integral category of time coordination (correspondingly, prospective and retrospective). In reality, though, it cannot be done, because the perfect expresses not only time in relative retrospect, but also the very connection of a prior process with a time-limit reflected in a subsequent event. Thus, the perfect forms of the verb display a mixed, intermediary character, which places them apart both from the relative posterior tense and the aspective development. The true nature of the perfect is temporal aspect reflected in its own opposition, which cannot be reduced to any other opposition of the otherwise recognized verbal categories. The suggested name for this category will be "retrospective coordination", or, contractedly, "retrospect". The categorial member opposed to the perfect, for the sake of terminological consistency, will be named "imperfect" (non-perfect). As an independent category, the retrospective coordination is manifested in the integral verb-form together with the manifestations of other categories, among them the aspective category of development. Thus, alongside the forms of perfect continuous and perfect indefinite, the

151

verb distinguishes also the forms of imperfect continuous and imperfect indefinite.

§ 2. At this point of our considerations, we should like once again to call the reader's attention to the difference between the categorial terminology and the definitions of categories.

A category, in normal use, cannot be represented twice in one and the same word-form. It follows from this that the integral verb-form cannot display at once more than one expression of each of the recognized verbal categories, though it does give a representative expression to all the verbal categories taken together through the corresponding obligatory featuring (which can be, as we know, either positive or negative). And this fact provides us with a safe criterion of categorial identification for cases where the forms under analysis display related semantic functions.

We have recognized in the verbal system of English two temporal categories (plus one "minor" category of futurity option) and two aspective categories. But does this mean that the English verb is "doubly" (or "triply", for that matter) inflected by the "grammatical category" of tense and the "grammatical category" of aspect? In no wise.

The course of our deductions has been quite the contrary. It is just because the verb, in its one and the same, at each time uniquely given integral form of use, manifests not one, but two expressions of time (for instance, past and future); it is because it manifests not one, but two expressions of aspect (for instance, continuous and perfect), that we have to recognize these expressions as categorially different. In other words, such universal grammatical notions as "time", "tense", "aspect", "mood" and others, taken by themselves, do not automatically presuppose any unique categorial systems. It is only the actual correlation of the corresponding grammatical forms in a concrete, separate language that makes up a grammatical category. In particular, when certain forms that come under the same meaningful grammatical heading are mutually exclusive, it means that they together make up a grammatical category. This is the case with the three Russian verbal tenses. Indeed, the Russian verbal form of the future cannot syntagmatically coexist with the present or past forms – these forms are mutually exclusive, thereby constituting one unified category of time (tense), existing in the three categorial forms: the present, the past, the future. In English, on the contrary, the future form of the verb can freely co-occur with the strongly marked past form, thereby making up a category radically different from the category manifested by the system of "present – past" discrimination. And it is the same case with the forms of the continuous and the perfect. Just because they can freely coexist in one and the same syntagmatic manifestation of the verb, we have to infer that they enter (in the capacity of oppositional markers) essentially different categories, though related to each other by their general aspective character.

§ 3. *The aspective category of development* is constituted by the opposition of the continuous forms of the verb to the non-continuous, or indefinite forms of the verb. The marked member of the opposition is the continuous, which is built up by the auxiliary *be* plus the present participle of the conjugated verb. In symbolic notation it is represented by the formula *be...ing*. The categorial meaning of the continuous is "action in progress"; the unmarked member of the opposition, the indefinite, leaves this meaning unspecified, i.e. expresses the non-continuous.

The evolution of views in connection with the interpretation of the continuous forms has undergone three stages.

The traditional analysis placed them among the tense-forms of the verb, defining them as expressing an action going on simultaneously with some other action. This temporal interpretation of the continuous was most consistently developed in the works of H. Sweet and O. Jespersen. In point of fact, the continuous usually goes with a verb which expresses a simultaneous action, but, as we have stated before, the timing of the action is not expressed by the continuous as such – rather, the immediate time-meaning is conveyed by the syntactic constructions, as well as the broader semantic context in which the form is used, since action in progress, by definition, implies that it is developing at a certain time point.

The correlation of the continuous with contextual indications of time is well illustrated on examples of complex sentences with *while*-clauses. Four combinations of the continuous and the indefinite are possible in principle in these constructions (for two verbs are used here, one in the principal clause and one in the subordinate clause, each capable of taking both forms in question), and all the four possibilities are realized in contexts of Modern English. *Cf*.:

While I *was typing*, Mary and Tom *were chatting* in the adjoining room. – While I *typed*, Mary and Tom *were chatting* in the adjoining room. – While I *was typing*, they *chatted* in the adjoining room. – While I *typed*, they *chatted* in the adjoining room.

153

Clearly, the difference in meaning between the verb-entries in the cited examples cannot lie in their time denotations, either absolutive, or relative. The time is shown by their tense-signals of the past (the past form of the auxiliary *be* in the continuous, or the suffix -(*e*)*d* in the indefinite). The meaningful difference consists exactly in the categorial semantics of the indefinite and continuous: while the latter shows the action in the very process of its realization, the former points it out as a mere fact.

On the other hand, by virtue of its categorial semantics of action in progress (of necessity, at a definite point of time), the continuous is usually employed in descriptions of scenes correlating a number of actions going on simultaneously – since all of them are actualy shown in progress, at the time implied by the narration. *Cf.*:

Standing on the chair, I could see in through the barred window into the hall of the Ayuntamiento and in there it was as it had been before. The priest *was standing*, and those who were left *were kneeling* in a half circle around him and they *were* all *praying*. Pablo *was sitting* on the big table in front of the Mayor's chair with his shotgun slung over his back. His legs *were hanging down* from the table and he *was rolling* a cigarette. Cuatro Dedos *was sitting* in the Mayor's chair with his feet on the table and he *was smoking* a cigarette. All the guards *were sitting* in different chairs of the administration, holding their guns. The key to the big door was on the table beside Pablo (E. Hemingway).

But if the actions are not progressive by themselves (i.e. if they are not shown as progressive), the description, naturally, will go without the continuous forms of the corresponding verbs. *E.g.*:

Inland, the prospect *alters*. There is an oval Maidan, and a long sallow hospital. Houses belonging to Eurasians *stand* on the high ground by the railway station. Beyond the railway – which *runs* parallel to the river – the land *sinks*, then *rises* again rather steeply. On the second rise *is laid* out the little civil station, and viewed hence Chandrapore *appears* to be a totally different place (E.M. Forster).

A further demonstration of the essentially non-temporal meaning of the continuous is its regular use in combination with the perfect, i.e. its use in the verb-form perfect continuous. Surely, the very idea of perfect is alien to simultaneity, so the continuous combined with the perfect in one and the same manifestation of the verb can only be understood as expressing aspectuality, i.e. action in progress.

154

Thus, the consideration of the temporal element in the continuous shows that its referring an action to a definite time-point, or its expressing simultaneity irrespective of absolutive time, is in itself an aspective, not a temporal factor.

At the second stage of the interpretation of the continuous, the form was understood as rendering a blend of temporal and aspective meanings – the same as the other forms of the verb obliquely connected with the factor of time, i.e. the indefinite and the perfect. This view was developed by I.P. Ivanova.

The combined temporal-aspective interpretation of the continuous, in general, should be appraised as an essential step forward, because, first, it introduced on an explicit, comprehensively grounded basis the idea of aspective meanings in the grammatical system of English; second, it demonstrated the actual connection of time and aspect in the integral categorial semantics of the verb. In fact, it presented a thesis that proved to be crucial for the subsequent demonstration, at the next stage of analysis, of the essence of the form on a strictly oppositional foundation.

This latter phase of study, initiated in the works of A.I. Smirnitsky, V.N. Yartseva and B.A. Ilyish, was developed further by B.S. Khaimovich and B.I. Rogovskaya and exposed in its most comprehensive form by L.S. Barkhudarov.

Probably the final touch contributing to the presentation of the category of development at this third stage of study should be still more explicit demonstration of its opposition working beyond the correlation of the continuous non-perfect form with the indefinite non-perfect form. In the expositions hitherto advanced the two series of forms – continuous and perfect – have been shown, as it were, too emphatically in the light of their mutual contrast against the primitive indefinite, the perfect continuous form, which has been placed somewhat separately, being rather interpreted as a "peculiarly modified" perfect than a "peculiarly modified" continuous. In reality, though, the perfect continuous is equally both perfect and continuous, the respective markings belonging to different, though related, categorial characteristics.

§ 4. The category of development, unlike the categories of person, number, and time, has a verbid representation, namely, it is represented in the infinitive. This fact, for its part, testifies to another than temporal nature of the continuous.

With the infinitive, the category of development, naturally, expresses the same meaningful contrast between action in progress and action not in progress as with the finite forms of the verb. *Cf.*:

Kezia and her grandmother *were taking* their siesta together. – – It was but natural for Kezia and her grandmother *to be taking* their siesta together. What *are* you *complaining* about? – – Is there really anything for you *to be complaining* about?

But in addition to this purely categorial distinction, the form of the continuous infinitive has a tendency to acquire quite a special meaning in combination with modal verbs, namely that of probability. This meaning is aspectual in a broader sense than the "inner character" of action: the aspectuality amounts here to an outer appraisal of the denoted process. *Cf.*:

Paul *must wait* for you, you needn't be in a hurry. Paul *must be waiting* for us, so let's hurry up.

The first of the two sentences expresses Paul's obligation to wait, whereas the second sentence renders the speaker's supposition of the fact.

The general meaning of probability is varied by different additional shades depending on the semantic type of the modal verb and the corresponding contextual conditions, such as uncertainty, incredulity, surprise, etc. *Cf.*:

But *can* she *be taking* Moyra's words so personally? If the flight went smoothly, they *may be approaching* the West Coast. You *must be losing* money over this job.

The action of the continuous infinitive of probability, in accord with the type of the modal verb and the context, may refer not only to the plane of the present, but also to the plane of the future. *Cf.*:

Ann *must be coming* soon, you'd better have things put in order.

The gerund and the participle do not distinguish the category of development as such, but the traces of progressive meaning are inherent in these forms, especially in the present participle, which itself is one of the markers of the category (in combination with the categorial auxiliary). In particular, these traces are easily disclosed in various syntactic participial complexes. *Cf.*:

The girl looked straight into my face, *smiling* enigmatically. → The girl *was smiling* enigmatically as she looked straight into my face. We heard the leaves above our heads *rustling* in the wind. →

We heard how the leaves above our heads *were rustling* in the wind.

However, it should be noted that the said traces of meaning are still traces, and they are more often than not subdued and neutralized.

§ 5. The opposition of the category of development undergoes various reductions, in keeping with the general regularities of the grammatical forms functioning in speech, as well as of their paradigmatic combinability.

The easiest and most regular neutralizational relations in the sphere continuous – indefinite are observed in connection with the subclass division of verbs into limitive and unlimitive, and within the unlimitive into actional and statal.

Namely, the unlimitive verbs are very easily neutralized in cases where the continuity of action is rendered by means other than aspective. *Cf.*:

The night is wonderfully silent. The stars *shine* with a fierce brilliancy, the Southern Cross and Canopus; there is not a breath of wind. The Duke's face seemed flushed, and more lined than some of his recent photographs showed. He *held* a glass in his hand.

As to the statal verbs, their development neutralization amounts to a grammatical rule. It is under this heading that the "never-used-in-the-continuous" verbs go, i.e. the uniques *be* and *have*, verbs of possession other than *have*, verbs of relation, of physical perceptions, of mental perceptions. The opposition of development is also neutralized easily with verbs in the passive voice, as well as with the infinitive, the only explicit verbid exposer of the category.

Worthy of note is the regular neutralization of the development opposition with the introductory verb supporting the participial construction of parallel action. *E.g.*:

The man *stood smoking* a pipe. (Not normally: The man *was standing smoking* a pipe.)

On the other hand, the continuous can be used transpositionally to denote habitual, recurrent actions in emphatic collocations. *Cf.*:

Miss Tillings said you *were* always *talking* as if there had been some funny business about me (M. Dickens).

In this connection, special note should be made of the broadening use of the continuous with unlimitive verbs, including verbs of statal existence. Here are some very typical examples:

I only heard a rumour that a certain member here present *has been seeing* the prisoner this afternoon (E.M. Forster). I had a horrid feeling she *was seeing* right through me and *knowing* all about me (A. Christie). What matters is, you*'re being* damn fools, both of you (A. Hailey).

Compare similar transpositions in the expressions of anticipated future:

Dr Aarons *will be seeing* the patient this morning, and I wish to be ready for him (A. Hailey). Soon we *shall be hearing* the news about the docking of the spaceships having gone through.

The linguistic implication of these uses of the continuous is indeed very peculiar. Technically it amounts to de-neutralizing the usually neutralized continuous. However, since the neutralization of the continuous with these verbs is quite regular, we have here essentially the phenomenon of reverse transposition – an emphatic reduction of the second order, serving the purpose of speech expressiveness.

We have considered the relation of unlimitive verbs to the continuous form in the light of reductional processes.

As for the limitive verbs, their standing with the category of development and its oppositional reductions is quite the reverse. Due to the very aspective quality of limitiveness, these verbs, first, are not often used in the continuous form in general, finding no frequent cause for it; but second, in cases when the informative purpose does demand the expression of an action in progress, the continuous with these verbs is quite obligatory and normally cannot undergo reduction under any conditions. It cannot be reduced, for otherwise the limitive meaning of the verb would prevail, and the informative purpose would not be realized. *Cf.*:

The plane *was* just *touching down* when we arrived at the airfield. The patient *was sitting up* in his bed, his eyes riveted on the trees beyond the window.

The linguistic paradox of these uses is that the continuous aspect with limitive verbs neutralizes the expression of their lexical aspect, turning them for the nonce into unlimitive verbs. And this is one of the many manifestations of grammatical relevance of lexemic categories.

§ 6. In connection with the problem of the aspective category of development, we must consider the forms of the verb built up with the help of the auxiliary *do*. These forms, entering the verbal system of the indefinite, have been described under different headings.

Namely, the auxiliary *do*, first, is presented in grammars as a means of building up interrogative constructions when the verb is used in the indefinite aspect. Second, the auxiliary *do* is described as a means of building up negative constructions with the indefinite form of the verb. Third, it is shown as a means of forming emphatic constructions of both affirmative declarative and affirmative imperative communicative types, with the indefinite form of the verb. Fourth, it is interpreted as a means of forming elliptical constructions with the indefinite form of the verb.

L.S. Barkhudarov was the first scholar who paid attention to the lack of accuracy, and probably linguistic adequacy, in these definitions. Indeed, the misinterpretation of the defined phenomena consists here in the fact that the *do*-forms are presented immediately as parts of the corresponding syntactic constructions, whereas actually they are parts of the corresponding verb-forms of the indefinite aspect. Let us compare the following sentences in pairs:

Fred *pulled* her hand to his heart. – – *Did* Fred *pull* her hand to his heart? You *want* me to hold a smile. – – You *don't want* me to hold a smile. In dreams people *change* into somebody else. – – In dreams people *do change* into somebody else. *Ask* him into the drawing-room. – – *Do ask* him into the drawing-room. Mike *liked* the show immensely, and Kitty *liked* it too. – – Mike liked the show immensely, and so *did* Kitty.

On the face of the comparison, we see only the construction-forming function of the analysed auxiliary, the cited formulations being seemingly vindicated both by the structural and the functional difference between the sentences: the right-hand constituent utterances in each of the given pairs has its respective *do*-addition. However, let us relate these right-hand utterances to another kind of categorial counterparts:

*Did* Fred *pull* her hand to his heart? – – *Will* Fred *pull* her hand to his heart? You *don't want* me to hold a smile. – – You *won't want* me to hold a smile. In dreams people *do change* into somebody else. – – In dreams people *will change* into somebody else. Mike liked the show immensely, and so *did* Kitty. – – Mike will like the show immensely, and so *will* Kitty.

Observing the structure of the latter series of constructional pairs, we see at once that their constituent sentences are built up on one and the same syntactic principle of a special treatment of the morphological auxiliary element. And here lies the necessary correction of the interpretation of *do*-forms. As a matter of fact, *do*-forms should be first of all described as the variant analytical indefinite forms of the verb that are effected to share the various constructional functions with the other analytical forms of the verb placing their respective auxiliaries in accented and otherwise individualized positions. This presentation, while meeting the demands of adequate description, at the same time is very convenient for explaining the formation of the syntactic constructional categories on the unified basis of the role of analytical forms of the verb. Namely, the formation of interrogative constructions will be explained simply as a universal word-order procedure of partial inversion (placing the auxiliary before the subject for all the categorial forms of the verb); the formation of the corresponding negative will be described as the use of the negative particle with the analytical auxiliary for all the categorial forms of the verb; the formation of the corresponding emphatic constructions will be described as the accent of the analytical auxiliaries, including the indefinite auxiliary; the formation of the corresponding reduced constructions will be explained on the lines of the representative use of the auxiliaries in general (which won't mar the substitute role of *do*).

For the sake of terminological consistency the analytical form in question might be called the "marked indefinite", on the analogy of the term "marked infinitive". Thus, the indefinite forms of the non-perfect order will be divided into the pure, or unmarked present and past indefinite, and the marked present and past indefinite. As we have pointed out above, the existence of the specifically marked present and past indefinite serves as one of the grounds for identifying the verbal primary time and the verbal prospect as different grammatical categories.

§ 7. *The category of retrospective coordination (retrospect)* is constituted by the opposition of the perfect forms of the verb to the non-perfect, or imperfect forms. The marked member of the opposition is the perfect, which is built up by the auxiliary *have* in combination with the past participle of the conjugated verb. In symbolic notation it is expressed by the formula *have ... en*.

The functional meaning of the category has been interpreted in linguistic literature in four different ways, each contributing to the evolution of the general theory of retrospective coordination.

The first comprehensively represented grammatical exposition of the perfect verbal form was the "tense view": by this view the perfect is approached as a peculiar tense form. The tense view of the perfect is presented in the works of H. Sweet, G. Curme, M. Bryant and J.R. Aiken, and some other foreign scholars. In Russian linguistic literature this view was consistently developed by N.F. Irtenyeva. The tense interpretation of the perfect was also endorsed by the well-known course of English Grammar by M.A. Ganshina and N.M. Vasilevskaya.

The difference between the perfect and non-perfect forms of the verb, according to the tense interpretation of the perfect, consists in the fact that the perfect denotes a secondary temporal characteristic of the action. Namely, it shows that the denoted action precedes some other action or situation in the present, past, or future. This secondary tense quality of the perfect, in the context of the "tense view", is naturally contrasted against the secondary tense quality of the continuous, which latter, according to N.F. Irtenyeva, intensely expresses simultaneity of the denoted action with some other action in the present, past, or future.

The idea of the perfect conveying a secondary time characteristic of the action is quite a sound one, because it shows that the perfect, in fact, coexists with the other, primary expression of time. What else, if not a secondary time meaning of priority, is rendered by the perfect forms in the following example:

Grandfather *has taken* his morning stroll and now is having a rest on the veranda.

The situation is easily translated into the past with the time correlation intact: → Grandfather *had taken* his morning stroll and was having a rest on the veranda.

With the future, the correlations is not so clearly pronounced. However, the reason for it lies not in the deficiency of the perfect as a secondary tense, but in the nature of the future time plane, which exists only as a prospective plane, thereby to a degree levelling the expression of differing timings of actions. Making allowance for the unavoidable prospective temporal neutralizations, the perfective priority expressed in the given situation can be clearly conveyed even in its future translations, extended by the exposition of the corresponding connotations:

→ By the time he is having a rest on the veranda, Grandfather *will* surely *have taken* his morning stroll. → Grandfather will have a rest on the veranda only after he *has taken* his morning stroll.

Laying emphasis on the temporal function of the perfect, the "tense view", though, fails to expose with the necessary distinctness its aspective function, by which the action is shown as successively or "transmissively" connected with a certain time limit. Besides, the purely oppositional nature of the form is not disclosed by this approach either, thus leaving the categorial status of the perfect undefined.

The second grammatical interpretation of the perfect was the "aspect view": according to this interpretation the perfect is approached as an aspective form of the verb. The aspect view is presented in the works of M. Deutschbein, E.A. Sonnenschein, A.S. West, and other foreign scholars. In Russian linguistic literature the aspective interpretation of the perfect was comprehensively developed by G.N. Vorontsova. This subtle observer of intricate interdependencies of language profoundly demonstrated the idea of the successive connection of two events expressed by the perfect, prominence given by the form to the transference or "transmission" of the accessories of a pre-situation to a post-situation. The great merit of G.N. Vorontsova's explanation of the aspective nature of the perfect lies in the fact that the resultative meaning ascribed by some scholars to the perfect as its determining grammatical function is understood in her conception within a more general destination of this form, namely as a particular manifestation of its transmissive functional semantics.

Indeed, if we compare the two following verbal situations, we shall easily notice that the first of them expresses result, while the second presents a connection of a past event with a later one in a broad sense, the general inclusion of the posterior situation in the sphere of influence of the anterior situation:

The wind *has dropped*, and the sun burns more fiercely than ever.

"*Have* you really *never been* to a ball before, Leila? But my child, how too weird – " cried the Sheridan girls.

The resultative implication of the perfect in the first of the above examples can be graphically shown by the diagnostic transformation, which is not applicable to the second example:

→ The sun burns ₊more fiercely than ever as a result of the wind *having dropped*.

At the same time, the plain resultative semantics quite evidently appears as a particular variety of the general transmissive meaning, by which a posterior event is treated as a successor of an anterior event on very broad lines of connection.

Recognizing all the merits of the aspect approach in question, however, we clearly see its two serious drawbacks. The first of them is that, while emphasizing the aspective side of the function of the perfect, it underestimates its temporal side, convincingly demonstrated by the tense view of the perfect described above. The second drawback, though, is just the one characteristic of the tense view, repeated on the respectively different material: the described aspective interpretation of the perfect fails to strictly formulate its oppositional nature, the categorial status of the perfect being left undefined.

The third grammatical interpretation of the perfect was the "tense-aspect blend view": in accord with this interpretation the perfect is recognized as a form of double temporal-aspective character, similar to the continuous. The tense-aspect interpretation of the perfect was developed in the works of I.P. Ivanova. According to I.P. Ivanova, the two verbal forms expressing temporal and aspective functions in a blend are contrasted against the indefinite form as their common counterpart of neutralized aspective properties.

The achievement of the tense-aspect view of the perfect is the fact that it demonstrates the actual double nature of the analysed verbal form, its inherent connection with both temporal and aspective spheres of verbal semantics. Thus, as far as the perfect is concerned, the tense-aspect view overcomes the one-sided approach to it peculiar both to the first and the second of the noted conceptions.

Indeed, the temporal meaning of the perfect is quite apparent in constructions like the following:

I *have lived* in this city long enough. I *haven't met* Charlie for years.

The actual time expressed ·by the perfect verbal forms used in the examples can be made explicit by time-test questions:

How long *have* you *lived* in this city? For how long *haven't* you met Charlie?

Now, the purely aspective semantic component of the perfect form will immediately be made prominent if the sentences were continued like that:

I *have lived* in this city long enough to show you all that is worth seeing here. I *haven't met* Charlie for years, and can hardly recognize him in a crowd.

The aspective function of the perfect verbal forms in both sentences, in its turn, can easily be revealed by aspect-test questions:

What can you do as a result of your *having lived* in this city for years? What is the consequence of your *not having met* Charlie for years?

However, comprehensively exposing the two different sides of the integral semantics of the perfect, the tense-aspect conception loses sight of its categorial nature altogether, since it leaves undisclosed how the grammatical function of the perfect is effected in contrast to the continuous or indefinite, as well as how the "categorial blend" of the perfect-continuous is contrasted against its three counterparts, i.e. the perfect, the continuous, the indefinite.

As we see, the three described interpretations of the perfect, actually complementing one another, have given in combination a broad and profound picture of the semantical content of the perfect verbal forms, though all of them have failed to explicitly explain the grammatical category within the structure of which the perfect is enabled to fulfil its distinctive function.

The categorial individuality of the perfect was shown as a result of study conducted by A.I. Smirnitsky. His conception of the perfect, the fourth in our enumeration, may be called the "time correlation view", to use the explanatory name he gave to the identified category. What was achieved by this brilliant thinker, is an explicit demonstration of the fact that the perfect form, by means of its oppositional mark, builds up its own category, different from both the "tense" (present – past – future) and the "aspect" (continuous – indefinite), and not reducible to either of them. The functional content of the category of "time correlation" («временная отнесенность») was defined as priority expressed by the perfect forms in the present, past or future contrasted against the non-expression of priority by the non-perfect forms. The immediate factor that gave cause to A.I. Smirnitsky to advance the new interpretation of the perfect was the peculiar structure of the perfect continuous form in which the perfect, the form of precedence, i.e. the form giving prominence to the idea of two times brought in contrast, coexists syntagmatically with the continuous, the form of simultaneity, i.e. the form expressing one time for two events, according to the "tense view" conception of it. The gist of reasoning here is that, since the two expressions of the same categorial semantics are impossible in one and the same verbal form, the perfect cannot be either an aspective form, granted the continuous expresses the category of aspect, or a temporal form, granted the continuous expresses the category of tense. The inference is that the category in question, the determining part of which is embodied in the perfect, is different from both the tense and the aspect, this difference being fixed by the special categorial term "time correlation".

The analysis undertaken by A.I. Smirnitsky is of outstanding significance not only for identifying the categorial status of the perfect, but also for specifying further the general notion of a grammatical category. It develops the very technique of this kind of identification.

Still, the "time correlation view" is not devoid of certain limitations. First, it somehow underestimates the aspective plane of the categorial semantics of the perfect, very convincingly demonstrated by G.N. Vorontsova in the context of the "aspect view" of the perfect, as well as by I.P. Ivanova in the context of the "tense-aspect blend view" of the perfect. Second, and this is far more important, the reasoning by which the category is identified, is not altogether complete in so far as it confuses the general grammatical notions of time and aspect with the categorial status of concrete word-forms in each particular language conveying the corresponding meanings. Some languages may canvey temporal or aspective meanings within the functioning of one integral category for each (as, for instance, the Russian language), while other languages may convey the same or similar kind of meanings in two or even more categories for each (as, for instance, the English language). The only true criterion of this is the character of the representation of the respective categorial forms in the actual speech manifestation of a lexeme. If a lexeme normally displays the syntagmatic coexistence of several forms distinctly identifiable by their own peculiar marks, as, for example, the forms of person, number, time, etc., it means that these forms in the system of language make up different grammatical categories. The integral grammatical meaning of any word-form (the concrete speech entry of a lexeme) is determined by the whole combination ("bunch") of the categories peculiar to the part of speech the lexeme belongs to. For instance, the verb-form *has been speaking* in the sentence "The Red Chief *has* just *been speaking*" expresses, in terms of immediately (positively) presented grammatical forms, the third person of the category of person, the singular of the category of number, the present of the category of time, the continuous of the category of development, the perfect of the category under analysis. As for the character of the determining meaning of any category, it may either be related to the meaning of some adjoining category, or may not – it depends on the actual categorial correlations that have shaped in a language in the course of its historical development. In particular, in Modern English, in accord with our knowledge of its structure, two major purely temporal categories are to be identified, i.e. primary time and prospective time, as well as two major aspective categories. One of the latter is the category of development. The other, as has been decided above, is the category of retrospective coordination featuring the perfect as the marked component form and the imperfect as its unmarked counterpart. We have considered it advisable to re-name the indicated category in order, first, to stress its actual retrospective property (in fact, what is strongly expressed in the temporal plane of the category, is priority of action, not any other relative time signification), and second, to reserve such a general term as "correlation" for more unrestricted, free manipulations in non-specified uses connected with grammatical analysis.

§ 8. Thus, we have arrived at the "strict categorial view" of the perfect, disclosing it as the marking form of a separate verbal category, semantically intermediate between aspective and temporal, but quite self-dependent in the general categorial system of the English verb. It is this interpretation of the perfect that gives a natural explanation to the "enigmatic" verbal form of the perfect continuous, showing that each categorial marker – both perfect and continuous – being separately expressed in the speech entry of the verbal lexeme, conveys its own part in the integral grammatical meaning of the entry. Namely, the perfect interprets the action in the light of priority and aspective transmission, while the continuous presents the same action as progressive. As a result, far from displaying any kind of semantic contradiction or discrepancy, the grammatical characterization of the action gains both in precision and vividness. The latter quality explains why this verbal form is gaining more and more ground in present-day colloquial English.

As a matter of fact, the specific semantic features of the perfect and the continuous in each integrating use can be distinctly exposed by separate diagnostic tests. *Cf.*:

A week or two ago someone related an incident to me with the suggestion that I should write a story on it, and since then I *have been thinking* it over (S. Maugham).

Testing for the perfect giving prominence to the expression of priority in retrospective coordination will be represented as follows: → I *have been thinking* over the suggestion for a week or two now.

Testing for the perfect giving prominence to the expression of succession in retrospective coordination will be made thus: → Since the time the suggestion was made I *have been thinking* it over.

Finally, testing for the continuous giving prominence to the expression of action in progress will include expansion: → Since the suggestion was made I *have been thinking* it over continually.

Naturally, both perfect indefinite and perfect continuous, being categorially characterized by their respective features, in normal use are not strictly dependent on a favourable contextual environment and can express their semantics in isolation from adverbial time indicators. *Cf.*:

Surprisingly, she did not protest, for she *had given* up the struggle (M. Dickens). "What *have* you *been doing* down there?" Miss Peel asked him. "I've *been looking* for you all over the play-ground" (M. Dickens).

The exception is the future perfect that practically always requires a contextual indicator of time due to the prospective character of posteriority, of which we have already spoken.

It should be noted that with the past perfect the priority principle is more distinct than with the present perfect, which again is explained semantically. In many cases the past perfect goes with the lexical indicators of time introducing the past plane as such in the microcontext. On the other hand, the transmissive semantics of the perfect can so radically take an upper hand over its priority semantics even in the past plane that the form is placed in a peculiar expressive contradiction with a lexical introduction of priority. In particular, it concerns constructions introduced by the subordinative conjunction *before*. *Cf.*:

It was his habit to find a girl who suited him and live with her as long as he was ashore. But he had forgotten her **before** the anchor *had come* dripping out of the water and been made fast. The sea was his home (J. Tey).

§ 9. In keeping with the general tendency, the category of retrospective coordination can be contextually neutralized, the imperfect as the weak member of the opposition filling in the position of neutralization. *Cf.*:

"I feel exactly like you," she said, "only different, because after all I *didn't produce* him; but, Mother, darling, it's all right..." (J. Galsworthy). Christine nibbled on Oyster Bienville. "I always *thought* it was because they spawned in summer" (A. Hailey).

In this connection, the treatment of the lexemic aspective division of verbs by the perfect is, correspondingly, the reverse, if less distinctly pronounced, of their treatment by the continuous. Namely, the expression of retrospective coordination is neutralized most naturally and freely with limitive verbs. As for the unlimitive verbs, these, by being used in the perfect, are rather turned into "limitive for the nonce". *Cf.*:

"I'm no beaten rug. I don't need to feel like one. I've *been* a teacher all my life, with plenty to show for it" (A. Hailey).

Very peculiar neutralizations take place between the forms of the present perfect – imperfect. Essentially these neutralizations signal instantaneous subclass migrations of the verb from a limitive to an unlimitive one. *Cf.*:

Where *do* you *come* from? (i.e. What is the place of your origin?) I *put* all my investment in London. (i.e. I keep all my money there.)

Characteristic colloquial neutralizations affect also some verbs of physical and mental perceptions. *Cf.*:

I *forget* what you've told me about Nick. I *hear* the management has softened their stand after all the hurly-burly!

The perfect forms in these contexts are always possible, being the appropriate ones for a mode of expression devoid of tinges of colloquialism.

§ 10. The categorial opposition "perfect versus imperfect" is broadly represented in verbids. The verbid representation of the opposition, though, is governed by a distinct restrictive regularity which may be formulated as follows: the perfect is used with verbids only in semantically strong positions, i.e. when its categorial meaning is made prominent. Otherwise the opposition is neutralized, the imperfect being used in the position of neutralization. Quite evidently this regularity is brought about by the intermediary lexico-grammatical features of verbids, since the category of retrospective coordination is utterly alien to the non-verbal parts of speech. The structural neutralization of the opposition is especially distinct with the present participle of the limitive verbs, its indefinite form very naturally expressing priority in the perfective sense. *Cf.*:

She came to Victoria to see Joy off, and Freddy Rigby came too, *bringing* a crowd of the kind of young people Rodney did not care for (M. Dickens).

But the rule of the strong position is valid here also. *Cf.*:

Her Auntie Phyll had too many children. *Having brought* up six in a messy, undisciplined way, she had started all over again with another baby late in life (M. Dickens).

With the gerund introduced by a preposition of time the perfect is more often than not neutralized. *E.g.*:

He was at Cambridge and after *taking* his degree decided to be a planter (S. Maugham).

*Cf.* the perfect gerund in a strong position:

The memory of *having met* the famous writer in his young days made him feel proud even now.

Less liable to neutralization is the infinitive. The category of retrospective coordination is for the most part consistently represented in its independent constructions, used as concise semi-predicative equivalents of syntactic units of full predication. *Cf.*:

It was utterly unbelievable for the man *to have* no competence whatsoever (simultaneity expressed by the imperfect). – – It was utterly unbelievable for the man *to have had* no competence whatsoever (priority expressed by the perfect).

The perfect infinitive of notional verbs used with modal predicators, similar to the continuous, performs the two types of functions. First, it expresses priority and transmission in retrospective coordination, in keeping with its categorial destination. Second, dependent on the concrete function of each modal verb and its equivalent, it helps convey gradations of probabilities in suppositions. *E.g.*:

He *may have warned* Christine, or again, he *may not have warned* her. Who can tell? Things *must have been* easier fifty years ago. You needn't worry, Miss Nickolson. The children are sure *to have been following* our instructions, it *can't have been otherwise*.

In addition, as its third type of function, also dependent on the individual character of different modal verbs, the perfect can render the idea of non-compliance with certain rule, advice, recommendation, etc. The modal verbs in these cases serve as signals of remonstrance (mostly the verbs *ought to* and *should*). *Cf.*:

Mary *ought to have thought* of the possible consequences. Now the situation can't be mended, I'm afraid.

The modal *will* used with a perfect in a specific collocation renders a polite, but officially worded statement of the presupposed hearer's knowledge of an indicated fact. *Cf.*:

"You *will* no doubt *have heard*, Admiral Morgan, that Lord Vaughan is going to replace Sir Thomas Lynch as Governor of Jamaica," Charles said, and cast a glance of secret amusement at the strong countenance of his most famous sailor (J. Tey). It *will not have escaped* your attention, Inspector, that the visit of the nuns was the same day that poisoned wedding cake found its way into that cottage (A. Christie).

Evident relation between the perfect and the continuous in their specific modal functions (i.e. in the use under modal government) can be pointed out as a testimony to the category of retrospective coordination being related to the category of development on the broad semantic basis of aspectuality.

## CHAPTER XVI

### VERB: VOICE

§ 1. The verbal category of voice shows the direction of the process as regards the participants of the situation reflected in the syntactic construction.

The voice of the English verb is expressed by the opposition of the passive form of the verb to the active form of the verb. The sign marking the passive form is the combination of the auxiliary *be* with the past participle of the conjugated verb (in symbolic notation: *be ... en* – see Ch. II, § 5). The passive form as the strong member of the opposition expresses reception of the action by the subject of the syntactic construction (i.e. the "passive" subject, denoting the object of the action); the active form as the weak member of the opposition leaves this meaning unspecified, i.e. it expresses "non-passivity".

In colloquial speech the role of the passive auxiliary can occasionally be performed by the verb *get* and, probably, *become.* Cf.:

Sam *got licked* for a good reason, though not by me. The young violinist *became admired* by all.

The category of voice has a much broader representation in the system of the English verb than in the system of the Russian verb, since in English not only transitive, but also intransitive objective verbs including prepositional ones can be used in the passive (the preposition being retained in the absolutive location). Besides, verbs taking not one, but two objects, as a rule, can feature both of them in the position of the passive subject. *E.g.*:

I've just *been rung up* by the police. The diplomat *was refused* transit facilities through London. She *was undisturbed* by the frown on his face. *Have* you ever *been told* that you're very good-looking? He *was said* to have been very wild in his youth. The dress *has* never *been tried on*. The child *will be looked after* all right. I *won't be talked to* like this. Etc.

Still, not all the verbs capable of taking an object are actually used in the passive. In particular, the passive form is alien to many verbs of the statal subclass (displaying a weak dynamic force), such as *have* (direct possessive meaning), *belong, cost, resemble, fail, misgive*, etc. Thus, in accord with their relation to the passive voice, all the verbs can be divided into two large sets: the set of passivized verbs and the set of non-passivized verbs.

A question then should be posed whether the category of voice is a full-representative verbal category, i.e. represented in the system of the verb as a whole, or a partial-representative category, confined only to the passivized verbal set. Considerations of both form and function tend to interpret voice rather as a full-representative cate-

---

gory, the same as person, number, tense, and aspect. Three reasons can be given to back this appraisal.

First, the integral categorial presentation of non-passivized verbs fully coincides with that of passivized verbs used in the active voice (*cf. takes – goes, is taking – is going, has taken – has gone*, etc.). Second, the active voice as the weak member of the categorial opposition is characterized in general not by the "active" meaning as such (i.e. necessarily featuring the subject as the doer of the action), but by the extensive non-passive meaning of a very wide range of actual significations, some of them approaching by their process-direction characteristics those of non-passivized verbs (*cf.* The door *opens* inside the room; The magazine *doesn't sell* well). Third, the demarcation line between the passivized and non-passivized sets is by no means rigid, and the verbs of the non-passivized order may migrate into the passivized order in various contextual conditions (*cf.* The bed *has not been slept* in; The house seems *not to have been lived* in for a long time).

Thus, the category of voice should be interpreted as being reflected in the whole system of verbs, the non-passivized verbs presenting the active voice form if not directly, then indirectly.

As a regular categorial form of the verb, the passive voice is combined in the same lexeme with other oppositionally strong forms of the verbal categories of the tense-aspect system, i.e. the past, the future, the continuous, the perfect. But it has a neutralizing effect on the category of development in the forms where the auxiliary *be* must be doubly employed as a verbid (the infinitive, the present participle, the past participle), so that the future continuous passive, as well as the perfect continuous passive are practically not used in speech. As a result, the future continuous active has as its regular counterpart by the voice opposition the future indefinite passive; the perfect continuous active in all the tense-forms has as its regular counterpart the perfect indefinite passive. *Cf.*:

The police *will be keeping* an army of reporters at bay.→An army of reporters *will be kept* at bay by the police. We *have been expecting* the decision for a long time.→The decision *has been expected* for a long time.

§ 2. The category of voice differs radically from all the other hitherto considered categories from the point of view of its referential qualities. Indeed, all the previously described categories reflect various characteristics of processes, both direct and oblique, as certain facts of reality existing irrespective of the speaker's perception. For instance, the verbal category of person expresses the personal relation of the process. The verbal number, together with person, expresses its person-numerical relation. The verbal primary time denotes the absolutive timing of the process, i.e. its timing in reference to the moment of speech. The category of prospect expresses the timing of the process from the point of view of its relation to the plane of posteriority. Finally, the analysed aspects characterize the respective inner qualities of the process. So, each of these categories does disclose some actual property of the process denoted by the verb, adding more and more particulars to the depicted processual situation. But we cannot say the same about the category of voice.

As a matter of fact, the situation reflected by the passive construction does not differ in the least from the situation reflected by the active construction – the nature of the process is preserved intact, the situational participants remain in their places in their unchanged quality. What is changed, then, with the transition from the active voice to the passive voice, is the subjective appraisal of the situation by the speaker, the plane of his presentation of it. It is clearly seen when comparing any pair of constructions one of which is the passive counterpart of the other. *Cf.:*

The guards *dispersed* the crowd in front of the Presidential Palace.→The crowd in front of the Presidential Palace *was dispersed* by the guards.

In the two constructions, the guards as the doer of the action, the crowd as the recepient of the action are the same; the same also is the place of action, i.e. the space in front of the Palace. The presentation planes, though, are quite different with the respective constructions, they are in fact mutually reverse. Namely, the first sentence, by its functional destination, features the act of the guards, whereas the second sentence, in accord with its meaningful purpose, features the experience of the crowd.

This property of the category of voice shows its immediate connection with syntax, which finds expression in direct transformational relations between the active and passive constructions.

The said fundamental meaningful difference between the two forms of the verb and the corresponding constructions that are built around them goes with all the concrete connotations specifically expressed by the active and passive presentation of the same event in various situational contexts. In particular, we find the object-experience-featuring achieved by the passive in its typical uses in cases when the subject is unknown or is not to be mentioned for certain reasons, or when the attention of the speaker is centred on the action as such. *Cf.*, respectively:

Another act of terrorism *has been committed* in Argentina. Dinner *was announced*, and our conversation stopped. The defeat of the champion *was* very much *regretted*.

All the functional distinctions of the passive, both categorial and contextual-connotative, are sustained in its use with verbids.

For instance, in the following passive infinitive phrase the categorial object-experience-featuring is accompanied by the logical accent of the process characterizing the quality of its situational object (expressed by the subject of the passive construction):

This is an event never *to be forgotten*.

*Cf.* the corresponding sentence-transform: This event *will* never *be forgotten*.

The gerundial phrase that is given below, conveying the principal categorial meaning of the passive, suppresses the exposition of the indefinite subject of the process:

After *being* wrongly *delivered*, the letter found its addressee at last.

*Cf.* the time-clause transformational equivalent of the gerundial phrase: After the letter *had been* wrongly *delivered*, it found its addressee at last.

The following passive participial construction in an absolutive position accentuates the resultative process:

The enemy batteries *having been put* out of action, our troops continued to push on the offensive.

*Cf.* the clausal equivalent of the construction: When the enemy batteries *had been put* out of action, our troops continued to push on the offensive.

The past participle of the objective verb is passive in meaning, and phrases built up by it display all the cited characteristics. *E.g.:*

*Seen* from the valley, the castle on the cliff presented a phantastic sight.

*Cf.* the clausal equivalent of the past participial phrase: When it *was seen* from the valley, the castle on the cliff presented a phantastic sight.

174

**§ 3.** The big problem in connection with the voice identification in English is the problem of "medial" voices, i.e. the functioning of the voice forms in other than the passive or active meanings. All the medial voice uses are effected within the functional range of the unmarked member of the voice opposition. Let us consider the following examples:

I *will shave* and *wash*, and be ready for breakfast in half an hour. I'm afraid Mary *hasn't dressed up* yet. Now I see your son *is* thoroughly *preparing* for the entrance examinations.

The indicated verbs in the given sentences are objective, transitive, used absolutely, in the form of the active voice. But the real voice meaning rendered by the verb-entries is not active, since the actions expressed are not passed from the subject to any outer object; on the contrary, these actions are confined to no other participant of the situation than the subject, the latter constituting its own object of the action performance. This kind of verbal meaning of the action performed by the subject upon itself is classed as "reflexive". The same meaning can be rendered explicit by combining the verb with the reflexive "self"-pronoun:

I *will shave myself*, *wash myself*; Mary *hasn't dressed herself up* yet; your son *is* thoroughly *preparing himself*.

Let us take examples of another kind:

The friends *will be meeting* tomorrow. Unfortunately, Nellie and Christopher *divorced* two years after their magnificent marriage. *Are* Phil and Glen *quarrelling* again over their toy cruiser?

The actions expressed by the verbs in the above sentences are also confined to the subject, the same as in the first series of examples, but, as different from them, these actions are performed by the subject constituents reciprocally: the friends will be meeting one another; Nellie divorced Christopher, and Christopher, in his turn, divorced Nellie; Phil is quarrelling with Glen, and Glen, in his turn, is quarrelling with Phil. This verbal meaning of the action performed by the subjects in the subject group on one another is called "reciprocal". As is the case with the reflexive meaning, the reciprocal meaning can be rendered explicit by combining the verbs with special pronouns, namely, the reciprocal pronouns: the friends will be meeting one another; Nellie and Christopher divorced each other; the children are quarrelling with each other.

The cited reflexive and reciprocal uses of verbs are open to consideration as special grammatical voices, called, respectively, "reflexive" and "reciprocal". The reflexive and reciprocal pronouns within the framework of the hypothetical voice identification of the uses in question should be looked upon as the voice auxiliaries.

That the verb-forms in the given collocations do render the idea of the direction of situational action is indisputable, and in this sense the considered verbal meanings are those of voice. On the other hand, the uses in question evidently lack a generalizing force necessary for any lingual unit type or combination type to be classed as grammatical. The reflexive and reciprocal pronouns, for their part, are still positional members of the sentence, though phrasemically bound with their notional kernel elements. The inference is that the forms are not grammatical-categorial; they are phrasal-derivative, though grammatically relevant.

The verbs in reflexive and reciprocal uses in combination with the reflexive and reciprocal pronouns may be called, respectively, "reflexivized" and "reciprocalized". Used absolutely, they are just reflexive and reciprocal variants of their lexemes.

Subject to reflexivization and reciprocalization may be not only natively reflexive and reciprocal lexemic variants, but other verbs as well. *Cf.*:

The professor *was arguing* with himself, as usual. The parties *have been accusing* one another vehemently.

To distinguish between the two cases of the considered phrasal-derivative process, the former can be classed as "organic", the latter as "inorganic" reflexivization and reciprocalization.

The derivative, i.e. lexemic expression of voice meanings may be likened, with due alteration of details, to the lexemic expression of aspective meanings. In the domain of aspectuality we also find derivative aspects, having a set of lexical markers (verbal post-positions) and generalized as limitive and non-limitive.

Alongside the considered two, there is still a third use of the verb in English directly connected with the grammatical voice distinctions. This use can be shown by the following examples:

The new paper-backs *are selling* excellently. The suggested procedure *will* hardly *apply* to all the instances. Large native cigarettes *smoked* easily and coolly. Perhaps the loin chop *will eat* better than it looks.

The actions expressed by the otherwise transitive verbs in the cited examples are confined to the subject, though not in a way of

176

active self-transitive subject performance, but as if going on of their own accord. The presentation of the verbal action of this type comes under the heading of the "middle" voice.

However, lacking both regularity and an outer form of expression, it is natural to understand the "middle" voice uses of verbs as cases of neutralizing reduction of the voice opposition. The peculiarity of the voice neutralization of this kind is, that the weak member of opposition used in the position of neutralization does not fully coincide in function with the strong member, but rather is located somewhere in between the two functional borders. Hence, its "middle" quality is truly reflected in its name. Compare the shown middle type neutralization of voice in the infinitive:

She was delightful *to look at*, witty *to talk to* – altogether the most charming of companions. You have explained so fully everything there is *to explain* that there is no need for me to ask questions.

§ 4. Another problem posed by the category of voice and connected with neutralizations concerns the relation between the morphological form of the passive voice and syntactical form of the corresponding complex nominal predicate with the pure link *be*. As a matter of fact, the outer structure of the two combinations is much the same. *Cf.*:

You may consider me a coward, but there you *are mistaken*. They *were* all *seized* in their homes.

The first of the two examples presents a case of a nominal predicate, the second, a case of a passive voice form. Though the constructions are outwardly alike, there is no doubt as to their different grammatical status. The question is, why?

As is known, the demarcation between the construction types in question is commonly sought on the lines of the semantic character of the constructions. Namely, if the construction expresses an action, it is taken to refer to the passive voice form; if it expresses a state, it is interpreted as a nominal predicate. *Cf.* another pair of examples:

The door *was closed* by the butler as softly as could be. The door on the left *was closed*.

The predicate of the first sentence displays the "passive of action", i.e. it is expressed by a verb used in the passive voice; the predicate of the second sentence, in accord with the cited semantic interpretation, is understood as displaying the "passive of state", i.e. as consisting of a link-verb and a nominal part expressed by a past participle.

Of course, the factor of semantics as the criterion of the dynamic force of the construction is quite in its place, since the dynamic force itself is a meaningful factor of language. But the "technically" grammatical quality of the construction is determined not by the meaning in isolation; it is determined by the categorial and functional properties of its constituents, first and foremost, its participial part. Thus, if this part, in principle, expresses processual verbality, however statal it may be in its semantic core, then the whole construction should be understood as a case of the finite passive in the categorial sense. *E.g.*:

The young practitioner *was* highly *esteemed* in his district.

If, on the other hand, the participial part of the construction doesn't convey the idea of processual verbality, in other words, if it has ceased to be a participle and is turned into an adjective, then the whole construction is to be taken for a nominal predicate. But in the latter case it is not categorially passive at all.

Proceeding from this criterion, we see that the predicate in the construction "You are mistaken" (the first example in the present paragraph) is nominal simply by virtue of its notional part being an adjective, not a participle. The corresponding non-adjectival participle would be used in quite another type of constructions. *Cf.*:

I *was* often *mistaken* for my friend Otto, though I never could tell why.

On the other hand, this very criterion shows us that the categorial status of the predicate in the sentence "The door *was closed*" is wholly neutralized in so far as it is categorially latent, and only a living context may de-neutralize it both ways. In particular, the context including the *by*-phrase of the doer (*e.g.* by the butler) de-neutralizes it into the passive form of the verb; but the context in the following example de-neutralizes it into the adjectival nominal collocation:

The door on the left *was closed*, and the door on the right *was open*.

Thus, with the construction in question the context may have both voice-suppressing, "statalizing" effect, and voice-stimulating, "processualizing" effect. It is very interesting to note that the role of processualizing stimulators of the passive can be performed, alongside action-modifying adverbials, also by some categorial forms of the verb itself, namely, by the future, the continuous, and the perfect – i.e. by the forms of the time-aspect order other than the indefinite imperfect past and present. The said contextual stimulators are especially important for limitive verbs, since their past participles combine the semantics of processual passive with that of resultative perfect. *Cf.*:

The fence *is painted*. – The fence *is painted* light green. – The fence *is to be painted*. – The fence *will be painted*. – The fence *has just been painted*. – The fence *is* just *being painted*.

The fact that the indefinite imperfect past and present are left indifferent to this gradation of dynamism in passive constructions bears one more evidence that the past and present of the English verb constitute a separate grammatical category distinctly different from the expression of the future (see Ch. XIV).

## CHAPTER XVII

## VERB: MOOD

§ 1. The category of mood, undoubtedly, is the most controversial category of the verb. On the face of it, the principles of its analysis, the nomenclature, the relation to other categories, in particular, to tenses, all this has received and is receiving different presentations and appraisals with different authors. Very significant in connection with the theoretical standing of the category are the following words by B.A. Ilyish: "The category of mood in the present English verb has given rise to so many discussions, and has been treated in so many different ways, that it seems hardly possible to arrive at any more or less convincing and universally acceptable conclusion concerning it" [Ilyish, 99].

Needless to say, the only and true cause of the multiplicity of opinion in question lies in the complexity of the category as such, made especially peculiar by the contrast of its meaningful intricacy against the scarcity of the English word inflexion. But, stressing the disputability of so many theoretical points connected with the English mood, the scholars are sometimes apt to forget the positive results already achieved in this domain during scores of years of both textual researches and the controversies accompanying them.

We must always remember that the knowledge of verbal structure, the understanding of its working in the construction of speech utterances have been tellingly deepened by the studies of the mood system within the general framework of modern grammatical theories, especially by the extensive investigations undertaken by scholars in the past three decades. The main contributions made in this field concern the more and more precise statement of the significance of the functional plane of any category; the exposition of the subtle paradigmatic correlations that, working on the same unchangeable verbal basis, acquire the status of changeable forms; the demonstration of the sentence-constructional value of the verb and its mood, the meaningful destination of it being realized at the level of the syntactic predicative unit as a whole. Among the scholars we are indebted to for this knowledge and understanding, to be named in the first place is A.I. Smirnitsky, whose theories revolutionized the presentation of English verbal grammar; then B.A. Ilyish, a linguist who skilfully demonstrated the strong and weak points of the possible approaches to the general problem of mood; then G.N. Vorontsova, L.S. Barkhudarov, I.B. Khlebnikova, and a number of others, whose keen observations and theoretical generalizations, throwing a new light on the analysed phenomena and discussed problems, at the same time serve as an incentive to further investigations in this interesting sphere of language study. It is due to the materials gathered and results obtained by these scholars that we venture the present, of necessity schematic, outline of the category under analysis.

§ 2. The category of mood expresses the character of connection between the process denoted by the verb and the actual reality, either presenting the process as a fact that really happened, happens or will happen, or treating it as an imaginary phenomenon, i.e. the subject of a hypothesis, speculation, desire. It follows from this that the functional opposition underlying the category as a whole is constituted by the forms of oblique mood meaning, i.e. those of unreality, contrasted against the forms of direct mood meaning, i.e. those of reality, the former making up the strong member, the latter, the weak member of the opposition. What is, though, the formal sign of this categorial opposition? What kind of morphological change makes up the material basis of the functional semantics of the oppositional contrast of forms? The answer to this question, evidently, can be obtained as a result of an observation of the relevant language data in the light of the two correlated presentations of the category, namely, a formal presentation and a functional presentation.

But before going into details of fact, we must emphasize, that the most general principle of the interpretation of the category of mood within the framework of the two approaches is essentially the same; it is the statement of the semantic content of the category as determining the reality factor of the verbal action, i.e. showing whether the denoted action is real or unreal.

In this respect, it should be clear that the category of mood, like the category of voice, differs in principle from the immanent verbal categories of time, prospect, development, and retrospective coordination. Indeed, while the enumerated categories characterize the action from the point of view of its various inherent properties, the category of mood expresses the outer interpretation of the action as a whole, namely, the speaker's introduction of it as actual or imaginary. Together with the category of voice, this category, not reconstructing the process by way of reflecting its constituent qualities, gives an integrating appraisal of the process and establishes its lingual representation in a syntactic context.

§ 3. The formal description of the category has its source in the traditional school grammar. It is through the observation of immediate differences in changeable forms that the mood distinctions of the verb were indicated by the forefathers of modern sophisticated descriptions of the English grammatical structure. These differences, similar to the categorial forms of person, number, and time, are most clearly pronounced with the unique verb *be*.

Namely, it is first and foremost with the verb *be* that the pure infinitive stem in the construction of the verbal form of desired or hypothetical action is made prominent. "*Be* it as you wish", "So *be* it", "*Be* what may", "The powers that *be*", "The insistence that the accused *be* present" – such and like constructions, though characterized by a certain bookish flavour, bear indisputable testimony to the fact that the verb *be* has a special finite oblique mood form, different from the direct indicative. Together with the isolated, notional *be*, as well as the linking *be*, in the capacity of the same mood form come also the passive manifestations of verbs with *be* in a morphologically bound position, *cf.*:

The stipulation that the deal *be made* without delay, the demand that the matter *be examined* carefully, etc.

By way of correlation with the oblique *be*, the infinitive stem of the other verbs is clearly seen as constituting the same form of the

181

considered verbal mood. Not only constructions featuring the third person singular without its categorial mark -(e)s, but also constructions of other personal forms of the verb are ordered under this heading. Thus, we distinguish the indicated mood form of the verb in sentences like "*Happen* what may", "God *forgive* us", "Long *live* our friendship", "It is important that he *arrive* here as soon as possible", and also "The agreement stipulates that the goods *pass* customs free", "It is recommended that the elections *start* on Monday", "My orders are that the guards *draw up*", etc.

Semantical observation of the constructions with the analysed verbal form shows that within the general meaning of desired or hypothetical action, it signifies different attitudes towards the process denoted by the verb and the situation denoted by the construction built up around it, namely, besides desire, also supposition, speculation, suggestion, recommendation, inducement of various degrees of insistence including commands.

Thus, the analysed form-type presents the *mood of attitudes*. Traditionally it is called "subjunctive", or in more modern terminological nomination, "subjunctive one". Since the term "subjunctive" is also used to cover the oblique mood system as a whole, some sort of terminological specification is to be introduced that would give a semantic alternative to the purely formal "subjunctive one" designation. Taking into account the semantics of the form-type in question, we suggest that it should be named the "spective" mood, employing just the Latin base for the notion of "attitudes". So, what we are describing now, is the spective form of the subjunctive mood, or, in keeping with the usual working linguistic parlance, simply the *spective mood*, in its pure, classical manifestation.

Going on with our analysis, we must consider now the imperative form of the verb, traditionally referred to as a separate, imperative mood.

In accord with the formal principles of analysis, it is easy to see that the verbal imperative morphemically coincides with the spective mood, since it presents the same infinitive stem, though in relation to the second person only. Turning to the semantics of the imperative, we note here as constitutive the meaning of attitudes of the general spective description. This concerns the forms both of *be* and the other verbs, cf.: *Be* on your guard! *Be* off! *Do be* careful with the papers! *Don't be* blue! *Do* as I ask you! *Put* down the address, will you? About *turn*!

As is known, the imperative mood is analysed in certain grammatical treatises as semantically direct mood, in this sense being likened to the indicative [Ganshina, Vasilevskaya, 200]. This kind of interpretation, though, is hardly convincing. The imperative form displays every property of a form of attitudes, which can easily be shown by means of equivalent transformations. *Cf.*:

*Be* off! → I demand that you *be* off. *Do be* careful with the papers! → My request is that you *do be* careful with the papers. *Do* as I ask you! → I insist that you *do* as I ask you. About *turn*! → I command that you *turn* about.

Let us take it for demonstrated, then, that the imperative verbal forms may be looked upon as a variety of the spective, i.e. its particular, if very important, manifestation.*

At this stage of study we must pay attention to how time is expressed with the analysed form. In doing so we should have in mind that, since the expression of verbal time is categorial, a consideration of it does not necessarily break off with the formal principle of observation. In this connection, first, we note that the infinitive stem taken for the building up of the spective is just the present-tense stem of the integral conjugation of the verb. The spective *be*, the irregular (suppletive) formation, is the only exception from this correlation (though, as we have seen, it does give the general pattern for the mood identification in cases other than the third person singular). Second, we observe that constructions with the spective, though expressed by the present-stem of the verb, can be transferred into the past plane context. *Cf.*:

It *was* recommended that the elections *start* on Monday. My orders *were* that the guards *draw up*. The agreement *stipulated* that the goods *pass* customs free.

This phenomenon marks something entirely new from the point of view of the categorial status of the verbal time in the indicative. Indeed, in the indicative the category of time is essentially absolutive, while in the sphere of the subjunctive (in our case, spective) the present stem, as we see, is used relatively, denoting the past in the context of the past.

---

* *Cf.* L.S. Barkhudarov's consideration of both varieties of forms under the same heading of "imperative".

Here our purely formal, i.e. morphemic consideration of the present stem of the subjunctive comes to an end. Moreover, remaining on the strictly formal ground in the strictly morphemic sense, we would have to state that the demonstrated system of the spective mood exhausts, or nearly exhausts, the entire English oblique mood morphology. See: [Бархударов, 1975, 129]. However, turning to functional considerations of the expression of the oblique mood semantics, we see that the system of the subjunctive, far from being exhausted, rather begins at this point.

§ 4. Observations of the materials undertaken on the comparative functional basis have led linguists to the identification of a number of construction types rendering the same semantics as is expressed by the spective mood forms demonstrated above. These generalized expressions of attitudes may be classed into the following three groups.

The first construction type of attitude series is formed by the combination *may/might* + Infinitive. It is used to express wish, desire, hope in the contextual syntactic conditions similar to those of the morphemic (native) spective forms. *Cf.*:

*May* it *be* as you wish! *May* it all *happen* as you desire! *May* success *attend* you. I hope that he *may be* safe. Let's pray that everything *might* still *turn* to the good, after all. *May* our friendship *live* long.

The second construction type of attitude series is formed by the combination *should* + Infinitive. It is used in various subordinate predicative units to express supposition, speculation, suggestion, recommendation, inducements of different kinds and degrees of intensity. *Cf.*:

Whatever they *should say* of the project, it must be considered seriously. It has been arranged that the delegation *should be received* by the President of the Federation. Orders were given that the searching group *should start* out at once.

The third construction type of the same series is formed by the combination *let* + Objective Substantive + Infinitive. It is used to express inducement (i.e. an appeal to commit an action) in relation to all the persons, but preferably to the first person plural and third person both numbers. The notional homonym *let*, naturally, is not taken into account. *Cf.*:

*Let's agree* to end this wait-and-see policy. Now *don't let's be* hearing any more of this. *Let him repeat* the accusation in Tim's presence. *Let our military forces be* capable and ready. *Let me try* to convince them myself.

All the three types of constructions are characterized by a high frequency occurrence, by uniformity of structure, by regularity of correspondence to the "pure", native morphemic spective form of the verb. For that matter, taken as a whole, they are more universal stylistically than the pure spective form, in so far as they are less bound by conventions of usage and have a wider range of expressive connotations of various kinds. These qualities show that the described constructions may safely be identified as functional equivalents of the pure spective mood. Since they specialize, within the general spective mood meaning, in semantic destination, the specialization being determined by the semantic type of their modal markers, we propose to unite them under the tentative heading of the "modal" spective mood forms, or, by way of the usual working contraction, the modal spective mood, as contrasted against the "pure" spective expressed by native morphemic means (morphemic zeroing).

The functional varieties of the modal spective, i.e. its specialized forms, as is evident from the given examples, should be classed as, first, the "desiderative" series (*may*-spective, the form of desire); second, the "considerative" series (*should*-spective, the form of considerations); third, the "imperative" series (*let*-spective, the form of commands).

We must stress that by terming the spective constructional forms "modal" we don't mean to bring down their grammatical value. Modality is part and parcel of predication, and the modern paradigmatic interpretation of syntactic constructions has demonstrated that all the combinations of modal verbs as such constitute grammatical means of sentence-forming. On the other hand, the relevance of medial morpho-syntactic factor in the structure of the forms in question cannot be altogether excluded from the final estimation of their status. The whole system of the English subjunctive mood is far from stabilized, it is just in the making, and all that we can say about the analysed spective forms in this connection is that they tend to quickly develop into rigidly "formalized" features of morphology.

Very important for confirming the categorial nature of the modal spective forms is the way they express the timing of the process.

The verbal time proper is neutralized with these forms and, considering their relation to the present-order pure spective, they can also be classed as "present" in this sense. As to the actual expression of time, it is rendered relatively, by means of the aspective category of retrospective coordination: the imperfect denotes the relative present (simultaneity and posteriority), while the perfect denotes the relative past (priority in the present and the past). This regularity, common for all the system of the subjunctive mood, is not always clearly seen in the constructions of the spective taken by themselves (i.e. without a comparison with the subjunctive of the past order, which is to be considered further) due to the functional destination of this mood.

The perfect is hardly ever used with the pure spective non-imperative. As far as the imperative is concerned, the natural time-aspect plane is here the present-oriented imperfect strictly relative to the moment of speech, since, by definition, the imperative is addressed to the listener. The occasional perfect with the imperative gives accent to the idea of some time-limit being transgressed, or stresses an urge to fulfil the action in its entirety. *Cf.*:

*Try and have done*, it's not so difficult as it seems. *Let's have finished* with the whole affair!

Still, when it is justified by the context, the regularity of expressing time through aspect is displayed by the specialized modal spective with the proper distinctness. *Cf.*:

I *wish* her plans *might succeed* (the present simultaneity – posteriority). – – I *wished* her plans *might succeed* (the past simultaneity – posteriority). I *wish* her plans *might have succeeded* (failure in the present priority). – – I *wished* her plans *might have succeeded* (failure in the past priority). Whatever the outcome of the conference *should be*, stalemate cannot be tolerated (the present simultaneity – posteriority). – – The commentator emphasized that, whatever the outcome of the conference *should be*, stalemate could not be tolerated (the past simultaneity – posteriority). Whatever the outcome of the conference *should have been*, stalemate cannot be tolerated (the present priority, the outcome of the conference is unknown). – – The commentator emphasized that, whatever the outcome of the conference *should have been*, stalemate could not be tolerated (the past priority, the outcome of the conference was unknown).

186

The perfect of the modal spective makes up for the deficiency of the pure spective which lacks the perfect forms. *Cf.*:

*Be* it so or otherwise, I see no purpose in our argument (simultaneity in the present). - - *Should* it *have been* otherwise, there might have been some purpose in our argument (priority in the present).

§ 5. As the next step of the investigation, we are to consider the forms of the subjunctive referring to the past order of the verb. The approach based on the purely morphemic principles leads us here also to the identification of the specific form of the conjugated *be* as the only native manifestation of the categorial expression of unreal process. *E.g.*:

Oh, that he *were* together with us now! If I *were* in your place, I'd only be happy. If it *were* in my power, I wouldn't hesitate to interfere.

As is the case with *be* in the present subjunctive (spective), the sphere of its past subjunctive use is not confined to its notional and linking functions, but is automatically extended to the broad imperfect system of the passive voice, as well as the imperfect system of the present continuous. *Cf.*:

If he *were given* the same advice by an outsider, he would no doubt profit by it; with the relatives it *might be* the other way about, I'm afraid. I'd repeat that you were right from the start, even though Jim himself *were putting down* each word I say against him.

Unfortunately, the cited case types practically exhaust the native past subjunctive distinctions of *be*, since with the past subjunctive, unlike the present, it is only the first and third persons singular that have the suppletive marking feature *were*. The rest of the forms coincide with the past indicative. Moreover, the discriminate personal finite *was* more and more penetrates into the subjunctive, thus liquidating the scarce remnants of differences between the subjunctive and the indicative of the past order as a whole. *Cf.*:

If he *was* as open-hearted as you are, it would make all the difference.

Thus, from here on we have to go beyond the morphemic principle of analysis and look for other discriminative marks of the subjunctive elsewhere. Luckily, we don't have to wander very far in search of them, but discover them in the explicitly distinctive, strikingly significant correlation of the aspective forms of retrospective coordination. These are clearly taken to signify the time of the imaginary process, namely, imperfect for the absolute and relative present, perfect for the absolute and relative past. Thereby, in union with the past verbal forms as such, the perfect-imperfect retrospective coordination system is made to mark the past subjunctive in universal contradistinction to the past and present indicative. This feature is all the more important, since it is employed not only in the structures patterned by the subjunctive *were* and those used in similar environmental conditions, but also in the further *would – should*-structures, in which the feature of the past is complicated by the feature of the posteriority, also reformed semantically. *Cf.:*

I*'m sure* if she *tried*, she *would manage* to master riding not later than by the autumn, for all her unsporting habits (simultaneity – posteriority in the present). – – I *was sure* if she *tried*, she *would manage* it by the next autumn (simultaneity – posteriority in the past). How much embarrassment *should* I *have been spared* if only I. *had known* the truth before! (priority of the two events in the present). – – I *couldn't keep* from saying that I *should have been spared* much embarrassment if only I *had known* the truth before (priority of the two events in the past).

The sought-for universal mark of the subjunctive, the "unknown quantity" which we have undertaken to find, is, then, the tense-retrospect shift noted in a preliminary way above, while handling the forms of the present (i.e. spective) subjunctive. The differential mark is unmistakable, both delimiting the present and past subjunctive in their different functional spheres (the present and the past verbal forms as such), and distinguishing the subjunctive as a whole from the indicative as a whole (the tense-retrospect shift taken in its entirety). The mark is explicit not by virtue of the grammatical system being just so many ready-made, unmovable sets of units and forms; it is explicit due to something very important existing in addition to the static correlations and interdependencies making up the base of the system. What renders it not only distinct, but absolutely essential, is the paradigmatic relations in dynamics of language functioning. It is this dynamic life of paradigmatic connections in the course of speech production and perception that turns the latent structural differences, if small and insignificant in themselves, into regular and accurate means of expression. The tense-retrospect shift analysed within the framework of the latent system is almost imperceptible, almost entirely hidden under the cover of morphemic identity. But this identity proves ephemeral the very moment the process of speech begins. The paradigmatic connections all come into life as if by magic; the different treatments of absolutive and relative tenses sharply contrast one against the other; the imperfect and perfect indicative antagonize those of the subjunctive; the tense-retrospect shift manifests its working in explicit structural formations of contexts and environments, not allowing grammatical misunderstandings between the participants of lingual communication.

Thus, having abandoned the exhausted formal approach in the traditional sense in order to seek the subjunctive distinctions on the functional lines, we return to formality all the same, though existing on a broader, dynamic, but none the less real basis.

As for the functional side of it, not yet looked into with the past subjunctive, it evidently differs considerably from that which we have seen in the system of the present subjunctive. The present subjunctive is a system of verbal forms expressing a hypothetical action appraised in various attitudes, namely, as an object of desire, wish, consideration, etc. The two parallel sets of manifestations of the present subjunctive, i.e. the pure spective and the modal spective, stand in variant functional inter-relations, conveying essentially identical basic semantics and partially complementing each other on the connotative and structural lines. As different from this, the past subjunctive is not a mood of attitudes. Rather, it is a mood of reasoning by the rule of contraries, the contraries being situations of reality opposed to the corresponding situations of unreality, i.e. opposed to the reflections of the same situations placed by an effort of thinking in different, imaginary connections with one another. Furthermore, the past subjunctive, unlike the present subjunctive, is not a system of two variant sets of forms, though, incidentally, it does present two sets of forms constituting a system. The difference is, that the systemic sets of the past subjunctive are functional invariants, semantically complementing each other in the construction of complex sentences reflecting the causal-conditional relations of events.

The most characteristic construction in which the two form-types occur in such a way that one constitutes the environment of the other is the complex sentence with a clause of unreal condition. The subjunctive form-type used in the conditional clause is the past unposterior; the subjunctive form-type used in the principal clause is the past posterior. By referring the verbal forms to the past, as well as to the posterior, we don't imply any actual significations effected by the forms either of the past, or of the posterior: the terms are purely technical, describing the outer structure, or morphemic derivation, of the verbal forms in question. The method by which both forms actualize the denotation of the timing of the process has been described above.

The subjunctive past unposterior is called by some grammarians "subjunctive two". Since we have reserved the term "subjunctive" for denoting the mood of unreality as a whole, another functional name should be chosen for this particular form-type of the subjunctive. "Spective" can't be used here for the simple reason that the analysed mood form differs in principle from the spective in so far as its main functions, with the exception of a few construction-types, do not express attitudes. So, to find an appropriate functional name for the mood form in question, we must consider the actual semantic role served by it in syntactic constructions.

We have already stated that the most typical use of the past unposterior subjunctive is connected with the expression of unreal actions in conditional clauses (see examples cited above). Further observations of texts show that, in principle, in all the other cases of its use the idea of unreal condition is, if not directly expressed, then implied by way of "subtext". These are constructions of concession and comparison, expressions of urgency, expressions of wish introduced independently and in object clauses. Let us examine them separately.

The syntactic clause featuring the analysed form in the context nearest to the clause of condition is the clause of concession. *E.g.*:

Even if he *had been* a commanding officer himself, he wouldn't have received a more solemn welcome in the mess. Even though it *were raining*, we'll go boating on the lake.

It is easy to see, that the so-called "concession" in the cited complex sentences presents a variety of condition. Namely, it is unreal or hypothetical condition which is either overcome or neglected. And it is expressed intensely. Thus, the transformational exposition of the respective implications will be the following:

...→In spite of the fact that he *was* not a commanding officer, he was given the most solemn welcome of the sort commanding officers were given. ...→We don't know whether it *will be raining* or not, but even in case it *is raining* we will go boating.

Comparisons with the subjunctive are expressed in adverbial clauses and in predicative clauses. In both cases condition is implied by way of contracted implication. *Cf.* an adverbial comparative clause:

She was talking to Bennie as if he *were* a grown person.

The inherent condition is exposed by re-constructing the logic of the imaginary situation: →She was talking to Bennie as she would be talking to him if he *were* a grown person.

A similar transformation applies to the predicative comparative clause:

It looks as if it *had been snowing* all the week.→It looks as it would look if it *had been snowing* all the week.

In the subjunctive expression of urgency (temporal limit) the implied urgent condition can be exposed by indicating a possible presupposed consequence. *Cf.*:

It is high time the right key to the problem *were found*. \*→ The finding of the right key to the problem *is* a condition that has long been necessary to realize; those interested would be satisfied in this case.

In clauses and sentences of wish featuring the subjunctive, the implied condition is dependent on the expressed desire of a situation contrary to reality, and on the regret referring to the existing stage of things. This can also be exposed by indicating a possible presupposed consequence. *Cf.* a complex sentence with an object clause of wish-subjunctive:

I wish my brain *weren't* in such a whirl all the time. \*→My brain not being in such a whirl all the time *is* a condition for my attending to matters more efficiently.

The wish-subjunctive in independent sentences has the same implication:

Oh, that the distress signals *had* only *been heard* when we could be in time to rescue the crew! \*→Our hearing the distress signals *was* a condition for the possibility of our being in time to rescue the crew. We are in despair that it *was* not so.

---

\* The symbol \*→ denotes approximate transformation.

As is indicated in grammars, modal verbs used in similar constructions display the functional features of the subjunctive, including the verb *would* which implies some effort of wilful activity. *Cf.*:

I wish he *could have come*! (The implication is that, unfortunately, he had no such possibility.) I wish he *would have come*! (The implication is that he had not come of his own free will.)

As we see, the subjunctive form under analysis in its various uses does express the unreality of an action which constitutes a condition for the corresponding consequence. Provided our observation is true, and the considered subjunctive uses are essentially those of stipulation, the appropriate explanatory term for this form of the subjunctive would be "stipulative". Thus, the subjunctive form-type which is referred to on the structural basis as the past unposterior, on the functional basis will be referred to as stipulative.

Now let us consider the form-type of the subjunctive which structurally presents the past posterior. As we have stated before, its most characteristic use is connected with the principal clause of the complex sentence expressing a situation of unreal condition: the principal clause conveys the idea of its imaginary consequence, thereby also relating to unreal state of events. *Cf.*:

If the peace-keeping force had not been on the alert, the civil war in that area *would have resumed* anew.

The consequential situation of fact is dependent on the conditional situation of fact as a necessity; and this factual correlation is preserved in reference to the corresponding imaginary situations. This can be shown by a transformation: →For the civil war in that area not to have resumed anew, the peace-keeping force *had to be* on the alert.

*Cf.* another example:

If two people were found with a great bodily resemblance, the experiment *would succeed.*→For the experiment to succeed, it *is necessary to find* two people with a great bodily resemblance.

In keeping with its functional meaning, this kind of consequence may be named a "consequence of necessity".

A consequence dependent on a "concessive" condition shown above has another implication. Two semantic varieties of clauses of consequence should be pointed out as connected with the said concessive condition and featuring the subjunctive mood. The first variety presents a would-be effected action in consequence of a would-be overcome unfavourable condition as a sort of challenge. *E.g.*:

I know Sam. Even if they had tried to cajole him into acceptance, he *would have* flatly *refused* to cooperate.

The second variety of concessive-conditional consequence featuring the subjunctive, as different from the "consequence of challenge", expresses neglect of a hypothetical situation. *Cf.*:

Even though weather-conditions were altogether forbidding, the reconnaissance flight *would start* as scheduled.

Apart from complex sentences, the past posterior form of the subjunctive can be used in independent sentences. It is easy to see, though, that these sentences are based on the presupposition of some condition, the consequence of which they express. It means that from the point of view of the analysed functions they practically do not differ from the constructions of consequence shown above. *Cf.*:

He *would be* here by now: he may have missed his train.→He may have missed his train, otherwise (i.e. if he hadn't missed it) he *would be* here by now.

As we see, the subjunctive form-type in question in the bulk of its uses essentially expresses an unreal consequential action dependent on an unreal stipulating action. In grammars which accept the idea of this form being a variety of the verbal mood of unreality, it is commonly called "conditional". However, the cited material tends to show that the term in this use is evidently inadequate and misleading. In keeping with the demonstrated functional nature of the analysed verbal form it would be appropriate, relying on the Latin etymology, to name it "consective". "Consective" in function, "past posterior" in structure – the two names will go together similar to the previously advanced pair "stipulative" – "past unposterior" for the related form of the subjunctive.

Thus, the functions of the two past form-types of the subjunctive are really different from each other on the semantic lines. On the other hand, this difference is of such a kind that the forms complement each other within one embedding syntactic construction, at the same time being manifestations of the basic integral mood of unreality. This allows us to unite both analysed form-types under one heading, opposed not only structurally, but also functionally to the heading of the spective mood. And the appropriate term for this united system of the past-tense subjunctive will be "conditional". Indeed, the name had to be rejected as the designation of the consequential (consective) form of the subjunctive taken separately, but it will be very helpful in showing the actual unity of the forms not only on the ground of their structure (i.e. the past tense order), but also from the point of view of their semantico-syntactic destination.

The conditional system of the subjunctive having received its characterization in functional terms, the simplified "numbering" terminology may also be of use for practical teaching purposes. Since the purely formal name for the stipulative mood-form, now in more or less common use, is "subjunctive two", it would stand to reason to introduce the term "subjunctive three" for the consective form of the subjunctive. For the sake of observing consistency and symmetry in terms, "modal subjunctive" will then receive the name "subjunctive four".

§ 6. We have surveyed the structure of the category of mood, trying to expose the correlation of its formal and semantic features, and also attempting to choose the appropriate terms of linguistic denotation for this correlation. The system is not a simple one, though its basic scheme is not so cumbersome as it would appear in the estimation of certain academic opinion. The dynamic scheme of the category has been much clarified of late in the diverse researches carried out by modern linguists.

One of the drawbacks of the descriptions of the category of mood in the existing manuals is the confusion of the functional (semantic) terms of analysis with the formal (categorial) terms of analysis.

To begin with, hardly convenient in this respect would appear the shifted nomination of the "oblique" tenses broadly used in grammars, i.e. the renaming of the past imperfect into the "present" and the past perfect into the simple "past". By this shift in terms the authors, naturally, meant to indicate the tense-shift of the "oblique moods", i.e. the functional difference of the tenses in the subjunctive mood from their counterparts in the indicative mood. But the term "tense" is clearly a categorial name which ought to be consistent with the formal structure of the category common for the whole of the verb. As a result of the terminological shift, the tense-structure of the verb receives a hindering reflection, the confusion being aggravated by the additional difficulty of contrasting the "present" tense of one system of the oblique moods (which is formally past) against the "present" tense of another system of the oblique moods (which is formally present).

Hardly consistent with adequacy would appear the division of the general mood system into several moods at the upper level of presentation. "Imperative", "subjunctive one", "subjunctive two", "conditional", "suppositional" – these are in fact shown in separate contrasts to the indicative, which hinders the observation of the common basis underlying the analysed category.

The notions "synthetical" moods and "analytical" moods, being formal, hardly meet the requirements of clarity in correlation, since, on the one hand, the "synthetical" formation in the English subjunctive is of a purely negative nature (no inflexion), and, on the other hand, the "analytical" oblique formations ("conditional", "suppositional") and the "synthetical" oblique formations ("subjunctive one", "subjunctive two") are asymmetrically related to the analytical and synthetical features of the temporal-aspective forms of the verb ("subjunctive one" plus part of "subjunctive two" against the "analytical moods" plus the other part of "subjunctive two").

Apparently inconsistent with the function of the referent form is the accepted name "conditional" by which the form-type of consequence is designated in contrast to the actual form-type of condition ("subjunctive two").

The attempted survey of the system of the English mood based on the recent extensive study of it and featuring oppositional interpretations, has been aimed at bringing in appropriate correlation the formal and the functional presentations of its structure.

We have emphasized that underlying the unity of the whole system is the one integral form of the subjunctive standing in opposition to the one integral form of the indicative. The formal mark of the opposition is the tense-retrospect shift in the subjunctive, the latter being the strong member of the opposition. The shift consists in the perfect aspect being opposed to the imperfect aspect, both turned into the relative substitutes for the absolutive past and present tenses of the indicative. The shift has been brought about historically, as has been rightly demonstrated by scholars, due to the semantic nature of the subjunctive, since, from the point of view of semantics, it is rather a mood of meditation and imagination.

The term "subjunctive" itself cannot be called a very lucky one: its actual motivation by the referent phenomena has long been lost so that at present it is neither formal, nor functional. The mood system of unreality designated by the name "subjunctive" might as well be called "conjunctive", another meaningless term, but stressing the unity of English with other Germanic languages. We have chosen the name "subjunctive", though, as a tribute to the purely English grammatical tradition. As for its unmotivated character, with a name of the most general order it might be considered as its asset, after all.

The subjunctive, the integral mood of unreality, presents the two sets of forms according to the structural division of verbal tenses into the present and the past. These form-sets constitute the two corresponding functional subsystems of the subjunctive, namely, the spective, the mood of attitudes, and the conditional, the mood of appraising causal-conditional relations of processes. Each of these, in its turn, falls into two systemic sub-sets, so that at the immediately working level of presentation we have the four subjunctive form-types identified on the basis of the strict correlation between their structure and their function: the pure spective, the modal spective, the stipulative conditional, the consective conditional.

For the sake of simplifying the working terminology and bearing in mind the existing practice, the described forms of the subjunctive can be called, respectively, *subjunctive one* (pure spective), *subjunctive two* (stipulative), *subjunctive three* (consective), *subjunctive four* (modal spective, or modal subjunctive). The functional correlation of these forms can be shown on a diagram (See Fig 3).

FORMS OF THE SUBJUNCTIVE MOOD

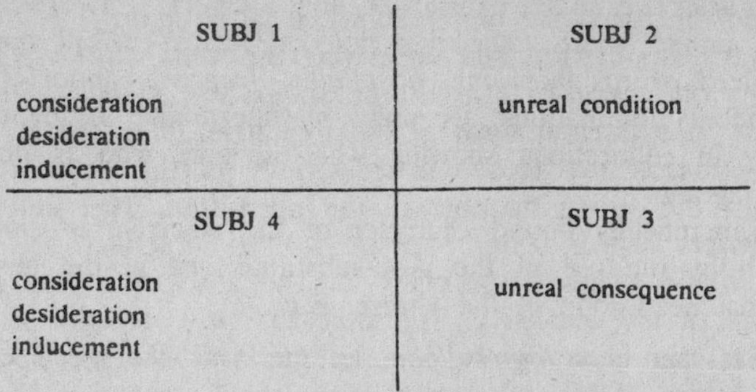

| SUBJ 1 | SUBJ 2 |
|---|---|
| consideration desideration inducement | unreal condition |
| SUBJ 4 | SUBJ 3 |
| consideration desideration inducement | unreal consequence |

Fig 3

The described system is not finished in terms of the historical development of language; on the contrary, it is in the state of making and change. Its actual manifestations are complicated by neutral-

196

izations of formal contrasts (such as, for instance, between the past indicative and the past subjunctive in reported speech); by neutralizations of semantic contrasts (such as, for instance, between the considerative modal spective and the desiderative modal spective); by fluctuating uses of the auxiliaries (*would – should*); by fluctuating uses of the finite *be* in the singular (*were – was*); etc. Our task in the objective study of language, as well as in language teaching, is to accurately register these phenomena, to explain their mechanism and systemic implications, to show the relevant tendencies of usage in terms of varying syntactic environments, topical contexts, stylistic preferences.

As we see, the category of mood, for all the positive linguistic work performed upon it, continues to be a tremendously interesting field of analytical observation. There is no doubt that its numerous particular properties, as well as its fundamental qualities as a whole, will be further exposed, clarified, and paradigmatically ordered in the course of continued linguistic research.

### C H A P T E R  XVIII

## ADJECTIVE

§ 1. The adjective expresses the categorial semantics of property of a substance. It means that each adjective used in the text presupposes relation to some noun the property of whose referent it denotes, such as its material, colour, dimensions, position, state, and other characteristics both permanent and temporary. It follows from this that, unlike nouns, adjectives do not possess a full nominative value. Indeed, words like *long, hospitable, fragrant* cannot effect any self-dependent nominations; as units of informative sequences they exist only in collocations showing what is long, who is hospitable, what is fragrant.

The semantically bound character of the adjective is emphasized in English by the use of the prop-substitute *one* in the absence of the notional head-noun of the phrase. *E.g.*:

I don't want *a yellow balloon*, let me have *the green one* over there.

On the other hand, if the adjective is placed in a nominatively self-dependent position, this leads to its substantivization. *E.g.*:

Outside it was a beautiful day, and the sun tinged the snow with *red*.

*Cf.*: The sun tinged the snow with the *red colour*.

Adjectives are distinguished by a specific combinability with nouns, which they modify, if not accompanied by adjuncts, usually in pre-position, and occasionally in post-position; by a combinability with link-verbs, both functional and notional; by a combinability with modifying adverbs.

In the sentence the adjective performs the functions of *an attribute* and *a predicative*. Of the two, the more specific function of the adjective is that of an attribute, since the function of a predicative can be performed by the noun as well. There is, though, a profound difference between the predicative uses of the adjective and the noun which is determined by their native categorial features. Namely, the predicative adjective expresses some attributive property of its noun-referent, whereas the predicative noun expresses various substantival characteristics of its referent, such as its identification or classification of different types. This can be shown on examples analysed by definitional and transformational procedures. *Cf.*:

You talk to people as if they *were a group*.→You talk to people as if they *formed a group*. Quite obviously, he *was a friend*.→His behaviour *was like that of a friend*.

*Cf.*, as against the above:

I will be *silent as a grave*.→I will be like a *silent grave*. Walker felt *healthy*.→Walker felt a *healthy man*. It was *sensational*.→That fact was a *sensational fact*.

When used as predicatives or post-positional attributes, a considerable number of adjectives, in addition to the general combinability characteristics of the whole class, are distinguished by a complementive combinability with nouns. The complement-expansions of adjectives are effected by means of prepositions. *E.g.: fond of, jealous of, curious of, suspicious of; angry with, sick with; serious about, certain about; happy about; grateful to, thankful to*, etc. Many such adjectival collocations render essentially verbal meanings and some of them have direct or indirect parallels among verbs. *Cf.: be fond of* – love, like; *be envious of* – envy; *be angry with* – resent; *be mad for, about* – covet; *be thankful to* – thank.

Alongside other complementive relations expressed with the help of prepositions and corresponding to direct and prepositional object-relations of verbs, some of these adjectives may render relations of addressee. *Cf.: grateful to, indebted to, partial to, useful for*.

To the derivational features of adjectives belong a number of suffixes and prefixes of which the most important are: *-ful* (hopeful),

*-less* (flawless), *-ish* (bluish), *-ous* (famous), *-ive* (decorative), *-ic* (basic); *un-* (unprecedented), *in-* (inaccurate), *pre-* (premature). Among the adjectival affixes should also be named the prefix *a-*, constitutive for the stative subclass which is to be discussed below.

As for the variable (demutative) morphological features, the English adjective, having lost in the course of the history of English all its forms of grammatical agreement with the noun, is distinguished only by the hybrid category of comparison, which will form a special subject of our study.

§ 2. All the adjectives are traditionally divided into two large subclasses: *qualitative* and *relative*.

*Relative* adjectives express such properties of a substance as are determined by the direct relation of the substance to some other substance. E.g.: wood – a *wooden* hut; mathematics – *mathematical* precision; history – a *historical* event; table – *tabular* presentation; colour – *coloured* postcards; surgery – *surgical* treatment; the Middle Ages – *mediaeval* rites.

The nature of this "relationship" in adjectives is best revealed by definitional correlations. *Cf.*: a *wooden* hut – a hut made of wood; a *historical* event – an event referring to a certain period of history; *surgical* treatment – treatment consisting in the implementation of surgery; etc.

*Qualitative* adjectives, as different from relative ones, denote various qualities of substances which admit of a quantitative estimation, i.e of establishing their correlative quantitative measure. The measure of a quality can be estimated as high or low, adequate or inadequate, sufficient or insufficient, optimal or excessive. *Cf.*: an *awkward* situation – a *very awkward* situation; a *difficult* task – *too difficult* a task; an *enthusiastic* reception – *rather* an *enthusiastic* reception; a *hearty* welcome – *not* a *very hearty* welcome; etc.

In this connection, the ability of an adjective to form degrees of comparison is usually taken as a formal sign of its qualitative character, in opposition to a relative adjective which is understood as incapable of forming degrees of comparison by definition. *Cf.*: a *pretty* girl – a *prettier* girl; a *quick* look – a *quicker* look; a *hearty* welcome – the *heartiest* of welcomes; a *bombastic* speech – the *most bombastic* speech.

However, in actual speech the described principle of distinction is not at all strictly observed, which is noted in the very grammar treatises putting it forward. Two typical cases of contradiction should be pointed out here.

In the first place, substances can possess such qualities as are incompatible with the idea of degrees of comparison. Accordingly, adjectives denoting these qualities, while belonging to the qualitative subclass, are in the ordinary use incapable of forming degrees of comparison. Here refer adjectives like *extinct, immobile, deaf, final, fixed,* etc.

In the second place, many adjectives considered under the heading of relative still can form degrees of comparison, thereby, as it were, transforming the denoted relative property of a substance into such as can be graded quantitatively. *Cf.:* a *mediaeval* approach – *rather* a *mediaeval* approach – a *far more mediaeval* approach; of a *military* design – of a *less military* design – of a *more military* design; a *grammatical* topic – a *purely grammatical* topic – the *most grammatical* of the suggested topics.

In order to overcome the demonstrated lack of rigour in the definitions in question, we may introduce an additional linguistic distinction which is more adaptable to the chances of usage. The suggested distinction is based on the evaluative function of adjectives. According as they actually give some qualitative evaluation to the substance referent or only point out its corresponding native property, all the adjective functions may be grammatically divided into "evaluative" and "specificative". In particular, one and the same adjective, irrespective of its being basically (i.e. in the sense of the fundamental semantic property of its root constituent) "relative" or "qualitative", can be used either in the evaluative function or in the specificative function.

For instance, the adjective *good* is basically qualitative. On the other hand, when employed as a grading term in teaching, i.e. a term forming part of the marking scale together with the grading terms *bad, satisfactory, excellent,* it acquires the said specificative value; in other words, it becomes a specificative, not an evaluative unit in the grammatical sense (though, dialectically, it does signify in this case a lexical evaluation of the pupil's progress). Conversely, the adjective *wooden* is basically relative, but when used in the broader meaning "expressionless" or "awkward" it acquires an evaluative force and, consequently, can presuppose a greater or lesser degree ("amount") of the denoted property in the corresponding referent. *E.g.:*

Bundle found herself looking into the expressionless, *wooden* face of Superintendent Battle (A. Christie). The superintendent was sitting behind a table and looking *more wooden* than ever (Ibid).

The degrees of comparison are essentially evaluative formulas, therefore any adjective used in a higher comparison degree (comparative, superlative) is thereby made into an evaluative adjective, if only for the nonce (see the examples above).

Thus, the introduced distinction between the evaluative and specificative uses of adjectives, in the long run, emphasizes the fact that the morphological category of comparison (comparison degrees) is potentially represented in the whole class of adjectives and is constitutive for it.

§ 3. Among the words signifying properties of a nounal referent there is a lexemic set which claims to be recognized as a separate part of speech, i.e. as a class of words different from the adjectives in its class-forming features. These are words built up by the prefix *a-* and denoting different states, mostly of temporary duration. Here belong lexemes like *afraid, agog, adrift, ablaze.* In traditional grammar these words were generally considered under the heading of "predicative adjectives" (some of them also under the heading of adverbs), since their most typical position in the sentence is that of a predicative and they are but occasionally used as pre-positional attributes to nouns.

Notional words signifying states and specifically used as predicatives were first identified as a separate part of speech in the Russian language by L.V. Shcherba and V.V. Vinogradov. The two scholars called the newly identified part of speech the "category of state" (and, correspondingly, separate words making up this category, "words of the category of state"). Here belong the Russian words mostly ending in -*о*, but also having other suffixes: *тепло, зябко, одиноко, радостно, жаль, лень,* etc. Traditionally the Russian words of the category of state were considered as constituents of the class of adverbs, and they are still considered as such by many Russian scholars.

On the analogy of the Russian "category of state", the English qualifying *a*-words of the corresponding meanings were subjected to a lexico-grammatical analysis and given the part-of-speech heading "category of state". This analysis was first conducted by B.A. Ilyish and later continued by other linguists. The term "words of the category of state", being rather cumbersome from the technical point of view, was later changed into "stative words", or "statives".

The part-of-speech interpretation of the statives is not shared by all linguists working in the domain of English, and has found both its proponents and opponents.

Probably the most consistent and explicit exposition of the part-of-speech interpretation of statives has been given by B.S. Khaimovich and B.I. Rogovskaya [Khaimovich, Rogovskaya, 199 ff]. Their theses supporting the view in question can be summarized as follows.

First, the statives, called by the quoted authors "adlinks" (by virtue of their connection with link-verbs and on the analogy of the term "adverbs"), are allegedly opposed to adjectives on a purely semantic basis, since adjectives denote "qualities", and statives-adlinks denote "states". Second, as different from adjectives, statives-adlinks are characterized by the specific prefix *a-*. Third, they allegedly do not possess the category of the degrees of comparison. Fourth, the combinability of statives-adlinks is different from that of adjectives in so far as they are not used in the pre-positional attributive function, i.e. are characterized by the absence of the right-hand combinability with nouns.

The advanced reasons, presupposing many-sided categorial estimation of statives, are undoubtedly serious and worthy of note. Still, a closer consideration of the properties of the analysed lexemic set cannot but show that, on the whole, the said reasons are hardly instrumental in proving the main idea, i.e. in establishing the English stative as a separate part of speech. The re-consideration of the stative on the basis of comparison with the classical adjective inevitably discloses the fundamental relationship between the two, – such relationship as should be interpreted in no other terms than identity at the part-of-speech level, though, naturally, providing for their distinct differentiation at the subclass level.

The first scholar who undertook this kind of re-consideration of the lexemic status of English statives was L.S. Barkhudarov, and in our estimation of them we essentially follow his principles, pointing out some additional criteria of argument.

First, considering the basic meaning expressed by the stative, we formulate it as "stative property", i.e. a kind of property of a nounal referent. As we already know, the adjective as a whole signifies not "quality" in the narrow sense, but "property", which is categorially divided into "substantive quality as such" and "substantive relation". In this respect, statives do not fundamentally differ from classical adjectives. Moreover, common adjectives and participles in adjective-type functions can express the same, or, more specifically, typologically the same properties (or "qualities" in a broader sense) as are expressed by statives.

Indeed, the main meaning types conveyed by statives are: the psychic state of a person *(afraid, ashamed, aware);* the physical state of a person *(astir, afoot);* the physical state of an object *(afire, ablaze, aglow);* the state of an object in space *(askew, awry, aslant).* Meanings of the same order are rendered by pre-positional adjectives. *Cf.*:

the *living* predecessor – the predecessor *alive;* *eager* curiosity – curiosity *agog;* the *burning* house – the house *afire;* a *floating* raft – a raft *afloat;* a *half-open* door – a door *adjar;* *slanting* ropes – ropes *aslant;* a *vigilant* man – a man *awake;* *similar* cases – cases *alike;* an *excited* crowd – a crowd *astir.*

It goes without saying that many other adjectives and participles convey the meanings of various states irrespective of their analogy with statives. *Cf.* such words of the order of psychic state as *despondent, curious, happy, joyful;* such words of the order of human physical state as *sound, refreshed, healthy, hungry;* such words of the order of activity state as *busy, functioning, active, employed,* etc.

Second, turning to the combinability characteristics of statives, we see that, though differing from those of the common adjectives in one point negatively, they basically coincide with them in the other points. As a matter of fact, statives are not used in attributive pre-position, but, like adjectives, they are distinguished by the left-hand categorial combinability both with nouns and link-verbs. *Cf.*:

The household was all *astir.* – – The household was all *excited.* – – It was strange to see the household *astir* at this hour of the day. – – It was strange to see the household *active* at this hour of the day.

Third, analysing the functions of the stative corresponding to its combinability patterns, we see that essentially they do not differ from the functions of the common adjective. Namely, the two basic functions of the stative are the predicative and the attribute. The similarity of functions leads to the possibility of the use of a stative and a common adjective in a homogeneous group. *E.g.*: Launches and barges moored to the dock were *ablaze* and *loud* with wild sound.

True, the predominant function of the stative, as different from the common adjective, is that of the predicative. But then, the important structural and functional peculiarities of statives uniting them in a distinctly separate set of lexemes cannot be disputed. What is disputed is the status of this set in relation to the notional parts of speech, not its existence or identification as such.

Fourth, from our point of view, it would not be quite consistent with the actual lingual data to place the stative strictly out of the category of comparison. As we have shown above, the category of comparison, is connected with the functional division of adjectives into evaluative and specificative. Like common adjectives, statives are subject to this flexible division, and so in principle they are included into the expression of the quantitative estimation of the corresponding properties conveyed by them. True, statives do not take the synthetic forms of the degrees of comparison, but they are capable of expressing comparison analytically, in cases where it is to be expressed. *Cf.*:

Of us all, Jack was the one *most aware* of the delicate situation in which we found ourselves. I saw that the adjusting lever stood *far more askew* than was allowed by the directions.

Fifth, quantitative considerations, though being a subsidiary factor of reasoning, tend to support the conjoint part-of-speech interpretation of statives and common adjectives. Indeed, the total number of statives does not exceed several dozen (a couple of dozen basic, "stable" units and, probably, thrice as many "unstable" words of the nature of coinages for the nonce [Жигадло, Иванова, Иофик, 170]). This number is negligible in comparison with the number of words of the otherwise identified notional parts of speech, each of them counting thousands of units. Why, then, an honour of the part-of-speech status to be granted to a small group of words not differing in their fundamental lexico-grammatical features from one of the established large word-classes?

As for the set-forming prefix *a-*, it hardly deserves a serious consideration as a formal basis of the part-of-speech identification of statives simply because formal features cannot be taken in isolation from functional features. Moreover, as is known, there are words of property not distinguished by this prefix, which display essential functional characteristics inherent in the stative set. In particular, here belong such adjectives as *ill, well, glad, sorry, worth (while), subject (to), due (to), underway,* and some others. On the other hand, among the basic statives we find such as can hardly be analysed into a genuine combination of the type "prefix + root", because their morphemic parts have become fused into one indivisible unit in the course of language history, *e.g. aware, afraid, aloof.*

Thus, the undertaken semantic and functional analysis shows that statives, though forming a unified set of words, do not constitute a separate lexemic class existing in language on exactly the same footing as the noun, the verb, the adjective, the adverb; rather it should be looked upon as a subclass within the general class of adjectives. It is essentially an adjectival subclass, because, due to their peculiar features, statives are not directly opposed to the notional parts of speech taken together, but are quite particularly opposed to the rest of adjectives. It means that the general subcategorization of the class of adjectives should be effected at the two levels: at the upper level the class will be divided into the subclass of stative adjectives and common adjectives; at the lower level the common adjectives fall into qualitative and relative, which division has been discussed in the foregoing paragraph.

As we see, our final conclusion about the lexico-grammatical nature of statives appears to have returned them into the lexemic domain in which they were placed by traditional grammar and from which they were alienated in the course of subsequent linguistic investigations. A question then arises, whether these investigations, as well as the discussions accompanying them, have served any rational purpose at all.

The answer to this question, though, can only be given in the energetic affirmative. Indeed, all the detailed studies of statives undertaken by quite a few scholars, all the discussions concerning their systemic location and other related matters have produced very useful results, both theoretical and practical.

The traditional view of the stative was not supported by any special analysis, it was formed on the grounds of mere surface analogies and outer correlations. The later study of statives resulted in the exposition of their inner properties, in the discovery of their historical productivity as a subclass, in their systemic description on the lines of competent inter-class and inter-level comparisons. And it is due to the undertaken investigations (which certainly will be continued) that we are now in a position, though having rejected the fundamental separation of the stative from the adjective, to name the subclass of statives as one of the peculiar, idiomatic lexemic features of Modern English.

§ 4. As is widely known, adjectives display the ability to be easily substantivized by conversion, i.e. by zero-derivation. Among the noun-converted adjectives we find both old units, well-established in the system of lexicon, and also new ones, whose adjectival etymology conveys to the lexeme the vivid colouring of a new coinage.

For instance, the words *a relative* or *a white* or *a dear* bear an unquestionable mark of established tradition, while such a noun as *a sensitive* used in the following sentence features a distinct flavour of purposeful conversion:

He was a regional man, a man who wrote about *sensitives* who live away from the places where things happen (M. Bradbury).

Compare this with the noun *a high* in the following example:

The weather report promises *a new high* in heat and humidity (Ibid.).

From the purely categorial point of view, however, there is no difference between the adjectives cited in the examples and the ones given in the foregoing enumeration, since both groups equally express constitutive categories of the noun, i.e. the number, the case, the gender, the article determination, and they likewise equally perform normal nounal functions.

On the other hand, among the substantivized adjectives there is a set characterized by hybrid lexico-grammatical features, as in the following examples:

The new bill concerning the wage-freeze introduced by the Labour Government cannot satisfy either *the poor*, or *the rich* (Radio Broadcast). A monster. The word conveyed *the ultimate* in infamy and debasement inconceivable to one not native to the times (J. Vance). The train, indulging all his English nostalgia for *the plushy* and *the genteel*, seemed to him a deceit (M. Bradbury).

The mixed categorial nature of the exemplified words is evident from their incomplete presentation of the part-of-speech characteristics of either nouns or adjectives. Like nouns, the words are used in the article form; like nouns, they express the category of number (in a relational way); but their article and number forms are rigid, not being subject to the regular structural change inherent in the normal expression of these categories. Moreover, being categorially unchangeable, the words convey the mixed adjectival-nounal semantics of property.

The adjectival-nounal words in question are very specific. They are distinguished by a high productivity and, like statives, are idiomatically characteristic of Modern English.

On the analogy of verbids these words might be called "adjectivids", since they are rather nounal forms of adjectives than nouns as such.

The adjectivids fall into two main grammatical subgroups, namely, the subgroup *pluralia tantum* (*the English, the rich, the unemployed, the uninitiated,* etc.), and the subgroup *singularia tantum* (*the invisible, the abstract, the tangible,* etc.). Semantically, the words of the first subgroup express sets of people (personal multitudes), while the words of the second group express abstract ideas of various types and connotations.

§ 5. The category of adjectival comparison expresses the quantitative characteristic of the quality of a nounal referent, i.e. it gives a relative evaluation of the quantity of a quality. The purely relative nature of the categorial semantics of comparison is reflected in its name.

The category is constituted by the opposition of the three forms known under the heading of degrees of comparison; the basic form (*positive degree*), having no features of comparison; the *comparative degree* form, having the feature of restricted superiority (which limits the comparison to two elements only); the *superlative degree* form, having the feature of unrestricted superiority.

It should be noted that the meaning of unrestricted superiority is in-built in the superlative degree as such, though in practice this form is used in collocations imposing certain restrictions on the effected comparison; thus, the form in question may be used to signify restricted superiority, namely, in cases where a limited number of referents are compared. *Cf.*:

Johnny was *the strongest boy* in the company.

As is evident from the example, superiority restriction is shown here not by the native meaning of the superlative, but by the particular contextual construction of comparison where the physical strength of one boy is estimated in relation to that of his companions.

Some linguists approach the number of the degrees of comparison as problematic on the grounds that the basic form of the adjective does not express any comparison by itself and therefore should be excluded from the category. This exclusion would reduce the category to two members only, i.e. the comparative and superlative degrees.

However, the oppositional interpretation of grammatical categories underlying our considerations does not admit of such an exclusion; on the contrary, the non-expression of superiority by the basic form is understood in the oppositional presentation of comparison as a pre-requisite for the expression of the category as such. In this expression of the category the basic form is the unmarked member, not distinguished by any comparison suffix or comparison auxiliary, while the superiority forms (i.e. the comparative and superlative) are the marked members, distinguished by the comparison suffixes or comparison auxiliaries.

That the basic form as the positive degree of comparison does express this categorial idea, being included in one and the same categorial series with the superiority degrees, is clearly shown by its actual uses in comparative syntactic constructions of equality, as well as comparative syntactic constructions of negated equality. *Cf.*:

The remark was *as bitter as* could be. The Rockies are not *so high as* the Caucasus.

These constructions are directly correlative with comparative constructions of inequality built around the comparative and superlative degree forms. *Cf.*:

That was *the bitterest* remark I have ever heard from the man. The Caucasus is *higher than* the Rockies.

Thus, both formally and semantically, the oppositional basis of the category of comparison displays a binary nature. In terms of the three degrees of comparison, at the upper level of presentation the superiority degrees as the marked member of the opposition are contrasted against the positive degree as its unmarked member. The superiority degrees, in their turn, form the opposition of the lower level of presentation, where the comparative degree features the functionally weak member, and the superlative degree, respectively, the strong member. The whole of the double oppositional unity, considered from the semantic angle, constitutes a gradual ternary opposition.

§ 6. The synthetical forms of comparison in -*er* and -(*e*)*st* coexist with the analytical forms of comparison effected by the auxiliaries *more* and *most*. The analytical forms of comparison perform a double function. On the one hand, they are used with the evaluative adjectives that, due to their phonemic structure (two-syllable words with the stress on the first syllable ending in other grapho-phonemic complexes than -er, -y, -le, -ow or words of more than two-syllable composition) cannot normally take the synthetic forms of comparison. In this respect, the analytical comparison forms are in categorial complementary distribution with the synthetic comparison forms. On the other hand, the analytical forms of comparison, as different from the synthetic forms, are used to express emphasis, thus complementing the synthetic forms in the sphere of this important stylistic connotation. *Cf.*:

The audience became *more* and *more noisy*, and soon the speaker's words were drowned in the general hum of voices.

The structure of the analytical degrees of comparison is meaningfully overt; these forms are devoid of the feature of "semantic idiomatism" characteristic of some other categorial analytical forms, such as, for instance, the forms of the verbal perfect. For this reason the analytical degrees of comparison invite some linguists to call in question their claim to a categorial status in English grammar.

In particular, scholars point out the following two factors in support of the view that the combinations of *more/most* with the basic form of the adjective are not the analytical expressions of the morphological category of comparison, but free syntactic constructions: first, the *more / most*-combinations are semantically analogous to combinations of *less / least* with the adjective which, in the general opinion, are syntactic combinations of notional words; second, the *most*-combination, unlike the synthetic superlative, can take the indefinite article, expressing not the superlative, but the elative meaning (i.e. a high, not the highest degree of the respective quality).

The reasons advanced, though claiming to be based on an analysis of actual lingual data, can hardly be called convincing as regards their immediate negative purpose.

Let us first consider the use of the *most*-combination with the indefinite article.

This combination is a common means of expressing elative evaluations of substance properties. The function of the elative *most*-construction in distinction to the function of the superlative *most*-construction will be seen from the following examples:

The speaker launched *a most significant* personal attack on the Prime Minister. *The most significant* of the arguments in a dispute is not necessarily *the most spectacular* one.

While the phrase "a most significant (personal) attack" in the first of the two examples gives the idea of rather a high degree of the quality expressed irrespective of any directly introduced or implied comparison with other attacks on the Prime Minister, the phrase "the most significant of the arguments" expresses exactly the superlative degree of the quality in relation to the immediately introduced comparison with all the rest of the arguments in a dispute; the same holds true of the phrase "the most spectacular one". It is this exclusion of the outwardly superlative adjective from a comparison that makes it into a simple elative, with its *most*-constituent turned from the superlative auxiliary into a kind of a lexical intensifier.

The definite article with the elative *most*-construction is also possible, if leaving the elative function less distinctly recognizable (in oral speech the elative *most* is commonly left unstressed, the absence of stress serving as a negative mark of the elative). *Cf.*:

I found myself in the *most awkward* situation, for I couldn't give a satisfactory answer to any question asked by the visitors.

Now, the synthetic superlative degree, as is known, can be used in the elative function as well, the distinguishing feature of the latter being its exclusion from a comparison. *Cf.*:

Unfortunately, our cooperation with Danny proved *the worst* experience for both of us. No doubt Mr. Snider will show you his collection of minerals with *the greatest* pleasure.

And this fact gives us a clue for understanding the expressive nature of the elative superlative as such – the nature that provides it with a permanent grammatico-stylistic status in the language. Indeed, the expressive peculiarity of the form consists exactly in the immediate combination of the two features which outwardly contradict each other: the categorial form of the superlative on the one hand, and the absence of a comparison on the other.

That the categorial form of the superlative (i.e. the superlative with its general functional specification) is essential also for the expression of the elative semantics can, however paradoxical it might appear, be very well illustrated by the elative use of the comparative degree. Indeed, the comparative combination featuring the elative comparative degree is constructed in such a way as to place it in the functional position of unrestricted superiority, i.e. in the position specifically characteristic of the superlative. *E.g.*:

Nothing gives me *greater* pleasure than to greet you as our guest of honour. There is nothing *more refreshing* than a good swim.

The parallelism of functions between the two forms of comparison (the comparative degree and the superlative degree) in such and like examples is unquestionable.

As we see, the elative superlative, though it is not the regular superlative in the grammatical sense, is still a kind of a specific, grammatically featured construction. This grammatical specification distinguishes it from common elative constructions which may be generally defined as syntactic combinations of an intensely high estimation. *E.g.*: an *extremely important* amendment; a matter of *exceeding* urgency; quite an *unparalleled* beauty; etc.

Thus, from a grammatical point of view, the elative superlative, though semantically it is "elevated", is nothing else but a degraded superlative, and its distinct featuring mark with the analytical superlative degree is the indefinite article: the two forms of the superlative of different functional purposes receive the two different marks (if not quite rigorously separated in actual uses) by the article determination treatment.

It follows from the above that the possibility of the *most*-combination to be used with the indefinite article cannot in any way be demonstrative of its non-grammatical character, since the functions of the two superlative combinations in question, the elative superlative and the genuine superlative, are different.

Moreover, the use of the indefinite article with the synthetic superlative in the degraded, elative function is not altogether impossible, though somehow such a possibility is bluntly denied by certain grammatical manuals. *Cf.*:

He made a *last* lame effort to delay the experiment; but Basil was impervious to suggestion (J. Vance).

But there is one more possibility to formally differentiate the direct and elative functions of the synthetic superlative, namely, by using the zero article with the superlative. This latter possibility is noted in some grammar books [Ganshina, Vasilevskaya, 85]. *Cf.*:

Suddenly I was seized with a sensation of *deepest* regret.

However, the general tendency of expressing the superlative elative meaning is by using the analytical form. Incidentally, in the Russian language the tendency of usage is reverse: it is the synthetic form of the Russian superlative that is preferred in rendering the elative function. *Cf.*: слушали с *живейшим* интересом; повторялась *скучнейшая* история; попал в *глупейшее* положение, etc.

§ 7. Let us examine now the combinations of *less/least* with the basic form of the adjective.

As is well known, the general view of these combinations definitely excludes them from any connection with categorial analytical forms. Strangely enough, this rejectionist view of the "negative degrees of comparison" is even taken to support, not to reject the morphological interpretation of the *more/most*-combinations.

The corresponding argument in favour of the rejectionist interpretation consists in pointing out the functional parallelism existing between the synthetic degrees of comparison and the *more/most*-combinations accompanied by their complementary distribution, if not rigorously pronounced (the different choice of the forms by different syllabo-phonetic forms of adjectives). The *less/least*-combinations, according to this view, are absolutely incompatible with the synthetic degrees of comparison, since they express not only different, but opposite meanings [Khaimovich, Rogovskaya, 77-78].

Now, it does not require a profound analysis to see that, from the grammatical point of view, the formula "opposite meaning" amounts to ascertaining the categorial equality of the forms compared. Indeed, if two forms express the opposite meanings, then they can only belong to units of the same general order. And we cannot but agree with B.A. Ilyish's thesis that "there seems to be no sufficient reason for treating the two sets of phrases in different ways, saying that 'more difficult' is an analytical form, while 'less difficult' is not" [Ilyish, 60]. True, the cited author takes this fact rather as demonstration that both types of constructions should equally be excluded from the domain of analytical forms, but the problem of the categorial status of the *more/most*-combinations has been analysed above.

Thus, the *less/least*-combinations, similar to the *more/most*-combinations, constitute specific forms of comparison, which may be called forms of "reverse comparison". The two types of forms cannot be syntagmatically combined in one and the same form of the word, which shows the unity of the category of comparison. The whole category includes not three, but five different forms, making up the two series – respectively, direct and reverse. Of these, the reverse series of comparison (the reverse superiority degrees, or "inferiority degrees", for that matter) is of far lesser importance than the direct one, which evidently can be explained by semantic reasons. As a matter of fact, it is more natural to follow the direct model of comparison based on the principle of addition of qualitative quantities than on the reverse model of comparison based on the principle of subtraction of qualitative quantities, since subtraction in general is a far more abstract process of mental activity than addition. And, probably, exactly for the same reason the reverse comparatives and superlatives are rivalled in speech by the corresponding negative syntactic constructions.

§ 8. Having considered the characteristics of the category of comparison, we can see more clearly the relation to this category of some usually non-comparable evaluative adjectives.

Outside the immediate comparative grammatical change of the adjective stand such evaluative adjectives as contain certain comparative sememic elements in their semantic structures. In particular, as we have mentioned above, here belong adjectives that are themselves grading marks of evaluation. Another group of evaluative non-comparables is formed by adjectives of indefinitely moderated quality, or, tentatively, "moderating qualifiers", such as *whitish, tepid, half-ironical, semi-detached*, etc. But the most peculiar lexemic group of non-comparables is made up by adjectives expressing the highest degree of a respective quality, which words can tentatively be called "adjectives of extreme quality", or "extreme qualifiers", or simply "extremals".

The inherent superlative semantics of extremals is emphasized by the definite article normally introducing their nounal combinations, exactly similar to the definite article used with regular collocations of the superlative degree. *Cf.*:

*The ultimate* outcome of the talks was encouraging. *The final* decision has not yet been made public.

On the other hand, due to the tendency of colloquial speech to contrastive variation, such extreme qualifiers can sometimes be modified by intensifying elements. Thus, "the final decision" becomes "a very final decision"; "the ultimate rejection" turns into "rather an ultimate rejection"; "the crucial role" is made into "quite a crucial role", etc. As a result of this kind of modification, the highest grade evaluative force of these words is not strengthened, but, on the contrary, weakened; the outwardly extreme qualifiers become degraded extreme qualifiers, even in this status similar to the regular categorial superlatives degraded in their elative use.

## CHAPTER XIX

# ADVERB

§ 1. The adverb is usually defined as a word expressing either property of an action, or property of another property, or circumstances in which an action occurs. This definition, though certainly informative and instructive, fails to directly point out the relation between the adverb and the adjective as the primary qualifying part of speech.

In an attempt to overcome this drawback, let us define the adverb as a notional word expressing a non-substantive property, that is, a property of a non-substantive referent. This formula immediately shows the actual correlation between the adverb and the adjective, since the adjective is a word expressing a substantive property.

Properties may be of a more particular, "organic" order, and a more general and detached, "inorganic" order. Of the organic properties, the adverb denotes those characterizing processes and other properties. Of the inorganic properties, the adverb denotes various circumstantial characteristics of processes or whole situations built around processes.

The above definition, approaching the adverb as a word of the secondary qualifying order, presents the entire class of adverbial words as the least self-dependent of all the four notional parts of speech. Indeed, as has been repeatedly pointed out, the truly complete nominative value is inherent only in the noun, which is the name of substances. The verb comes next in its self-dependent nominative force, expressing processes as dynamic relations of substances, i.e. their dynamic relational properties in the broad sense. After that follow qualifying parts of speech – first the adjective denoting qualifications of substances, and then the adverb denoting qualifications of non-substantive phenomena which find themselves within the range of notional signification.

As we see, the adverb is characterized by its own, specific nominative value, providing for its inalienable status in the system of the parts of speech. Hence, the complaints of some linguists that the adverb is not rigorously defined and in fact presents something like a "dump" for those words which have been rejected by other parts of speech can hardly be taken as fully justified. On the other hand, since the adverb does denote qualifications of the second order, not of the first one like the adjective, it includes a great number of semantically weakened words which are in fact intermediate between notional and functional lexemes by their status and often display features of pronominal nature.

§ 2. In accord with their categorial meaning, adverbs are characterized by a combinability with verbs, adjectives and words of adverbial nature. The functions of adverbs in these combinations consist in expressing different adverbial modifiers. Adverbs can also refer to whole situations; in this function they are considered under the heading of situation-"determinants". Cf.:

The woman was crying *hysterically*. (an adverbial modifier of manner, in left-hand contact combination with the verb-predicate) Wilson looked at him *appraisingly*. (an adverbial modifier of manner, in left-hand distant combination with the verb-predicate) Without undressing she sat down to the poems, *nervously* anxious to like them... (an adverbial modifier of property qualification, in right-hand combination with a post-positional stative attribute-adjective) You've gotten awfully brave, *awfully* suddenly. (an adverbial modifier of intensity, in right-hand combination with an adverb-aspective determinant of the situation) *Then* he stamps his boots *again* and advances into the room. (two adverbial determinants of the situation: the first – of time, in right-hand combination with the modified predicative construction; the second – of recurrence, in left-hand combination with the modified predicative construction)

Adverbs can also combine with nouns acquiring in such cases a very peculiar adverbial-attributive function, essentially in post-position, but in some cases also in pre-position. E.g.:

The world *today* presents a picture radically different from what it was before the Second World War. Our vigil *overnight* was rewarded by good news: the operation seemed to have succeeded. Franklin D. Roosevelt, the *then* President of the United States, proclaimed the "New Deal" – a new Government economic policy.

The use of adverbs in outwardly attributive positions in such and like examples appears to be in contradiction with the functional destination of the adverb – a word that is intended to qualify a nonnounal syntactic element by definition.

However, this seeming inconsistence of the theoretical interpretation of adverbs with their actual uses can be clarified and resolved in the light of the syntactic principle of nominalization elaborated within the framework of the theory of paradigmatic syntax (see further). In accord with this principle, each predicative syntactic construction paradigmatically correlates with a noun-phrase displaying basically the same semantic relations between its notional constituents. A predicative construction can be actually changed into a nounphrase, by which change the dynamic situation expressed by the predicative construction receives a static name. Now, adverbs-determinants modifying in constructions of this kind the situation as a whole, are preserved in the corresponding nominalized phrases without a change in their inherent functional status. *Cf.*:

The world that exists *today*.→The world *today*. We kept vigil *overnight*.→Our vigil *overnight*. *Then* he was the President.→The *then* President.

These paradigmatic transformational correlations explain the type of connection between the noun and its adverbial attribute even in cases where direct transformational changes would not be quite consistent with the concrete contextual features of constructions. What is important here is the fact that the adverb used to modify a noun actually relates to the whole corresponding situation underlying the noun-phrase.

§ 3. In accord with their word-building structure adverbs may be *simple* and *derived*.

Simple adverbs are rather few, and nearly all of them display functional semantics, mostly of pronominal character: *here, there, now, then, so, quite, why, how, where, when*.

The typical adverbial affixes in affixal derivation are, first and foremost, the basic and only productive adverbial suffix *-ly (slowly, tiredly, rightly, firstly)*, and then a couple of others of limited distribution, such as *-ways (sideways, crossways)*, *-wise (clockwise)*, *-ward(s) (homewards, seawards, afterwards)*. The characteristic adverbial prefix is *a- (away, ahead, apart, across)*.

Among the adverbs there are also peculiar composite formations and phrasal formations of prepositional, conjunctional and other types: *sometimes, nowhere, anyhow; at least, at most, at last; to and fro; upside down;* etc.

Some authors include in the word-building sets of adverbs also formations of the type *from outside, till now, before then*, etc. However, it is not difficult to see that such formations differ in principle from the ones cited above. The difference consists in the fact that their parts are semantically not blended into an indivisible lexemic unity and present combinations of a preposition with a peculiar adverbial substantive – a word occupying an intermediary lexico-grammatical status between the noun and the adverb. This is most clearly seen on ready examples liberally offered by English texts of every stylistical standing. *E.g.*:

The pale moon looked at me *from above. By now* Sophie must have received the letter and very soon we shall hear from her. The departure of the delegation is planned *for later* this week.

The freely converted adverbial substantives in prepositional collocations belong to one of the idiomatic characteristics of English, and may be likened, with due alteration of details, to partially substantivized adjectives of the adjectivid type (see Ch. XVIII, § 4). On this analogy the adverbial substantives in question may be called "adverbids".

Furthermore, there are in English some other peculiar structural types of adverbs which are derivationally connected with the words of non-adverbial lexemic classes by conversion. To these belong both adverbs of full notional value and adverbs of half-notional value.

A peculiar set of converted notional adverbs is formed by adjective-stem conversives, such as *fast, late, hard, high, close, loud, tight,* etc. The peculiar feature of these adverbs consists in the fact that practically all of them have a parallel form in *-ly,* the two component units of each pair often differentiated in meaning or connotation. *Cf.*: to work *hard – hardly* to work at all; to fall *flat* into the water – to refuse *flatly*; to speak *loud* – to criticize *loudly*; to fly *high* over the lake – to raise a *highly* theoretical question; etc.

Among the adjective-stem converted adverbs there are a few words with the non-specific *-ly* originally in-built in the adjective: *daily, weekly, lively, timely,* etc.

The purely positional nature of the conversion in question, i.e. its having no support in any differentiated categorial paradigms, can be reflected by the term "fluctuant conversives" which we propose to use as the name of such formations.

As for the fluctuant conversives of weakened pronominal semantics, very characteristic of English are the adverbs that positionally interchange with prepositions and conjunctive words: *before, after, round, within,* etc. *Cf.*: never *before* – never *before* our meeting; somewhere *round – round* the corner; not to be found *within – within* a minute; etc.

Of quite a different nature are preposition-adverb-like elements which, placed in post-position to the verb, form a semantic blend with it. By combining with these elements, verbs of broader meaning

' are subjected to a regular, systematic multiplication of their semantic functions. *E.g.*: to give – to give *up*, to give *in*, to give *out*, to give *away*, to give *over*, etc.; to set – to set *up*, to set *in*, to set *forth*, to set *off*, to set *down*, etc.; to get – to get *on*, to get *off*, to get *up*, to get *through*, to get *about*, etc.; to work – to work *up*, to work *in*, to work *out*, to work *away*, to work *over*, etc.; to bring – to bring *about*, to bring *up*, to bring *through*, to bring *forward*, to bring *down*, etc.

The function of these post-positional elements is either to impart an additional aspective meaning to the verb-base, or to introduce a lexical modification to its fundamental semantics. *E.g.*: to bring *about* – to cause to happen; to reverse; to bring *up* – to call attention to; to rear and educate; to bring *through* – to help overcome a difficulty or danger; to save (a sick person); to bring *forward* – to introduce for discussion; to carry to the next page (the sum of figures); to bring *down* – to kill or wound; to destroy; to lower (as prices, etc.).

The lexico-grammatical standing of the elements in question has been interpreted in different ways. Some scholars have treated them as a variety of adverbs (H. Palmer, A. Smirnitsky); others, as preposition-like functional words (I. Anichkov, N. Amosova); still others, as peculiar prefix-like suffixes similar to the German separable prefixes (Y. Zhluktenko); finally, some scholars have treated these words as a special set of lexical elements functionally intermediate between words and morphemes (B.A. Ilyish; B.S. Khaimovich and B.I. Rogovskaya). The cited variety of interpretations, naturally, testifies to the complexity of the problem. Still, we cannot fail to see that one fundamental idea is common to all the various theories advanced, and that is the idea of the functional character of the analysed elements. Proceeding from this idea, we may class these words as a special functional set of particles, i.e. words of semi-morphemic nature, correlative with prepositions and conjunctions.

As for the name to be given to the words for their descriptive identification, out of the variety of those already existing ("postpositions", "adverbial word-morphemes", "adverbial postpositions", etc.) we would prefer the term "postpositives" introduced by N. Amosova. While evading the confusion with classical "postpositions" developed in some languages of non-Indo-European types (i.e. post-nounal analogues of prepositions), this term is fairly convenient for descriptive purposes and at the same time is neutral categorially, i.e. it easily admits of additional specifications of the nature of the units in question in the course of their further linguistic study.

§ 4. Adverbs are commonly divided into *qualitative*, *quantitative* and *circumstantial*.

By qualitative such adverbs are meant as express immediate, inherently non-graded qualities of actions and other qualities. The typical adverbs of this kind are qualitative adverbs in *-ly*. E.g.:

The little boy was crying *bitterly* over his broken toy. The *plainly* embarrassed Department of Industry confirmed the fact of the controversial deal.

The adverbs interpreted as "quantitative" include words of degree. These are specific lexical units of semi-functional nature expressing quality measure, or gradational evaluation of qualities. They may be subdivided into several very clearly pronounced sets.

The first set is formed by adverbs of high degree. These adverbs are sometimes classed as "intensifiers": *very, quite, entirely, utterly, highly, greatly, perfectly, absolutely, strongly, considerably, pretty, much.* The second set includes adverbs of excessive degree (direct and reverse) also belonging to the broader subclass of intensifiers: *too, awfully, tremendously, dreadfully, terrifically.* The third set is made up of adverbs of unexpected degree: *surprisingly, astonishingly, amazingly.* The fourth set is formed by adverbs of moderate degree: *fairly, comparatively, relatively, moderately, rather.* The fifth set includes adverbs of low degree: *slightly, a little, a bit.* The sixth set is constituted by adverbs of approximate degree: *almost, nearly.* The seventh set includes adverbs of optimal degree: *enough, sufficiently, adequately.* The eighth set is formed by adverbs of inadequate degree: *insufficiently, intolerably, unbearably, ridiculously.* The ninth set is made up of adverbs of under-degree: *hardly, scarcely.*

As we see, the degree adverbs, though usually described under the heading of "quantitative", in reality constitute a specific variety of qualitative words, or rather some sort of intermediate qualitative-quantitative words, in so far as they are used as quality evaluators. In this function they are distinctly different from genuine quantitative adverbs which are directly related to numerals and thereby form sets of words of pronominal order. Such are numerical-pronominal adverbs like *twice, thrice, four times*, etc.; *twofold, threefold, manifold*, etc.

Thus, we will agree that the first general subclass of adverbs is formed by qualitative adverbs which are subdivided into qualitative adverbs of full notional value and degree adverbs – specific functional words.

Circumstantial adverbs are also divided into notional and functional.

The functional circumstantial adverbs are words of pronominal nature. Besides quantitative (numerical) adverbs mentioned above, they include adverbs of time, place, manner, cause, consequence. Many of these words are used as syntactic connectives and question-forming functionals. Here belong such words as *now, here, when, where, so, thus, how, why,* etc.

As for circumstantial adverbs of more self-dependent nature, they include two basic sets: first, adverbs of time; second, adverbs of place: *today, tomorrow, already, ever, never, shortly, recently, seldom, early, late; homeward, eastward, near, far, outside, ashore,* etc. The two varieties express a general idea of temporal and spatial orientation and essentially perform deictic (indicative) functions in the broader sense. Bearing this in mind, we may unite them under the general heading of "orientative" adverbs, reserving the term "circumstantial" to syntactic analysis of utterances.

Thus, the whole class of adverbs will be divided, first, into nominal and pronominal, and the nominal adverbs will be subdivided into qualitative and orientative, the former including genuine qualitative adverbs and degree adverbs, the latter falling into temporal and local adverbs, with further possible subdivisions of more detailed specifications.

As is the case with adjectives, this lexemic subcategorization of adverbs should be accompanied by a more functional and flexible division into evaluative and specificative, connected with the categorial expression of comparison. Each adverb subject to evaluational grading by degree words expresses the category of comparison, much in the same way as, mutatis mutandis, adjectives do. Thus, not only qualitative, but also orientative adverbs, providing they come under the heading of evaluative, are included into the categorial system of comparison. *Cf.:* quickly – quicker – quickest – less quickly – least quickly; frequently – more frequently – most frequently – less frequently – least frequently; ashore – more ashore – most ashore – less ashore – least ashore, etc.

Barring the question of the uses of articles in comparative-superlative collocations, all the problems connected with the adjectival degrees of comparison retain their force for the adverbial degrees of comparison, including the problem of elative superlative.

§ 5. Among the various types of adverbs, those formed from adjectives by means of the suffix -*ly* occupy the most representative place and pose a special problem.

The problem is introduced by the very regularity of their derivation, the rule of which can be formulated quite simply: each evaluative (or, to keep to lexical tradition, qualitative) adjective has a parallel adverb in -*ly*. *E.g.*: silent – silently, slow – slowly, tolerable – tolerably, pious – piously, sufficient – sufficiently, tired – tiredly, explosive – explosively, etc.

This regularity of formation accompanied by the general qualitative character of semantics gave cause to A.I. Smirnitsky to advance the view that both sets of words belong to the same part of speech, the qualitative adverbs in -*ly* being in fact adjectives of specific combinability [Смирницкий, 1959, 174-175].

The strong point of the adjectival interpretation of qualitative adverbs in -*ly* is the demonstration of the actual similarity between the two lexemic sets in their broader evaluative function, which fact provides for the near-identity of the adjectival and adverbial grammatical categories of comparison. On the whole, however, the theory in question is hardly acceptable for the mere reason that derivative relations in general are not at all relations of lexico-grammatical identity; for that matter, they are rather relations of non-identity, since they actually constitute a system of production of one type of lexical units from another type of lexical units. As for the types of units belonging to the same or different lexemic classes, this is a question of their actual status in the system of lexicon, i.e. in the lexemic paradigm of nomination reflecting the fundamental correlations between the lexemic sets of language (see Ch. IV, § 8). Since the English lexicon does distinguish adjectives and adverbs; since adjectives are substantive-qualifying words in distinction to adverbs, which are non-substantive qualifying words; since, finally, adverbs in -*ly* do preserve this fundamental non-substantive-qualification character – there cannot be any question of their being "adjectives" in any rationally conceivable way. As for the regularity or irregularity of derivation, it is absolutely irrelevant to the identification of their class-lexemic nature.

Thus, the whole problem is not a problem of part-of-speech identity; it is a problem of inter-class connections, in particular, of inter-class systemic division of functions, and, certainly, of the correlative status of the compared units in the lexical paradigm of nomination.

But worthy of attention is the relation of the adverbs in question to adverbs of other types and varieties, i.e. their intra-class correlations. As a matter of fact, the derivational features of other adverbs, in sharp contrast to the -*ly*-adverbs, are devoid of uniformity to such an extent that practically all of them fall into a multitude of minor non-productive derivational groups. Besides, the bulk of notional qualitative adverbs of other than -*ly*-derivation have -*ly*-correlatives (both of similar and dissimilar meanings and connotations). These facts cannot but show that adverbs in -*ly* should be looked upon as the standard type of the English adverb as a whole.

C H A P T E R  XX

## SYNTAGMATIC CONNECTIONS OF WORDS

§ 1. Performing their semantic functions, words in an utterance form various syntagmatic connections with one another.

One should distinguish between syntagmatic groupings of notional words alone, syntagmatic groupings of notional words with functional words, and syntagmatic groupings of functional words alone.

Different combinations of notional words (notional phrases) have a clearly pronounced self-dependent nominative destination, they denote complex phenomena and their properties in their inter-connections, including dynamic inter-connections (semi-predicative combinations). *Cf.*: a sudden trembling; a soul in pain; hurrying along the stream; to lead to a cross-road; strangely familiar; so sure of their aims.

Combinations of a notional word with a functional word are equivalent to separate words by their nominative function. Since a functional word expresses some abstract relation, such combinations, as a rule, are quite obviously non-self-dependent; they are, as it were, stamped as artificially isolated from the context. *Cf.*: in a low voice; with difficulty; must finish; but a moment; and Jimmy; too cold; so unexpectedly.

We call these combinations "formative" ones. Their contextual dependence ("synsemantism") is quite natural; functionally they may be compared to separate notional words used in various marked grammatical forms (such as, for instance, indirect cases of nouns).

*Cf.: Eng.* Mr. Snow's – of Mr. Snow; him – to him; *Russ.* Иванов – к Иванову; лесом – через лес.

Expanding the cited formative phrases with the corresponding notional words one can obtain notional phrases of contextually self-dependent value ("autosemantic" at their level of functioning). *Cf.: Eng.* Mr. Snow's considerations – the considerations of Mr. Snow; gave it him – gave it to him; *Russ.* позвонили Иванову – позвонили к Иванову; шли лесом – шли через лес.

In this connection we should remember that among the notional word-classes only the noun has a full nominative force, for it directly names a substance. Similarly, we may assert that among various phrase-types it is the noun-phrase that has a full phrasal nominative force (see further).

As for syntagmatic groupings of functional words, they are essentially analogous to separate functional words and are used as connectors and specifiers of notional elements of various status. *Cf.:* out of; up to; so that; such as; must be able; don't let's.

Functional phrases of such and like character constitute limited groups supplementing the corresponding subsets of regular one-item functional words, as different from notional phrases which, as free combinations, form essentially open subsets of various semantic destinations.

§ 2. Groupings of notional words fall into two mutually opposite types by their grammatical and semantic properties.

Groupings of the first type are constituted by words related to one another on an equal rank, so that, for a case of a two-word combination, neither of them serves as a modifier of the other. Depending on this feature, these combinations can be called "equipotent".

Groupings of the second type are formed by words which are syntactically unequal in the sense that, for a case of a two-word combination, one of them plays the role of a modifier of the other. Due to this feature, combinations of the latter type can be called "dominational".

§ 3. Equipotent connection in groupings of notional words is realised either with the help of conjunctions (syndetically), or without the help of conjunctions (asyndetically). *Cf.:* prose and poetry; came and went; on the beach or in the water; quick but not careless; no sun, no moon; playing, chatting, laughing; silent, immovable, gloomy; Mary's, not John's.

In the cited examples, the constituents of the combinations form logically consecutive connections that are classed as coordinative. Alongside these, there exist equipotent connections of a non-consecutive type, by which a sequential element, although equal to the foregoing element by its formal introduction (coordinative conjunction), is unequal to it as to the character of nomination. The latter type of equipotent connections is classed as "cumulative".

The term "cumulation" is commonly used to mean connections between separate sentences. By way of restrictive indications, we may speak about "inner cumulation", i.e. cumulation within the sentence, and, respectively, "outer cumulation".

Cumulative connection in writing is usually signalled by some intermediary punctuation stop, such as a comma or a hyphen. *Cf.*: *Eng.* agreed, but reluctantly; quick – and careless; satisfied, or nearly so. *Russ.* сыт, но не очень; согласен, или почти согласен; дал – да неохотно.

Syndetic connection in a word-combination can alternate with asyndetic connection, as a result of which the whole combination can undergo a semantically motivated subgrouping. *Cf.*:

He is a little man *with irregular features, soft dark eyes and a soft voice, very shy, with a gift of mimicry and a love of music* (S. Maugham).

In enumerative combinations the last element, in distinction to the foregoing elements, can be introduced by a conjunction, which underlines the close of the syntagmatic series. *Cf.*:

All about them happy persons were enjoying the good things of life, talking, laughing, *and* making merry (S. Maugham).

The same is true about combinations formed by repetition. *E.g.*:

There were rows of books, books *and* books everywhere.

§ 4. Dominational connection, as different from equipotent connection, is effected in such a way that one of the constituents of the combination is principal (dominating) and the other is subordinate (dominated). The principal element is commonly called the "kernel", "kernel element", or "head-word"; the subordinate element, respectively, the "adjunct", "adjunct-word", "expansion".

Dominational connection is achieved by different forms of the word (categorial agreement, government), connective words (prepositions, i.e. prepositional government), word-order.

Dominational connection, like equipotent connection, can be both consecutive and cumulative. *Cf.*: a careful observer – – an observer, seemingly careful; definitely out of the point – – out of the point, definitely; will be helpful in any case – – will be helpful, at least in some cases.

The two basic types of dominational connection are bilateral (reciprocal, two-way) domination and monolateral (one-way) domination. Bilateral domination is realized in predicative connection of words, while monolateral domination is realized in completive connection of words.

§ 5. The predicative connection of words, uniting the subject and the predicate, builds up the basis of the sentence. The reciprocal nature of this connection consists in the fact that the subject dominates the predicate determining the person of predication, while the predicate dominates the subject, determining the event of predication, i.e. ascribing to the predicative person some action, or state, or quality. This difference in meaning between the elements of predication, underlying the mutually opposite directions of domination, explains the seeming paradox of the notion of reciprocal domination, exposing its dialectic essence. Both directions of domination in a predicative group can be demonstrated by a formal test.

The domination of the subject over the predicate is exposed by the reflective character of the verbal category of person and also the verbal category of number which is closely connected with the former.

The English grammatical forms of explicit subject-verb agreement (concord) are very scarce (the inflexion marking the third person singular present, and some special forms of the verb *be*). Still, these scarce forms are dynamically correlated with the other, grammatically non-agreed forms. *Cf.*: he went – he goes – – I went – I go.

But apart from the grammatical forms of agreement, the predicative person is directly reflected upon the verb-predicate as such; the very semantics of the person determines the subject reference of the predicative event (action, state, quality). Thus, the subject unconditionally dominates over the predicate by its specific substantive categories in both agreed, and non-agreed forms of predicative connection.

As for the predicate dominating the subject in its own sphere of grammatical functions, this fact is clearly demonstrated by the correlation of the sentence and the corresponding noun-phrase. Namely, the transformation of the sentence into the noun-phrase places the predicate in the position of the head-word, and the subject, in the position of the adjunct. *Cf.*:

The train arrived. → The arrival of the train.

Alongside fully predicative groupings of the subject and the finite verb-predicate, there exist in language partially predicative groupings formed by a combination of a non-finite verbal form (verbid) with a substantive element. Such are infinitival, gerundial, and participial constructions.

The predicative person is expressed in the infinitival construction by the prepositional *for*-phrase, in the gerundial construction by the possessive or objective form of the substantive, in the participial construction by the nominative (common) form of the substantive. *Cf.*:

*The pupil* understands his mistake → *for the pupil* to understand his mistake → *the pupil('s)* understanding his mistake → *the pupil* understanding his mistake.

In the cited semi-predicative (or potentially-predicative) combinations the "event"-expressing element is devoid of the formal agreement with the "person"-expressing element, but the two directions of domination remain valid by virtue of the very predicative nature of the syntactic connection in question (although presented in an incomplete form).

Thus, among the syntagmatic connections of the reciprocal domination the two basic subtypes are distinguished: first, complete predicative connections, second, incomplete predicative connections (semi-predicative, potentially-predicative connections).

§ 6. The completive, one-way connection of words (monolateral domination) is considered as subordinative on the ground that the outer syntactic status of the whole combination is determined by the kernel element (head-word). *Cf.*:

She would be reduced to a nervous wreck. → She would be reduced to a wreck. → She would be reduced. That woman was astonishingly beautiful. → That woman was beautiful.

In the cited examples the head-word can simply be isolated through the deletion of the adjunct, the remaining construction being structurally complete, though schematic. In other cases, the head-word cannot be directly isolated, and its representative nature is to be exposed, for instance, by diagnostic questions. *Cf.*:

Larry greeted the girl heartily. → Whom did Larry greet? → How did Larry greet the girl?

The questions help demonstrate that the verb is presupposed as the kernel in its lines of connections, i.e. objective and adverbial ones.

All the completive connections fall into two main divisions: objective connections and qualifying connections.

Objective connections reflect the relation of the object to the process and are characterized as, on the whole, very close. By their form these connections are subdivided into non-prepositional (word-order, the objective form of the adjunct substantive) and prepositional, while from the semantico-syntactic point of view they are classed as direct (the immediate transition of the action to the object) and indirect or oblique (the indirect relation of the object to the process). Direct objective connections are non-prepositional, the preposition serving as an intermediary of combining words by its functional nature. Indirect objective connections may be both prepositional and non-prepositional. Since, on the other hand, some prepositional objective connections, in spite of their being indirect, still come very near to direct ones in terms of closeness of the process-substance relation expressed, all the objective connections may be divided into "narrow" and "broader". Semantically, narrow prepositional objective connections are then to be classed together with direct objective connections, the two types forming the corresponding subclasses of non-prepositional (direct) and prepositional (indirect) narrow objective connections of words. *Cf.*:

He remembered *the man*. I won't stand *any more nonsense*. I sympathized *with the child*. They were working *on the problem*. Etc.

*Cf.* examples of broader indirect objective connections, both non-prepositional and prepositional:

Will you show *me* the picture? *Who(m)* did he buy it *for?* Tom peeped *into the hall.* Etc.

Further subdivision of objective connections is realized on the basis of subcategorizing the elements of objective combinations, and first of all the verbs; thus, we recognize objects of immediate action, of perception, of speaking, etc.

Objective connection may also combine an adjunct substance word with a kernel word of non-verbal semantics (such as a state or a property word), but the meaning of some processual relation is still implied in the deep semantic base of such combinations all the same. *Cf.: aware* of John's presence → *am aware; crazy* about her → *got crazy* about her; *full* of spite → *is full* of spite; etc.

Qualifying completive connections are divided into attributive and adverbial. Both are expressed in English by word-order and prepositions.

Attributive connection unites a substance with its attribute expressed by an adjective or a noun. *E.g.:* an *enormous* appetite; an *emerald* ring; a woman *of strong character*; the case *for the prosecution*; etc.

Adverbial connection is subdivided into primary and secondary.

The primary adverbial connection is established between the verb and its adverbial modifiers of various standings. *E.g.:* to talk *glibly*; to come *nowhere*; to receive (a letter) *with surprise*; to throw (one's arms) *round a person's neck*; etc.

The secondary adverbial connection is established between the non-verbal kernel expressing a quality and its adverbial modifiers of various standings. *E.g.: marvellously* becoming; *very much* at ease; *strikingly* alike; *no longer* oppressive; *unpleasantly* querulous; etc.

§ 7. Different completive noun combinations are distinguished by a feature that makes them into quite special units on the phrasemic level of language. Namely, in distinction to all the other combinations of words they are directly related to whole sentences, i.e. predicative combinations of words. This fact was illustrated above when we described the verbal domination over the subject in a predicative grouping of words (see § 5). Compare some more examples given in the reverse order:

The arrival of the train → The train arrived. The baked potatoes→The potatoes are baked. The gifted pupil → The pupil has a gift.

Completive combinations of adjectives and adverbs (adjective-phrases and adverb-phrases), as different from noun combinations (noun-phrases), are related to predicative constructions but indirectly, through the intermediary stage of the corresponding noun-phrase. *Cf.*: utterly neglected – utter neglect – The neglect is utter; very carefully – great carefulness – The carefulness is great; speechlessly reproachful – speechless reproach – The reproach is speechless.

These distinctions of completive word combinations are very important to understand for analysing paradigmatic relations in syntax (see further).

### CHAPTER XXI

### SENTENCE: GENERAL

§ 1. The sentence is the immediate integral unit of speech built up of words according to a definite syntactic pattern and distinguished by a contextually relevant communicative purpose. Any coherent connection of words having an informative destination is effected within the framework of the sentence. Therefore the sentence is the main object of syntax as part of the grammatical theory.

The sentence, being composed of words, may in certain cases include only one word of various lexico-grammatical standings. *Cf.*:

Night. Congratulations. Away! Why? Certainly.

The actual existence of one-word sentences, however, does not contradict the general idea of the sentence as a special syntactic combination of words, the same as the notion of one-element set in mathematics does not contradict the general idea of the set as a combination of certain elements. Moreover, this fact cannot lead even to the inference that under some circumstances the sentence and the word may wholly coincide: a word-sentence as a unit of the text is radically different from a word-lexeme as a unit of lexicon, the differentiation being inherent in the respective places occupied by the sentence and the word in the hierarchy of language levels. While the word is a component element of the word-stock and as such is a nominative unit of language, the sentence, linguistically, is a predicative utterance-unit. It means that the sentence not only names some referents with the help of its word-constituents, but also, first, presents these referents as making up a certain situation, or, more specifically, a situational event, and second, reflects the connection between the nominal denotation of the event, on the one hand, and objective reality, on the other, showing the time of the event, its being real or unreal, desirable or undesirable, necessary or unnecessary, etc. *Cf.*:

I am satisfied, the experiment has succeeded. I would have been satisfied if the experiment had succeeded. The experiment seems to have succeeded – why then am I not satisfied?

Thus, even one uninflected word making up a sentence is thereby turned into an utterance-unit expressing the said semantic complex through its concrete contextual and consituational connections. By way of example, compare the different connections of the word-sentence "night" in the following passages:

1) Night. Night and the boundless sea, under the eternal star-eyes shining with promise. Was it a dream of freedom coming true? 2) Night? Oh no. No night for me until I have worked through the case. 3) Night. It pays all the day's debts. No cause for worry now, I tell you.

Whereas the utterance "night" in the first of the given passages refers the event to the plane of reminiscences, the "night" of the second passage presents a question in argument connected with the situation wherein the interlocutors are immediately involved, while the latter passage features its "night" in the form of a proposition of reason in the flow of admonitions.

It follows from this that there is another difference between the sentence and the word. Namely, unlike the word, the sentence does not exist in the system of language as a ready-made unit; with the exception of a limited number of utterances of phraseological citation, it is created by the speaker in the course of communication. Stressing this fact, linguists point out that the sentence, as different from the word, is not a unit of language proper; it is a chunk of text built up as a result of speech-making process, out of different units of language, first of all words, which are immediate means for making up contextually bound sentences, i.e. complete units of speech.

It should be noted that this approach to the sentence, very consistently exposed in the works of A.I. Smirnitsky, corresponds to the spirit of traditional grammar from the early epoch of its development. Traditional grammar has never regarded the sentence as part of the system of means of expression; it has always interpreted the sentence not as an implement for constructing speech, but as speech itself, i.e. a portion of coherent flow of words of one speaker containing a complete thought.

Being a unit of speech, the sentence is intonationally delimited. Intonation separates one sentence from another in the continual flow of uttered segments and, together with various segmental means of expression, participates in rendering essential communicative-predicative meanings (such as, for instance, the syntactic meaning of interrogation in distinction to the meaning of declaration). The role of intonation as a delimiting factor is especially important for sentences which have more than one predicative centre, in particular more than one finite verb. *Cf.*:

1) The class *was over*, the noisy children *filled* the corridors. 2) The class *was over*. The noisy children *filled* the corridors.

Special intonation contours, including pauses, represent the given speech sequence in the first case as one compound sentence, in the second case as two different sentences (though, certainly, connected both logically and syntactically).

On the other hand, as we have stated elsewhere, the system of language proper taken separately, and the immediate functioning of this system in the process of intercourse, i.e. speech proper, present an actual unity and should be looked upon as the two sides of one dialectically complicated substance – the human language in the broad sense of the term. Within the framework of this unity the sentence itself, as a unit of communication, also presents the two different sides, inseparably connected with each other. Namely, within each sentence as an immediate speech element of the communication process, definite standard synactico-semantic features are revealed which make up a typical model, a generalized pattern repeated in an indefinite number of actual utterances. This complicated predicative pattern does enter the system of language. It exists at its own level in the hierarchy of lingual segmental units in the capacity of a "linguistic sentence" and as such is studied by grammatical theory.

Thus, the sentence is characterized by its specific category of predication which establishes the relation of the named phenomena to actual life. The general semantic category of modality is also defined by linguists as exposing the connection between the named objects and surrounding reality. However, modality, as different from predication, is not specifically confined to the sentence; this is a broader category revealed both in the grammatical elements of language and its lexical, purely nominative elements. In this sense, every word expressing a definite correlation between the named substance and objective reality should be recognized as modal. Here belong such lexemes of full notional standing as "probability", "desirability", "necessity" and the like, together with all the derivationally relevant words making up the corresponding series of the lexical paradigm of nomination; here belong semi-functional words and phrases of probability and existential evaluation, such as *perhaps, may be, by all means*, etc.; here belong, further, word-particles of specifying modal semantics, such as *just, even, would-be*, etc.; here belong, finally, modal verbs expressing a broad range of modal meanings which are actually turned into elements of predicative semantics in concrete, contextually-bound utterances.

As for predication proper, it embodies not any kind of modality, but only syntactic modality as the fundamental distinguishing feature of the sentence. It is the feature of predication, fully and explicitly expressed by a contextually relevant grammatical complex, that identifies the sentence as opposed to any other combination of words having a situational referent.

The centre of predication in a sentence of verbal type (which is the predominant type of sentence-structure in English) is a finite verb. The finite verb expresses essential predicative meanings by its categorial forms, first of all, the categories of tense and mood (the category of person, as we have seen before, reflects the corresponding category of the subject). However, proceeding from the principles of sentence analysis worked out in the Russian school of theoretical syntax, in particular, in the classical treatises of V.V. Vinogradov, we insist that predication is effected not only by the forms of the finite verb connecting it with the subject, but also by all the other forms and elements of the sentence establishing the connection between the named objects and reality, including such means of expression as intonation, word order, different functional words. Besides the purely verbal categories, in the predicative semantics are included such syntactic sentence meanings as purposes of communication (declaration – interrogation – inducement), modal probability, affirmation and negation, and others, which, taken together, provide for the sentence to be identified as a unit forming its own, proposemic level of lingual hierarchy.

§ 2. From what has been said about the category of predication, we see quite clearly that the general semantic content of the sen-

232

tence is not at all reduced to predicative meanings only. Indeed, in order to establish the connection between some substance and reality, it is first necessary to name the substance ifself. This latter task is effected in the sentence with the help of its nominative means. Hence, the sentence as a lingual unit performs not one, but two essential signemic (meaningful) functions: first, substance-naming, or nominative finction; second, reality-evaluating, or predicative function.

The terminological definition of the sentence as a predicative unit gives prominence to the main feature distinguishing the sentence from the word among the meaningful lingual units (signemes). However, since every predication is effected upon a certain nomination as its material semantic base, we gain a more profound insight into the difference between the sentence and the word by pointing out the two-aspective meaningful nature of the sentence. The semantics of the sentence presents a unity of its nominative and predicative aspects, while the semantics of the word, in this sense, is monoaspective.

Some linguists do not accept the definition of the sentence through predication, considering it to contain tautology, since, allegedly, it equates the sentence with predication ("the sentence is predication, predication is the sentence"). However, the identification of the two aspects of the sentence pointed out above shows that this negative attitude cannot be accepted as justified; the real content of the predicative interpretation of the sentence has nothing to do with definitions of the "vicious circle" type. In point of fact, as follows from the given exposition of predication, predicative meanings do not exhaust the semantics of the sentence; on the contrary, they presuppose the presence in the sentence of meanings of quite another nature, which form its deeper nominative basis. Predicative functions work upon this deep nominative basis, and as a result the actual utterance-sentence is finally produced.

On the other hand, we must also note a profound difference between the nominative function of the sentence and the nominative function of the word. The nominative meaning of the syntagmatically complete average sentence (an ordinary proposemic nomination) reflects a processual situation or event that includes a certain process (actional or statal) as its dynamic centre, the agent of the process, the objects of the process, and also the various conditions and circumstances of the realization of the process. This content of the proposemic event, as is known from school grammar, forms the basis of the traditional syntactic division of the sentence into its nominative parts. In other words, the identification of traditional syntactic parts of the sentence is nothing else than the nominative division of the sentence. *Cf.*:

The pilot was steering the ship out of the harbour. – – The old pilot was carefully steering the heavily loaded ship through the narrow straits out of the harbour.

Any separate (notional) part of the sentence (subject, object, etc.) can denote a wide range of the elements of the reflected situation. For instance, the subject of the sentence, besides denoting the agent of the action (as in the example above), may point out the object of the action, the addressee of the action, the instrument with which the action is performed, the time and place of it, etc. *Cf.*:

The ship was carefully steered by the pilot. The pilot was entrusted with the ship's safety. The rudder, obeying the helmsman, steadily directed the boat among the reefs. The quiet evening saw the boat sailing out into the open sea...

The semantic reflections of the elements of the situation, in contrast to the parts of the sentence, are sometimes referred to as the "semantic roles" of the sentence, or the "deep cases" of it.

However, no matter what the concrete referential meaning of any part of the sentence might be, it is only through those nominative, syntactically determined sentence constituents that the situation together with its various elements can be reflected. Thus, it must be clearly understood that what is called the "semantic roles" of the sentence is in fact the situational meanings of its syntactic parts.

As is easily seen, no separate word, be it composed of so many stems, can express the described situation-nominative semantics of the proposition. Even hyperbolically complicated artificial words such as are sometimes coined for various expressive purposes by authors of fiction cannot have means of organizing their root components analogous to the means of arranging the nominative constituents of the sentence.

Quite different in this respect is a nominal phrase – a compound signemic unit made up of words and denoting a complex phenomenon of reality analysable into its component elements together with various relations between them. Comparative observations of predicative and non-predicative combinations of words have unmistakably shown that among the latter there are quite definite constructions which are actually capable of realizing nominations of proposemic situations. These are word combinations of full nominative value represented by expanded substantive phrases. It is these combinations that, by their nominative potential, directly correspond to sentences expressing typical proposemic situations. *Cf.*:

... → The pilot's steering of the ship out of the harbour. ... → The old pilot's careful steering of the heavily loaded ship through the narrow straits out of the harbour.

In other words, between the sentence and the substantive wordcombination of the said full nominative type, direct transformational relations are established: the sentence, interpreted as an element of paradigmatics, is transformed into the substantive phrase, or "nominalized", losing its processual-predicative character. Thus, syntactic nominalization, while depriving the sentence of its predicative aspect (and thereby, naturally, destroying the sentence as an immediate communicative unit), preserves its nominative aspect intact.

The identification of nominative aspect of the sentence effected on the lines of studying the paradigmatic relations in syntax makes it possible to define more accurately the very notion of predication as the specific function of the sentence.

The functional essence of predication has hitherto been understood in linguistics as the expression of the relation of the utterance (sentence) to reality, or, in more explicit presentation, as the expression of the relation between the content of the sentence and reality. This kind of understanding predication can be seen, for instance, in the well-known "Grammar of the Russian Language" published by the Academy of Sciences of the USSR, where it is stated that "the meaning and purpose of the general category of predication forming the sentence consists in referring the content of the sentence to reality".[*] Compare with this the definition advanced by A.I. Smirnitsky, according to which predication is understood as "referring the utterance to reality" [Смирницкий, 1957, 102].

The essential principles of this interpretation of predication can be expressed even without the term "predication" as such. The latter approach to the exposition of the predicative meaning of the sentence can be seen, for instance, in the course of English grammar by M.A. Ganshina and N.M. Vasilevskaya, who wrote: "Every sentence shows the relation of the statement to reality from the point of view of the speaker" [Ganshina, Vasilevskaya, 321].

---

[*] Грамматика русского языка. М., 1960. Т. 2, Ч. I, с. 79 – 80.

Now, it is easily noticed that the cited and similar definitions of predication do not explicitly distinguish the two cardinal sides of the sentence content, namely, the nominative side and the predicative side. We may quite plausibly suppose that the non-discrimination of these two sides of sentence meaning gave the ultimate cause to some scholars for their negative attitude towards the notion of predication as the fundamental factor of sentence forming.

Taking into consideration the two-aspective character of the sentence as a signemic unit of language, predication should now be interpreted not simply as referring the content of the sentence to reality, but as referring the nominative content of the sentence to reality. It is this interpretation of the semantico-functional nature of predication that discloses, in one and the same generalized presentation, both the unity of the two identified aspects of the sentence, and also their different, though mutually complementary meaningful roles.

CHAPTER XXII

ACTUAL DIVISION OF THE SENTENCE

§ 1. The notional parts of the sentence referring to the basic elements of the reflected situation form, taken together, the nominative meaning of the sentence. For the sake of terminological consistency, the division of the sentence into notional parts can be just so called – the "nominative division" (its existing names are the "grammatical division" and the "syntactic division"). The discrimination of the nominative division of the sentence is traditional; it is this type of division that can conveniently be shown by a syntagmatic model, in particular, by a model of immediate constituents based on the traditional syntactic analysis (see Ch. XXIV).

Alongside the nominative division of the sentence, the idea of the so-called "actual division" of the sentence has been put forward in theoretical linguistics. The purpose of the actual division of the sentence, called also the "functional sentence perspective", is to reveal the correlative significance of the sentence parts from the point of view of their actual informative role in an utterance, i.e. from the point of view of the immediate semantic contribution they make to the total information conveyed by the sentence in the context of connected speech. In other words, the actual division of the sentence in fact exposes its informative perspective.

The main components of the actual division of the sentence are the *theme* and the *rheme*. The theme expresses the starting point of the communication, i.e. it denotes an object or a phenomenon about which something is reported. The rheme expresses the basic informative part of the communication, its contextually relevant centre. Between the theme and the rheme are positioned intermediary, transitional parts of the actual division of various degrees of informative value (these parts are sometimes called "transition").

The theme of the actual division of the sentence may or may not coincide with the subject of the sentence. The rheme of the actual division, in its turn, may or may not coincide with the predicate of the sentence – either with the whole predicate group or its part, such as the predicative, the object, the adverbial.

Thus, in the following sentences of various emotional character the theme is expressed by the subject, while the rheme is expressed by the predicate:

Max bounded forward. Again Charlie is being too clever! Her advice can't be of any help to us.

In the first of the above sentences the rheme coincides with the whole predicate group. In the second sentence the adverbial introducer *again* can be characterized as a transitional element, i.e. an element informationally intermediary between the theme and the rheme, the latter being expressed by the rest of the predicate group. The main part of the rheme – the "peak" of informative perspective – is rendered in this sentence by the intensified predicative *too clever*. In the third sentence the addressee object *to us* is more or less transitional, while the informative peak, as in the previous example, is expressed by the predicative *of any help*.

In the following sentences the correlation between the nominative and actual divisions is the reverse: the theme is expressed by the predicate or its part, while the rheme is rendered by the subject:

Through the open window came the purr of an approaching motor car. Who is coming late but John! There is a difference of opinion between the parties.

Historically, the theory of actual division of the sentence is connected with the logical analysis of the proposition. The principal parts of the proposition, as is known, are the logical subject and the logical predicate. These, like the theme and the rheme, may or may not coincide, respectively, with the subject and the predicate of the sentence. The logical categories of subject and predicate are prototypes of the linguistic categories of theme and rheme. However, if logic analyses its categories of subject and predicate as the meaningful components of certain forms of thinking, linguistics analyses the categories of theme and rheme as the corresponding means of expression used by the speaker for the sake of rendering the informative content of his communications.

§ 2. The actual division of the sentence finds its full expression only in a concrete context of speech, therefore it is sometimes referred to as the "contextual" division of the sentence. This can be illustrated by the following example:

Mary is fond of poetry.

In the cited sentence, if we approach it as a stylistically neutral construction devoid of any specific connotations, the theme is expressed by the subject, and the rheme, by the predicate. This kind of actual division is "direct". On the other hand, a certain context may be built around the given sentence in the conditions of which the order of actual division will be changed into the reverse: the subject will turn into the exposer of the rheme, while the predicate, accordingly, into the exposer of the theme. *Cf.*:

"Isn't it surprising that Tim is so fond of poetry?" – "But you are wrong. Mary is fond of poetry, not Tim."

The actual division in which the rheme is expressed by the subject is to be referred to as "inverted".

§ 3. The close connection of the actual division of the sentence with the context in the conditions of which it is possible to divide the informative parts of the communication into those "already known" by the listener and those "not yet known" by him, gave cause to the recognized founder of the linguistic theory of actual division J. Mathesius to consider this kind of sentence division as a purely semantic factor sharply opposed to the "formally grammatical" or "purely syntactic" division of the sentence (in our terminology called its "nominative" division).

One will agree that the actual division of the sentence will really lose all connection with syntax if its components are to be identified solely on the principle of their being "known" or "unknown" to the listener. However, we must bear in mind that the informative value of developing speech consists not only in introducing new words that denote things and phenomena not mentioned before; the informative value of communications lies also in their disclosing various new relations between the elements of reflected events, though the elements themselves may be quite familiar to the listener. The expression of a certain aspect of these relations, namely, the correlation of the said elements from the point of view of their immediate significance in a given utterance produced as a predicative item of a continual speech, does enter the structural plane of language. This expression becomes part and parcel of the structural system of language by the mere fact that the correlative informative significance of utterance components are rendered by quite definite, generalized and standardized lingual constructions. The functional purpose of such constructions is to reveal the meaningful centre of the utterance (i.e. its rheme) in distinction to the starting point of its content (i.e. its theme).

These constructions do not present any "absolutely formal", "purely differential" objects of language which are filled with semantic content only in the act of speech communication. On the contrary, they are bilateral signemic units in exactly the same sense as other meaningful constructions of language, i.e. they are distinguished both by their material form and their semantics. It follows from this that the constructional, or immediately systemic side of the phenomenon which is called the "actual division of the sentence" belongs to no other sphere of language than syntax. And the crucial syntactic destination of the whole aspect of the actual division is its rheme-identifying function, since an utterance is produced just for the sake of conveying the meaningful content expressed by its central informative part, i.e. by the rheme.

§ 4. Among the formal means of expressing the distinction between the theme and the rheme investigators name such structural elements of language as word-order patterns, intonation contours, constructions with introducers, syntactic patterns of contrastive complexes, constructions with articles and other determiners, constructions with intensifying particles.

The difference between the actual division of sentences signalled by the difference in their word-order patterns can be most graphically illustrated by the simplest type of transformations. *Cf.*:

The winner of the competition stood on the platform in the middle of the hall. → On the platform in the middle of the hall stood the winner of the competition. Fred didn't notice the flying balloon. → The one who didn't notice the flying balloon was Fred. Helen should be the first to receive her diploma. → The first to receive her diploma should be Helen.

In all the cited examples, i.e. both base sentences and their transforms, the rheme (expressed either by the subject or by an element of the predicate group) is placed towards the end of the sentence, while the theme is positioned at the beginning of it. This kind of positioning the components of the actual division corresponds to the natural development of thought from the starting point of communication to its semantic centre, or, in common parlance, from the "known data" to the "unknown (new) data". Still, in other contextual conditions, the reversed order of positioning the actual division components is used, which can be shown by the following illustrative transformations:

It was unbelievable to all of them. → Utterly unbelievable it was to all of them. Now you are speaking magic words, Nancy. → Magic words you are speaking now, Nancy. You look so well! → How well you look!

It is easily seen from the given examples that the reversed order of the actual division, i.e. the positioning of the rheme at the beginning of the sentence, is connected with emphatic speech.

Among constructions with introducers, the *there*-pattern provides for the rhematic identification of the subject without emotive connotations. *Cf.*:

Tall birches surrounded the lake. → There were tall birches surrounding the lake. A loud hoot came from the railroad. → There came a loud hoot from the railroad.

Emphatic discrimination of the rheme expressed by various parts of the sentence is achieved by constructions with the anticipatory *it. Cf.*:

Grandma gave them *a moment's deep consideration.* → It was a moment's deep consideration that Grandma gave them. She had just escaped *something simply awful.* → It was something simply awful that she had just escaped. At that moment *Laura* joined them. → It was Laura who joined them at that moment.

Syntactic patterns of contrastive complexes are used to expose the rheme of the utterance in cases when special accuracy of distinction is needed. This is explained by the fact that the actual division as such is always based on some sort of antithesis or "contraposition" (see further), which in an ordinary speech remains implicit. Thus, a syntactic contrastive complex is employed to make explicative the inner contrast inherent in the actual division by virtue of its functional nature. This can be shown on pairs of nominatively cognate examples of antithetic constructions where each member-construction will expose its own contrastively presented element. *Cf.*:

The costume is meant *not for your cousin, but for you. - - The costume, not the frock,* is meant for you, my dear. The strain told *not so much on my visitor as on myself. - - The strain of the situation, not the relaxation of it,* was what surprised me.

Determiners, among them the articles, used as means of forming certain patterns of actual division, divide their functions so that the definite determiners serve as identifiers of the theme while the indefinite determiners serve as identifiers of the rheme. *Cf.*:

*The man* walked up and down the platform. - - *A man* walked up and down the platform. *The whole book* was devoted to the description of a tiny island on the Pacific. - - *A whole book* is needed to describe that tiny island on the Pacific. I'm sure *Nora's knitting needles* will suit you. - - I'm sure *any knitting needles* will suit you.

Intensifying particles identify the rheme, commonly imparting emotional colouring to the whole of the utterance. *Cf.*:

Mr. Stores had a part in the general debate. → *Even Mr. Stores* had a part in the general debate. Then he sat down in one of the armchairs. → *Only then* did he sit down in one of the armchairs. We were impressed by what we heard and saw. → We were *so impressed* by what we heard and saw.

As for intonation as a means of realizing the actual division, it might appear that its sphere is relatively limited, being confined to oral speech only. On closer consideration, however, this view of rheme-identifying role of intonation proves inadequate. To appreciate the true status of intonation in the actual division of the sentence, one should abstract oneself from "paper syntax" (description of written texts) and remember that it is phonetical speech, i.e. articulately pronounced utterances that form the basis of human language as a whole. As soon as the phonetical nature of language is duly taken account of, intonation with its accent-patterns presents itself not as a limited, but as a universal and indisputable means of expressing the actual division in all types and varieties of lingual contexts. This universal rheme-identifying function of intonation has been described in treatises on logic, as well as in traditional philological literature, in terms of "logical accent". The "logical accent", which amounts linguistically to the "rhematic accent", is inseparable from the other rheme-identifying means described above, especially from the word-order patterns. Moreover, all such means in written texts in fact represent the logical accent, i.e. they indicate its position either directly or indirectly. This can be seen on all the examples hitherto cited in the present chapter.

§ 5. While recognizing the logical accent as a means of effecting the actual division, we must strictly distinguish between the elements immediately placed under the phonetical, "technical" stress, and the sentence segments which are identified as the informative centre of communication, in the true sense of the term.

Technically, not only notional, but functional units as well can be phrasally stressed in an utterance, which in modern printed texts is shown by special graphical ways of identification, such as italics, bold type, etc. *Cf.*:

"I can't bring along someone who isn't invited." – "But I *am* invited!" said Miss Casement (I. Murdoch). Moreover, being a highly intelligent young woman, she'd be careful *not* to be the only one affected (A. Christie).

However, it would be utterly incorrect to think that in such instances only those word-units are logically, i.e. rhematically, marked out as are stressed phonetically. As a matter of fact, functional elements cannot express any self-dependent nomination; they do not exist by themselves, but make up units of nomination together with the notional elements of utterances whose meanings they specify. Thus, the phrasal phonetical stress, technically making prominent some functional element, thereby identifies as rhematic the corresponding notional part ("knot") of the utterance as a whole. It is such notional parts that are real members of the opposition "theme – rheme", not their functional constituents taken separately. As for the said functional constituents themselves, these only set up specific semantic bases on which the relevant rhematic antitheses are built up.

§ 6. The actual division, since it is effected upon the already produced nominative sentence base providing for its contextually relevant manifestation, enters the predicative aspect of the sentence. It makes up part of syntactic predication, because it strictly meets the functional purpose of predication as such, which is to relate the nominative content of the sentence to reality (see. Ch. XXI). This predicative role of the actual division shows that its contextual relevance is not reduced to that of a passive, concomitant factor of expression. On the contrary, the actual division is an active means of expressing functional meanings, and, being organically connected with the context, it is not so much context-governed as it is context-governing: in fact, it does build up concrete contexts out of constructional sentence-models chosen to reflect different situations and events.

One of the most important manifestations of the immediate contextual relevance of the actual division is the regular deletion (ellipsis) of the thematic parts of utterances in dialogue speech. By this syntactic process, the rheme of the utterance or its most informative part (peak of informative perspective) is placed in isolation, thereby being graphically presented to the listener. *Cf.*:

"You've got the letters?" – "*In my bag*" (G.W. Target). "How did you receive him?" – "*Coldly*" (J. Galsworthy).

In other words, the thematic reduction of sentences in the context, resulting in a constructional economy of speech, performs an informative function in parallel with the logical accent: it serves to accurately identify the rheme of the utterance.

<h3 style="text-align:center">C H A P T E R XXIII</h3>

<h2 style="text-align:center">COMMUNICATIVE TYPES OF SENTENCES</h2>

§ 1. The sentence is a communicative unit, therefore the primary classification of sentences must be based on the communicative principle. This principle is formulated in traditional grammar as the "purpose of communication".

The purpose of communication, by definition, refers to the sentence as a whole, and the structural features connected with the expression of this sentential function belong to the fundamental, constitutive qualities of the sentence as a lingual unit.

In accord with the purpose of communication three cardinal sentence-types have long been recognized in linguistic tradition: first, the *declarative* sentence; second, the *imperative* (*inducive*) sentence; third, the *interrogative* sentence. These communicative sentence-types stand in strict opposition to one another, and their inner properties of form and meaning are immediately correlated with the corresponding features of the listener's responses.

Thus, the declarative sentence expresses a statement, either affirmative or negative, and as such stands in systemic syntagmatic correlation with the listener's responding signals of attention, of appraisal (including agreement or disagreement), of fellow-feeling. *Cf.*:

"I think," he said, "that Mr. Desert should be asked to give us his reasons for publishing that poem." – "Hear, hear!" said the K.C. (J. Galsworthy). "We live very quietly here, indeed we do; my niece here will tell you the same." – "Oh, come, I'm not such a fool as that," answered the squire (D. du Maurier).

The imperative sentence expresses inducement, either affirmative or negative. That is, it urges the listener, in the form of request or command, to perform or not to perform a certain action. As such, the imperative sentence is situationally connected with the corresponding "action response" (Ch. Fries), and lingually is systemically correlated with a verbal response showing that the inducement is either complied with, or else rejected. *Cf.*:

"Let's go and sit down up there, Dinny." – "Very well" (J. Galsworthy). "Then marry me." – "Really, Alan, I never met anyone with so few ideas" (J. Galsworthy). "Send him back!" he said again. – "Nonsense, old chap" (J. Aldridge).

Since the communicative purpose of the imperative sentence is to make the listener act as requested, silence on the part of the latter (when the request is fulfilled), strictly speaking, is also linguistically relevant. This gap in speech, which situationally is filled in by the listener's action, is set off in literary narration by special comments and descriptions. *Cf.*:

"Knock on the wood." – Retan's man leaned forward and knocked three times on the barrera (E. Hemingway). "Shut the piano," whispered Dinny; "let's go up." – Diana closed the piano without noise and rose (J. Galsworthy).

The interrogative sentence expresses a question, i.e. a request for information wanted by the speaker from the listener. By virtue of this communicative purpose, the interrogative sentence is naturally connected with an answer, forming together with it a question-answer dialogue unity. *Cf.*:

"What do you suggest I should do, then?" said Mary helplessly. – "If I were you I should play a waiting game," he replied (D. du Maurier).

Naturally, in the process of actual communication the interrogative communicative purpose, like any other communicative task, may sporadically not be fulfilled. In case it is not fulfilled, the question-answer unity proves to be broken; instead of a needed answer the speaker is faced by silence on the part of the listener, or else he receives the latter's verbal rejection to answer. *Cf.*:

"Why can't you lay off?" I said to her. But she didn't even notice me (R.P. Warren). "Did he know about her?" – "You'd better ask him" (S. Maugham).

Evidently, such and like reactions to interrogative sentences are not immediately relevant in terms of environmental syntactic featuring.

§ 2. Ways of expressing different purposes of communication of the speaker, i.e. his "communicative intentions", are studied by the branch of linguistics called "pragmatic linguistics", or contractedly "pragmalinguistics". In accord with the principles of pragmalinguistics, communicative intentions of the speaker are realized in his "speech acts", each of them characterized by a definite communicative intention underlying it. Such are statements of fact, conjectures, confirmations, refutations, agreements, disagreements, commands, requests, greetings at meeting, greetings at parting, exhortations, recommendations, applications for information, supplications, promises, menaces, etc. Among such and like speech acts classified as pragmatic utterance types, two mutually opposed and crucially important types are pointed out, namely "constative utterances" ("constatives") and "performative utterances" ("performatives"). Whereas constatives express the speaker's reflections of reality as they are, performatives render such verbal actions of the speaker as immediately constitute his social functions. In other words, the performative is the pronouncement by the speaker of such an action of his, as is embodied in the pronouncement itself: pronouncing this kind of utterance, the speaker *performs* his complete function; hence the term "performative utterance". *E.g.*:

I declare the conference open. (Indeed, I open the conference by pronouncing this sentence. My act of opening the conference is *performed* by declaring it open.) I disapprove of this decision! (My act of disapproving the decision is *performed* by this utterance of disapproval.)

The performative utterance includes (or implies) the pronoun of the first person singular (the direct indication of the speaker), while its verb is used only in the form of the present tense of the indicative mood, active.

It is, no doubt, quite important and necessary to study the semantics of the sentence from the point of view of the speaker's intention inherent in it. However, it must be clearly understood that performative utterances are not to be looked upon as standing in absolute isolation from the rest of the sentence-patterns of language. Far from being isolated, they are part and parcel of the syntactic system as a whole, forming regular structural and functional correlations with other predicative constructions. *E.g.*:

I declare the conference open. (Performative). – I declared the conference open. (Constative: real fact in the past). – I would have declared the conference open if... (Constative: unreal fact in the past). – He declares the conference open. (Constative: action of a third person in the present). Etc.

Thus, structural and functional considerations on purely linguistic lines (i.e. identifying and analysing lingual facts as *means* of expressing ideas) demonstrate that, peculiar as they might be from the logical point of view, performative utterances in the long run belong to the declarative type of sentences. Furthermore, the whole set of performative utterance types at any given level of generalization is subject to syntactic communicative sentence type identification based on the character of the actual division of the sentence shown above.

§ 3. An early attempt to revise the traditional communicative classification of sentences was made by the American scholar Ch. Fries who classed them, as a deliberate challenge to the "accepted routine", not in accord with the purposes of communication, but according to the responses they elicit [Fries, 29-53].

In Fries's system, as a universal speech unit subjected to communicative analysis was chosen not immediately a sentence, but an utterance unit (a "free" utterance, i.e. capable of isolation) understood as a continuous chunk of talk by one speaker in a dialogue. The sentence was then defined as a minimum free utterance.

Utterances collected from the tape-recorded corpus of dialogues (mostly telephone conversations) were first classed into "situation utterances" (eliciting a response), and "response utterances". Situation single free utterances (i.e. sentences) were further divided into three groups:

1) Utterances that are regularly followed by oral responses only. These are greetings, calls, questions. *E.g.*:

Hello! Good-bye! See you soon! ... Dad! Say, dear! Colonel Howard! ... Have you got moved in? What are you going to do for the summer? ...

2) Utterances regularly eliciting action responses. These are requests or commands. *E.g.*:

Read that again, will you? Oh, wait a minute! Please have him call Operator Six when he comes in! Will you see just exactly what his status is?

3) Utterances regularly eliciting conventional signals of attention to continuous discourse. These are statements. *E.g.*:

I've been talking with Mr. D – in the purchasing department about our type-writer. ( – Yes?). That order went in March seventh. However it seems that we are about eighth on the list. ( – I see). Etc.

Alongside the described "communicative" utterances, i.e. utterances directed to a definite listener, another, minor type of utterances were recognized as not directed to any listener but, as Ch. Fries puts it, "characteristic of situations such as surprise, sudden pain, disgust, anger, laughter, sorrow" [Fries, 53]. *E.g.*:

Oh, oh! Goodness! My God! Darn! Gosh! Etc.

Such and like interjectional units were classed by Ch. Fries as "noncommunicative" utterances.

Observing the given classification, it is not difficult to see that, far from refuting or discarding the traditional classification of sentences built up on the principle of the "purpose of communication", it rather confirms and specifies it. Indeed, the very purpose of communication inherent in the addressing sentence is reflected in the listener's response. The second and third groups of Ch. Fries's "communicative" sentences-utterances are just identical imperative and declarative types both by the employed names and definition. As for the first group, it is essentially heterogeneous, which is recognized by the investigator himself, who distinguishes in its composition three communicatively different subgroups. One of these ("C") is constituted by "questions", i.e. classical interrogative sentences. The other two, viz. greetings ("A") and calls ("B"), are syntactically not cardinal, but, rather, minor intermediary types, making up the periphery of declarative sentences (greetings – statements of conventional goodwill at meeting and parting) and imperative sentences (calls – requests for attention). As regards "noncommunicative" utterances – interjectional units, they are devoid of any immediately expressed intellective semantics, which excludes them from the general category of sentence as such (see further).

Thus, the undertaken analysis should, in point of fact, be looked upon as an actual application of the notions of communicative sentence-types to the study of oral speech, resulting in further specifications and development of these notions.

§ 4. Alongside the three cardinal communicative sentence-types, another type of sentences is recognized in the theory of syntax, namely, the so-called *exclamatory* sentence. In modern linguistics it has been demonstrated that exclamatory sentences do not possess any complete set of qualities that could place them on one and the same level with the three cardinal communicative types of sentences. The property of exclamation should be considered as an accompanying feature which is effected within the system of the three cardinal communicative types of sentences.* In other words, each of the cardinal communicative sentence-types can be represented in the two variants, viz. non-exclamatory and exclamatory. For instance, with the following exclamatory sentences-statements it is easy to identify their non-exclamatory declarative prototypes:

What a very small cabin it was! (K. Mansfield) ← It was a very small cabin. How utterly she had lost count of events! (J. Galsworthy) ← She had lost count of events. Why, if it isn't my lady! (J. Erskine) ← It is my lady.

Similarly, exclamatory questions are immediately related in the syntactic system to the corresponding non-exclamatory interrogative sentences. *E.g.*:

Whatever do you mean, Mr. Critchlow? (A. Bennett) ← What do you mean? Then why in God's name did you come? (K. Mansfield) ← Why did you come?

Imperative sentences, naturally, are characterized by a higher general degree of emotive intensity than the other two cardinal communicative sentence-types. Still, they form analogous pairs, whose constituent units are distinguished from each other by no other feature than the presence or absence of exclamation as such. *E.g.*:

---

* See: Грамматика русского языка. М., 1960. Т. 2. Синтаксис, ч. I, с. 353; 365 и сл.

Francis, will you please try to speak sensibly! (E. Hemingway) ← Try to speak sensibly. Don't you dare to compare me to common people! (B. Shaw) ← Don't compare me to common people. Never so long as you live say I made you do that! (J. Erskine) ← Don't say I made you do that.

As is seen from the given examples, all the three pairs of variant communicative types of sentences (non-exclamatory – exclamatory for each cardinal division) make up distinct semantico-syntactic oppositions effected by regular grammatical means of language, such as intonation, word-order and special constructions with functional-auxiliary lexemic elements. It follows from this that the functional-communicative classification of sentences specially distinguishing emotive factor should discriminate, at the lower level of analysis, between the six sentence-types forming, respectively, three groups (pairs) of cardinal communicative quality.

§ 5. The communicative properties of sentences can further be exposed in the light of the theory of actual division of the sentence.

The actual division provides for the informative content of the utterance to be expressed with the due gradation of its parts according to the significance of their respective role in the context. But any utterance is formed within the framework of the system of communicative types of sentences. And as soon as we compare the communication-purpose aspect of the utterance with its actual division aspect we shall find that each communicative sentence-type is distinguished by its specific actual division features, which are revealed first and foremost in the nature of the rheme as the meaningful nucleus of the utterance.

The strictly declarative sentence immediately expresses a certain proposition. By virtue of this, the actual division of the declarative sentence presents itself in the most developed and complete form. The rheme of the declarative sentence makes up the centre of some statement as such. This can be distinctly demonstrated by a question-test directly revealing the rhematic part of an utterance. Cf.:

The next instant she had recognized him. → What had she done the next instant?

The pronominal what-question clearly exposes in the example the part "(had) recognized him" as the declarative rheme, for this part is placed within the interrogative-pronominal reference. In other words, the tested utterance with its completed actual division is the only answer to the cited potential question; the utterance has been produced by the speaker just to express the fact of "his being recognized".

Another transformational test for the declarative rheme is the logical superposition. The logical superposition consists in transforming the tested construction into the one where the rheme is placed in the position of the logically emphasized predicate. By way of example let us take the second sentence in the following sequence:

And I was very uneasy. All sorts of forebodings assailed me.

The logical superposition of the utterance is effected thus: → What assailed me was all sorts of forebodings.

This test marks out the subject of the utterance "all sorts of forebodings" as the rheme, because it is just this part of the utterance that is placed in the emphatic position of the predicate in the superpositional transform.

Similar diagnostic procedures expose the layer-structure of the actual division in composite syntactic constructions. For instance, in the following complex sentence rhematic question-tests easily reveal the three declarative rhemes on the three consecutive syntactic layers:

I knew that Mr. Wade had been very excited by something that he had found out.

Test for the first syntactic layer: What did I know?

Test for the second syntactic layer: What state was Mr. Wade in?

Test for the third syntactic layer: What made him excited? (By what was he excited?)

The strictly imperative sentence, as different from the strictly declarative sentence, does not express by its immediate destination any statement of fact, i.e. any proposition proper. It is only based on a proposition, without formulating it directly. Namely, the proposition underlying the imperative sentence is reversely contrasted against the content of the expressed inducement, since an urge to do something (affirmative inducement) is founded on the premise that something is not done or is otherwise not affected by the wanted action, and, conversely, an urge not to do something (negative inducement) is founded on the directly opposite premise. Cf.:

250

Let's go out at once! (The premise: We are in.) Never again take that horrible woman into your confidence, Jerry! (The premise: Jerry has taken that horrible woman into his confidence.)

Thus, the rheme of the imperative utterance expresses the informative nucleus not of an explicit proposition, but of an inducement – a wanted (or unwanted) action together with its referential attending elements (objects, qualities, circumstances).

Due to the communicative nature of the inducement addressed to the listener, its thematic subject is usually zeroed, though it can be represented in the form of direct address. *Cf.*:

Don't try to sidetrack me (J. Braine). Put that dam' dog down, Fleur; I can't see your face (J. Galsworthy). Kindly tell me what you meant, Wilfrid (J. Galsworthy).

Inducements that include in the address also the speaker himself, or are directed, through the second person medium, to a third person (persons) present their thematic subjects explicitly in the construction. *E.g.*:

I say, Bob, let's try to reconstruct the scene as it developed. Please don't let's quarrel over the speeds now. Let her produce the document if she has it.

The whole composition of an ordinary imperative utterance is usually characterized by a high informative value, so that the rheme proper, or the informative peak, may stand here not so distinctly against the background information as in the declarative utterance. Still, rhematic testing of imperative utterances does disclose the communicative stratification of their constituents. Compare the question-tests of a couple of the cited examples:

Put that dam' dog down, Fleur. → What is Fleur to do with the dog? Kindly tell me what you meant, Wilfrid. → What is Wilfrid to tell the speaker?

As for the thematic, and especially the subrhematic (transitional) elements of the imperative utterance, they often are functionally charged with the type-grading of inducement itself, i.e. with making it into a command, prohibition, request, admonition, entreaty, etc. Compare, in addition to the cited, some more examples to this effect:

Let us at least remember to admire each other (L. Hellman). Oh, please stop it... Please, please stop it (E. Hemingway). Get out before I break your dirty little neck (A. Hailey).

The second-person inducement may include the explicit pronominal subject, but such kind of constructions should be defined as of secondary derivation. They are connected with a complicated informative content to be conveyed to the listener-performer, expressing, on the one hand, the choice of the subject out of several persons-participants of the situation, and on the other hand, appraisals rendering various ethical connotations (in particular, the type-grading of inducement mentioned above). Cf.:

"What about me?" she asked. – "Nothing doing. You go to bed and sleep" (A. Christie). Don't you worry about me, sir. I shall be all right (B.K. Seymour).

At a further stage of complication, the subject of the inducement may be shifted to the position of the rheme. E.g.:

"... We have to do everything we can." – "You do it," he said. "I'm tired" (E. Hemingway).

The essentially different identifications of the rheme in the two imperative utterances of the cited example can be proved by transformational testing: ... → What we have to do is (to do) everything we can. ... → The person who should do it is you.

The inducement with the rhematic subject of the latter type may be classed as the "(informatively) shifted inducement".

§ 6. As far as the strictly interrogative sentence is concerned, its actual division is uniquely different from the actual division of both the declarative and the imperative sentence-types.

The unique quality of the interrogative actual division is determined by the fact that the interrogative sentence, instead of conveying some relatively self-dependent content, expresses an inquiry about information which the speaker (as a participant of a typical question-answer situation) does not possess. Therefore the rheme of the interrogative sentence, as the nucleus of the inquiry, is informationally open (gaping); its function consists only in marking the rhematic position in the response sentence and programming the content of its filler in accord with the nature of the inquiry.

Different types of questions present different types of open rhemes.

In the pronominal ("special") question, the nucleus of inquiry is expressed by an interrogative pronoun. The pronoun is immediately connected with the part of the sentence denoting the object or phenomenon about which the inquiry ("condensed" in the pronoun) is made. The gaping pronominal meaning is to be replaced in the answer by the wanted actual information. Thus, the rheme of the answer is the reverse substitute of the interrogative pronoun: the two make up a rhematic unity in the broader question-answer construction. As for the thematic part of the answer, it is already expressed in the question, therefore in common speech it is usually zeroed. E.g.:

"Why do you think so?" – "Because mostly I keep my eyes open, miss, and I talk to people" (A. Hailey).

The superpositional rhematic test for the pronominal question may be effected in the following periphrastic-definitional form: → The question about your thinking so is: why?

For the sake of analytical convenience this kind of superposition may be reduced as follows: → You think so – why?

Compare some more pronominal interrogative superpositions:

What happens to a man like Hawk Harrap as the years go by? (W. Saroyan). → To a man like Hawk Harrap, as the years go by – what happens? How do you make that out, mother? (E.M. Forster) → You make that out, mother, – how? How's the weather in the north? (D. du Maurier) → The weather in the north – how is it? What's behind all this? (A. Hailey) → Behind all this is – what?

The rheme of non-pronominal questions is quite different from the one described. It is also open, but its openness consists in at least two semantic suggestions presented for choice to the listener. The choice is effected in the response; in other words, the answer closes the suggested alternative according to the interrogative-rhematic programme inherent in it. This is clearly seen in the structure of ordinary, explicit alternative questions. E.g.: Will you take it away or open it here? (Th. Dreiser)

The superposition of the utterance may be presented as follows: → You in relation to it – will take (it) away, will open (it) here?

The alternative question may have a pronominal introduction, emphasizing the open character of its rheme. Cf.:

In which cave is the offence alleged, the Buddhist or the Jain? (E.M. Forster)

The superposition: → The offence is alleged – in the Buddhist cave, in the Jain cave?

Thus, in terms of rhematic reverse substitution, the pronominal question is a question of unlimited substitution choice, while the alternative question is a question of a limited substitution choice, the substitution of the latter kind being, as a rule, expressed implicitly. This can be demonstrated by a transformation applied to the first, of the two cited examples of alternative questions: Will you take it away or open it here? → Where will you handle it – take it away or open it here?

The non-pronominal question requiring either confirmation or negation ("general" question of *yes-no* response type) is thereby implicitly alternative, though the inquiry inherent in it concerns not the choice between some suggested facts, but the choice between the existence or non-existence of an indicated fact. In other words, it is a question of realized rhematic substitution (or of "no substitution choice"), but with an open existence factor (true to life or not true to life?), which makes up its implicitly expressed alternative. This can be easily shown by a superposition: Are they going to stay long? → They are going to stay – long, not long?

The implicit alternative question can be made into an explicit one, which as a rule is very emphatic, i.e. stylistically "forced". The negation in the implied alternative part is usually referred to the verb. *Cf.*: → Are they going to stay long, or are they not going to stay long?

The cited relation of this kind of question to interrogative reverse substitution (and, together with it, the open character of its rheme) is best demonstrated by the corresponding pronominal transformation: → How long are they going to stay – long (or not long)?

As we see, the essential difference between the two types of alternative questions, the explicit one and the implicit one, remains valid even if the latter is changed into an explicit alternative question (i.e. into a stylistically forced explicit alternative question). This difference is determined by the difference in the informative composition of the interrogative constructions compared.

In general terms of meaning, the question of the first type (the normal explicit alternative question) should be classed as the alternative question of fact, since a choice between two or more facts is required by it; the question of the second type (the implicit alternative question) should be classed as the alternative question of truth, since it requires the statement of truth or non-truth of the indi-

254

cated fact. In terms of actual division, the question of the first type should be classed as the polyperspective alternative question (biperspective, triperspective, etc.), because it presents more than one informative perspectives (more than one actual divisions) for the listener's choice; the question of the second type, as opposed to the polyperspective, should be classed as the monoperspective alternative question, because its both varieties (implicit and explicit) express only one informative perspective, which is presented to the listener for the existential *yes-no* appraisal.

§ 7. The exposition of the fundamental role of actual division in the formation of the communicative sentence-types involves, among other things, the unequivocal refutation of recognizing by some linguists the would-be "purely exclamatory sentence" that cannot be reduced to any of the three demonstrated cardinal communicative types.[*]

Indeed, by "purely exclamatory sentences" are meant no other things than interjectional exclamations of ready-made order such as "Great Heavens!", "Good Lord!", "For God's sake!", "Fiddle-dee-dee!", "Oh, I say!" and the like, which, due to various situational conditions, find themselves in self-dependent, proposemically isolated positions in the text. *Cf.*:

"Oh, for God's sake!" – "Oh, for God's sake!" the boy had repeated (W. Saroyan). "Ah!" said Lady Mont. "That reminds me" (J. Galsworthy).

As is seen from the examples, the isolated positions of the interjectional utterances do not make them into any meaningfully articulate, grammatically predicated sentences with their own informative perspective (either explicit, or implicit). They remain not signals of proposemically complete thoughts, not "communicative utterances" (see above), but mere symptoms of emotions, consciously or unconsciously produced shouts of strong feelings. Therefore the highest rank that they deserve in any relevant linguistic classification of "single free units of speech" is "non-sentential utterances" (which is just another name for Ch. Fries's "noncommunicative utterances").

Of quite another nature are exclamatory sentences with emphatic introducers derived on special productive syntactic patterns. *Cf.*:

---

[*] The existence of the "purely exclamatory sentence" is defended, in particular, by B.A. Ilyish in his cited book (p. 186-187).

Oh, that Mr. Thornspell hadn't been so reserved! How silly of you! If only I could raise the necessary sum! Etc.

These constructions also express emotions, but they are meaningfully articulate and proposemically complete. They clearly display a definite nominative composition which is predicated, i.e. related to reality according to the necessary grammatical regularities. And they inevitably belong to quite a definite communicative type of sentences, namely, to the declarative type.

§ 8. The vast set of constructional sentence models possessed by language is formed not only by cardinal, monofunctional communicative types; besides these, it includes also intermediary predicative constructions distinguished by mixed communicative features. The true nature of such intermediary constructions can be disclosed in the light of the actual division theory combined with the general theory of paradigmatic oppositions.

Observations conducted on the said principles show that intermediary communicative sentence models may be identified between all the three cardinal communicative correlations (viz., statement – question, statement – inducement, inducement – question); they have grown and are sustained in language as a result of the transference of certain characteristic features from one communicative type of sentences to another.

§ 9. In the following dialogue sequence the utterance which is declarative by its formal features, at the same time contains a distinct pronominal question:

"*I wonder why they come to me about it.* That's your job, sweetheart." – I looked up from Jasper, my face red as fire. "Darling," I said, "I meant to tell you before, but – but I forgot" (D. du Maurier).

Semantico-syntactic comparison of the two utterances produced by the participants of the cited dialogue clearly shows in the initial utterance the features inherently peculiar to the interrogative communicative type, namely, its open rhematic part ("why they come to me about it") and the general programming character of its actual division in relation to the required response.

Compare some more examples of a similar nature:

"But surely I may treat him as a human being." – "Most certainly not" (B. Shaw). "I don't disturb you, I hope, Mr

Cokane." – "By no means" (B. Shaw). "Wait a second, you haven't told me your address." – "Oh, I'm staying at the Hotel du Phare" (A. Christie). "I should like to hear your views on that," replied Utterson (R.L. Stevenson).

As is seen from the examples, utterances intermediary between statements and questions convey meanings and connotations that supplement the direct programming of the answer effected by strictly monofunctional, cardinal interrogative constructions. Namely, they render the connotation of insistence in asking for information, they express a more definite or less definite supposition of the nature of information possessed by the listener, they present a suggestion to the listener to perform a certain action or imply a request for permisson to perform an action, etc.

On the other hand, in the structural framework of the interrogative sentence one can express a statement. This type of utterance is classed as the "rhetorical question" – an expressive construction that has been attracting the closest attention of linguistic observers since ancient times.

A high intensity of declarative functional meaning expressed by rhetorical questions is best seen in various proverbs and maxims based on this specifically emphatic predicative unit. *Cf.*:

Can a leopard change his spots? Can man be free if woman be a slave? O shame! Where is thy blush? Why ask the Bishop when the Pope's around? Who shall decide when the doctors disagree?

Compare rhetorical questions in stylistically freer, more common forms of speech:

That was my mission, you imagined. It was not, but where was I to go? (O. Wilde) That was all right; I meant what I said. Why should I feel guilty about it? (J. Braine) How could I have ever thought I could get away with it! (J. Osborne)

It should be noted that in living speech responses to rhetorical questions exactly correspond to responses elicited by declarative sentences: they include signals of attention, appraisals, expressions of fellow feeling, etc. *Cf.*:

"How can a woman be expected to be happy with a man who insists on treating her as if she were a perfectly rational being?" – "My dear!" (O. Wilde)

A rhetorical question in principle can be followed by a direct answer, too. However, such an answer does not fill up the rheme of the rhetorical question (which, as different from the rheme of a genuine question, is not at all open), but emphatically accentuates its intensely declarative semantic nature. An answer to a rhetorical question also emphasizes its affirmative or negative implication which is opposite to the formal expression of affirmation or negation in the outer structure of the question. *Cf.*:

"What more can a gentleman desire in this world?" – "Nothing more, I am quite sure" (O. Wilde).

Due to these connotations, the answer to a rhetorical question can quite naturally be given by the speaker himself:

Who, being in love, is poor? Oh, no one (O. Wilde).

The declarative nature of the rhetorical question is revealed also in the fact that it is not infrequently used as an answer to a genuine question – namely, in cases when an expressive, emphatic answer is needed. *Cf.*:

"Do you expect to save the country, Mr Mangan?" – "Well, who else will?" (B. Shaw)

Rhetorical questions as constructions of intermediary communicative nature should be distinguished from such genuine questions as are addressed by the speaker to himself in the process of deliberation and reasoning. The genuine quality of the latter kind of questions is easily exposed by observing the character of their rhematic elements. *E.g.*:

Had she had what was called a complex all this time? Or was love always sudden like this? A wild flower seeding on a wild wind? (J. Galsworthy)

The cited string of questions belongs to the inner speech of a literary personage presented in the form of non-personal direct speech. The rhemes of the questions are definitely open, i.e. they are typical of ordinary questions in a dialogue produced by the speaker with an aim to obtain information from his interlocutor. This is clearly seen from the fact that the second question presents an alternative in relation to the first question; as regards the third question, it is not a self-dependent utterance, but a specification, cumulatively attached to the foregoing construction.

258

Genuine questions to oneself as part of monologue deliberations can quite naturally be followed by corresponding responses, forming various kinds of dialogue within monologue. *Cf.*:

Was she tipsy, week-minded, or merely in love? Perhaps all three! (J. Galsworthy). My God! What shall I do? I dare not tell her who this woman really is. The shame would kill her (O. Wilde).

§ 10. The next pair of correlated communicative sentence types between which are identified predicative constructions of intermediary nature are declarative and imperative sentences.

The expression of inducement within the framework of a declarative sentence is regularly achieved by means of constructions with modal verbs. *E.g.*:

You ought to get rid of it, you know (C.P. Snow). "You can't come in," he said. "You mustn't get what I have" (E. Hemingway). Well, you must come to me now for anything you want, or I shall be quite cut up (J. Galsworthy). "You might as well sit down," said Javotte (J. Erskine).

Compare semantically more complex constructions in which the meaning of inducement is expressed as a result of interaction of different grammatical elements of an utterance with its notional lexical elements:

"And if you'll excuse me, Lady Eileen, I think it's time you were going back to bed." The firmness of his tone admitted of no parley (A. Christie). If you have anything to say to me, Dr Trench, I will listen to you patiently. You will then allow me to say what I have to say on my part (B. Shaw).

Inducive constructions, according to the described general tendency, can be used to express a declarative meaning complicated by corresponding connotations. Such utterances are distinguished by especially high expressiveness and intensity. *E.g.*:

The Forsyte in him said: "Think, feel, and you're done for!" (J. Galsworthy)

Due to its expressiveness this kind of declarative inducement, similar to rhetorical questions, is used in maxims and proverbs. *E.g.*:

Talk of the devil and he will appear. Roll my log and I will roll yours. Live and learn. Live and let live.

Compare also corresponding negative statements of the formal imperative order:

Don't count your chickens before they are hatched. Don't cross the bridge till you get to it.

§ 11. Imperative and interrogative sentences make up the third pair of opposed cardinal communicative sentence types serving as a frame for intermediary communicative patterns.

Imperative sentences performing the essential function of interrogative sentences are such as induce the listener not to action, but to speech. They may contain indirect questions. *E.g.*:

"Tell me about your upbringing." – "I should like to hear about yours" (E.J. Howard). "Please tell me what I can do. There must be something I can do." – "You can take the leg off and that might stop it..." (E. Hemingway).

The reverse intermediary construction, i.e. inducement effected in the form of question, is employed in order to convey such additional shades of meaning as request, invitation, suggestion, softening of a command, etc. *E.g.*:

"Why don't you get Aunt Em to sit instead, Uncle? She's younger than I am any day, aren't you, Auntie?" (J. Galsworthy). "Would – would you like to come?" – "I would," said Jimmy heartily. "Thanks ever so much, Lady Coote" (A. Christie).

Additional connotations in inducive utterances having the form of questions may be expressed by various modal constructions. *E.g.*:

Can I take you home in a cab? (W. Saroyan) "Could you tell me," said Dinny, "of any place close by where I could get something to eat?" (J. Galsworthy) I am really quite all right. Perhaps you will help me up the stairs? (A. Christie)

In common use the expression of inducement is effected in the form of a disjunctive question. The post-positional interrogative tag imparts to the whole inducive utterance a more pronounced or less pronounced shade of a polite request or even makes it into a pleading appeal. *Cf.*:

Find out tactfully what he wants, will you? (J. Tey). And you will come too, Basil, won't you? (O. Wilde)

§ 12. The undertaken survey of lingual facts shows that the combination of opposite cardinal communicative features displayed by communicatively intermediary sentence patterns is structurally systemic and functionally justified. It is justified because it meets quite definite expressive requirements. And it is symmetrical in so far as each cardinal communicative sentence type is characterized by the same tendency of functional transposition in relation to the two other communicative types opposing it. It means that within each of the three cardinal communicative oppositions two different intermediary communicative sentence models are established, so that at a further level of specification, the communicative classification of sentences should be expanded by six subtypes of sentences of mixed communicative features. These are, first, mixed sentence patterns of declaration (interrogative-declarative, imperative-declarative); second, mixed sentence patterns of interrogation (declarative-interrogative, imperative-interrogative); third, mixed sentence patterns of inducement (declarative-imperative, interrogative-imperative). All the cited intermediary communicative types of sentences belong to living, productive syntactic means of language and should find the due reflection both in theoretical linguistic description and in practical language teaching.

## CHAPTER XXIV

## SIMPLE SENTENCE: CONSTITUENT STRUCTURE

§ 1. The basic predicative meanings of the typical English sentence, as has already been pointed out, are expressed by the finite verb which is immediately connected with the subject of the sentence. This predicative connection is commonly referred to as the "predicative line" of the sentence. Depending on their predicative complexity, sentences can feature one predicative line or several (more than one) predicative lines; in other words, sentences may be, respectively, "monopredicative" and "polypredicative". Using this distinction, we must say that the simple sentence is a sentence in which only one predicative line is expressed. *E.g.*:

Bob has never *left* the stadium. Opinions *differ*. This *may happen* any time. The offer *might have been* quite fair. Etc.

According to this definition, sentences with several predicates re-ferring to one and the same subject cannot be considered as simple. *E.g.*:

I *took* the child in my arms and *held* him.

It is quite evident that the cited sentence, although it includes only one subject, expresses two different predicative lines, since its two predicates are separately connected with the subject. The content of the sentence reflects two closely connected events that happened in immediate succession: the first – "my taking the child in my arms"; the second – "my holding him".

Sentences having one verb-predicate and more than one subject to it, if the subjects form actually separate (though interdependent) predicative connections, cannot be considered as simple, either. *E.g.*:

*The door* was open, and also the *front window*.

Thus, the syntactic feature of strict monopredication should serve as the basic diagnostic criterion for identifying the simple sentence in contrast to sentences of composite structures of various systemic standings.

§ 2. The simple sentence, as any sentence in general, is orga-nized as a system of function-expressing positions, the content of the functions being the reflection of a situational event. The nominative parts of the simple sentence, each occupying a notional position in it, are subject, predicate, object, adverbial, attribute, parenthetical enclo-sure, addressing enclosure; a special, semi-notional position is occu-pied by an interjectional enclosure. The parts are arranged in a hier-archy, wherein all of them perform some modifying role. The ulti-mate and highest object of this integral modification is the sentence as a whole, and through the sentence, the reflection of the situation (situational event).

Thus, the subject is a person-modifier of the predicate. The predicate is a process-modifier of the subject-person. The object is a substance-modifier of a processual part (actional or statal). The ad-verbial is a quality-modifier (in a broad sense) of a processual part or the whole of the sentence (as expressing an integral process in-herent in the reflected event). The attribute is a quality-modifier of a substantive part. The parenthetical enclosure is a detached speaker-bound modifier of any sentence-part or the whole of the sentence. The addressing enclosure (address) is a substantive modifier of the destination of the sentence and hence, from its angle, a modifier of the sentence as a whole. The interjectional enclosure is a speaker-bound emotional modifier of the sentence.

All the said modifiers may be expressed either singly (single modifiers) or collectively, i.e. in a coordinative combination (co-modifiers, in particular, homogeneous ones).

The traditional scheme of sentence parsing shows many essential traits of the said functional hierarchy. On the scheme presented graphically, sentence-parts connected by bonds of immediate domination are placed one under the other in a successive order of subordination, while sentence-parts related to one another equipotently are placed in a horizontal order. Direct connections between the sentence-parts are represented by horizontal and vertical lines.

By way of example, let us take an ordinary English sentence featuring the basic modifier connections, and see its traditional parsing presentation (Fig. 4):

The small lady listened to me attentively.

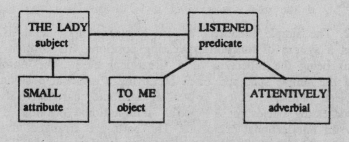

Fig. 4

The scheme clearly shows the basic logical-grammatical connections of the notional constituents of the sentence. If necessary, it can easily be supplemented with specifying linguistic information, such as indications of lexico-grammatical features of the sentence parts the same as their syntactic sub-functions.

However, observing the given scheme carefully, we must note its one serious flaw. As a matter of fact, while distinctly exposing the *subordination ranks* of the parts of the sentence, it fails to consistently present their genuine *linear order* in speech.

This drawback is overcome in another scheme of analysis called the "model of immediate constituents" (contractedly, the "IC-model").

The model of immediate constituents is based on the group-parsing of the sentence which has been developed by traditional grammar together with the sentence-part parsing scheme. It consists in dividing the whole of the sentence into two groups: that of the subject and that of the predicate, which, in their turn, are divided into their sub-group constituents according to the successive subordinative order of the latter. Profiting by this type of analysis, the IC-model explicitly exposes the binary hierarchical principle of subordinative connections, showing the whole structure of the sentence as made up by binary immediate constituents. As for equipotent (coordinative) connections, these are, naturally, non-binary, but, being of a more primitive character than subordinative connections, they are included in the analysis as possible inner subdivisions of subordinative connections.

Thus, structured by the IC-model, the cited sentence at the upper level of analysis is looked upon as a united whole (the accepted symbol S); at the next lower level it is divided into two maximal constituents – the subject noun-phrase (NP-subj) and the predicate verb-phrase (VP-pred); at the next lower level the subject noun-phrase is divided into the determiner (det) and the rest of the phrase to which it semantically refers (NP), while the predicate noun-phrase is divided into the adverbial (DP, in this case simply D) and the rest of the verb-phrase to which it semantically refers; the next level stages of analysis include the division of the first noun-phrase into its adjective-attribute constituent (AP, in this case A) and the noun constituent (N), and correspondingly, the division of the verb-phrase into its verb constituent (V or Vf – finite verb) and object noun-phrase constituent (NP-obj), the latter being, finally, divided into the preposition constituent (prp) and noun constituent (N). As we see, the process of syntactic IC-analysis continues until the word-level of the sentence is reached, the words being looked upon as the "ultimate" constituents of the sentence.

The described model of immediate constituents has two basic versions. The first is known as the "analytical IC-diagram", the second, as the "IC-derivation tree". The analytical IC-diagram commonly shows the groupings of sentence constituents by means of vertical and horizontal lines (see Fig. 5). The IC-derivation tree shows the groupings of sentence constituents by means of branching nodes: the nodes symbolize phrase-categories as unities, while the branches mark their division into constituents of the corresponding sub-categorial standings (see Fig. 6).

| THE | SMALL | LADY | LISTENED | TO prp | ME NP-pro | ATTENTIVELY. |
|---|---|---|---|---|---|---|
| | A | N | V | | NP | |
| det | | NP | VP | | | D |
| NP-subj | | | | | | VP-pred |

Fig. 5

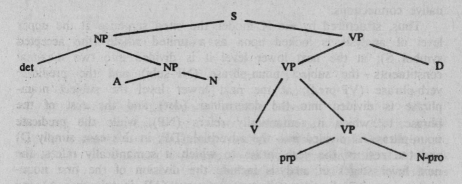

Fig. 6

§ 3. When analysing sentences in terms of syntagmatic connections of their parts, two types of subordinative relations are exposed: on the one hand, *obligatory* relations, i.e. such as are indispensable for the existence of the syntactic unit as such; on the other hand, *optional* relations, i.e. such as may or may not be actually represented in the syntactic unit. These relations, as we have pointed out elsewhere, are at present interpreted in terms of syntactic valency (combining power of the word) and are of especial importance for the characteristic of the verb as the central predicative organizer of the notional stock of sentence constituents. Comparing the IC-representation of the sentence with the pattern of obligatory syntactic positions directly determined by the valency of the verb-predicate, it is easy to see that this pattern reveals the essential generalized model of the sentence, its semantico-syntactic backbone. For instance, in the cited sentence this pattern will be expressed by the string *"The lady listened to me"*, the attribute *small* and the adverbial *attentively* being the optional parts of the sentence. The IC-model of this key-string of the sentence is logically transparent and easily grasped by the mind (see Fig. 7).

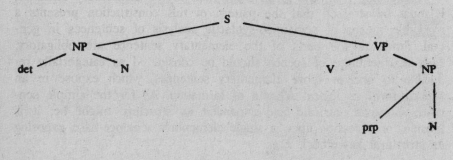

Fig. 7

Thus, the idea of verbal valency, answering the principle of dividing all the notional sentence parts into obligatory and optional, proves helpful in gaining a further insight into the structure of the simple sentence; moreover, it is of crucial importance for the modern definition of the simple sentence.

In terms of valencies and obligatory positions first of all the category of "elementary sentence" is to be rocognized; this is a sentence all the positions of which are obligatory. In other words, this is a sentence which, besides the principal parts, includes only complementive modifiers; as for supplementive modifiers, they find no place in this type of predicative construction.

After that the types of expansion should be determined which do not violate the syntactic status of the simple sentence, i.e. do not change the simple sentence into a composite one. Taking into consideration the strict monopredicative character of the simple sentence as its basic identification predicative feature, we infer that such expansions should not complicate the predicative line of the sentence by any additional predicative positions.

Finally, bearing in mind that the general identification of obligatory syntactic positions affects not only the principal parts of the sentence but is extended to the complementive secondary parts, we define the *unexpanded simple sentence* as a monopredicative sentence formed only by obligatory notional parts. The *expanded simple sentence* will, accordingly, be defined as a monopredicative sentence which includes, besides the obligatory parts, also some optional parts, i.e. some supplementive modifiers which do not constitute a predicative enlargement of the sentence.

Proceeding from the given description of the elementary sentence, it must be stressed that the pattern of this construction presents a workable means of semantico-syntactic analysis of sentences in general. Since all the parts of the elementary sentence are obligatory, each real sentence of speech should be conside d as categorially reducible to one or more elementary sentences, which expose in an explicit form its logical scheme of formation. As for the simple sentence, however intricate and expanded its structure might be, it is formed, of necessity, upon a single elementary sentence-base exposing its structural key-model. *E.g.*:

The tall trees by the island shore were shaking violently in the gusty wind.

This is an expanded simple sentence including a number of optional parts, and its complete analysis in terms of a syntagmatic parsing is rather intricate. On the other hand, applying the idea of the elementary sentence, we immediately reveal that the sentence is built upon the key-string "The trees were shaking", i.e. on the syntagmatic pattern of an intransitive verb.

As we see, the notions "elementary sentence" and "sentence model" do not exclude each other, but, on the contrary, supplement each other: a model is always an abstraction, whereas an elementary sentence can and should be taken both as an abstract category (in the capacity of the "model of an elementary sentence") and as an actual utterance of real speech.

§ 4. The subject-group and the predicate-group of the sentence are its two constitutive "members", or, to choose a somewhat more specific term, its "axes" (in the Russian grammatical tradition – «составы предложения»). According as both members are present in the composition of the sentence or only one of them, sentences are classed into "two-member" and "one-member" ones.

Scholars point out that "genuine" one-member sentences are characterized not only as expressing one member in their outer structure; in addition, as an essential feature, they do not imply the other member on the contextual lines. In other words, in accord with this view, elliptical sentences in which the subject or the predicate is contextually omitted, are analysed as "two-member" sentences [Ilyish, 190, 252].

We cannot accept the cited approach because, in our opinion, it is based on an inadequate presupposition that in the system of language there is a strictly defined, "absolute" demarcation line between the two types of constructions. In reality, though, each one-member sentence, however pure it might appear from the point of view of non-association with an ellipsis, still, on closer observation, does expose traits of this association.

For instance, the sentence "Come on!" exemplifying one of the classical one-member sentence varieties, implies a situational person (persons) stimulated to perform an action, i.e. the subject of the event. Similarly, the construction "All right!" rendering agreement on the part of the speaker, is a representative unit standing for a normal two-member utterance in its contextual-bound implication plane, otherwise it would be senseless.

Bearing in mind the advanced objection, our approach to the syntactic category of axis part of the sentence is as follows.

All simple sentences of English should be divided into *two-axis* constructions and *one-axis* constructions.

In a two-axis sentence, the subject axis and the predicate axis are directly and explicitly expressed in the outer structure. This concerns all the three cardinal communicative types of sentences. *E.g.*:

The books come out of the experiences. What has been happening here? You better go back to bed.

In a one-axis sentence only one axis or its part is explicitly expressed, the other one being non-presented in the outer structure of the sentence. *Cf.*:

"Who will meet us at the airport?" – "Mary."

The response utterance is a one-axis sentence with the subject-axis expressed and the predicate-axis implied: → *Mary will meet us at the airport. Both the non-expression of the predicate and its actual implication in the sub-text are obligatory, since the complete two-axis construction renders its own connotations.

"And what is your opinion of me?" – "Hard as nails, absolutely ruthless, a born intriguer, and as self-centred as they make 'em."

The response utterance is a one-axis sentence with the predicate-axis expressed (partially, by its predicative unit) and the subject-axis (together with the link-verb of the predicate) implied: → *You are hard as nails, etc.

"I thought he might have said something to you about it." – "Not a word."

The response utterance is a one-axis sentence with the predicate-axis partially expressed (by the object) and the subject-axis together with the verbal part of the predicate-axis implied: → *He said not a word to me.

"Glad to see you after all these years!"

The sentence is a one-axis unit with the predicate-axis expressed and the subject-axis implied as a form of familiarity: → *I am glad to see you ...

All the cited examples belong to "elliptical" types of utterances in so far as they possess quite definite "vacant" positions or zero-positions capable of being supplied with the corresponding fillers implicit in the situational contexts. Since the restoration of the absent axis in such sentences is, so to speak, "free of avail", we class them as "free" one-axis sentences. The term "elliptical" one-axis sentences can also be used, though it is not very lucky here; indeed, "ellipsis" as a sentence-curtailing process can in principle affect both two-axis and one-axis sentences, so the term might be misleading.

Alongside the demonstrated free one-axis sentences, i.e. sentences with a direct contextual axis-implication, there are one-axis sentences without a contextual implication of this kind; in other words, their absent axis cannot be restored with the same ease and, above all, semantic accuracy.

By way of example, let us read the following passage from S. Maugham's short story "Appearance and Reality":

Monsieur Le Sueur was a man of action. He went straight up to Lisette and smacked her hard on her right cheek with his left hand

and then smacked her hard on the left cheek with his right hand. "Brute," screamed Lisette.

The one-axis sentence used by the heroine does imply the *you*-subject and can, by association, be expanded into the two-axis one "You are a brute" or "You brute", but then the spontaneous "scream-style" of the utterance in the context (a cry of indignation and revolt) will be utterly distorted.

Compare another context, taken from R. Kipling's "The Light That Failed":

"... I'm quite miserable enough already." – "Why? Because you're going away from Mrs Jennett?" – "No." – "From me, then?" No answer for a long time. Dick dared not look at her.

The one-axis sentence "No answer for a long time" in the narrative is associated by variant lingual relations with the two-axis sentence "There was no answer...". But on similar grounds the association can be extended to the construction "He received no answer for a long time" or "No answer was given for a long time" or some other sentence supplementing the given utterance and rendering a like meaning. On the other hand, the peculiar position in the text clearly makes all these associations into remote ones: the two-axis version of the construction instead of the existing one-axis one would destroy the expressive property of the remark conveying Dick's strain by means of combining the author's line of narration with the hero's inner perception of events.

Furthermore, compare the psychologically tense description of packing up before departure given in short, deliberately disconnected nominative phrase-sentences exposing the heroine's disillusions (from D. du Maurier's "Rebecca"):

Packing up. The nagging worry of departure. Lost keys, unwritten labels, tissue paper lying on the floor. I hate it all.

Associations referring to the absent axes in the cited sentences are indeed very vague. The only unquestionable fact about the relevant implications is that they should be of demonstrative-introductory character making the presented nominals into predicative names.

As we see, there is a continuum between the one-axis sentences of the free type and the most rigid ones exemplified above. Still, since all the constructions of the second order differ from those of the first order just in that they are not free, we choose to class them as "fixed" one-axis sentences.

Among the fixed one-axis sentences quite a few subclasses are to be recognized, including nominative (nominal) constructions, greeting formulas, introduction formulas, incentives, excuses, etc. Many of such constructions are related to the corresponding two-axis sentences not by the mentioned "vague" implication, but by representation; indeed, such one-axis sentence-formulas as affirmations, negations, certain ready-made excuses, etc., are by themselves not word-sentences, but rather sentence-representatives that exist only in combination with the full-sense antecedent predicative constructions. *Cf.*:

"You can't move any farther back?" – "No." (*I.e.* "I can't move any farther back"). "D'you want me to pay for your drink?" – "Yes, old boy." (*I.e.* "Yes, I want you to pay for my drink, old boy"). Etc.

As for the isolated exclamations of interjectional type ("Good Lord!", "Dear me!" and the like), these are not sentences by virtue of their not possessing the inner structure of actual division even through associative implications (see Ch. XXII).

Summing up what has been said about the one-axis sentences we must stress the two things: first, however varied, they form a minor set within the general system of English sentence patterns; second, they all are related to two-axis sentences either by direct or by indirect association.

§ 5. The semantic classification of simple sentences should be effected at least on the three bases: first, on the basis of the *subject categorial meanings*; second, on the basis of the *predicate categorial meanings*; third, on the basis of the *subject-object relation*.

Reflecting the categories of the subject, simple sentences are divided into *personal* and *impersonal*. The further division of the personal sentences is into *human* and *non-human*; human – into *definite* and *indefinite*; non-human – into *animate* and *inanimate*. The further essential division of impersonal sentences is into *factual* (*It rains, It is five o'clock*) and *perceptional* (*It smells of hay here*).

The differences in subject categorial meanings are sustained by the obvious differences in subject – predicate combinability.

Reflecting the categories of the predicate, simple sentences are divided into *process featuring* ("verbal") and, in the broad sense, *substance featuring* (including substance as such and substantive

271

quality – "nominal"). Among the process featuring sentences *actional* and *statal* ones are to be discriminated (*The window is opening – The window is glistening in the sun*); among the substance featuring sentences *factual* and *perceptional* ones are to be discriminated (*The sea is rough – The place seems quiet*).

Finally, reflecting the subject – object relation, simple sentences should be divided into *subjective* (*John lives in London*), *objective* (*John reads a book*) and *neutral* or "*potentially*" *objective* (*John reads*), capable of implying both the transitive action of the syntactic person and the syntactic person's intransitive characteristic.

<br>

### CHAPTER XXV

## SIMPLE SENTENCE: PARADIGMATIC STRUCTURE

§ 1. Traditional grammar studied the sentence from the point of view of its syntagmatic structure: the sentence was approached as a string of certain parts fulfilling the corresponding syntactic functions. As for paradigmatic relations, which, as we know, are inseparable from syntagmatic relations, they were explicitly revealed only as part of morphological descriptions, because, up to recent times, the idea of the sentence model with its functional variations was not developed. Moreover, some representatives of early modern linguistics, among them F. de Saussure, specially noted that it was quite natural for morphology to develop paradigmatic (associative) observations, while syntax "by its very essence" should concern itself with the linear connections of words.

Thus, the sentence was traditionally taken at its face value as a ready unit of speech, and systemic connections between sentences were formulated in terms of classifications. Sentences were studied and classified according to the purpose of communication, according to the types of the subject and predicate, according to whether they are simple or composite, expanded or unexpanded, compound or complex, etc.

In contemporary modern linguistics paradigmatic structuring of lingual connections and dependencies has penetrated into the would-be "purely syntagmatic" sphere of the sentence. The paradigmatic approach to this element of rendering communicative information, as we have mentioned before, marked a new stage in the development of the science of language; indeed, it is nothing else than paradigmatic approach that has provided a comprehensive theoretical ground for treating the sentence not only as a ready unit of speech, but also and above all as a meaningful lingual unit existing in a pattern form.

§ 2. Paradigmatics finds its essential expression in a system of oppositions making the corresponding meaningful (functional) categories. Syntactic oppositions are realized by correlated sentence patterns, the observable relations between which can be described as "transformations", i.e. as transitions from one pattern of certain notional parts to another pattern of the same notional parts. These transitions, being oppositional, at the same time disclose derivational connections of sentence patterns. In other words, some of the patterns are to be approached as base patterns, while others, as their transforms.

For instance, a question can be described as transformationally produced from a statement; a negation, likewise, can be presented as transformationally produced from an affirmation. E.g.:

You are fond of the kid. → Are you fond of the kid?
You are fond of the kid. → You are not fond of the kid.

Why are the directions of transitions given in this way and not vice versa? – Simply because the ordinary affirmative statement presents a positive expression of a fact in its purest form, maximally free of the speaker's connotative appraisals.

Similarly, a composite sentence, for still more evident reasons, is to be presented as derived from two or more simple sentences. E.g.:

He turned to the waiter. + The waiter stood in the door. → He turned to the waiter who stood in the door.

These transitional relations are implicitly inherent in the syntagmatic classificational study of sentences. But modern theory, exposing them explicitly, has made a cardinal step forward in so far as it has interpreted them as regular derivation stages comparable to categorial form-making processes in morphology and word-building.

And it is on these lines that the initial, basic element of syntactic derivation has been found, i.e. a syntactic unit serving as a "sentence-root" and providing an objective ground for identifying syntactic categorial oppositions. This element is known by different names, such as the "basic syntactic pattern", the "structural sentence scheme", the "elementary sentence model", the "base sentence", though as the handiest in linguistic use should be considered the *"kernel sentence"* due to its terminological flexibility combined with a natural individualizing force.

Structurally the kernel sentence coincides with the elementary sentence described in the previous chapter. The difference is, that the pattern of the kernel sentence is interpreted as forming the base of a paradigmatic derivation in the corresponding sentence pattern series.

Thus, syntactic derivation should not be understood as an immediate change of one sentence into another one; a pronounced or written sentence is a finished utterance that thereby cannot undergo any changes. Syntactic derivation is to be understood as paradigmatic production of more complex pattern constructions out of kernel pattern constructions as their structural bases. The description of this production ("generation") may be more detailed and less detailed, i.e. it can be effected in more generalized and less generalized terms, depending on the aim of the scholar. The most concrete presentation concerns a given speech utterance analysed into its derivation history on the level of the word-forms.

By way of example let us take the following English sentence: *I saw him come.*

This sentence is described in scholar grammar as a sentence with a complex object, which is syntagmatically adequate, though incomplete from the systemic point of view. The syntagmatic description is supplemented and re-interpreted within the framework of the paradigmatic description presenting the sentence in question as produced from the two kernel sentences: *I saw him. + He came. → I saw him come.*

In a more generalized, categorial-oriented paradigmatic presentation the sentence will be shown as a transformational combination of the two kernel pattern-formulas:

$$N_{1pro}^{subj} - V_{1f} - N_{2pro}^{obj} + N_{2pro}^{subj}$$
$$N_{1pro}^{subj} - V_{1f} - N_{2pro}^{obj} - V_{2inf} \quad - V_{2f} \rightarrow$$

The same may be given in terms of the IC-derivation tree diagrams (see Fig. 8). The indices specifying the basic symbols can vary in accord with the concrete needs of analysis and demonstration.

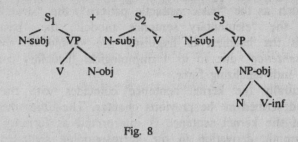

Fig. 8

§ 3. The derivation of genuine sentences lying on the "surface" of speech out of kernel sentences lying in the "deep base" of speech can be analysed as a process falling into sets of elementary transformational steps or procedures. These procedures make up six major classes.

The first class includes steps of *"morphological arrangement"* of the sentence, i.e. morphological changes expressing syntactically relevant categories, above all, the predicative categories of the finite verb: tense, aspect, voice, mood. The syntactic role of these forms of morphological change (systematized into morphological paradigms) consists in the fact that they make up parts of the more general syntactico-paradigmatic series. *E.g.:*

John + start (the kernel base string) → John starts. John will be starting. John would be starting. John has started. Etc.

The second class of the described procedures includes various uses of functional words (*functional expansion*). From the syntactic point of view these words are transformers of syntactic constructions in the same sense as the categorial morphemes (*e.g.* inflexions) are transformers of lexemes, i.e. morphological constructions. *E.g.:*

He understood my request. → He seemed to understand my request. Now they consider the suggestion. → Now they do consider the suggestion.

The third class of syntactic derivational procedures includes the processes of *substitution*. Among the substitutes we find personal pronouns, demonstrative-substitute pronouns, indefinite-substitute pronouns, as well as substitutive combinations of half-notional words. *Cf.*:

The pupils ran out of the classroom. → They ran out of the classroom. I want another pen, please. → I want another one, please.

The fourth class of the procedures in question is formed by processes of *deletion*, i.e. elimination of some elements of the sentence in various contextual conditions. As a result of deletion the corresponding reduced constructions are produced. *E.g.*:

Would you like a cup of tea? → A cup of tea? It's a pleasure! → Pleasure!

The fifth class of syntactic derivational procedures includes processes of *positional arrangement*, in particular, permutations (changes of the word-order into the reverse patterns). *E.g.*:

The man is here. → Is the man here? Jim ran in with an excited cry. → In ran Jim with an excited cry.

The sixth class of syntactic derivational procedures is formed by processes of *intonational arrangement*, i.e. application of various functional tones and accents. This arrangement is represented in written and typed speech by punctuation marks, the use of different varieties of print, the use of various modes of underlining and other graphical means. *E.g.*:

We must go. → We must go? We? Must go?? You care nothing about what I feel. → You care nothing about what *I* feel!

The described procedures are all functionally relevant, i.e. they serve as syntactically meaningful dynamic features of the sentence. For various expressive purposes they may be applied either singly or, more often than not, in combination with one another. *E.g.*:

We finish the work.→We are not going to finish it.

For the production of the cited sentence-transform the following procedures are used: morphological change, introduction of functional words, substitution, intonational arrangement. The functional (meaningful) outcome of the whole process is the expression of the modal future combined with a negation in a dialogue response. *Cf.*:

Are we ever going to finish the work? → Anyway, we are not going to finish it today!

**§ 4.** The derivational procedures applied to the kernel sentence introduce it into two types of derivational relations in the sentential paradigmatic system: first, the "constructional" relations; second, the "predicative" relations. The constructional derivation effects the formation of more complex clausal structures out of simpler ones; in other words, it provides for the expression of the nominative-notional syntactic semantics of the sentence. The predicative derivation realizes the formation of predicatively different units not affecting the constructional volume of the base; in other words, it is responsible for the expression of the predicative syntactic semantics of the sentence. Both types of derivational procedures form the two subsystems within the general system of syntactic paradigmatics.

**§ 5.** As part of the *constructional system* of syntactic paradigmatics, kernel sentences, as well as other, expanded base-sentences undergo derivational changes into clauses and phrases.

The transformation of a base sentence into a clause can be called "clausalization". By way of clausalization a sentence is changed into a subordinate or coordinate clause in the process of subordinative or coordinative combination of sentences. The main clausalizing procedures involve the use of conjunctive words – subordinators and coordinators. Since a composite sentence is produced from minimum two base sentences, the derivational processes of composite sentence production are sometimes called "two-base transformations".

For example, two kernel sentences *They arrived* and *They relieved me of my fears* (→*I was relieved of my fears*), combined by subordinative and coordinative clausalizing, produce the following constructions:

→ When they arrived I was relieved of my fears. → If they arrive, I shall be relieved of my fears. → Even though they arrive, I shan't be relieved of my fears. Etc. → They arrived, and I was relieved of my fears. → They arrived, but I was not relieved of my fears. Etc.

The transformation of a base sentence into a phrase can be called "phrasalization". By phrasalization a sentence is transformed either into a semi-predicative construction (a semi-clause), or into a nominal phrase.

Nominal phrases are produced by the process of nominalization, i.e. nominalizing phrasalization which we have analyzed before (see Ch. XX). Nominalization may be complete, consisting in completely depriving the sentence of its predicative aspect, or partial, consisting

277

in partially depriving the sentence of its predicative aspect. Partial nominalization in (English produces infinitive and gerundial phrases. By other types of phrasalization such semi-clauses are derived as complex objects of infinitive and participial types, various participial constructions of adverbial status and some other, minor complexes. The resulting constructions produced by the application of the cited phrasalizing procedures in the process of derivational combination of base sentences will be both simple expanded sentences (in case of complete nominalization) and semi-composite sentences (in case of various partial nominalizations and other phrasalizations). *Cf.*:

→ On their arrival I was relieved of my fears. → They arrived to relieve me of my fears. → They arrived relieving me of my fears. → Having arrived, they did relieve me of my fears. Etc.

As is seen from the examples, each variety of derivational combination of concrete sentences has its own semantic purpose expressed by the procedures employed.

§ 6. As part of the *predicative system* of syntactic paradigmatics, kernel sentences, as well as expanded base-sentences, undergo such structural modifications as immediately express the predicative functions of the sentence, i.e. the functions relating the nominative meanings of the sentence to reality. Of especial importance in this respect is the expression of predicative functions by sentences which are elementary as regards the set of their notional constituents: being elementary from the point of view of nominative semantics, these sentences can be used as genuine, ordinary utterances of speech. Bearing in mind the elementary nominative nature of its constructional units, we call the system of sentences so identified the "Primary Syntactic System" (*Lat.* "Prima Systema Syntactica").

To recognize a primary sentence in the text, one must use the criteria of elementary sentence structure identification applied to the notional constituents of the sentence, irrespective of the functional meanings rendered by it. For instance, the notionally minimal negative sentence should be classed as primary, though not quite elementary (kernel) in the paradigmatic sense, negation being not a notional, but a functional sentence factor. *Cf.*:

I have met the man. → I have not met the man. → I have never met the man.

Any composite (or semi-composite) sentence is analysable into two or more primary sentences (i.e. sentences elementary in the notional sense). E.g.:

Is it a matter of no consequence that I should find you with a young man wearing my pyjamas? ← Is it a matter of no consequence? + I should find you with a (young) man. + The (young) man is wearing my pyjamas.

The kernel sentence can also have its representation in speech, being embodied by the simplest sentential construction not only in the notional, but also in the functional sense. In other words, it is an elementary sentence which is non-interrogative, non-imperative, non-negative, non-modal, etc. In short, in terms of syntactic oppositions, this is the "weakest" construction in the predicative oppositional space of the primary syntactic system.

§ 7. The predicative functions expressed by primary sentence patterns should be divided into the two types: first, *lower* functions; second, *higher* functions. The lower functions include the expression of such morphological categories as tenses and aspects; these are of "factual", "truth-stating" semantic character. The higher functions are "evaluative" in the broad sense of the word; they immediately express the functional semantics of relating the nominative content of the sentence to reality.

The principal predicative functions expressed by syntactic categorial oppositions are the following.

First, question as opposed to statement. Second, inducement as opposed to statement. Third, negation as opposed to affirmation. Fourth, unreality as opposed to reality. Fifth, probability as opposed to fact. Sixth, modal identity (*seem to do, happen to do, prove to do*, etc.) as opposed to fact. Seventh, modal subject-action relation as opposed to fact (*can do, may do*, etc.). Eighth, specified actual subject-action relation as opposed to fact. Ninth, phase of action as opposed to fact. Tenth, passive action as opposed to active action. Eleventh, specialized actual division (specialized perspective) as opposed to non-specialized actual division (non-specialized perspective). Twelfth, emphasis (emotiveness) as opposed to emotional neutrality (unemotiveness).

Each opposition of the cited list forms a categorial set which is rather complex. For instance, within the framework of the question – statement opposition, pronominal and alternative questions are identified with their manifold varieties; within the system of phase of action, specialized subsets are identified rendering the phase of beginning, the phase of duration, the phase of end, etc. The total supersystem of all the pattern-forms of a given sentence base constitutes its general syntactic paradigm of predicative functions. This paradigm is, naturally, extremely complicated so that it is hardly observable if presented on a diagram. This fact shows that the volume of functional meanings rendered by a sentence even at a very high level of syntactic generalization is tremendous. At the same time the derivation of each functional sentence form in its paradigmatically determined position in the system is simple enough in the sense that it is quite explicit. This shows the dynamic essence of the paradigm in question; the paradigm exactly answers the needs of expression at every given juncture of actual communication.

§ 8. All the cited oppositions-categories may or may not be represented in a given utterance by their strong function members. In accord with this oppositional regularity, we advance the notion of the "predicative load" of the sentence. The predicative load is determined by the total volume of the strong members of predicative oppositions (i.e. by the sum of positive values of the corresponding differential features) actually represented in the sentence.

The sentence, by definition, always expresses predication, being a predicative unit of language. But, from the point of view of the comparative volume of the predicative meanings actually expressed, the sentence may be predicatively "loaded" or "non-loaded". If the sentence is predicatively "non-loaded", it means that its construction is kernel elementary at the accepted level of categorial generalization. Consequently, such a sentence will be characterized in oppositional terms as non-interrogative, non-inducive, non-negative, non-real, non-probable, non-modal-identifying, etc., down to the last of the recognized predicative oppositions. If, on the other hand, the sentence is predicatively "loaded", it means that it renders at least one of the strong oppositional meanings inherent in the described categorial system. Textual observations show that predicative loads amounting to one or two positive feature values (strong oppositional members) may be characterized as more or less common; hence, we consider such a load as "light" and, correspondingly, say that the sentence in this case is predicatively "lightly" loaded. As for sentences whose predicative load exceeds two positive feature values, they stand out of the common, their functional semantics showing clear signs of intricacy. Accordingly, we consider such loads as "heavy", and of sentences characterized by these loads we say that they are "heavily" loaded. Predicative loads amounting to four feature values occur but occasionally, they are too complicated to be naturally grasped by the mind.

To exemplify the cited theses, let us take as a derivation sentence-base the construction *The thing bothers me*. This sentence, in the above oppositional sense, is predicatively "non-loaded", or has the "zero predicative load". The predicative structure of the sentence can be expanded by the expression of the modal subject-action relation, for instance, the ability relation. The result is: → *The thing can bother me*; the predicative load of the sentence has grown to 1. This construction, in its turn, can be used as a derivation base for a sentence of a higher predicative complexity; for instance, the feature of unreality can be added to it: → *The thing could bother me (now)*. The predicative load of the sentence has grown to 2. Though functionally not simple, the sentence still presents a more or less ordinary English construction. To continue with our complicating it, we may introduce in the sentence the feature of passivity: → *I could be bothered (by the thing now)*. The predicative semantics expressed has quite clearly changed into something beyond the ordinary; the sentence requires a special context to sound natural. Finally, to complicate the primary construction still further, we may introduce a negation in it: → *I could not be bothered (by the thing now)*. As a result we are faced by a construction that, in the contextual conditions of real speech, expresses an intricate set of functional meanings and stylistic connotations. *Cf.*:

It "...Wilmet and Henrietta Bentworth have agreed to differ already." – "What about?" – "Well, I couldn't be bothered, but I think it was about the P.M., or was it Portulaca? – they differ about everything" (J. Galsworthy).

The construction is indeed semantically complicated; but all its meaningful complexity is linguistically resolved by the demonstrated semantico-syntactic oppositional analysis showing the stage-to-stage growth of the total functional meaning of the sentence in the course of its paradigmatic derivation.

# CHAPTER XXVI

## COMPOSITE SENTENCE AS A POLYPREDICATIVE CONSTRUCTION

§ 1. The composite sentence, as different from the simple sentence, is formed by two or more predicative lines. Being a polypredicative construction, it expresses a complicated act of thought, i.e. an act of mental activity which falls into two or more intellectual efforts closely combined with one another. In terms of situations and events this means that the composite sentence reflects two or more elementary situational events viewed as making up a unity; the constitutive connections of the events are expressed by the constitutive connections of the predicative lines of the sentence, i.e. by the sentential polypredication.

Each predicative unit in a composite sentence makes up a clause in it, so that a clause as part of a composite sentence corresponds to a separate sentence as part of a contextual sequence. *E.g.*:

When I sat down to dinner I looked for an opportunity to slip in casually the information that I had by accident run across the Driffields; but news travelled fast in Blackstable (S. Maugham).

The cited composite sentence includes four clauses which are related to one another on different semantic grounds. The sentences underlying the clauses are the following:

I sat down to dinner. I looked for an opportunity to slip in casually the information. I had by accident run across the Driffields. News travelled fast in Blackstable.

The correspondence of a predicative clause to a separate sentence is self-evident. On the other hand, the correspondence of a composite sentence to a genuine, logically connected sequence of simple sentences (underlying its clauses) is not evident at all; moreover, such kind of correspondence is in fact not obligatory, which is the very cause of the existence of the composite sentence in a language. Indeed, in the given example the independent sentences reconstructed from the predicative clauses do not make up any coherently presented situational unity; they are just so many utterances each expressing an event of self-sufficient significance. By way of rearrangement and the use of semantic connectors we may make them into a more or less explanatory situational sequence, but the exposition of the genuine logic of events, i.e. their presentation as natural parts of a unity achieved by the composite sentence will not be, and is not to be replaced in principle. *Cf.*:

I ran by accident across the Driffields. At some time later on I sat down to dinner. While participating in the general conversation, I looked for an opportunity to slip in casually the information about my meeting them. But news travelled fast in Blackstable.

The logical difference between the given composite sentence and its contextually coherent de-compositional presentation is that whereas the composite sentence exposes as its logical centre, i.e. the core of its purpose of communication, the intention of the speaker to inform his table-companions of a certain fact (which turns out to be already known to them), the sentential sequence expresses the events in their natural temporal succession, which actually destroys the original purpose of communication. Any formation of a sentential sequence more equivalent to the given composite sentence by its semantic status than the one shown above has to be expanded by additional elucidative prop-utterances with back-references; and all the same, the resulting contextual string, if it is intended as a real informational substitute for the initial composite, will hardly be effected without the help of some kind of essentially composite sentence constructions included in it (let the reader himself try to construct an equivalent textual sequence meeting the described semantic requirements).

As we see, the composite sentence in its quality of a structural unit of language is indispensable for language by its own purely semantic merits, let alone its terseness, as well as intellectual elegance of expression.

§ 2. As is well known, the use of composite sentences, especially long and logically intricate ones, is characteristic of literary written speech rather than colloquial oral speech. This unquestionable fact is explained by three reasons: one relating to the actual *needs of expression*; one relating to the *possibilities of production*; and one relating to the *conditions of perception*.

That the composite sentence structure answers the special needs of written mode of lingual expression is quite evident. It is this type of speech that deals with lengthy reasonings, descriptions, narrations, all presenting abundant details of intricate correlations of logical premises and inferences, of situational foreground and background, of sequences of events interrupted by cross-references and parenthetical comments. Only a composite sentence can adequately and within reasonable bounds of textual space fulfil these semantic requirements.

Now, the said requirements, fortunately, go together with the fact that in writing it is actually possible to produce long composite sentences of complicated, but logically flawless structure (the second of the advanced reasons). This is possible here because the written sentence, while in the process of being produced, is open to various alterations: it allows corrections of slips and errors; it can be subjected to curtailing or expanding; it admits of rearranging and reformulating one's ideas; in short, it can be prepared. This latter factor is of crucial importance, so that when considering the properties of literary written speech we must always bear it in mind. Indeed, from the linguistic point of view written speech is above all prepared, or "edited" speech: it is due to no other quality than being prepared before its presentation to the addressee that this mode of speech is structurally so tellingly different from colloquial oral speech. Employing the words in their broader sense, we may say that literary written speech is not just uttered and gone, but is always more carefully or less carefully composed in advance, being meant for a future use of the reader, often for his repeated use. In contrast to this, genuine colloquial oral speech is uttered each time in an irretrievably complete and final form, each time for one immediate and fleeting occasion.

We have covered the first two reasons explaining the composite sentence of increased complexity as a specific feature of written speech. The third reason, referring to the conditions of perception, is inseparable from the former two. Namely, if written text provides for the possibility for its *producer* to return to the beginning of each sentence with the aim of assessing its form and content, of rearranging or recomposing it altogether, it also enables the *reader*, after he has run through the text for the first time, to go back to its starting line and re-read it with as much care as will be required for the final understanding of each item and logical connection expressed by its wording or implied by its construction. Thus, the length limit imposed on the sentence by the recipient's immediate (operative) memory can in writing be practically neglected; the volume of the written sentence is regulated not by memory limitations as such, but by the considerations of optimum logical balance and stylistic well-formedness.

§ 3. Logic and style being the true limiters of the written sentence volume, two dialectically contrasted active tendencies can be observed in the sentence construction of modern printed texts. According to the first tendency, a given unity of reasons in meditation, a natural sequence of descriptive situations or narrative events is to be reflected in one *composite sentence*, however long and structurally complicated it might prove. According to the second, directly opposite tendency, for a given unity of reflected events or reasons, each of them is to be presented by one separate *simple sentence*, the whole complex of reflections forming a multisentential paragraph. The two tendencies are always in a state of confrontation, and which of them will take an upper hand in this or that concrete case of text production has to be decided out of various considerations of form and meaning relating to both contextual and con-situational conditions (including, among other things, the general purpose of the work in question, as well as the preferences and idiosyncrasies of its users).

Observe, for instance, the following complex sentence of mixed narrative-reasoning nature:

Once Mary waved her hand as she recognized her driver, but he took no notice of her, only whipping his horses the harder, and she realized with a rather helpless sense of futility that so far as other people were concerned she must be considered in the same light as her uncle, and that even if she tried to walk to Boduin or Launceston no one would receive her, and the door would be shut in her face (D. du Maurier).

The sentence has its established status in the expressive context of the novel, and in this sense it is unrearrangeable. On the other hand, its referential plane can be rendered by a multisentential paragraph, plainer in form, but somewhat more natural to the unsophisticated perceptions:

Once Mary recognized her driver. She waved her hand to him. But he took no notice of her. He only whipped his horses the harder. And she realized that so far as other people were concerned she must be considered in the same light as her uncle. This gave her a rather helpless sense of futility. Even if she tried to walk to Boduin or Launceston no one would receive her. Quite the contrary, the door would be shut in her face.

One long composite sentence has been divided into eight short sentences. Characteristically, though, in our simplification we could not do without the composite sentence structure as such: two of the sentential units in the adaptation (respectively, the fourth and the sixth) have retained their compositive features, and these structural properties seem to be indispensable for the functional adequacy of the rearranged passage.

The cited example of syntactic re-formation of text will help us formulate the following composition rule of good non-fiction (neutral) prose style: in neutral written speech each sentence construction should be as simple as can be permitted by the semantic context.

§ 4. We have emphatically pointed out in due course (see Ch. I) the oral basis of human language: the primary lingual matter is phonetical, so that each and every lingual utterance given in a graphic form has essentially a representative character, its speech referent being constructed of so many phones organized in a rhythmo-melodical sequence. On the other hand, and this has also been noted before, writing in a literary language acquires a relatively self-sufficient status in so far as a tremendous proportion of what is actually written in society is not meant for an oral reproduction at all: though read and re-read by those to whom it has been addressed, it is destined to remain "silent" for ever. The "silent" nature of written speech with all its peculiarities leads to the development of specifically written features of language, among which, as we have just seen, the composite sentence of increased complexity occupies one of the most prominent places. Now, as a natural consequence of this development, the peculiar features of written speech begin to influence oral speech, whose syntax becomes liable to display ever more syntactic properties directly borrowed from writing.

Moreover, as a result of active interaction between oral and written forms of language, a new variety of speech has arisen that has an intermediary status. This type of speech, being explicitly oral, is at the same time prepared and edited, and more often than not it is directly reproduced from the written text, or else from its epitomized version (theses). This intermediary written-oral speech should be given a special linguistic name, for which we suggest the term "scripted speech", i.e. speech read from the script. Here belong such forms of lingual communication as public report speech, lecturer speech, preacher speech, radio- and television-broadcast speech, each of them existing in a variety of subtypes.

By way of example let us take the following passage from President Woodrow Wilson's address to the Congress urging it to authorize the United States' entering the World War (1917):

But the right is more precious than peace, and we shall fight for the things which we have always carried nearest our hearts, – for democracy, for the right of those who submit to authority to have a voice in their own governments, for the rights and liberties of small nations, for a universal dominion of right by such a concert of free

286

peoples as shall bring peace and safety to all nations and make the world itself at last free.

The text presents a typical case of political scripted speech with a clear tinge of solemnity, its five predicative units being complicated by parallel constructions of homogeneous objects (*for*-phrases) adding to its high style emphasis.

Compare the above with a passage from President Franklin D. Roosevelt's second inaugural address (1937):

In this nation I see tens of millions of its citizens – a substantial part of its whole population – who at this very moment are denied the greater part of what the very lowest standards of today call the necessities of life.

The sentence is not a long one, but its bookish background, although meant for oral uttering before an audience, is most evident: a detached appositional phrase, consecutive subordination, the very nature of the last appositional clausal complex of commenting type, all these features being carefully prepared to give the necessary emphasis to the social content of the utterance aimed at a public success.

Compare one more example – a passage from Bernard Shaw's paper read before the Medico-Legal Society in London (1909):

Nevertheless, trade in medical advice has never been formally recognized, and never will be; for you must realize that, whereas competition in ordinary trade and business is founded on an elaborate theoretic demonstration of its benefits, there has never been anyone from Adam Smith to our own time who has attempted such a demonstration with regard to the medical profession. The idea of a doctor being a tradesman with a pecuniary interest in your being ill is abhorrent to every thoughtful person.

The scripted nature of the cited sentential sequence is clearly seen from its arrangement as an expressive climax built upon a carefully balanced contrastive composite construction.

§ 5. We have hitherto defended the thesis of the composite sentence of increased complexity being specifically characteristic of literary written speech. On the other hand, we must clearly understand that the composite sentence as such is part and parcel of the general syntactic system of language, and its use is an inalienable feature of any normal expression of human thought in intercourse. This is demonstrated by cases of composite sentences that could not be adequately reduced to the corresponding sets of separate simple sentences in their natural contexts (see above). Fictional literature, presenting in its works a reflection of language as it is spoken by the people, gives us abundant illustrations of the broad use of composite sentences in genuine colloquial speech both of dialogue and monologue character.

Composite sentences display two principal types of construction: *hypotaxis* (subordination) and *parataxis* (coordination). Both types are equally representative of colloquial speech, be it refined by education or not. In this connection it should be noted that the initial rise of hypotaxis and parataxis as forms of composite sentences can be traced back to the early stages of language development, i.e. to the times when language had no writing. Profuse illustrations of the said types of syntactic relations are contained, for instance, in the Old English epic "Beowulf" (dated presumably from the end of the VII c. A.D.) As is known, the text of the poem shows all the basic forms of sentential composition including the grammatically completed presentation of reported speech, connection of clauses on various nominal principles (objective, subjective, predicative, attributive), connection of clauses on various adverbial principles (temporal, local, conditional, causal, etc.). *E.g.*:

> Secȝe ic þe to soðe, sunu Ecȝlafes,
> þæt næfre Ȝrendel swa fela ȝryra ȝefremede,
> atol æȝlæca, ealdre þinum,
> Hynðo on Heorote, ȝif þin hiȝe wære,
> sefa swa searo-ȝrim, swa þu self talast;
> ac he hafað onfunden, þæt he þa fæhðe ne þearf,
> atole ecȝ-þræce, eower leode
> swiðe onsittan, Siȝe-Scyldinȝa.[*]

Compare the tentative prose translation of the cited text into Modern English (with the corresponding re-arrangements of the word-order patterns):

Truly I say onto thee, oh Son Egglaf, that never would Grendel, the abominable monster, have done so many terrible deeds to your chief, (so many) humiliating acts in Heorot, if thy soul (and) heart had been as bold as thou thyself declarest; but he has found that he

---

[*] From: Beowulf/Ed. by A.J. Wyatt. New edition revised with introduction and notes by R.W. Chambers. Cambr., 1933, verses 590-597.

need not much fear the hostile sword-attack of your people, the Victorious Skildings.

Needless to say, the forms of composite sentences in prewriting periods of language history cannot be taken as a proof that the structure of the sentence does not develop historically in terms of perfecting its expressive qualities. On the contrary, the known samples of Old English compared with their modern rendering are quite demonstrative of the fact that the sentence does develop throughout the history of language; moreover, they show that the nature and scope of the historical structural change of the sentence is not at all a negligible matter. Namely, from the existing lingual materials we see that the primitive, not clearly identified forms of subordination and coordination, without distinct border points between separate sentences, have been succeeded by such constructions of syntactic composition as are distinguished first and foremost by the clear-cut logic of connections between their clausal predicative parts. However, these materials, and among them the cited passage, show us at the same time that the composite sentence, far from being extraneous to colloquial speech, takes its origin just in the oral colloquial element of human speech as such: it is inherent in the very oral nature of developing language.

§ 6. The two main types of the connection of clauses in a composite sentence, as has been stated above, are subordination and coordination. By coordination the clauses are arranged as units of syntactically equal rank, i.e. equipotently; by subordination, as units of unequal rank, one being categorially dominated by the other. In terms of the positional structure of the sentence it means that by subordination one of the clauses (subordinate) is placed in a notional position of the other (principal). This latter characteristic has an essential semantic implication clarifying the difference between the two types of polypredication in question. As a matter of fact, a subordinate clause, however important the information rendered by it might be for the whole communication, presents it as naturally supplementing the information of the principal clause, i.e. as something completely premeditated and prepared even before its explicit expression in the utterance. This is of especial importance for post-positional subordinate clauses of circumstantial semantic nature. Such clauses may often shift their position without a change in semantico-syntactic status. *Cf.:*

I could not help blushing with embarrassment when I looked at him. → When I looked at him I could not help blushing with embarrassment. The board accepted the decision, though it didn't quite meet their plans. → Though the decision didn't quite meet their plans, the board accepted it.

The same criterion is valid for subordinate clauses with a fixed position in the sentence. To prove the subordinate quality of the clause in the light of this consideration, we have to place it in isolation – and see that the isolation is semantically false. *E.g.:*

But all the books were so neatly arranged, they were so clean, that I had the impression they were very seldom read. → *But all the books were so neatly arranged, they were so clean. That I had the impression they were very seldom read. I fancy that life is more amusing now than it was forty years ago. → *I fancy that life is more amusing now. Than it was forty years ago.

As for coordinated clauses, their equality in rank is expressed above all in each sequential clause explicitly corresponding to a new effort of thought, without an obligatory feature of premeditation. In accordance with the said quality, a sequential clause in a compound sentence refers to the whole of the leading clause, whereas a subordinate clause in a complex sentence, as a rule, refers to one notional constituent (expressed by a word or a phrase) in a principal clause [Khaimovich, Rogovskaya, 278]. It is due to these facts that the position of a coordinate clause is rigidly fixed in all cases, which can be used as one of the criteria of coordination in distinction to subordination. Another probe of rank equality of clauses in coordination is a potential possibility for any coordinate sequential clause to take either the copulative conjunction *and* or the adversative conjunction *but* as introducers. *Cf.:*

That sort of game gave me horrors, so I never could play it. → That sort of game gave me horrors, and I never could play it. The excuse was plausible, only it was not good enough for us. → The excuse was plausible, but it was not good enough for us.

§ 7. The means of combining clauses into a polypredicative sentence are divided into *syndetic*, i.e. conjunctional, and *asyndetic*, i.e. non-conjunctional. The great controversy going on among linguists about this division concerns the status of syndeton and asyndeton versus coordination and subordination. Namely, the question under consideration is whether or not syndeton and asyndeton equally express the two types of syntactic relations between clauses in a composite sentence.

According to the traditional view, all composite sentences are to be classed into compound sentences (coordinating their clauses) and complex sentences (subordinating their clauses), syndetic or asyndetic types of clause connection being specifically displayed with both classes. However, this view has of late been subjected to energetic criticism; the new thesis formulated by its critics is as follows: the "formal" division of clause connection based on the choice of connective means should be placed higher in the hierarchy than the "semantic" division of clause connection based on the criterion of syntactic rank. That is, at the higher level of classification all the composite sentences should be divided into syndetic and asyndetic, while at the lower level the syndetic composite sentences (and only these) should be divided into compound and complex ones in accordance with the types of the connective words used. The cited principle was put forward by N.S. Pospelov as part of his syntactic analysis of Russian, and it was further developed by some other linguists.

But the new approach to coordination and subordination has not been left unchallenged. In particular, B.A. Ilyish with his characteristic discretion in formulating final decisions has pointed out serious flaws in the non-traditional reasoning resulting first of all from mixing up strictly grammatical criteria of classification with general semantic considerations [Ilyish, 318 ff.].

Indeed, if we compare the following asyndetic composite sentences with their compound syndetic counterparts on the basis of paradigmatic approach, we shall immediately expose unquestionable equality in their semantico-syntactic status. E.g.:

My uncle was going to refuse, but we didn't understand why. → My uncle was going to refuse, we didn't understand why. She hesitated a moment, and then she answered him. → She hesitated a moment, then she answered him.

The equality of the compound status of both types of sentences is emphatically endorsed when compared with the corresponding complex sentences in transformational constructional paradigmatics. Cf.:

... → We didn't understand why my uncle was going to refuse.
... → After she hesitated a moment she answered him.

On the other hand, bearing in mind the in-positional nature of a subordinate clause expounded above, it would be altogether irrational to deny a subordinate status to the asyndetic attributive, objective or predicative clauses of the commonest order. *Cf.*:

They've given me a position I could never have got without them. → They've given me a position which I could never have got without them. We saw at once it was all wrong. → We saw at once that it was all wrong. The fact is he did accept the invitation. → The fact is that he did accept the invitation.

Now, one might say, as is done in some older grammatical treatises, that the asyndetic introduction of a subordinate clause amounts to the omission of the conjunctive word joining it to the principal clause. However, in the light of the above paradigmatic considerations, the invalidity of this statement in the context of the discussion appears to be quite obvious: as regards the "omission" or "non-omission" of the conjunctive introducer the compound asyndetic sentence should be treated on an equal basis with the complex asyndetic sentence. In other words, if we defend the idea of the omission of the conjunction with asyndetic *subordinate clauses*, we must apply this principle also to asyndetic *coordinate clauses*. But the idea of the omission of the conjunction expounded in its purest, classical form has already been demonstrated in linguistics as fallacious, since asyndetic connection of clauses is indisputably characterized by its own functional value; it is this specific value that vindicates and supports the very existence of asyndetic polypredication in the system of language. Moreover, many true functions of asyndetic polypredication in contradistinction to the functions of syndetic polypredication were aptly disclosed in the course of investigations conducted by the scholars who sought to refute the adequacy of coordinate or subordinate interpretation of clausal asyndeton. So, the linguistic effort of these scholars, though not convincing in terms of classification, has, on the whole, not been in vain; in the long run, it has contributed to the deeper insight into the nature of the composite sentence as a polypredicative combination of words.

§ 8. Besides the classical types of coordination and subordination of clauses, we find another case of the construction of composite sentence, namely, when the connection between the clauses combined in a polypredicative unit is expressly loose, placing the sequential clause in a syntactically detached position. In this loosely connected composite, the sequential clause information is presented rather as an afterthought, an idea that has come to the mind of the speaker after the completion of the foregoing utterance, which latter, by this new utterance forming effort, is forcibly made into the clausal fore-part of a composite sentence. This kind of syntactic connection, the traces of which we saw when treating the syntagmatic bonds of the word, comes under the heading of cumulation. Its formal sign is often the tone of sentential completion followed by a shorter pause than an inter-sentential one, which intonational complex is represented in writing by a semi-final punctuation mark, such as a semicolon, a dash, sometimes a series of periods. *Cf.*:

It was just the time that my aunt and uncle would be coming home from their daily walk down the town and I did not like to run the risk of being seen with people whom they would not at all approve of; so I asked them to go on first, as they would go more quickly than I (S. Maugham).

Cumulation as here presented forms a type of syntactic connection intermediary between clausal connection and sentential connection. Thus, the very composite sentence (loose composite) formed by it is in fact a unit intermediary between one polypredicative sentence and a group of separate sentences making up a contextual sequence.

There is good reason to interpret different parenthetical clauses as specific cumulative constructions, because the basic semantico-syntactic principle of joining them to the initially planned sentence is the same, i.e. presenting them as a detached communication, here – of an introductory or commenting-deviational nature. *E.g.*:

He was sent for very suddenly this morning, *as I have told you already*, and he only gave me the barest details before his horse was saddled and he was gone (D. du Maurier). Unprecedented in scale and lavishly financed (*£100,000 was collected in 1843 and 9,000,000 leaflets distributed*) this agitation had all the advantages that the railways, cheap newspapers and the penny post could give (A.L. Morton).

If this interpretation is accepted, then the whole domain of cumulation should be divided into two parts: first, the *continuative cumulation*, placing the cumulated clause in post-position to the expanded predicative construction; second, the *parenthetical cumulation*, placing the cumulated clause in inter-position to the expanded predicative construction. The inter-position may be made even into a pre-position as its minor particular case (here belong mostly constructions introduced by the conjunction *as*: *as we have seen*, *as I have said*, etc.). This paradox is easily explained by the type of relation between the clauses: the parenthetical clause (i.e. parenthetically cumulated) only gives a background to the essential information of the expanded original clause. And, which is very important, it can shift its position in the sentence without causing any change in the information rendered by the utterance as a whole. *Cf.*:

He was sent for very suddenly this morning, *as I have told you already.* → He was sent for, *as I have told you already,* very suddenly this morning. → *As I have told you already,* he was sent for very suddenly this morning.

§ 9. In the composite sentences hitherto surveyed, the constitutive predicative lines are expressed separately and explicitly: the described sentence types are formed by minimum two clauses each having a subject and a predicate of its own. Alongside these "completely" composite sentences, there exist constructions in which one explicit predicative line is combined with another one, the latter being not explicitly or completely expressed. To such constructions belong, for instance, sentences with homogeneous predicates, as well as sentences with verbid complexes. *Cf.*:

Philip *ignored* the question and *remained* silent. I *have* never before *heard* her *sing.* She *followed* him in, *bending* her head under the low door.

That the cited utterances do not represent classical, explicitly constructed composite sentence-models admits of no argument. At the same time, as we pointed out elsewhere (see Ch. XXIV), they cannot be analysed as genuine simple sentences, because they contain not one, but more than one predicative lines, though presented in fusion with one another. This can be demonstrated by explanatory expanding transformations. *Cf.*:

... → Philip ignored the question, (and) he remained silent. ... → I have never before heard how she sings. ... → As she followed him in, she bent her head under the low door.

The performed test clearly shows that the sentences in question are derived each from two base sentences, so that the systemic status of the resulting constructions is in fact intermediary between the simple sentence and the composite sentence. Therefore these predicative constructions should by right be analysed under the heading of semi-composite sentences.

It is easy to see that functionally semi-composite sentences are directly opposed to composite-cumulative sentences: while the latter are over-expanded, the former are under-expanded, i.e. they are concisely deployed. The result of the predicative blend is terseness of expression, which makes semi-composite constructions of especial preference in colloquial speech.

Thus, composite sentences as polypredicative constructions exist in the two type varieties as regards the degree of their predicative explicitness: first, composite sentences of complete composition; second, composite sentences of concise composition. Each of these types is distinguished by its own functional specification, occupies a permanent place in the syntactic system of language and so deserves a separate consideration in a grammatical description.

## CHAPTER XXVII

## COMPLEX SENTENCE

§ 1. The complex sentence is a polypredicative construction built up on the principle of subordination. It is derived from two or more *base sentences* one of which performs the role of a matrix in relation to the others, the *insert sentences*. The matrix function of the corresponding base sentence may be more rigorously and less rigorously pronounced, depending on the type of subordinative connection realized.

When joined into one complex sentence, the matrix base sentence becomes the principal clause of it and the insert sentences, its subordinate clauses.

The complex sentence of minimal composition includes two clauses – a principal one and a subordinate one. Although the principal clause positionally dominates the subordinate clause, the two form a semantico-syntactic unity within the framework of which they are in fact interconnected, so that the very existence of either of them is supported by the existence of the other.

The subordinate clause is joined to the principal clause either by a subordinating connector (subordinator), or, with some types of clauses, asyndetically. The functional character of the subordinative connector is so explicit that even in traditional grammatical descriptions of complex sentences this connector was approached as a transformer of an independent sentence into a subordinate clause. *Cf.*:

Moyra left the room. → (I do remember quite well) that Moyra left the room. → (He went on with his story) after Moyra left the room. → (Fred remained in his place) though Moyra left the room.

→ (The party was spoilt) because Moyra left the room. → (It was a surprise to us all) that Moyra left the room...

This paradigmatic scheme of the production of the subordinate clause vindicates the possible interpretation of contact-clauses in asyndetic connection as being joined to the principal clause by means of the "zero"-connector. *Cf.*: → (How do you know) ∅ Moyra left the room?

Needless to say, the idea of the zero-subordinator simply stresses the fact of the meaningful (functional) character of the asyndetic connection of clauses, not denying the actual absence of connector in the asyndetic complex sentence.

The minimal, two-clause complex sentence is the main volume type of complex sentences. It is the most important type, first, in terms of frequency, since its textual occurrence by far exceeds that of multi-clause complex sentences; second, in terms of its paradigmatic status, because a complex sentence of any volume is analysable into a combination of two-clause complex sentence units.

§ 2. The structural features of the principal clause differ with different types of subordinate clauses. In particular, various types of subordinate clauses specifically affect the principal clause from the point of view of the degree of its completeness. As is well known from elementary grammatical descriptions, the principal clause is markedly incomplete in complex sentences with the subject and predicative subordinate clauses. *E.g.*:

And why we descend to their level is a mystery to me. (The gaping principal part outside the subject clause: "– is a mystery to me".) Your statement was just what you were expected to say. (The gaping principal part outside the predicative clause: "Your statement was just – ")

Of absolutely deficient character is the principal clause of the complex sentence that includes both subject and predicative subordinate clauses: its proper segment, i.e. the word-string standing apart from the subordinate clauses, is usually reduced to a sheer finite link-verb. *Cf.*: How he managed to pull through is what baffles me. (The principal clause representation: " – is – ")

A question arises whether the treatment of the subject and predicative clauses as genuinely subordinate ones is rational at all. Indeed, how can the principal clause be looked upon as syntactically (positionally) dominating such clauses as perform the functions of its main syntactic parts, in particular, that of the subject? How can the link-verb, itself just a little more than an auxiliary element, be taken as the "governing predicative construction" of a complex sentence?

However, this seeming paradox is to be definitely settled on the principles of paradigmatic theory. Namely, to understand the status of the "deficiently incomplete and gaping" principal clause we must take into consideration the matrix nature of the principal clause in the sentence: the matrix presents the upper-level positional scheme which is to be completed by predicative constructions on the lower level. In case of such clauses as subject and predicative, these are all the same subordinated to the matrix by way of being its embedded elements, i.e. the fillers of the open clausal positions introduced by it. Since, on the other hand, the proper segment of the principal clause, i.e. its "nucleus", is predicatively deficient, the whole of the clause should be looked upon as merged with the corresponding filler-subordinate clauses. Thus, among the principal clauses there should be distinguished merger principal clauses and non-merger principal clauses, the former characterizing complex sentences with clausal deployment of their main parts, the latter characterizing complex sentences with clausal deployment of their secondary parts.

§ 3. The principal clause dominates the subordinate clause positionally, but it doesn't mean that by its syntactic status it must express the central informative part of the communication. The information perspective in the simple sentence does not repeat the division of its constituents into primary and secondary, and likewise the information perspective of the complex sentence is not bound to duplicate the division of its clauses into principal and subordinate. The actual division of any construction, be it simple or otherwise, is effected in the context, so it is as part of a continual text that the complex sentence makes its clauses into rheme-rendering and theme-rendering at the complex-sentence information level.

When we discussed the problem of the actual division of the sentence, we pointed out that in a neutral context the rhematic part of the sentence tends to be placed somewhere near the end of it (see Ch. XXII, § 4). This holds true both for the simple and complex sentences, so that the order of clauses plays an important role in distributing primary and secondary information among them. *Cf.*:

The boy was friendly with me because I allowed him to keep the fishing line.

In this sentence approached as part of stylistically neutral text the principal clause placed in the front position evidently expresses the starting point of the information delivered, while the subordinate clause of cause renders the main sentential idea, namely, the speaker's explanation of the boy's attitude. The "contraposition" presupposed by the actual division of the whole sentence is then like this: "Otherwise the boy wouldn't have been friendly". Should the clause-order of the utterance be reversed, the informative roles of the clauses will be re-shaped accordingly:

As I allowed the boy to keep the fishing line, he was friendly with me.

Of course, the clause-order, the same as word-order in general, is not the only means of indicating the correlative informative value of clauses in complex sentences; intonation plays here also a crucial role, and it goes together with various lexical and constructional rheme-forming elements, such as emphatic particles, constructions of meaningful antithesis, patterns of logical accents of different kinds.

Speaking of the information status of the principal clause, it should be noted that even in unemphatic speech this predicative unit is often reduced to a sheer introducer of the subordinate clause, the latter expressing practically all the essential information envisaged by the communicative purpose of the whole of the sentence. *Cf.*:

*You see* that mine is by far the most miserable lot. *Just fancy* that James has proposed to Mary! *You know, kind sir*, that I am bound to fasting and abstinence.

The principal clause-introducer in sentences like these performs also the function of keeping up the conversation, i.e. of maintaining the immediate communicative connection with the listener. This function is referred to as "phatic". Verbs of speech and especially thought are commonly used in phatic principals to specify "in passing" the speaker's attitude to the information rendered by their rhematic subordinates:

*I think* there's much truth in what we hear about the matter. *I'm sure* I can't remember her name now.

Many of these introducer principals can be re-shaped into parenthetical clauses on a strictly equivalent basis by a mere change of position:

There's much truth, *I think*, in what we hear about the matter. I can't remember her name now, *I'm sure*.

§ 4. Of the problems discussed in linguistic literature in connection with the complex sentence, the central one concerns the principles of classification of subordinate clauses. Namely, the two different bases of classification are considered as competitive in this domain: the first is *functional*, the second is *categorial*.

According to the *functional principle*, subordinate clauses are to be classed on the analogy of the positional parts of the simple sentence, since it is the structure of the simple sentence that underlies the essential structure of the complex sentence (located at a higher level). In particular, most types of subordinate clauses meet the same functional question-tests as the parts of the simple sentence. The said analogy, certainly, is far from being absolute, because no subordinate clause can exactly repeat the specific character of the corresponding non-clausal part of the sentence; moreover, there is a deep difference in the functional status even between different categorial types of the same parts of the sentence, one being expressed by a word-unit, another by a word-group, still another by a substitute. *Cf.*:

You can see my state. → You can see my wretched state. → You can see my state being wretched. → You can see that my state is wretched. → You can see that. → What can you see?

Evidently, the very variety of syntactic forms united by a central function and separated by specific sub-functions is brought about in language by the communicative need of expressing not only rough and plain ideas, but also innumerable variations of thought reflecting the ever developing reality.

Furthermore, there are certain (and not at all casual) clauses that do not find ready correspondences among the non-clausal parts of the sentence at all. This concerns, in particular, quite a number of adverbial clauses.

Still, a general functional analogy (though not identity) between clausal and lexemic parts of the sentence does exist, and, which is very important, it reflects the underlying general similarity of their semantic purpose. So, the functional classification of subordinate clauses on the simple sentence-part analogy does reflect the essential properties of the studied syntactic units and has been proved useful and practicable throughout many years of application to language teaching.

Now, according to the *categorial principle*, subordinate clauses are to be classed by their inherent nominative properties irrespective of their immediate positional relations in the sentence. The nominative properties of notional words are reflected in their part-of-speech classification. A question arises, can there be any analogy between types of subordinate clauses and parts of speech?

One need not go into either a detailed research or heated argument to see that no direct analogy is possible here. This is made clear by the mere reason that a clause is a predicative unit expressing an event, while a lexeme is a pure naming unit used only as material for the formation of predicative units, both independent and dependent.

On the other hand, if we approach the categorial principle of the characterization of clauses on a broader basis than drawing plain part-of-speech analogies, we shall find it both plausible and helpful.

As a matter of fact, from the point of view of their general nominative features all the subordinate clauses can be divided into three categorial-semantic groups. The first group includes clauses that name an event as a certain fact. These pure fact-clauses may be terminologically defined as *"substantive-nominal"*. Their substantive-nominal nature is easily checked by a substitute test:

*That his letters remained unanswered* annoyed him very much. → *That fact* annoyed him very much. The woman knew only too well *what was right and what was wrong.* → The woman knew *those matters* well.

The second group of clauses also name an event-fact, but, as different from the first group, this event-fact is referred to as giving a characteristic to some substantive entity (which, in its turn, may be represented by a clause or a phrase or a substantive lexeme). Such clauses, in compliance with our principle of choosing explanatory terminology, can be tentatively called *"qualification-nominal".* The qualification-nominal nature of the clauses in question, as is the case with the first group of clauses, is proved through the corresponding replacement patterns:

The man *who came in the morning* left a message. → *That* man left a message. Did you find a place *where we could make a fire*?→Did you find *such kind of* place?

Finally, the third group of clauses make their event-nomination into a dynamic relation characteristic of another event or a process or a quality of various descriptions. In keeping with the existing practices, it will be quite natural to call these clauses *"adverbial".*

Adverbial clauses are best tested not by a replacement, but by a definitive transformation. *Cf.*:

Describe the picture *as you see it.* → Describe the picture *in the manner you see it.* All will be well *if we arrive in time.* → All will be well *on condition that we arrive in time.*

§ 5. When comparing the two classifications in the light of the systemic principles, it is easy to see that only by a very superficial observation they could be interpreted as alternative (i.e. contradicting each other). In reality they are mutually complementary, their respective bases being valid at different levels of analysis. The categorial features of clauses go together with their functional sentence-part features similar to the categorial features of lexemes going together with their functional characteristics as parts of the simple sentence.

Subordinate clauses are introduced by functional connective words which effect their derivation from base sentences. Categorially these sentence subordinators (or subordinating clausalizers) fall into the two basic types: those that occupy a notional position in the derived clause, and those that do not occupy such a position. The non-positional subordinators are referred to as *pure conjunctions.* Here belong such words as *since, before, until, if, in case, because, so that, in order that, though, however, than, as if,* etc. The positional subordinators are in fact *conjunctive substitutes.* The main positional subordinators are the pronominal words *who, what, whose, which, that, where, when, why, as.* Some of these words are double-functional (bifunctional), entering also the first set of subordinators; such are the words *where, when, that, as,* used both as conjunctive substitutes and conjunctions. Together with these the zero subordinator should be named, whose polyfunctional status is similar to the status of the subordinator *that.* The substitute status of positional subordinators is disclosed in their function as "relative" pronominals, i.e. pronominals referring to syntagmatic antecedents. *Cf.*:

That was the day *when* she was wearing her pink dress. Sally put on her pink dress *when* she decided to join the party downstairs.

The relative pronominal *when* in the first of the cited sentences syntagmatically replaces the antecedent *the day,* while the conjunction *when* in the second sentence has no relative pronominal status. From the point of view of paradigmatics, though, even the second *when* cannot be understood as wholly devoid of substitute force, since it remains associated systemically with the adverb *then,* another abstract indicator of time. So, on the whole the non-substitute use of the double-functional subordinators should be described not as utterly "non-positional", but rather as "semi-positional".

On the other hand, there is another aspect of categorial difference between the subordinators, and this directly corresponds to the nature of clauses they introduce. Namely, nominal clauses, being clauses of fact, are introduced by subordinators of fact (conjunctions and conjunctive subordinators), while adverbial clauses, being clauses of adverbial relations, are introduced by subordinators of relational semantic characteristics (conjunctions). This difference holds true both for monofunctional subordinators and bifunctional subordinators. Indeed, the subordinate clauses expressing time and place and, correspondingly, introduced by the subordinators *when* and *where* may be used both as nominal nominators and adverbial nominators. The said difference is quite essential, though outwardly it remains but slightly featured. *Cf.*:

I can't find the record *where you put it yesterday.* I forget *where I put the record yesterday.*

It is easy to see that the first place-clause indicates the place of action, giving it a situational periphrastic definition, while the second place-clause expresses the object of a mental effort. Accordingly, the subordinator *where* in the first sentence introduces a place description as a background of an action, while the subordinator *where* in the second sentence introduces a place description as a fact to be considered. The first *where* and the second *where* differ by the force of accent (the first is unstressed, the second is stressed), but the main marking difference between them lies in the difference between the patterns of their use, which difference is noted by the chosen terms "nominal" and "adverbial". This can easily be illustrated by a question-replacement test: ... → Where can't I find the record? ... → What do I forget?

Likewise, the corresponding subdivision of the nominal subordinators and the clauses they introduce can be checked and proved on the same lines. *Cf.*:

The day *when we met* is unforgettable. → *Which day* is unforgettable? *When we met* is of no consequence now. → *What* is of no consequence now?

The first *when*-pattern is clearly disclosed by the test as a qualification-nominal, while the second, as a substantive-nominal.

Thus, the categorial classification of clauses is sustained by the semantic division of the subordinators which are distinguished as *substantive-nominal* clausalizers, *qualification-nominal* clausalizers and *adverbial* clausalizers. Since, on the other hand, substantive nomination is primary in categorial rank, while qualification nomination is secondary, in terms of syntactic positions all the subordinate clauses are to be divided into three groups: first, clauses of *primary nominal positions* to which belong subject, predicative and object clauses; second, clauses of *secondary nominal positions* to which belong attributive clauses; third, clauses of *adverbial positions*.

§ 6. Clauses of primary nominal positions – subject, predicative, object – are interchangeable with one another in easy reshufflings of sentence constituents. *Cf.:*

*What you saw at the exhibition* is just *what I want to know.* → *What I want to know* is just *what you saw at the exhibition.* → I just want to know *what you saw at the exhibition.*

However, the specific semantic functions of the three respective clausal positions are strictly preserved with all such interchanges, so that there is no ground to interpret positional rearrangements like the ones shown above as equivalent.

The *subject clause*, in accordance with its functional position, regularly expresses the theme at the upper level of the actual division of the complex sentence. The thematic property of the clause is well exposed in its characteristic uses with passive constructions, as well as constructions in which the voice opposition is neutralized. *E.g.:*

*Why he rejected the offer* has never been accounted for. *What small reputation the town does possess* derives from two things.

It should be noted that in modern colloquial English the formal position of the subject clause in a complex sentence is open to specific contaminations (syntactic confusions on the clausal level). Here is one of the typical examples:

*Just because you say I wouldn't have* (seen a white elephant – *M.B.*) doesn't prove anything (E. Hemingway).

The contamination here consists in pressing into one construction the clausal expression of cause and the expression of the genuine theme-subject to which the predicate of the sentence refers. The logical implication of the statement is that the event in question cannot be taken as impossible by the mere reason of the interlocutor's considering it as such. Thus, what can be exposed of the speaker's idea by way of "de-contaminating" the utterance is approximately like this: *"Your saying that I wouldn't have* doesn't prove anything."

Another characteristic type of syntactic contamination of the subject-clause pattern is its use as a frame for an independent sentence. *E.g.:*

*You just get yourselves into trouble* is what happens (M. Bradbury).

The cited contamination presents a feature of highly emotional speech. The utterance, as it were, proves to be a living illustration of the fact that where strong feelings are concerned the logic of lingual construction is liable to be trespassed upon. The logic in question can be rehabilitated by a substitution pattern: *"You just get yourselves into trouble,* this is what happens."

As is known, the equivalent subject-clausal function can be expressed by the construction with an anticipatory pronoun (mostly the anticipatory *it*). This form of expression, emphasizing the rheme-clause of the sentence, at the same time presents the information of the subject clause in a semantically stronger position than the one before the verb. Therefore the anticipatory construction is preferred in cases when the content of the subject clause is not to be wholly overbalanced or suppressed by the predicate of the sentence. *E.g.:*

*How he managed to pull through* is a miracle. → *It* is a miracle *how he managed to pull through.*

Some scholars analyse the clause introduced by the anticipatory construction as presenting two possibilities of interpretation which stand in opposition to each other. According to the first and more traditional view, this is just a subject clause introduced by the anticipatory *it*, while in the light of the second, the clause introduced by *it* is appositive. In our opinion, the latter explanation is quite rational; however, it cannot be understood as contrary to the "anticipatory" theory. Indeed, the appositive type of connection between the introducer *it* and the introduced clause is proved by the very equivalent transformation of the non-anticipatory construction into the anticipatory one; but the exposition of the appositive character of the clause does not make the antecedent *it* into something different from an introductory pronominal element. Thus, the interpretation of the subject clause referring to the introducer *it* as appositive, in fact, simply explains the type of syntactic connection underlying the anticipatory formula.

304

The *predicative clause*, in conformity with the predicative position as such, performs the function of the nominal part of the predicate, i.e. the part adjoining the link-verb. The link-verb is mostly expressed by the pure link *be*, not infrequently we find here also the specifying links *seem* and *look*; the use of other specifying links is occasional. *E.g.*:

The trouble is *that I don't know Fanny personally*. The question is *why the decision on the suggested innovation is still delayed*. The difficulty seems *how we shall get in touch with the chief before the conference*. After all those years of travelling abroad, John has become *what you would call a man of will and experience*.

Besides the conjunctive substitutes, the predicative clause, the same as other nominal clauses, can be introduced by some conjunctions (*that, whether, as if, as though*). The predicative clause introduced by the conjunctions *as if, as though* has an adverbial force, which is easily shown by contrast:

She looks *as though she has never met him*. → She behaves *as though she has never met him*.

While considering subordinate clauses relating to the finite *be* in the principal clause, care should be taken to strictly discriminate between the linking and non-linking (notional) representations of the verb. Indeed, the linking *be* is naturally followed by a predicative clause, while the notional *be*, featuring verbal semantics of existence, cannot join a predicative. *Cf.*:

It*'s because he's weak* that he needs me. This *was because he had just arrived*.

The cited sentences have been shown by B.A. Ilyish as examples of predicative clauses having a non-conventional nominal-clause conjunction [Ilyish, 276-277]. However, the analysis suggested by the scholar is hardly acceptable, since the introducing *be* in both examples does not belong to the class of links.

The predicative clause in a minimal complex sentence regularly expresses its rheme. Therefore there is an essential informative difference between the two functional uses of a categorially similar nominal clause: that of the predicative and that of the subject. *Cf.*:

The impression is *that he is quite competent*. *That he is quite competent* is the impression.

The second sentence (of an occasional status, with a sentence-stress on the link-verb), as different from the first, suggests an implication of a situational antithesis: the impression may be called in question, or it may be contrasted against another trait of the person not so agreeable as the one mentioned, etc.

The same holds true of complex sentences featuring subordinate clauses in both subject and predicative positions. *Cf.*:

*How she gets there* is *what's troubling me* (→ I am troubled). *What's troubling me* is *how she gets there* (→ How is she to get there?).

The peculiar structure of this type of sentence, where two nominal clauses are connected by a short link making up all the outer composition of the principal clause, suggests the scheme of a balance. For the sake of convenient terminological discrimination, the sentence may be so called – a "complex balance".

The third type of clauses considered under the heading of clauses of primary nominal positions are object clauses.

The *object clause* denotes an object-situation of the process expressed by the verbal constituent of the principal clause.

The object position is a strong substantive position in the sentence. In terms of clausal relations it means that the substantivizing force of the genuine object-clause derivation is a strongly pronounced nominal clause-type derivation. This is revealed, in particular, by the fact that object clauses can be introduced not only non-prepositionally, but also, if not so freely, prepositionally. *Cf.*:

They will accept with grace *whatever he may offer.* She stared *at what seemed a faded photo of Uncle Jo taken half a century before.* I am simply puzzled *by what you are telling me about the Carfairs.*

On the other hand, the semantic content of the object clause discriminates three types of backgrounds: first, an immediately substantive background; second, an adverbial background; third, an uncharacterized background of general event. This differentiation depends on the functional status of the clause-connector, that is on the sentence-part role it performs in the clause. *Cf.*:

We couldn't decide *whom we should address.* The friends couldn't decide *where they should spend their vacation.*

The object clause in the first of the cited sentences is of a substantive background (*We should address* – whom), whereas the object clause in the second sentence is of adverbial-local background (*They should spend their vacation* – where).

The plot of the novel centred *on what might be called a far-fetched, artificial situation*. The conversation centred *on why that clearly formulated provision of international law had been violated*.

The first object clause in the above two sentences is of substantive background, while the second one is of an adverbial-causal background.

Object clauses of general event background are introduced by conjunctions:

Now he could prove *that the many years he had spent away from home had not been in vain*.

The considered background features of subordinate clauses, certainly, refer to their inner status and therefore concern all the nominal clauses, not only object ones. But with object clauses they are of especial contrastive prominence, which is due to immediate dependence of the object clause on the valency of the introducing (subordinating) verb.

An extremely important set of clause-types usually included into the vast system of object clauses is formed by clauses presenting chunks of speech and mental-activity processes. These clauses are introduced by the verbs of speech and mental activity (*Lat.* "verba sentiendi et declarandi"), whose contextual content they actually expose. *Cf.*:

Who says *the yacht hasn't been properly prepared for the voyage*? She wondered *why on earth she was worrying so much, when obviously the time had come to end the incident and put it out of mind*.

The two sentences render by their subordinate clauses speech of the non-author (non-agent) plane: in the first, actual words of some third person are cited, in the second, a stream of thought is presented which is another form of the existence of speech (i.e. inner speech). The chunk of talk rendered by this kind of presentation may not necessarily be actually pronounced or mentally produced by a denoted person; it may only be suggested or imagined by the speaker; still, even in the latter case we are faced by lingually (grammatically) the same kind of non-author speech-featuring complex construction. *Cf.*:

Do you mean to say *that the story has a moral?*

Not all the clauses introduced by the verbs in question belong to this type. In principle, these clauses are divided into the ones *exposing* the content of a mental action (as shown above) and the ones *describing* the content of a mental action, such as the following:

You may tell me *whatever you like.* Will you tell me *what the matter is?*

The object clauses in the cited sentences, as different from the foregoing examples, describe the information allowed by the speaker-author (the first sentence) or wanted by the speaker-author (the second sentence), thereby not differing much from non-speech-rendering clauses. As for the speech-rendering object clauses, they are quite special, and it is by right that, as a rule, they are treated in grammar books under the separate heading of "rules of reported speech". Due to their semantic nature, they may be referred to as "reportive" clauses, and the same term will helpfully apply to the corresponding sentences as wholes. Indeed, it is in reportive sentences that the principal clause is more often than not reduced to an introductory phrase akin to a parenthesis of additionally specifying semantics, so that the formally subordinate clause practically absorbs all the essential information rendered by the sentence. *Cf.*:

*Wainright said* that Eastin would periodically report to him. → Periodically, *Wainright said*, Eastin would report to him (A. Hailey).

§ 7. Subordinate clauses of secondary nominal positions include attributive clauses of various syntactic functions. They fall into two major classes: "descriptive" attributive clauses and "restrictive" ("limiting") attributive clauses.

The descriptive attributive clause exposes some characteristic of the antecedent (i.e., its substantive referent) as such, while the restrictive attributive clause performs a purely identifying role, singling out the referent of the antecedent in the given situation. The basis of this classification, naturally, has nothing to do with the artistic properties of the classified units: a descriptive clause may or may not possess a special expressive force depending on the purpose and mastery of the respective text production. Moreover, of the two attributive clause classes contrasted, the restrictive class is distinguished as the more concretely definable one, admitting of the oppositional interpretation as the "marked element": the descriptive class then will be oppositionally interpreted as the "non-restrictive" one, which precisely explains the correlative status of the two types of subordinate clauses.

It should be noted that, since the difference between descriptive and restrictive clauses lies in their functions, there is a possibility of one and the same clausal unit being used in both capacities, depending on the differences of the contexts. *Cf.*:

At last we found a place *where we could make a fire*. The place *where we could make a fire* was not a lucky one.

The subordinate clause in the first of the cited examples informs the listener of the quality of the place (→ *We found such a place*) thereby being descriptive, while the same clause in the second example refers to the quality in question as a mere mark of identification (→ *The place was not a lucky one*) and so is restrictive.

Descriptive clauses, in their turn, distinguish two major subtypes: first, "ordinary" descriptive clauses; second, "continuative" descriptive clauses.

The ordinary descriptive attributive clause expresses various situational qualifications of nounal antecedents. The qualifications may present a constant situational feature or a temporary situational feature of different contextual relations and implications. *Cf.*:

It gave me a strange sensation to see a lit up window in a big house *that was not lived in*. He wore a blue shirt *the collar of which was open at the throat.* They were playing such a game *as could only puzzle us.*

The continuative attributive clause presents a situation on an "equal domination basis with its principal clause, and so is attributive only in form, but not in meaning. It expresses a new predicative event (connected with the antecedent) which somehow continues the chain of situations reflected by the sentence as a whole. *Cf.*:

In turn, the girls came singly before Brett, *who frowned, blinked, bit his pencil, and scratched his head with it, getting no help from the audience,* who applauded each girl impartially and hooted at every swim suit, as if they could not see hundreds any day round the swimming pool (M. Dickens).

It has been noted in linguistic literature that such clauses are essentially not subordinate, but coordinate, and hence they make up with their principal clause not a complex, but a compound sentence. As a matter of fact, for the most part such clauses are equal to coordinate clauses of the copulative type, and their effective test is the replacement of the relative subordinator by the combination *and* + substitute. *Cf.*:

I phoned to Mr. Smith, *who recognized me at once and invited me to his office.* → I phoned to Mr. Smith, *and he recognized me at once*...

Still, the form of the subordinate clause is preserved by the continuative clause, the contrast between a dependent form and an independent content constituting the distinguishing feature of this syntactic unit as such. Thus, what we do see in continuative clauses is a case of syntactic transposition, i.e. the transference of a subordinate clause into the functional sphere of a coordinate clause, with the aim of achieving an expressive effect. This transpositional property is especially prominent in the *which*-continuative clause that refers not to a single nounal antecedent, but to the whole principal clause. *E.g.*:

The tower clock struck the hour, *which changed the train of his thoughts.* His pictures were an immediate success on the varnishing day, *which was nothing to wonder.*

The construction is conveniently used in descriptions and reasonings.

To attributive clauses belongs also a vast set of appositive clauses which perform an important role in the formation of complex sentences. The appositive clause, in keeping with the general nature of apposition, does not simply give some sort of qualification to its antecedent, but defines or elucidates its very meaning in the context. Due to this specialization, appositive clauses refer to substantive antecedents of abstract semantics. Since the role of appositive clauses consists in bringing about contextual limitations of the meaning of the antecedent, the status of appositive clauses in the general system of attributive clauses is intermediary between restrictive and descriptive.

In accordance with the type of the governing antecedent, all the appositive clauses fall into three groups: first, appositive clauses of *nounal relation;* second, appositive clauses of *pronominal relation;* third, appositive clauses of *anticipatory relation.*

Appositive clauses of nounal relation are functionally nearer to restrictive attributive clauses than the rest. They can introduce information of a widely variable categorial nature, both nominal and adverbial. The categorial features of the rendered information are defined by the type of the antecedent.

The characteristic antecedents of nominal apposition are abstract nouns like *fact, idea, question, plan, suggestion, news, information,* etc. *Cf.*:

The news *that Dr. Blare had refused to join the Antarctic expedition* was sensational. We are not prepared to discuss the question *who will chair the next session of the Surgical Society.*

The nominal appositive clauses can be tested by transforming them into the corresponding clauses of primary nominal positions through the omission of the noun-antecedent or translating it into a predicative complement. *Cf.*:

... → *That Dr. Blare had refused to join the Antarctic expedition* was sensational. → *That Dr. Blare had refused to join the Antarctic expedition* was sensational news.

The characteristic antecedents of adverbial apposition are abstract names of adverbial relations, such as *time, moment, place, condition, purpose,* etc. *Cf.*:

We saw him at the moment *he was opening the door of his Cadillac.* They did it with the purpose *that no one else might share the responsibility for the outcome of the venture.*

As is seen from the examples, these appositive clauses serve a mixed or double function, i.e. a function constituting a mixture of nominal and adverbial properties. They may be tested by transforming them into the corresponding adverbial clauses through the omission of the noun-antecedent and, if necessary, the introduction of conjunctive adverbializers. *Cf.*:

... → We saw him as he was opening the door of his Cadillac. ... → They did it so that no one else might share the responsibility for the outcome of the venture.

Appositive clauses of pronominal relation refer to an antecedent expressed by an indefinite or demonstrative pronoun. The constructions serve as informatively limiting and attention focusing means in contrast to the parallel non-appositive constructions. *Cf.*:

I couldn't agree with all *that she was saying in her irritation.* → I couldn't agree with *what she was saying in her irritation.* (Limitation is expressed.) That *which did strike us* was the inspector's utter ignorance of the details of the case. → *What did strike us* was the inspector's utter ignorance of the details of the case. (The utterances are practically equivalent, the one with a clausal apposition being somewhat more intense in its delimitation of the desired focus of attention.)

Appositive clauses of anticipatory relation are used in constructions with the anticipatory pronoun (namely, the anticipatory *it*, occasionally the demonstratives *this, that*). There are two varieties of these constructions – subjective and objective. The subjective clausal apposition is by far the basic one, both in terms of occurrence (it affects all the notional verbs of the vocabulary, not only transitive) and functional range (it possesses a universal sentence-transforming force). Thus, the objective anticipatory apposition is always interchangeable with the subjective anticipatory apposition, but not vice versa. *Cf.*:

I would consider it (this) a personal offence *if they didn't accept the forwarded invitation.* → It would be a personal offence (to me) *if they didn't accept the forwarded invitation.* You may depend on it *that the letters won't be left unanswered.* → It may be depended on *that the letters won't be left unanswered.*

The anticipatory appositive constructions, as is widely known, constitute one of the most peculiar typological features of English syntax. Viewed as part of the general appositive clausal system here presented, it is quite clear that the exposure of their appositive nature does not at all contradict their anticipatory interpretation, nor does it mar or diminish their "idiomatically English" property so emphatically pointed out in grammar books.

The unique role of the subjective anticipatory appositive construction, as has been stated elsewhere, consists in the fact that it is used as a universal means of rheme identification in the actual division of the sentence.

§ 8. Clauses of adverbial positions constitute a vast domain of syntax which falls into many subdivisions each distinguishing its own field of specifications, complications, and difficulties of analysis. The structural peculiarities and idiosyncrasies characterizing the numerous particular clause models making up the domain are treated at length in grammatical manuals of various practical purposes; here our concern will be to discuss some principal issues of their functional semantics and classification.

Speaking of the semantics of these clauses, it should be stressed that as far as the level of generalized clausal meanings is concerned, semantics in question is of absolute syntactic relevance; accordingly, the traditional identification of major adverbial clause models based on "semantic considerations" is linguistically rational, practically helpful, and the many attempts to refute it in the light of the "newly advanced, objective, consistently scientific" criteria have not resulted in creating a comprehensive system capable of competing with the traditional one in its application to textual materials.

On the other hand, it would be a mistake to call in question the usefulness of the data obtained by the latest investigations. Indeed, if their original negative purpose has failed, the very positive contribution of the said research efforts to theoretical linguistics is not to be overlooked: it consists in having studied the actual properties of the complicated clausal system of the sentence, above all the many-sided correlation between structural forms and functional meanings in the making of the systemic status of each clausal entity that admits of a description as a separate unit subtype.

Proceeding from the said insights, the whole system of adverbial clauses is to be divided into four groups.

The first group includes clauses of *time* and clauses of *place*. Their common semantic basis is to be defined as "localization" – respectively, temporal and spatial. Both types of clauses are subject to two major subdivisions, one concerning the local identification, the other concerning the range of functions.

Local identification is essentially determined by subordinators. According to the choice of connector, clauses of time and place are divided into general and particularizing. The general local identification is expressed by the non-marking conjunctions *when* and *where*. Taken by themselves, they do not introduce any further specifications in the time or place correlations between the two local clausal events (i.e. principal and subordinate). As for the particularizing local identification, it specifies the time and place correlations of the two events localizing the subordinate one before the principal, parallel with the principal, after the principal, and possibly expressing further subgradations of these correspondences.

With subordinate clauses of time the particularizing localization is expressed by such conjunctions as *while, as, since, before, after, until, as soon as, now that, no sooner than*, etc. E.g.:

We lived here in London *when the war ended. While the war was going on* we lived in London. We had lived in London all through the war *until it ended. After the war ended* our family moved to Glasgow. Etc.

With clauses of place proper the particularizing localization is ex-

313

pressed but occasionally, mostly by the prepositional conjunctive combinations *from where* (bookish equivalent – *whence*) and *to where*. *E.g.*:

The swimmers gathered *where the beach formed a small promontory*. The swimmers kept abreast of one another *from where they started*.

For the most part, however, spatial specifications in the complex sentence are rendered not by place-clauses proper, but by adverbial-appositive clauses. *Cf.*:

We decided not to go back to the place *from where we started on our journey*.

From the functional point of view, clauses of localization should be divided into "direct" (all the above ones) and "transferred", the latter mostly touching on matters of reasoning. *E.g.*:

*When you speak of the plain facts* there can't be any question of argument. But I can't agree with you *where the principles of logic are concerned*.

A special variety of complex sentence with a time clause is presented by a construction in which the main predicative information is expressed in the subordinate clause, the actual meaning of temporal localization being rendered by the principal clause of the sentence. *E.g.*:

Alice was resting in bed *when Humphrey returned*. He brought his small charge into the room and presented her to her "aunt" (D.E. Stevenson).

The context clearly shows that the genuine semantic accents in the first sentence of the cited passage is to be exposed by the reverse arrangement of subordination: it is Humphrey's actions that are relevant to the developing situation, not Alice's resting in bed: → Humphrey returned when Alice was resting in bed...

This type of complex sentence is known in linguistics as "inversive"; what is meant by the term, is semantics taken against the syntactic structure. The construction is a helpful stylistic means of literary narration employed to mark a transition from one chain of related events to another one.

The second group of adverbial clauses includes clauses of *manner* and *comparison*. The common semantic basis of their functions can be defined as "qualification", since they give a qualification to the

314

action or event rendered by the principal clause. The identification of these clauses can be achieved by applying the traditional question-transformation test of the *how*-type, with the corresponding variations of specifying character (for different kinds of qualification clauses). *Cf.*:

He spent the Saturday night *as was his wont.* → How did he spend the Saturday night? You talk to people *as if they were a group.* → How do you talk to people? I planned to give my mother a length of silk for a dress, as thick and heavy *as it was possible to buy.* → How thick and heavy the length of silk was intended to be?

All the adverbial qualification clauses are to be divided into "factual" and "speculative", depending on the real or unreal propositional event described by them.

The discrimination between manner and comparison clauses is based on the actual comparison which may or may not be expressed by the considered clausal construction of adverbial qualification. The semantics of comparison is inherent in the subordinators *as if, as though, than*, which are specific introducers of comparison clauses. On the other hand, the subordinator *as*, both single and in the combinations *as ... as, not so ... as*, is unspecific in this sense, and, so invites for a discrimination test to be applied in dubious cases. It should be noted that more often than not a clausally expressed manner in a complex sentence is rendered by an appositive construction introduced by phrases with the broad-meaning words *way* and *manner. E.g.*:

Mr. Smith looked at me in *a way that put me on the alert.*

Herein lies one of the needed procedures of discrimination, which is to be formulated as the transformation of the tested clause into an appositive *that-* or *which*-clause: the possibility of the transformation marks the clause of manner, while the impossibility of the transformation (i.e. the preservation of the original *as*-clause) marks the clause of comparison. *Cf.*:

Mary received the guests as nicely *as Aunt Emma had taught her* → ... in a (very) nice way that Aunt Emma had taught her. (The test marks the clause as that of manner.) Mary received the guests as nicely *as Aunt Emma would have done.* → ... in as nice a way as Aunt Emma would have done. (The test marks the clause as comparative.)

Clauses of comparison are subdivided into those of equality (subordinators *as, as ... as, as if, as though*) and those of inequality (subordinators *not so ... as, than*). The discontinuous introducers mark, respectively, a more intense rendering of the comparison in question. *Cf.*:

That summer he took *a longer holiday than he had done for many years*. For many years he hadn't taken *so long a holiday as he was offered that summer*.

With clauses of comparison it is very important to distinguish the contracted expression of predication, i.e. predicative zeroing, especially for cases where a clause of comparison as such is combined with a clause of time. Here predicative zeroing may lead to the rise of peculiarly fused constructions which may be wrongly understood. By way of example, let us take the sentence cited in B.A. Ilyish's book: *Do you find Bath as agreeable as when I had the honour of making the enquiry before?* (J. Austen)

B.A. Ilyish analyses the construction as follows: "The *when*-clause as such is a temporal clause: it indicates the time when an action ("his earlier enquiry") took place. However, being introduced by the conjunction *as*, which has its correlative, another *as*, in the main clause, it is at the same time a clause of comparison" [Ilyish, 299].

But time and comparison are absolutely different characteristics, so that neither of them can by definition be functionally used for the other. They may go together only in cases when time itself forms the basis of comparison (*I came later than Mr. Jerome did*). As far as the analysed example is concerned, its clause of time renders no other clausal meaning than temporal; the clausal comparison proper is expressed reductionally, its sole explicit representative being the discontinuous introducer *as ... as*. Thus, the true semantics of the cited comparison is to be exposed by paradigmatic de-zeroing: → Do you find Bath as agreeable *as it was* when I had the honour of making the enquiry before?

The applied principle of analysis of contamination time-comparison clauses for its part supports the zero-conception of other outwardly non-predicative comparative constructions, in particular those introduced by *than*. *Cf.*:

Nobody could find the answer quicker *than John*. → Nobody could find the answer quicker *than John did (could do)*.

The third and most numerous group of adverbial clauses includes "classical" clauses of different *circumstantial semantics*, i.e. semantics connected with the meaning of the principal clause by various circumstantial associations; here belong clauses of *attendant event, condition, cause, reason, result (consequence), concession, purpose*. Thus, the common semantic basis of all these clauses can be defined as "circumstance". The whole group should be divided into two subgroups, the first being composed by clauses of *"attendant circumstance"*; the second, by clauses of *"immediate circumstance"*.

Clauses of attendant circumstance are not much varied in structure or semantics and come near to clauses of time. The difference lies in the fact that, unlike clauses of time, the event described by a clause of attendant circumstance is presented as some sort of background in relation to the event described by the principal clause. Clauses of attendant circumstance are introduced by the conjunctions *while* and *as*. E.g.:

*As (while) the reception was going on,* Mr. Smiles was engaged in a lively conversation with the pretty niece of the hostess.

The construction of attendant circumstance may be taken to render contrast; so all the clauses of attendant circumstance can be classed into "contrastive" (clauses of contrast) and "non-contrastive". The non-contrastive clause of circumstance has been exemplified above. Here is an example of contrastive attendant circumstance expressed clausally:

Indeed, there is but this difference between us – that he wears fine clothes *while I go in rags*, and that *while I am weak from hunger* he suffers not a little from overfeeding (O. Wilde).

As is clear from the example, a complex sentence with a contrastive clause of attendant circumstance is semantically close to a compound sentence, i.e. a composite sentence based on coordination.

Clauses of immediate circumstance present a vast and complicated system of constructions expressing different explanations of events, reasonings and speculations in connection with them. The system should relevantly be divided into "factual" clauses of circumstance and "speculative" clauses of circumstance depending on the real or unreal predicative denotations expressed. This division is of especial significance for complex sentences with conditional clauses (real condition, problematic condition, unreal condition). Other types of circumstantial clauses express opposition between factual and speculative semantics with a potential relation to some kind of condition inherent in the deep associations of the syntactic constructions. E.g.:

*Though she disapproved of their endless discussions,* she had to put up with them. (Real concession) → *Though she may disapprove of their discussions,* she will have to put up with them. (Speculative concession) → *If she disapproved (had disapproved) of their discussions,* why would she put up (have put up) with them? (Speculative condition)

The argument was so unexpected *that for a moment Jack lost his ability to speak.* (Real consequence) → The argument was so unexpected *that it would have frustrated Jack's ability to speak if he had understood the deep meaning of it.* (Speculative consequence, based on the speculative condition)

Each type of clauses of circumstance presents its own problems of analysis. On the other hand, it must be pointed out that all the types of these clauses are inter-related both semantically and paradigmatically, which may easily be shown by the corresponding transformations and correlations. Some of such correlations have been shown on the examples above. Compare also:

He opened the window wide *that he might hear the conversation below.* (Purpose) → *Unless he wanted to hear the conversation below* he wouldn't open the window. (Condition) → *As he wanted to hear the conversation below,* he opened the window wide and listened. (Cause) → *Though he couldn't hear properly the conversation below,* he opened the window and listened. (Concession) → The voices were so low *that he couldn't hear the conversation through the open window.* (Consequence) → *If he hadn't opened the window wide* he couldn't have heard the conversation. (Condition)

Certain clausal types of circumstance are closely related to non-circumstantial clausal types. In particular, this kind of connection is observed between conditional clauses and time clauses and finds its specifically English expression in the rise of the contaminated *if-and-when*-clauses:

*If and when the discussion of the issue is renewed,* both parties will greatly benefit by it.

Another important variety of clauses of mixed syntactic semantics is formed by concessive clauses introduced by the connectors ending in *-ever.* E.g.:

*Whoever calls,* I'm not at home. *However tempting the offer might be,* Jim is not in a position to accept it.

Clauses of mixed adverbial semantics present an interesting field of paradigmatic study.

The fourth group of adverbial clauses is formed by *parenthetical* or *insertive* constructions. Parenthetical clauses, as has been stated elsewhere, are joined to the principal clause on a looser basis than the other adverbial clauses; still, they do form with the principal clause a syntactic sentential unity, which is easily proved by the procedure of diagnostic elimination. *Cf.:*

Jack has called here twice this morning, *if I am not mistaken.* → (*) Jack has called here twice this morning.

As is seen from the example, the elimination of the parenthesis changes the meaning of the whole sentence from problematic to assertive: the original sense of the utterance is lost, and this shows that the parenthesis, though inserted in the construction by a loose connection, still forms an integral part of it.

As to the subordinative quality of the connection, it is expressed by the type of the connector used. In other words, parenthetical predicative insertions can be either subordinative or coordinative, which is determined by the contextual content of the utterance and exposed by the connective introducer of the clause. *Cf.* a coordinate parenthetical clause:

Jim said, *and I quite agree with him,* that it would be in vain to appeal to the common sense of the organizers.

*Cf.* the subordinate correlative of the cited clause:

Jim said, *though I don't quite agree with him,* that it would be in vain to appeal to the common sense of the organizers.

Parenthetical clauses distinguish two semantic subtypes. Clauses of the first subtype, illustrated by the first example in this paragraph, are "introductory", they express different modal meanings. Clauses of the second subtype, illustrated by the latter example, are "deviational", they express commenting insertions of various semantic character. Deviational parenthesis marks the loosest possible syntactic connection of clauses combined into a composite sentence.

§ 9. Clauses in a complex sentence may be connected with one another more closely and less closely, similar to the parts of a simple sentence. The intensity of connection between the clauses directly reflects the degree of their proposemic self-dependence and is therefore an essential characteristic of the complex sentence as a whole. For instance, a predicative clause or a direct object clause are connected with the principal clause so closely that the latter cannot exist without them as a complete syntactic unit. Thus, this kind of clausal connection is obligatory. *Cf*.:

The matter is, *we haven't received all the necessary instructions yet.* → (*) The matter· is – ... I don't know *what Mike is going to do about his damaged bike.* → (*) I don't know – ...

As different from this, an ordinary adverbial clause is connected with the principal clause on a looser basis, it can be deleted without destroying the principal clause as an autonomous unit of information. This kind of clausal connection is optional. *Cf*.:

The girl gazed at him *as though she was struck by something extraordinary in his appearance.* → The girl gazed at him.

The division of subordinative clausal connections into obligatory and optional was employed by the Russian linguist N.S. Pospelov (1950) for the introduction of a new classification of complex sentences. According to his views, all the complex sentences of minimal structure (i.e consisting of one principal clause and one subordinate clause) should be classed as "one-member" complex sentences and "two-member" complex sentences. One-member complex sentences are distinguished by an obligatory subordinative connection, while two-member complex sentences are distinguished by an optional subordinative connection. The obligatory connection is determined both by the type of the subordinate clause (subject, predicative, object clauses) and the type of the introduction of the clause (demonstrative correlation). The optional connection characterizes adverbial clauses of diverse functions and attributive clauses of descriptive type. Semantically, one-member complex sentences are understood as reflecting one complex logical proposition, and two-member complex sentences as reflecting two logical propositions connected with each other on the subordinative principle.

The rational character of the advanced conception is quite obvious. Its strong point is the fact that it consistently demonstrates the correlation between form and meaning in the complex sentence structure. Far from rejecting the traditional teaching of complex sentences, the "member conception" is based on its categories and develops them further, disclosing such properties of subordinative connections which were not known to the linguistic science before.

Speaking not only of the complex sentence of minimal composition, but in terms of complex sentences in general, it would be appropriate to introduce the notions of "monolythic" and "segregative" sentence structures. Obligatory subordinative connections underlie monolythic complexes, while optional subordinative connections underlie segregative complexes.

Monolythic complex sentences fall into four basic types.

The first of them is formed by *merger* complex sentences, i.e. sentences with subject and predicative subordinate clauses. The subordinate clausal part of the merger monolyth complex, as has been shown above (see § 2), is fused with its principal clause. The corresponding construction of syntactic anticipation should also be considered under this heading. *Cf.*:

It was at this point *that Bill had come bustling into the room.* → (•) It was at this point – ...

The second subtype of complex sentences in question is formed by constructions whose subordinate clauses are dependent on the obligatory right-hand valency of the verb in the principal clause. We can tentatively call these constructions *"valency" monolyth* complexes. Here belong complexes with object clauses and valency-determined adverbial clauses: from the point of view of subordinative cohesion they are alike. *Cf.*:

I don't know *when I'm beaten.* → (•) I don't know – ... Put the book *where you've taken it from.* → (•) Put the book – ... Her first shock was *when she came down.* → (•) Her first shock was – ...

The third subtype of monolythic complex sentences is formed by constructions based on subordinative correlations – *"correlation" monolythic* complexes. *E.g.*:

His nose was as unkindly short *as his upper lip was long.* You will enjoy such a sight *as you are not likely to see again.* The *more I think of it,* the more I'm convinced of his innocence.

Restrictive attributive clauses should be included into this subtype of correlation monolyths irrespective of whether or not their correlation scheme is explicitly expressed. *Cf.*:

This is the same report *as was submitted last week.* This is the report *that was submitted last week.*

Finally, the fourth subtype of monolythic complex sentences is formed by constructions whose obligatory connection between the principal and subordinate clauses is determined only by the linear order of clausal positions. *Cf.*:

*If he comes,* tell him to wait. → (•) If he comes – ...

As is easily seen, such *"arrangement"* monolythic complexes are not "organically" monolythic, as different from the first three monolyth subtypes; positional re-arrangement deprives them of this quality, changing the clausal connection from obligatory into optional:

Tell him to wait *if he comes.* → Tell him to wait.

The rest of the complex sentences are characterized by segregative structure, the maximum degree of syntactic option being characteristic of subordinative parenthetical connection.

§ 10. Complex sentences which have two or more subordinate clauses discriminate two basic types of subordination arrangement: *parallel* and *consecutive*.

Subordinate clauses immediately referring to one and the same principal clause are said to be subordinated "in parallel" or "co-subordinated". Parallel subordination may be both homogeneous and heterogeneous. For instance, the two clauses of time in the following complex sentence, being embedded on the principle of parallel subordination, are homogeneous – they depend on the same element (the principal clause as a whole), are connected with each other coordinatively and perform the same function:

*When he agrees to hear me, and when we have spoken the matter over,* I'll tell you the result.

Homogeneous arrangement is very typical of object clauses expressing reported speech. *E.g.*:

Mrs. Lewin had warned her *that Cadover was an extraordinary place, and that one must never be astonished by anything* (A. Huxley).

By heterogeneous parallel subordination, co-subordinate clauses mostly refer to different elements in the principal clause. *E.g.*:

The speakers *who represented different nations and social strata* were unanimous in their call for peace *which is so ardently desired by the common people of the world*.

As different from parallel subordination, consecutive subordination presents a hierarchy of clausal levels. In this hierarchy one subordinate clause is commonly subordinated to another, making up an uninterrupted gradation. This kind of clausal arrangement may be called "direct" consecutive subordination. *E.g.*:

I've no idea *why she said she couldn't call on us at the time I had suggested*.

322

Alongside direct consecutive subordination there is another form of clausal hierarchy which is formed without an immediate domination of one subordinate clause over another. For instance, this is the case when the principal clause of a complex multi-level sentence is built up on a merger basis, i.e. includes a subject or predicative clause. E.g.:

*What he saw* made him wince *as though he had been struck.*

In the cited sentence the comparative subordinate clause is dominated by the whole of the principal clause which includes a subordinate propositional unit in its syntactic position of the subject. Thus, the subordinative structure of the sentence is in fact consecutive, though not directly consecutive. This type of hierarchical clausal arrangement may be called "oblique" consecutive subordination; it is of minor importance for the system of subordination perspective as a whole.

The number of consecutive levels of subordination gives the evaluation of the "depth" of subordination perspective – one of the essential syntactic characteristics of the complex sentence. In the first three examples cited in the current paragraph this depth is estimated as 1; in the fourth example (direct consecutive subordination) it equals 3; in the fifth example (oblique consecutive subordination) it equals 2. The subordination perspective of complex sentences used in ordinary colloquial speech seldom exceeds three consecutive clausal levels.

## C H A P T E R  XXVIII

## COMPOUND SENTENCE

§ 1. The compound sentence is a composite sentence built on the principle of coordination. Coordination, the same as subordination, can be expressed either syndetically (by means of coordinative connectors) or asyndetically.

The main semantic relations between the clauses connected coordinatively are copulative, adversative, disjunctive, causal, consequential, resultative. Similar semantic types of relations are to be found between independent, separate sentences forming a continual text. As is known, this fact has given cause to some scholars to deny the existence of the compound sentence as a special, regular form of the composite sentence.[*]

---

[*] See: *Иофик Л.Л.* Сложное предложение в новоанглийском языке. Л., 1968.

The advanced thesis to this effect states that the so-called "compound sentence" is a fictitious notion developed under the school influence of written presentation of speech; what is fallaciously termed the "compound sentence" constitutes in reality a sequence of semantically related independent sentences not separated by full stops in writing because of an arbitrary school convention.

To support this analysis, the following reasons are put forward: first, the possibility of a falling, finalizing tone between the coordinated predicative units; second, the existence, in written speech, of independently presented sentences introduced by the same conjunctions as the would-be "coordinate clauses"; third, the possibility of a full stop-separation of the said "coordinate clauses" with the preservation of the same semantic relations between them.

We must admit that, linguistically, the cited reasons are not devoid of a rational aspect, and, which is very important, they appeal to the actual properties of the sentence in the text. However, the conception taken as a whole gives a false presentation of the essential facts under analysis and is fallacious in principle.

As a matter of fact, there is a substantial semantico-syntactic difference between the compound sentence and the corresponding textual sequence of independent sentences. This difference can escape the attention of the observer when tackling isolated sentences, but it is explicitly exposed in the contexts of continual speech. Namely, by means of differences in syntactic distributions of predicative units, different distributions of the expressed ideas are achieved, which is just the coordinative syntactic functions in action; by means of combining or non-combining predicative units into a coordinative polypredicative sequence the corresponding closeness or looseness of connections between the reflected events is shown, which is another aspect of coordinative syntactic functions. It is due to these functions that the compound sentence does not only exist in the syntactic system of language, but occupies in it one of the constitutive places.

By way of example, let us take a textual sequence of independent monopredicative units:

Jane adored that actor. Hockins could not stand the sight of him. Each was convinced of the infallibility of one's artistic judgment. That aroused prolonged arguments.

Given the "negative" theory of the compound sentence is correct, any coordinative-sentential re-arrangements of the cited sentences must be indifferent as regards the sense rendered by the text. In practice, though, it is not so. In particular, the following arrangement of the predicative units into two successive compound sentences is quite justified from the semantico-syntactic point of view:

→ Jane adored that actor, but Hockins could not stand the sight of him. Each was convinced of the infallibility of one's judgment, and that aroused prolonged arguments.

As different from this, the version of arranging the same material given below cannot be justified in any syntactic or semantic sense:

→ *Jane adored that actor. But Hockins could not stand the sight of him, each was convinced of the infallibility of one's judgment. And that aroused prolonged arguments.

On the other hand, some *subordinate* clauses of a complex sentence can also be separated in the text, thus being changed into specific independent sentences. Still, no one would seek to deny the existence of complex sentence patterns based on optional subordinative connections. *Cf.*:

Suddenly Laura paused *as if she was arrested by something invisible from here.* → Suddenly Laura paused. *As if she was arrested by something invisible from here.*

As for the factor of intonation, it should indeed be invariably taken into account when considering general problems of sentence identification. The propositional intonation contour with its final delimitation pause is one of the constitutive means of the creation and existence of the sentence as a lingual phenomenon. In particular, the developing intonation pattern in the process of speech sustains the semantic sentence strain from the beginning of the sentence up to the end of it. And there is a profound difference between the intonation patterns of the sentence and those of the clause, no matter how many traits of similarity they may possess, including finalizing features. Moreover, as is known, the tone of a coordinate clause, far from being rigorously falling, can be rising as well. The core of the matter is that the speaker has intonation at his disposal as a means of forming sentences, combining sentences, and separating sentences. He actively uses this means, grouping the same syntactic strings of words now as one composite sentence, now as so many simple sentences, with the corresponding more essential or less essential changes in meanings, of his own choice, which is determined by concrete semantic and contextual conditions.

Thus, the idea of the non-existence of the compound sentence in English should be rejected unconditionally. On the other hand, it should be made clear that the formulation of this negative idea as such has served us a positive cause, after all: its objective scientific merit, similar to some other inadequate ideas advanced in linguistics at different times, consists in the very fact that it can be used as a means of counter-argumentation in the course of research work, as a starting point for new insights into the deep nature of lingual phenomena in the process of theoretical analysis sustained by observation.

§ 2. The compound sentence is derived from two or more base sentences which, as we have already stated above, are connected on the principle of coordination either syndetically or asyndetically. The base sentences joined into one compound sentence lose their independent status and become coordinate clauses – parts of a composite unity. The first clause is "leading" (the "leader" clause), the successive clauses are "sequential". This division is essential not only from the point of view of outer structure (clause-order), but also in the light of the semantico-syntactic content: it is the sequential clause that includes the connector in its composition, thus being turned into some kind of dependent clause, although the type of its dependence is not subordinative. Indeed, what does such a predicative unit signify without its syntactic leader?

The coordinating connectors, or coordinators, are divided into conjunctions proper and semi-functional clausal connectors of adverbial character. The main coordinating conjunctions, both simple and discontinuous, are: *and, but, or, nor, neither, for, either ... or, neither ... nor*, etc. The main adverbial coordinators are: *then, yet, so, thus, consequently, nevertheless, however*, etc. The adverbial coordinators, unlike pure conjunctions, as a rule can shift their position in the sentence (the exceptions are the connectors *yet* and *so*). *Cf.*:

Mrs. Dyre stepped into the room, *however* the host took no notice of it. → Mrs. Dyre stepped into the room, the host, *however*, took no notice of it.

The intensity of cohesion between the coordinate clauses can become loose, and in this case the construction is changed into a cumulative one (see Ch. XXVI). *E.g.*:

Nobody ever disturbed him while he was at work; it was one of the unwritten laws.

As has been stated elsewhere, such cases of cumulation mark the intermediary status of the construction, i.e. its place in syntax between a composite sentence and a sequence of independent sentences.

§ 3. When approached from the semantico-syntactic point of view, the connection between the clauses in a compound sentence should be analysed into two basic types: first, the *unmarked* coordinative connection; second, the *marked* coordinative connection.

The unmarked coordinative connection is realized by the coordinative conjunction *and* and also asyndetically. The unmarked semantic nature of this type of connection is seen from the fact that it is not specified in any way and requires a diagnostic exposition through the marked connection. The exposition properly effected shows that each of the two series of compound predicative constructions falls into two principal subdivisions. Namely, the syndetic *and*-constructions discriminate, first, simple copulative relations and, second, broader, non-copulative relations. The asyndetic constructions discriminate, first, simple enumerative relations and, second, broader, non-enumerative relations. *Cf.* examples of the primary connective meanings of the constructions in question:

You will have a great deal to say to her, and she will have a great deal to thank you for. She was tall and slender, her hair was light chestnut, her eyes had a dreamy expression.

The broader connective meanings of the considered constructions can be exposed by equivalent substitutions:

The money kept coming in every week, *and* the offensive gossip about his wife began to be replaced by predictions of sensational success. → The money kept coming in every week, *so* the offensive gossip about his wife began to be replaced by predictions of sensational success. The boy obeyed, the request was imperative. → The boy obeyed, *for* the request was imperative.

The marked coordinative connection is effected by the pure and adverbial coordinators mentioned above. Each semantic type of connection is inherent in the marking semantics of the connector. In particular, the connectors *but, yet, still, however*, etc. express different varieties of adversative relations of clauses; the discontinuous connectors *both ... and, neither ... nor* express, correspondingly, positive and negative (exclusive) copulative relations of events; the connectors *so, therefore, consequently* express various subtypes of clausal consequence, etc.

In order to give a specification to the semantics of clausal relations, the coordinative conjunction can be used together with an accompanying functional particle-like or adverb-like word. As a result, the marked connection, as it were, becomes doubly marked. In particular, the conjunction *but* forms the conjunctive specifying combinations *but merely, but instead, but also* and the like; the conjunction *or* forms the characteristic coordinative combinations *or else, or rather, or even*, etc. *Cf*.:

The workers were not prepared to accept the conditions of the administration, *but instead* they were considering a mass demonstration. She was frank with him, *or rather* she told him everything concerning the mere facts of the incident.

The coordinative specifiers combine also with the conjunction *and*, thus turning the unmarked coordinative connection into a marked one. Among the specifiers here used are included the adverbial coordinators *so, yet, consequently* and some others. *E.g*.:

The two friends didn't dispute over the issue afterwards, *and yet* there seemed a hidden discord growing between them.

It should be specially noted that in the described semantic classification of the types of coordinative relations, the asyndetic connection is not included in the upper division of the system, which is due to its non-specific functional meaning. This fact serves to sustain the thesis that asyndetic connection of clauses is not to be given such a special status in syntax as would raise it above the discrimination between coordination and subordination.

§ 4. It is easily seen that coordinative connections are correlated semantically with subordinative connections so that a compound sentence can often be transformed into a complex one with the preservation of the essential relational semantics between the clauses. The coordinative connections, as different from subordinative, besides the basic opposition to the latter by their ranking quality, are more general, they are semantically less discriminatory, less "refined". That is why the subordinative connection is regularly used as a diagnostic model for the coordinative connection, while the reverse is an exception rather than a rule. *Cf*.:

Our host had rung the bell on our entrance and now a Chinese cook came in with more glasses and several bottles of soda. → *On our entrance, as our host had rung the bell*, a Chinese cook came in with more glasses and several bottles of soda. There was nothing else to do, so Alice soon began talking again. → Alice soon began talking again *because there was nothing else to do*.

328

Speaking of the diagnostic role of subordinative constructions in relation to coordinative, it should be understood that this is of especial importance for the unmarked constructions, in particular for those realized by the conjunction *and*.

On the other hand, the coordinative connection of clauses is in principle not reducible to the subordinative connection, which fact, as in other similar cases of correlations, explains the separate and parallel existence of both types of clausal connection in language. This can be illustrated by the following example: *I invited Mike to join us, but he refused.*

It would appear at first sight that the subordinative diagnostic-specifying exposition of the semantic relations between the clauses of the cited sentence can be achieved by the concessive construction: *Though I invited Mike to join us, he refused.* But the proper observation of the corresponding materials shows that this diagnosis is only valid for part of the possible contexts. Suffice it to give the following two contextual expansions to the sentence in question, of which only one corresponds to the cited diagnosis.

The first expansion: You are mistaken if you think that Mike was eager to receive an invitation to join us. *I invited him, but he refused.*

The given concessive reading of the sentence is justified by the context: the tested compound sentence is to be replaced here by the above complex one on a clear basis of equivalence.

The second expansion: It was decided to invite either Mike or Jesse to help us with our work. *First I invited Mike, but he refused.* Then we asked Jesse to join us.

It is quite clear that the devised concessive diagnosis is not at all justified by this context: what the analysed construction does render here, is a stage in a succession of events, for which the use of a concessive model would be absurd.

§ 5. The length of the compound sentence in terms of the number of its clausal parts (its predicative volume), the same as with the complex sentence, is in principle unlimited; it is determined by the informative purpose of the speaker. The commonest type of the compound sentence in this respect is a two-clause construction.

On the other hand, predicatively longer sentences than two-clause ones, from the point of view of semantic correlation between the clauses, are divided into "open" and "closed" constructions. Copulative and enumerative types of connection, if they are not varied in the final sequential clause, form "open" coordinations. These are used as descriptive and narrative means in a literary text, *Cf.*:

They visited house after house. They went over them thoroughly, examining them from the cellars in the basement to the attics under the roof. *Sometimes* they were too large *and sometimes* they were too small; *sometimes* they were too far from the center of things *and sometimes* they were too close; *sometimes* they were too expensive *and sometimes* they wanted too many repairs; *sometimes* they were too stuffy *and sometimes* they were too airy; *sometimes* they were too dark *and sometimes* they were too bleak. Roger always found a fault that made the house unsuitable (S. Maugham).

In the multi-clause compound sentence of a closed type the final part is joined on an unequal basis with the previous ones (or one), whereby a finalization of the expressed chain of ideas is achieved. The same as open compound sentences, closed compound constructions are very important from the point of view of a general text arrangement. The most typical closures in such compound sentences are those effected by the conjunctions *and* (for an asyndetic preceding construction) and *but* (both for an asyndetic and copulative syndetic preceding construction). *Cf.*, respectively:

His fingernails had been cleaned, his teeth brushed, his hair combed, his nostrils cleared and dried, *and* he had been dressed in formal black by somebody or other (W. Saroyan). Pleasure may turn a heart to stone, riches may make it callous, *but* sorrow – oh, sorrow cannot break it (O. Wilde).

The structure of the closed coordinative construction is most convenient for the formation of expressive climax.

### CHAPTER XXIX

### SEMI-COMPLEX SENTENCE

§ 1. In accord with the principles laid down in the introductory description of composite sentences (Ch. XXVI), the semi-composite sentence is to be defined as a sentence with more than one predicative lines which are expressed in fusion. For the most part, one of these lines can be identified as the leading or dominant, the others making the semi-predicative expansion of the sentence. The expanding semi-predicative line in the minimal semi-composite sentence is either wholly fused with the dominant (complete) predicative line of the construction, or partially fused with it, being weakened as a result of the fusing derivational transformation.

The semi-composite sentence displays an intermediary syntactic character between the composite sentence and the simple sentence. Its immediate syntagmatic structure ("surface" structure) is analogous to that of an expanded simple sentence, since it possesses only one completely expressed predicative unit. Its derivational structure ("deep" structure), on the other hand, is analogous to that of a composite sentence, because it is derived from two or more completely predicative units – its base sentences.

There are two different causes of the existence of the semi-composite sentence in language, each of them being essentially important in itself.

The first cause is the tendency of speech to be economical. As a result of this tendency, reductional processes are developed which bring about semi-blending of sentences. The second cause is that, apart from being economical, the semi-composite sentence fulfills its own purely semantic function, different from the function of the composite sentence proper (and so supplementing it). Namely, it is used to show that the events described in the corresponding sentence parts are more closely connected than the events described in the parts of the composite sentence of complete composition. This function is inherent in the structure – it reflects the speaker's view of reality, his presentation of it. Thus, for different reasons and purposes the same two or several events can be reflected now by one type of structure, now by another type of structure, the corresponding "pleni"- and semi-constructions existing in the syntactic system of language as pairs of related and, for that matter, synonymically related functions. *E.g.*:

*The sergeant gave a quick salute to me*, and then he put his squad in motion. → *Giving a· quick salute ·to me*, the sergeant put his squad in motion. → *With a quick salute to me*, the sergeant put his squad in motion.

The two connected events described by the cited sentences are, first, the sergeant's giving a salute to the speaker, and, second, the sergeant's putting his squad in motion. The first sentence, of the pleni-composite type, presents these situationally connected events in separate processual descriptions as they happened one after the other, the successive order being accentuated by the structural features of the construction, in particular, its sequential coordinate clause. The second sentence, of the semi-composite participial-expanded type, expresses a semantic ranking of the events in the situational blend, one of them standing out as a dominant event, the other as a by-event. In the presentation of the third construction, belonging to the primitivized type of semi-composition (maximum degree of blending), the fusion of the events is shown as constituting a unity in which the attendant action (the sergeant's salute) forms simply a background detail in relation to the immediately reflected occurrence (the sergeant's putting the squad in motion).

According to the ranking structure of the semi-composite sentences, they should be divided into *semi-complex* and *semi-compound* ones. These constructions correspond to the complex and compound sentences of complete composition (i.e., respectively, *pleni-complex* and *pleni-compound* sentences).

§ 2. The semi-complex sentence is a semi-composite sentence built up on the principle of subordination. It is derived from minimum two base sentences, one matrix and one insert. In the process of semi-complexing, the insert sentence is transformed into a partially depredicated construction which is embedded in one of the syntactic positions of the matrix sentence. In the resulting construction, the matrix sentence becomes its dominant part and the insert sentence, its subordinate semi-clause.

The semi-complex sentences fall into a number of subtypes. Their basic division is dependent on the character of predicative fusion: this may be effected either by the process of *position-sharing* (*word-sharing*), or by the process of direct *linear expansion*. The sentences based on position-sharing fall into those of *subject-sharing* and those of *object-sharing*. The sentences based on semi-predicative linear expansion fall into those of *attributive complication*, *adverbial complication*, and *nominal-phrase complication*. Each subtype is related to a definite complex sentence (pleni-complex sentence) as its explicit structural prototype.

§ 3. Semi-complex sentences of subject-sharing are built up by means of the two base sentences overlapping round the common subject. *E.g.*:

*The man* stood. + *The man* was silent. → *The man* stood silent.

*The moon* rose. + *The moon* was red. → *The moon* rose red.

From the syntagmatic point of view, the predicate of these sentences forms the structure of the "double predicate" because it expresses two essential functions at once: first, the function of a verbal type (the verb component of the predicate); second, the function of a nominal type (the whole combination of the verb with the nominal component). The paradigmatic analysis shows that the verb of the double predicate, being on the surface a notional link-verb, is in fact a quasi-link.

In the position of the predicative of the construction different categorial classes of words are used with their respective specific meanings and implications: nouns, adjectives, participles both present and past. *Cf.*:

Sam returned from the polar expedition *a grown-up man*. They waited *breathless*. She stood *bending over the child's bed*. We stared at the picture *bewildered*.

Observing the semantic content of the given constructions, we see that, within the bounds of their functional differences, they express two simultaneous events – or, rather, the simultaneity of the event described by the complicator expansion with that described by the dominant part. At the same time the construction gives informative prominence not to its dominant, but to the complicator, and corresponds to the pleni-complex sentence featuring the complicator event in the principal clause placed in post-position. *Cf.*:

The moon rose *red*. → As the moon rose *it was red*. She stood *bending over the child's bed*. → As she stood *she was bending over the child's bed*.

In the subject-sharing semi-composites with reflexivised dominant verbs of intense action the idea of change is rendered. *E.g.:*

He spoke himself *hoarse*. → As he spoke *he became hoarse*. (Further diagnosis: He spoke and spoke until he became hoarse.)

Apart from the described types of subject-sharing sentences there is a variety of them featuring the dominant verb in the passive. *E.g.:*

The idea *has never been considered* a wise one. The company *was ordered* to halt.

These sentences have active counterparts as their paradigmatic derivation bases which we analyse below as semi-complex sentences of object sharing.

**§ 4.** Semi-complex sentences of object-sharing, as different from those of subject-sharing, are built up of two base sentences overlapping round the word performing different functions in them: in the matrix sentence it is the object, in the insert sentence it is the subject. The complicator expansion of such sentences is commonly called the "complex object". *E.g.*:

We saw *him.* + *He* approached us. → We saw *him* approach us (approaching us). They painted *the fence.* + *The fence* was (became) green. → They painted *the fence* green.

Some dominant verbs of such constructions are not used in the same essential meaning outside the constructions, in particular, some causative verbs, verbs of liking and disliking, etc. *Cf.*:

*I *made* him. + He obeyed. → I *made* him obey.

This fact, naturally, reflects a very close unity of the constituents of such constructions, but, in our opinion, it cannot be looked upon as excluding the constructions from the syntactic subsystem in question; rather, the subsystem should be divided into the subsets of "free" object-sharing and "bound" object-sharing.

The adjunct to the shared object is expressed by an infinitive, a present or past participle, an adjective, a noun, depending on the structural type of the insert sentence (namely, on its being verbal or nominal).

As is seen from the above, the paradigmatic (derivational) explanation of the sentence with a "complex object" saves much descriptive space and, which is far more important, is at once generalizing and practicable.* As for the relations between the two connected events expressed by the object-sharing sentence, they are of the three basic types: first, relations of *simultaneity* in the same place; second, relations of *cause* and *result*; third, relations of *mental attitude* towards the event (events thought of, spoken of, wished for, liked or disliked, etc.). All these types of relations can be explicated by the corresponding transformations of the semi-complex sentences into pleni-complex sentences.

Simultaneity in the same place is expressed by constructions with dominant verbs of perceptions (*see, hear, feel, smell,* etc.). *E.g.*:

---

* *Cf.* the classical "syntagmatic" explanation of constructions with complex objects in the cited B.A. Ilyish's book, p. 257 ff.

He felt the morning breeze *gently touching his face.* → He felt the morning breeze *as it was gently touching his face.* I never heard the word *pronounced like that.* → I never heard the word *as it was pronounced like that.*

Cause and result relations are rendered by constructions with dominant causative verbs taking three types of complex objects: an unmarked infinitival complex object (the verbs *make, let, get, have, help*); a nounal or adjectival complex object (the verbs *call, appoint, keep, paint,* etc.); a participial complex object (the verbs *set, send, keep,* etc.). *Cf.*:

I helped Jo *find the photo.* → I helped Jo *so that he found the photo.* The cook beat the meat *soft.* → The cook beat the meat *so that it was (became) soft.*

Different mental presentations of the complicator event are effected, respectively, by verbs of mental perceptions and thinking (*think, believe, expect, find,* etc.); verbs of speech (*tell, ask, report, announce,* etc.); verbs of wish: verbs of liking and disliking. *Cf.*:

You will find *many things strange here.* → You will find *that many things are strange here.* I didn't mean *my words to hurt you.* → I didn't mean *that my words should hurt you.*

Semi-complex sentences of the object-sharing type, as we have stated above, are closely related to sentences of the subject-sharing type. Structurally this is expressed in the fact that they can be transformed into the passive, their passive counterparts forming the corresponding subject-sharing constructions. *Cf.*:

We *watched the plane disappear* behind the distant clouds. → *The plane was watched to disappear* behind the distant clouds. They *washed the floor clean.* → *The floor was washed clean.*

Between the two series of constructions, i.e. active and passive, equivalence of the event-relations is observed, so that the difference in their basic meaning is inherent in the difference between the verbal active and passive as such.

§ 5. Semi-complex sentences of attributive complication are derived from two base sentences having an identical element that occupies the position of the subject in the insert sentence and any notional position in the matrix sentence. The insert sentence is usually an expanded one. By the semi-complexing process, the insert sentence drops out its subject-identical constituent and is transformed into a semi-predicative post-positional attribute to the antecedent element in the matrix sentence. *E.g.*:

*The waves* sent out fine spray. + *The waves* rolled over the dam. → *The waves* rolling over the dam sent out fine spray. I came in late for *the supper*. + *The supper* was served in the dining-room. → I came in late for *the supper* served in the dining-room.

The analogy between post-positional attributes (especially of a detached type) and attributive subordinate clauses has always been pointed out in grammar books of various destination. The common pre-positional attribute is devoid of a similar 'half-predicative character and is not to be considered as forming a semi-composite construction with the dominant predicative unit. *Cf.*:

The *bored* family switched off the TV. – The family, *bored*, switched off the TV.

As for the possible detachment of the defining element (construction) in pre-position, this use is rather to be analysed as adverbial, not attributive, the circumstantial semantic component prevailing over the attributive one in this case. *Cf.*:

*Bored*, the family switched off the TV. → *As the family was bored*, it switched off the TV.

Naturally, the existence of some intermediary types cannot be excluded, which should be exposed in due course by the corresponding contextual observation.

As is seen, the base syntactic material for producing attributively complicated semi-composites is similar to the derivation base of position-sharing semi-composites. The essential difference between the constructions, though, lies in the character of joining their clausal parts: while the process of overlapping deprives the position-sharing expansion of any self-dependent existence, however potential it might be, the process of linear expansion with the attributive complication preserves the autonomous functional role of the semi-clause. The formal test of it is the possibility of inserting into the construction a relative conjunctive plus the necessary verbal element, changing the attributive semi-clause into the related attributive pleni-clause. *E.g.*:

This is a novel *translated from the French*. → This is a novel *which has been translated from the French*.

This test resembles a reconstruction, since an attributive complication in many respects resembles a reduced clause. The position-sharing expansion does not admit of this kind of procedure: the very process of overlapping puts it out of the question. The other factor of difference is the obligatory status of the position-sharing expansion (even in constructions of "free" object sharing) against the optional status of the attributive complicator.

The attributive semi-clause may contain in its head position a present participle, a past participle and an adjective. The present participial attributive semi-clause corresponds to the attributive subordinate clause with a verbal predicate in the active. *E.g.*:

We found dry ground at the base of a tree *looking toward the sun.* → We found dry ground at the base of a tree *that looked toward the sun.*

Naturally, the present participial semi-clause of the attributive type cannot express an event prior to the event of the dominant clause. So, an attributive clause of complete predicative character expressing such an event has no parallel in a participial attributive semi-clause. *E.g.*:

The squad *that picked me up* could have been scouts. → (*) The squad *picking me up*...

The past participial attributive semi-clause corresponds to the passive attributive subordinate clause. *E.g.*:

You can never rely on the information *received from that office.* → You can never rely on the information *which is received from that office.*

The adjectival attributive semi-clause corresponds to the nominal attributive subordinate clause. *E.g.*:

We admired the lilies *white against the blue water.* → We admired the lilies *which were white against the blue water.*

Semi-complex sentences of participial attributive complication formed by introducer constructions resemble subject-sharing semi-complex sentences. *Cf.*:

There is a river *flowing through the town.* → There is a river *which flows through the town.* This is John *speaking.* → This is John *who is speaking.*

Still closer to the subject-sharing semi-composite sentence stands the peculiar introducer or demonstrative construction whose attributive semi-clause has a finite verb predicate. This specific semi-complex sentence, formed much on the pattern of common subject overlapping, is called the "apo-koinou" construction (Greek "with a common element"). E.g.:

It was you *insisted on coming*, because you didn't like restaurants (S. O'Casey). He's the one *makes the noise at night* (E. Hemingway). And there's nothing more *can be done* (A. Christie).

The apo-koinou construction is considered here under the heading of the semi-complex sentence of attributive complication on the ground of its natural relation to the complex sentence with an attributive subordinate clause, similar to any common semi-complex sentence of the type in question. The apo-koinou construction should be classed as a familiar colloquialism of occasional use.

§ 6. Semi-complex sentences of adverbial complication are derived from two base sentences one of which, the insert sentence, is predicatively reduced and embedded in an adverbial position of the other one, the matrix sentence. E.g.:

*The task was completed.* + The task seemed a very easy one. → The task, *when completed*, seemed a very easy one. *The windows were closed.* + She did not hear the noise in the street. → *The windows being closed*, she did not hear the noise in the street.

The subject of the insert sentence may be either identical with that of the matrix sentence (the first of the above examples) or not identical with it (the second example). This feature serves as the first fundamental basis for classifying the semi-complex sentences in question, since in the derived adverbial semi-clause the identical subject is dropped out and the non-identical subject is preserved. It will be reasonable to call the adverbial semi-clause of the first type (i.e. referring to the subject of the dominant clause) the "conjoint" semi-clause. The adverbial complicator expansion of the second type (i.e. having its own subject) is known under the name of the "absolute construction" (it will further be referred to as "absolutive").

The given classification may be formulated for practical purposes as the "rule of the subject", which will run as follows: by adverbializing semi-complexing the subject of the insert sentence is deleted if it is identical with the subject of the matrix sentence.

The other classificational division of adverbial semi-clauses concerns the representation of the predicate position. This position is only partially predicative, the role of the partial predicate being performed by the participle, either present or past. The participle is derived from the finite verb of the insert sentence; in other words, the predicate of the insert sentence is participialized in the semi-clause. Now, the participle-predicate of the adverbial semi-clause may be dropped out if the insert sentence presents a nominal or existential construction (the finite verb *be*). Thus, in accord with this feature of their outer structure, adverbial semi-clauses are divided into participial and non-participial. *E.g.:*

One day Kitty had an accident. + She *was swinging in the garden*. → One day Kitty had an accident while *swinging in the garden*. (The participle is not to be deleted, being of an actional character.) He *is very young*. + He is quite competent in this field. → Though *being very young*, he is quite competent in this field. → Though *very young*, he is quite competent in this field. (The participle can be deleted, being of a linking nature.) She spoke as if *being in a dream*. → She spoke as if *in a dream*. (The predicate can be deleted, since it is expressed by the existential *be*.)

The two predicate types of adverbial semi-clauses, similar to the two subject types, can be briefly presented by the "rule of the predicate" as follows: by adverbializing semi-complexing the verb-predicate of the insert sentence is participialized, and may be deleted if it is expressed by *be*.

Conjoint adverbial semi-clauses are either introduced by adverbial subordinator conjunctions or joined to the dominant clause asyndetically. The adverbial semantics expressed is temporal, broader local, causal, conditional, comparative. *Cf.* syndetic introduction of adverbial semi-clauses:

He was silent *as if not having heard the call.* → ... *as if he had not heard the call.* Read on *unless told otherwise.* → ... *unless you are told otherwise. Although kept out of the press*, the event is widely known in the diplomatic circles. → *Although it is kept out of the press... When in London*, the tourists travelled in double-deckers. → *When they were in London...*

Asyndetic introduction of adverbial semi-clauses is characteristic of temporal and causal constructions. *Cf.:*

*Working on the book*, the writer travelled much about the country. → *When working on the book... Dialling her number*, she made a mistake. → *While dialling her number... Being tired*, I could not accept the invitation. → *As I was tired...*

As for the absolutive adverbial semi-clauses, they are joined to the dominant clause either asyndetically, or, mostly for the purpose of emphasis, by the conjunction *with*. The adverbial semantics of the absolutive complicator expansion is temporal, causal, and attendant-circumstantial. *E.g.*:

*Everything being settled*, Moyra felt relieved. → *As everything was settled... Two days having elapsed*, the travellers set out on their way. → *When two days had elapsed... With all this work waiting for me*, I can't afford to join their Sunday outing. → *As all this work is waiting for me...*

The rule of the predicate is observed in absolutive complicators the same as in conjoint adverbial complicators. Its only restriction concerns impersonal sentences where the link-verb is not to be deleted. *Cf.*:

*The long luncheon over*, the business friend would bow and go his way. → *When the long luncheon was over... It being very hot*, the children gladly ran down to the lake. → *As it was very hot...*

§ 7. Semi-complex sentences of nominal phrase complication are derived from two base sentences one of which, the insert sentence, is partially nominalized (changed into a verbid phrase of infinitival or gerundial type) and embedded in one of the nominal and prepositional adverbial positions of the other sentence serving as the matrix. The nominal verbid constructions meet the demands both of economy and expressiveness, and they are widely used in all the functional orders of speech. The gerundial phrase is of a more substantive semantic character, the infinitival phrase, correspondingly, of a more processual semantic character. The gerundial nominalization involves the optional change of the noun subject into the possessive, while the infinitival nominalization involves the use of the preposition *for* before the subject. *E.g.*:

*Tom's coming late* annoyed his mother. → *The fact that Tom came late* annoyed his mother. *For him to come so late* was unusual. → It was unusual that he came so late.

The rule of the subject exposed in connection with the adverbial semi-complexing (see above) applies also to the process of partial nominalization and is especially important here. It concerns the two types of subject deletion: first, its contextual identification; second, its referring to a general (indefinite) person. Thus, the rule can be formulated in this way: the subject of the verbid phrase is deleted when it is either identified from the context (usually, but not necessarily, from the matrix sentence) or denotes an indefinite person. *Cf.* the contextual identification of the subject:

*We are definite* about it. → *Our being definite* about it. → Let's postpone *being definite* about it. *Mary has recovered* so soon. → *For Mary to have recovered* so soon. → Mary is happy *to have recovered* so soon.

*Cf.* the indefinite person identification of the subject:

*One avoids* quarrels with strangers. → *One's avoiding* quarrels with strangers. → *Avoiding* quarrels with strangers is always a wise policy. *One loves* spring. → *For one to love* spring. → It's but natural *to love* spring.

A characteristic function of the infinitive phrase is its use with subordinative conjunctions in nominal semi-clauses. The infinitive in these cases implies modal meanings of obligation, admonition, possibility, etc. *E.g.*:

I wondered *where to go.* → I wondered *where I was to go.* The question is *what to do next.* → The question is *what we should do next.*

In contrast with nominal uses of infinitive phrases, gerundial phrases are widely employed as adverbial semi-clauses introduced by prepositions. Semi-clauses in question are naturally related to the corresponding adverbial pleni-clauses. *Cf.*:

*In writing the letter* he dated it wrong. → *While he was writing the letter* he dated it wrong. She went away *without looking back.* → As she went away *she didn't look back.* I cleaned my breast *by telling you everything.* → I cleaned my breast *because I told you everything.*

The prepositional use of gerundial adverbial phrases is in full accord with the substantival syntactic nature of the gerund, and this feature differentiates in principle the gerundial adverbial phrase from the participial adverbial phrase as a positional constituent of the semi-complex sentence.

## CHAPTER XXX

## SEMI-COMPOUND SENTENCE

§ 1. The semi-compound sentence is a semi-composite sentence built up on the principle of coordination. Proceeding from the outlined grammatical analysis of the composite sentence, the structure of the semi-compound sentence is derivationally to be traced back to minimum two base sentences having an identical element belonging to one or both of their principal syntactic positions, i.e. either the subject, or the predicate, or both. By the process of semi-compounding, the sentences overlap round the identical element sharing it in coordinative fusion, which can be either syndetic or asyndetic. Thus, from the formal point of view, a sentence possessing coordinated notional parts of immediately sentential reference (directly related to its predicative line) is to be treated as semi-compound. But different structural types of syntactic coordination even of direct sentential reference (coordinated subjects, predicates, objects, adverbial modifiers) display very different implications as regards semi-compounding composition of sentences.

By way of a general statement we may say that, other things being equal, the closer the coordinative group is related to the verb-predicate of the sentence, and at the same time the looser the interconnection between its components (coordinated elements), the more directly and explicitly it functions as a factor of sentence semi-compounding.

For instance, coordinated subjects connected asyndetically in an enumerative sequence or forming a plain copulative syndetic string can hardly be taken as constituting so many separately identified predicative lines with the verbal constituent of the sentence. As different from this, two subject-groups connected adversatively or antithetically are more "live" in their separate relation to the predicative centre; the derivative reference of such a sentence to the two source predicative constructions receives some substantiality. *E.g.*:

There was *nothing* else, only *her face* in front of me. → There was nothing else in front of me. + There was only her face in front of me.

Substantially involved in the expression of semi-compounding is a combination of two subjects relating to one predicate when the subjects are discontinuously positioned, so that the first starts the utterance, while the second concludes it with some kind of process-referred introduction. *Cf.*:

*The entrance door* stood open, and also *the door of the living-room*. → The entrance door stood open. + The door of the living-room stood also open.

However, if we turn our attention to genuine coordinations of predicates (i.e. coordinations of non-repetitive or otherwise primitivizing type), both verbal and nominal, we shall immediately be convinced of each element of the group presenting its own predicative centre relating to the one subject axis of the sentence, thereby forming a strictly compounding fusion of the predicative lines expressed. This fact is so trivially clear that it does not seem to require a special demonstration.

Hence, we will from now on treat the corresponding sentence-patterns with coordinate predicate phrases as featuring classes of constructions that actually answer the identifying definition of semi-compound sentence; in our further exposition we will dwell on some structural properties and functional semantics of this important sentence type so widely represented in the living English speech in all its lingual divisions, which alone displays an unreservedly clear form of sentential semi-compounding out of the numerous and extremely diversified patterns of syntactic coordination.

§ 2. The semi-compound sentence of predicate coordination is derived from minimum two base sentences having identical subjects. By the act of semi-compounding, one of the base sentences in most cases of textual occurrence becomes the leading clause of complete structure, while the other one is transformed into the sequential coordinate semi-clause (expansion) referring to the same subject. *E.g.*:

The soldier *was badly wounded.* + The soldier *stayed in the ranks.* → The soldier *was badly wounded*, but *stayed in the ranks*. He *tore the photograph in half.* + He *threw the photograph in the fire.* → He *tore the photograph in half and threw it in the fire.*

The rare instances contradicting the given rule concern inverted constructions where the intense fusion of predicates in overlapping round the subject placed in the end position deprives the leading clause of its unbroken, continuous presentation. *Cf.*:

*Before him lay* the road to fame. + The road to fame *lured him.* → *Before him lay and lured him* the road to fame.

In the case of a nominal predicate, the sequential predicative complement can be used in a semi-compound pattern without its linking part repeated. *E.g.*:

343

My manner *was matter-of-fact,* and *casual.* The savage *must have been asleep* or *very tired.*

The same holds true about coordinated verbids related to a common finite verb in the function of an auxiliary or otherwise. *E.g.*:

The tiger *was at large* and *burning* with rage. He *could not recall* the face of the peasant girl or *remember* the feel of her.

By the number of bases joined (and predicate phrases representing them), semi-compound sentences may be two-base (minimal) or multi-base (more than minimal two-base). The coordinated expansion is connected with the leading part either syndetically or asyndetically.

The syndetic formation of the semi-compound sentence expresses, first, copulative connection of events; then contrast, either comparative or adversative; furthermore, disjunction (alternation), consequence, limitation, elucidation. The conjunctive elements effecting this syndetic semi-compounding of sentences are both pure conjunctions and also words of adverbial nature. The pure conjunction *and*, the same as with pleni-compound sentences, expresses the *unmarked* semantic type of semi-compounding; the rest of the connectors render various *marked* types of it. The pure conjunctions used for semi-compounding, besides the copulative *and*, are monoconjunctions *but, or, nor*, and double (discontinuous) conjunctions *both ... and, not only ... but also, either ... or, neither ... nor.* The conjunctive adverbials are *then, so, just, only.*

Here are some examples of double-conjunctional formations expressing, respectively, disjunction, simple copulative relation, copulative antithesis, copulative exclusion:

They *either* went for long walks over the fields, *or* joined in a quiet game of chess on the veranda. That great man was *both* a soldier *and* a born diplomat. Mary *not only* put up with his presence, *but* tried to be hospitable. I am *neither* for the proposal, *nor* against the proposal; *nor* participating in that sham discussion of theirs at all.

*Cf.* instances of conjunctive-adverbial introduction of predicate expansion rendering the functional meanings of action ordering (*then*), of adversative-concessive relation (*yet*), of consequence (*so*), of limitation (*just*):

His beady eyes searched the clearing, *then* came back to my face. He was the tallest and bravest, *yet* was among those to give up life. I knew then that she was laughing, *so* laughed with her. The Colonel didn't enlarge on the possible outcome of their adventure, *just* said a few words of warning against the abrupt turns of the mountain-pass.

With semi-compound sentences, similar to pleni-compound sentences, but on a larger scale, conjunctions combine with particle-like elements of modal-adverbial description. These elements supplement and specify the meaning of the conjunction, so that they receive the status of sub-conjunction specifiers, and the pairs "conjunction plus sub-conjunctive" become in fact regular conjunctive-coordinative combinations. Here belong such combinations as *and then, and perhaps, and probably, and presently, and so, and consequently,* etc.; *but merely, but only, but instead, but nevertheless,* etc.; *or else, or even, or rather,* etc. The specifications given by the sub-conjunctives are those of change of events, probability evaluation, consequence in reasoning, concessive contrast, limiting condition, intensity gradation, and many others, more specific ones. *E.g.*:

He waited for some moments longer *and then* walked down to the garden to where, on the terrace, the jeep was parked (H.E. Bates). She lived entirely apart from the contemporary literary world *and probably* was never in the company of anyone more talented than herself (J. Austen). To his relief, she was not giving off the shifting damp heat of her anger, *but instead* was cool, decisive, material (J. Updike). For several hours I discussed this with you, *or rather* vented exhaustive rewordings upon your silent phantom (J. Updike).

§ 3. Of all the diversified means of connecting base sentences into a semi-compound construction the most important and by far the most broadly used is the conjunction *and*. Effecting the unmarked semi-compounding connection of sentences, it renders the widest possible range of syntactic relational meanings; as for its frequency of occurrence, it substantially exceeds that of all the rest of the conjunctives used for semi-compounding taken together.

The functional meanings expressed by the *and*-semi-compound patterns can be exposed by means of both coordinative and subordinative correlations. Here are some basic ones:

The officer parked the car at the end of the terrace *and* went into the Mission. → The officer parked the car ..., *then* went into the Mission (Succession of events, inviting a coordinative exposition).

Suddenly the door burst open *and* Tommy rushed in panting for breath. → *As* the door burst open, Tommy rushed in ... ("Successive simultaneity" of actions, inviting a subordinative exposition). Patterton gavelled for attention *and* speedily disposed of several routine matters. → Patterton gavelled for attention *so that* he could dispose and did dispose of several routine matters (Purpose in successive actions, inviting a subordinative exposition). Her anger and emotion grew, *and* finally exploded. → Her anger and emotion grew *to the degree that* they finally exploded (Successive actions in gradation, inviting a subordinative exposition). He just miscalculated *and* won't admit it. → *Though* he miscalculated, he won't admit it (Concession in opposition, inviting a subordinative exposition). Mary promised to come *and* he was determined to wait. → He was determined to wait *because* Mary had promised to come (Cause and consequence, inviting a subordinative exposition).

Among the various connective meanings expressed by the conjunction *and* in combination with the corresponding lexemic constituents of the sentence there are two standing very prominent, due to the regular correlations existing between such constructions and semi-complex patterns with verbid phrases – infinitival and participial.

The first construction expresses a subsequent action of incidental or unexpected character:

He leaped up in time *to see the Colonel rushing out of the door* (H.E. Bates). → He leaped up in time *and saw the Colonel rushing out of the door.* Walker woke in his bed at the bourbon house *to hear a strange hum and buzz in the air* (M. Bradbury). → Walker woke in his bed at the bourbon house *and heard a strange hum and buzz in the air.*

In these constructions the leading clause, as a rule, includes verbs of positional or psychological change, while the expansion, correspondingly, features verbs of perceptions. As is seen from the examples, it is the semi-compound pattern that diagnoses the meaning of the pattern with the infinitive, not the reverse. The infinitive pattern for its part makes up an expressive stylistic device by virtue of its outward coincidence with an infinitive pattern of purpose: the unexpectedness of the referent action goes together with the contextual unexpectedness of the construction.

The participial construction expresses a parallel attendant event that serves as a characteristic to the event rendered by the leading clause:

He sat *staring down the gardens, trying to remember whether this was the seventh or eighth day since the attack had begun* (H.E. Bates). → He was sitting *and staring down the gardens, and was trying to remember...* Rage flamed up in him, *contorting his own face* (M. Puzo). → Rage flamed up in him *and contorted his own face.*

With the participial pattern, the same as with the infinitival one, the diagnostic construction is the semi-compound sentence, not vice versa.

The nature of the shown correlations might be interpreted as a reason for considering the relations between the head-verb and the verbid in the tested patterns as coordinative, not subordinative. However, on closer analysis we must admit that diagnosis of this kind is called upon to expose the hidden meanings, but not to level up the differences between units of opposed categorial standings. The verbid patterns remain part of the system of semi-complex sentences because of the hierarchical ranking of their notional positions, while the correlation with semi-compound sentences simply explains their respective semantic properties.

§ 4. The asyndetic formation of the semi-compound sentence stands by its functional features close to the syndetic *and*-formation in so far as it does not give a rigorous characterization (semantic mark) to the introduced expansion. At the same time its functional range is incomparably narrower than that of the *and*-formation.

The central connective meaning distinguishing the asyndetic connection of predicative parts in semi-compound sentences is enumeration of events, either parallel or consecutive. In accord with the enumerative function, asyndetic semi-compounding more often than not is applied to a larger set of base sentences than the minimal two. *E.g.*:

He *closed* the door behind him with a shaking hand, *found* the old car in its parking place, *drove* along with the drifting lights. They *talked, laughed, were perfectly happy* late into the night.

Asyndetic semi-compound sentences are often used to express gradation of intensity going together with a general emphasis. *E.g.*:

He would in truth *give up the shop, follow her to Paris, follow her also to the château in the country* (D. du Maurier). He *never took the schoolbag again, had refused to touch it* (J. Updike).

Characteristic of enumerative and gradational semi-compound sentences is the construction where the first two parts are joined asyndetically, and the third part syndetically, by means of the conjunction *and*. In such three-base constructions the syndetic expansion finalizes the sentence both structurally and semantically, making it into an intensely complete utterance. *E.g.:*

He knows his influence, struts about *and considers himself a great duellist.* They can do it, have the will to do it, *and are actually doing it.*

Of the meanings other than enumerative rendered by the construction in question, the most prominent is elucidation combined with various connotations, such as consequence, purpose, additional characteristics of the basic event. *Cf.:*

The sight of him made me feel young again: *took me back to the beaches, the Ardennes, the Reichswald, and the Rhine.* I put an arm round her, *tried to tease her into resting.*

§ 5. The number of predicative parts in a semi-compound sentence is balanced against the context in which it is used, and, naturally, is an essential feature of its structure. This number may be as great as seven, eight, or even more.

The connection-types of multi-base semi-compound sentences are syndetic, asyndetic, and mixed.

The syndetic semi-compound sentences may be homosyndetic (i.e. formed by so many entries of one and the same conjunctive) and heterosyndetic (i.e. formed by different conjunctives). The most important type of homosyndetic semi-compounding is the *and*-type. Its functional meaning is enumeration combined with copulation. *E.g.:*

A harmless young man going nowhere in particular was *knocked down and trodden on and rose* to fight back *and was punched* in the head by a policeman in mistake for someone else *and hit* the policeman back *and ended* in more trouble than if he had been on the party himself (M. Dickens).

A series of successive events is intensely rendered by a homosyndetic construction formed with the help of the conjunctive *then. E.g.:*

You *saw* the flash, *then heard* the crack, *then saw* the smoke ball distort and thin in the wind (E. Hemingway).

Another conjunctive pattern used in homosyndetic semi-compounding is the *or*-type in its different variants. *E.g.*:

After dinner we *sat* in the yard of the inn on hard chairs, *or paced* about the platform *or stumbled* between the steel sleepers of the permanent way (E. Waugh). Babies never *cried or got* the wind *or were sick* when Nurse Morrison fed them (M. Dickens).

By heterosyndetic semi-compounding the parts of the sentence are divided into groups according to the meanings of the conjunctives. *Cf.*:

A native woman in a sarong *came and looked* at them, *but vanished* when the doctor addressed her (S. Maugham). Ugly *sat* in the bow *and barked* arrogantly at passing boats, *or stood* rockily peering in the river (M. Dickens).

The asyndetic connections in semi-compound sentences, within their range of functions, are very expressive, especially when making up long enumerations-gradations. *E.g.*:

He *had enjoyed* a sharp little practice in Split, *had meddled* before the war in anti-Serbian politics, *had found* himself in an Italian prison, *had been let out* when the partisans briefly "liberated" the coast, *had been swept up* with them in the retreat (E. Waugh).

In the mixed syndetic-asyndetic semi-compound sentence various groupings of coordinated parts are effected. *E.g.*:

He *spun* completely round, *then fell forward* on his knees, *rose* again *and limped* slowly on (E. Waugh).

In cases where multi-base semi-compound sentences are formed around one and the same subject-predicate combination, they are very often primitivized into a one-predicate sentence with coordinated secondary parts. Of these sentences, a very characteristic type is presented by a construction with a string of adverbial groups. This type of sentence expresses an action (usually, though not necessarily, a movement) or a series of actions continued through a sequence of consecutive place and time situations. *E.g.*:

Then she took my hand, and *we went down the steps of the tower together, and through the court and to the walls of the rock-place* (D. du Maurier).

The construction is very dynamic, its adverbial constituents preserve clear traces of the corresponding predications, and therefore it approaches the genuine semi-compound sentence of predicate coordination by its semantic nature.

§ 6. The semi-compound sentence of predicate coordination immediately correlates with a compound sentence of complete composition having identical subjects. Both constructions are built upon the same set of base sentences, use the same connective means and reflect the same situation. *E.g.*:

*She looked* at him *and saw* again the devotion, the humility in his eyes. → *She looked* at him and *she saw* again the devotion, the humility in his eyes (The latter sentence – from D. du Maurier). *The officer received* the messengers, took their letters, *and* though I stood with them, completely *ignored* me. → *The officer received* the messengers, took their letters, *and* though I stood with them, *he* completely *ignored* me (The latter sentence – from H.E. Stover).

A question arises whether the compared sentences are absolutely the same in terms of functions and semantics, or whether there is some kind of difference between them which causes them to be used discriminately.

In an attempt to expose the existing functional difference between the two constructions, it has been pointed out that base sentences with identical subjects are connected not into a semi-compound, but into a compound sentence (of complete composition) in the three main cases: first, when the leading sentence is comparatively long; second, when the finite verbs in the two sentences are of different structure; third, when the second sentence is highly emotional.[*] These tentative formulations should rather be looked upon as practical guides, for they do correspond to the existing tendencies of living speech. But the tendencies lack absolute regularity and, which is far more significant, they do not present complete lingual facts by themselves, but rather are particular manifestations of a general and fundamental mechanism at work. This mechanism is embodied in the actual division of the sentence: as a matter of fact, observations of the relevant contexts show that the structure of the actual division in the two types of sentences is essentially different. Namely, whereas the actual division of the compound sentence with identical subjects presents two (or more) separate informative perspectives characterized by identical themes and different rhemes, the actual di-

---

[*] *Irtenyeva N.F., Shapkin A.P., Blokh M.Y.* The Structure of the English Sentence. M., 1969, p. 110.

vision of the semi-compound sentence presents only one perspective, analysed into one theme and one, though complex, rheme; the latter falls into two or more constituent rhemes (sub-rhemes) in various concrete contexts.

The sub-rhemes may be of equal importance from the informational point of view, as in the following example:

We were met by a guide who *spoke excellent English* and *had a head full of facts.*

The sub-rhemes may be of unequal informative importance, the predicative expansion rendering the basic semantic content of the sentence. *E.g.:*

She *gave us her address* and *asked us to come and see her.*

The coordinated predicate groups may also be informatively fused into an essentially simple rheme, i.e. into a phrase making up a close informative unity. *E.g.:*

He *took out his diary and began to write.* The man *looked up and laughed.*

As different from the semi-compound construction with its exposed informative properties, the very identity of the subject themes in a compound sentence of complete composition is a factor making it into a communicatively intense, logically accented syntactic unit (compare the examples given at the beginning of the paragraph).

CHAPTER XXXI

SENTENCE IN THE TEXT

§ 1. We have repeatedly shown throughout the present work that sentences in continual speech are not used in isolation; they are interconnected both semantically-topically and syntactically.

Inter-sentential connections have come under linguistic investigation but recently. The highest lingual unit which was approached by traditional grammar as liable to syntactic study was the sentence; scholars even specially stressed that to surpass the boundaries of the sentence was equal to surpassing the boundaries of grammar.

In particular, such an outstanding linguist as L. Bloomfield, while recognizing the general semantic connections between sentences in the composition of texts as linguistically relevant, at the same time pointed out that the sentence is the largest grammatically arranged linguistic form, i.e. it is not included into any other linguistic form by a grammatical arrangement.[*]

However, further studies in this field have demonstrated the inadequacy of the cited thesis. It has been shown that sentences in speech do come under broad grammatical arrangements, do combine with one another on strictly syntactic lines in the formation of larger stretches of both oral talk and written text.

It should be quite clear that, supporting the principle of syntactic approach to arrangement of sentences into a continual text, we do not assert that any sequence of independent sentences forms a syntactic unity. Generally speaking, sentences in a stretch of uninterrupted talk may or may not build up a coherent sequence, wholly depending on the purpose of the speaker. *E.g.*:

BARBARA. Dolly: don't be insincere. Cholly: fetch your concertina and play something for us (B. Shaw).

The cited sequence of two sentences does not form a unity in either syntactic or semantic sense, the sentences being addressed to different persons on different reasons. A disconnected sequence may also have one and the same communication addressee, as in the following case:

DUCHESS OF BERWIC... I like him so much. I am quite delighted he's gone! How sweet you're looking! Where do you get your gowns? And now I must tell you how sorry I am for you, dear Margaret (O. Wilde).

But disconnected sequences like these are rather an exception than the rule. Moreover, they do not contradict in the least the idea of a continual topical text as being formed by grammatically interconnected sentences. Indeed, successive sentences in a disconnected sequence mark the corresponding transitions of thought, so each of them can potentially be expanded into a connected sequence bearing on one unifying topic. Characteristically, an utterance of a personage in a work of fiction marking a transition of thought (and breaking the syntactic connection of sentences in the sequence) is usually introduced by a special author's comment. *E.g.*:

"You know, L.S., you're rather a good sport." *Then his tone grew threatening again.* "It's a big risk I'm taking. It's the biggest risk I've ever had to take" (C.P. Snow).

---

[*] See: *Bloomfield L.* Language. N.Y., 1933, p. 170.

As we see, the general idea of a sequence of sentences forming a text includes two different notions. On the one hand, it presupposes a succession of spoken or written utterances irrespective of their forming or not forming a coherent semantic complex. On the other hand, it implies a strictly topical stretch of talk, i.e. a continual succession of sentences centering on a common informative purpose. It is this latter understanding of the text that is syntactically relevant. It is in this latter sense that the text can be interpreted as a lingual entity with its two distinguishing features: first, *semantic (topical) unity*; second, *semantico-syntactic cohesion*.

§ 2. The primary division of sentence sequences in speech should be based on the communicative direction of their component sentences. From this point of view monologue sequences and dialogue sequences are to be discriminated.

In a monologue, sentences connected in a continual sequence are directed from one speaker to his one or several listeners. Thus, the sequence of this type can be characterized as a one-direction sequence. *E.g.*:

We'll have a lovely garden. We'll have roses in it and daffodils and a lovely lawn with a swing for little Billy and little Barbara to play on. And we'll have our meals down by the lily pond in summer (K. Waterhouse and H. Hall).

The first scholars who identified a succession of such sentences as a special syntactic unit were the Russian linguists N.S. Pospelov and L.A. Bulakhovsky. The former called the unit in question a "complex syntactic unity", the latter, a "super-phrasal unity". From consistency considerations, the corresponding English term used in this book is the "supra-sentential construction" (see Ch. I).

As different from this, sentences in a dialogue sequence are uttered by the speakers-interlocutors in turn, so that they are directed, as it were, to meet one another; the sequence of this type, then, should be characterized as a two-direction sequence. *E.g.*:

"Annette, what have you done?" – "I've done what I had to do" (S. Maugham).

It must be noted that two-direction sequences can in principle be used within the framework of a monologue text, by way of an "inner dialogue" (i.e. a dialogue of the speaker with himself). *E.g.*:

What were they jabbering about now in Parliament? *Some twopenny-ha'penny tax!* (J. Galsworthy).

On the other hand, one-direction sequences can be used in a dialogue, when a response utterance forms not a rejoinder, but a continuation of the stimulating utterance addressed to the same third party, or to both speakers themselves as a collective self-addressee, or having an indefinite addressee. *E.g.:*

ST. ERTH. All the money goes to fellows who don't know a horse from a haystack. – CANYNGE (*profoundly*). And care less. Yes! We want men racing to whom a horse means something (J. Galsworthy). ELYOT. I'm glad we didn't go out tonight. AMANDA. Or last night. ELYOT. Or the night before. AMANDA. There's no reason to, really, when we're cosy here (N. Coward).

Thus, the direction of communication should be looked upon as a deeper characteristic of the sentence-sequence than its outer, purely formal presentation as either a monologue (one man's speech) or a dialogue (a conversation between two parties). In order to underline these deep distinguishing features of the two types of sequences, we propose to name them by the types of sentence connection used. The formation of a one-direction sequence is based on syntactic cumulation of sentences, as different from syntactic composition of sentences making them into one composite sentence. Hence, the supra-sentential construction of one-direction communicative type can be called a cumulative sequence, or a "cumuleme". The formation of a two-direction sequence is based on its sentences being positioned to meet one another. Hence, we propose to call this type of sentence connection by the term "occursive", and the supra-sentential construction based on occursive connection, by the term "occurseme".

Furthermore, it is not difficult to see that from the hierarchical point of view the occurseme as an element of the system occupies a place above the cumuleme. Indeed, if the cumuleme is constructed by two or more sentences joined by cumulation, the occurseme can be constructed by two or more cumulemes, since the utterances of the interlocutors can be formed not only by separate sentences, but by cumulative sequences as well. *E.g.:*

"Damn you, stop talking about my wife. If you mention her name again I swear I'll knock you down." – "Oh no, you won't. You're too great a gentleman to hit a feller smaller than yourself" (S. Maugham).

As we see, in formal terms of the segmental lingual hierarchy, the supra-proposemic level (identified in the first chapter of the book) can be divided into two sublevels: the lower one at which cumulemic connection of sentences are identified, and the higher one at which occursemic connection of sentences are identified. On the other hand, a fundamental difference between the two units in question should be carefully noted lying beyond the hierarchy relation, since the occurseme, as different from the cumuleme, forms part of a conversation, i.e. is essentially produced not by one, but by two or several speakers, or, linguistically, not by one, but by two or several individual sub-lingual systems working in communicative contact.

As for the functional characteristic of the two higher segmental units of language, it is representative of the function of the text as a whole. The signemic essence of the text is exposed in its topic. The monologue text, or "discourse", is then a topical entity; the dialogue text, or "conversation", is an exchange-topical entity. The cumuleme and occurseme are component units of these two types of texts, which means that they form, respectively, subtopical and exchange-subtopical units as regards the embedding text as a whole. Within the framework of the system of language, however, since the text as such does not form any "unit" of it, the cumuleme and occurseme can simply be referred to as topical elements (correspondingly, topical and exchange-topical), without the "sub"-specification.

§ 3. Sentences in a cumulative sequence can be connected either "prospectively" or "retrospectively".

Prospective ("epiphoric", "cataphoric") cumulation is effected by connective elements that relate a given sentence to one that is to follow it. In other words, a prospective connector signals a continuation of speech: the sentence containing it is semantically incomplete. Very often prospective connectors are notional words that perform the cumulative function for the nonce. *E.g.*:

I tell you, *one of two things* must happen. *Either* out of that darkness some new creation will come to supplant us as we have supplanted the animals, *or* the heavens will fall in thunder and destroy us (B. Shaw).

The prospective connection is especially characteristic of the texts of scientific and technical works. *E.g.*:

Let me add *a word of caution* here. The solvent vapour drain enclosure must be correctly engineered and constructed to avoid the possibility of a serious explosion (From a technical journal).

As different from prospective cumulation, retrospective (or "anaphoric") cumulation is effected by connective elements that relate a given sentence to the one that precedes it and is semantically complete by itself. Retrospective cumulation is the more important type of sentence connection of the two; it is the basic type of cumulation in ordinary speech. *E.g.*:

What curious "class" sensation was *this*? Or was *it* merely fellow-feeling with the hunted, a tremor at the way things found one out? (J. Galsworthy).

§ 4. On the basis of the functional nature of connectors, cumulation is divided into two fundamental types: *conjunctive* cumulation and *correlative* cumulation.

Conjunctive cumulation is effected by conjunction-like connectors. To these belong, first, regular conjunctions, both coordinative and subordinative; second, adverbial and parenthetical sentence-connectors (*then, yet, however, consequently, hence, besides, moreover, nevertheless*, etc.). Adverbial and parenthetical sentence-connectors may be both specialized, i.e. functional and semi-functional words, and non-specialized units performing the connective functions for the nonce. *E.g.*:

There was an indescribable agony in his voice. *And* as if his own words of pain overcame the last barrier of his self-control, he broke down (S. Maugham). There was no train till nearly eleven, and she had to bear her impatience as best she could. *At last* it was time to start, and she put on her gloves (S. Maugham).

Correlative cumulation is effected by a pair of elements one of which, the "succeedent", refers to the other, the "antecedent", used in the foregoing sentence; by means of this reference the succeeding sentence is related to the preceding one, or else the preceding sentence is related to the succeeding one. As we see, by its direction correlative cumulation may be either retrospective or prospective, as different from conjunctive cumulation which is only retrospective.

Correlative cumulation, in its turn, is divided into substitutional connection and representative connection. Substitutional cumulation is based on the use of substitutes. *E.g.*:

Spolding woke me with the apparently noiseless efficiency of the trained housemaid. *She* drew the curtains, placed a can of hot water in my basin, covered it with the towel, and retired (E.J. Howard).

356

A substitute may have as its antecedent the whole of the preceding sentence or a clausal part of it. Furthermore, substitutes often go together with conjunctions, effecting cumulation of mixed type. *E.g.*:

And as I leaned over the rail methought that all the little stars in the water were shaking with austere merriment. *But it* may have been only the ripple of the steamer, after all (R. Kipling).

Representative correlation is based on representative elements which refer to one another without the factor of replacement. *E.g.*:

She should be here soon. I must tell Phipps, I am not in to *any one else* (O. Wilde). I went home. Maria accepted *my departure* indifferently (E.J. Howard).

Representative correlation is achieved also by repetition, which may be complicated by different variations. *E.g.*:

Well, the night was beautiful, and the great thing not to be a pig. *Beauty* and *not being a pig*! Nothing much else to it (J. Galsworthy).

§ 5. A cumuleme (cumulative supra-sentential construction) is formed by two or more independent sentences making up a topical syntactic unity. The first of the sentences in a cumuleme is its "leading" sentence, the succeeding sentences are "sequential".

The cumuleme is delimited in the text by a finalizing intonation contour (cumuleme-contour) with a prolonged pause (cumuleme-pause); the relative duration of this pause equals two and a half moras ("mora" – the conventional duration of a short syllable), as different from the sentence-pause equalling only two moras.

The cumuleme, like a sentence, is a universal unit of language in so far as it is used in all the functional varieties of speech. For instance, the following cumuleme is part of the author's speech of a work of fiction:

The boy winced at this. It made him feel hot and uncomfortable all over. He knew well how careful he ought to be, and· yet, do what he could, from time to time his forgetfulness of the part betrayed him into unreserve (S. Butler).

Compare a cumuleme in a typical newspaper article:

We have come a long way since then, of course. Unemployment insurance is an accepted fact. Only the most die-hard reactionaries, of the Goldwater type, dare to come out against it (from *Canadian Press*).

Here is a sample cumuleme of scientific-technical report prose:

To some engineers who apply to themselves the word "practical" as denoting the possession of a major virtue, applied research is classed with pure research as something highbrow they can do without. To some business men, applied research is something to have somewhere in the organisation to demonstrate modernity and enlightenment. And people engaged in applied research are usually so satisfied in the belief that what they are doing is of interest and value that they are not particularly concerned about the niceties of definition (from a technical journal).

Poetical text is formed by cumulemes, too:

She is not fair to outward view, | As many maidens be; | Her loveliness I never knew | Until she smiled on me. | Oh, then I saw her eye was bright, | A well of love, a spring of light (H. Coleridge).

But the most important factor showing the inalienable and universal status of the cumuleme in language is the indispensable use of cumulemes in colloquial speech (which is reflected in plays, as well as in conversational passages in works of various types of fiction).

The basic semantic types of cumulemes are "factual" (narrative and descriptive), "modal" (reasoning, perceptive, etc.), and mixed. Here is an example of a narrative cumuleme:

Three years later, when Jane was an Army driver, she was sent one night to pick up a party of officers who had been testing defences on the cliff. She found the place where the road ran between a cleft almost to the beach, switched off her engine and waited, hunched in her great-coat, half asleep, in the cold black silence. She waited for an hour and woke in a fright to a furious voice coming out of the night (M. Dickens).

Compare this with modal cumulemes of various topical standings:

She has not gone? I thought she gave a second performance at two? (S. Maugham) (A reasoning cumuleme of perceptional variety)

Are you kidding? Don't underrate your influence, Mr. O'Keefe. Dodo's in. Besides, I've lined up Sandra Straughan to work with her (A. Hailey). (A remonstrative cumuleme)

Don't worry. There will be a certain amount of unpleasantness but I will have some photographs taken that will be very useful at the inquest. There's the testimony of the gunbearers and the driver too. You're perfectly all right (E. Hemingway). (A reasoning cumuleme expressing reassurance) Etc.

§ 6. As we have stated above (see: Ch. I, § 5) cumuleme (super-sentential construction) correlates with a separate sentence which is placed in the text in a topically significant position. In printed text this correlation leads to the formation of one-sentence paragraph that has the same topical function as a multi-sentence paragraph from the point of view of the communicative content of the text. *E.g.:*

The fascists may spread over the land, blasting their way with weight of metal brought from other countries. They may advance aided by traitors and by cowards. They may destroy cities and villages and try to hold the people in slavery. But you cannot hold any people in slavery.

*The Spanish people will rise again as they have always risen before against tyranny* (E. Hemingway).

In the cited passage the sentence-paragraph marks a transition from the general to the particular, and by its very isolation in the text expressively stresses the author's belief in the invincible will of the Spanish people who are certain to smash their fascist oppressors in the long run.

Thus, from the point of view of style, the regular function of the one-sentence paragraph is expressive emphasis.

And it is direct correlation between one-sentence paragraphs and multi-sentence paragraphs that enables us to identify the general elementary unit-segment of text as being built either by a cumuleme or by a single sentence. The communicative function of this unit is topical. We call this unit the "dicteme" (see p. 17).

It must be noted that though the dicteme in written (printed) text is normally represented by a paragraph, these two units are not identical.

In the first place, the paragraph is a stretch of written (printed) literary text delimited by a new (indented) line at the beginning and an incomplete line at the close. As different from this, the dicteme, as we have just seen, is essentially a feature of all the varieties of speech, both oral and written, both literary and colloquial.

In the second place, the paragraph is a polyfunctional unit of written speech and as such is used not only for the written representation of a dicteme, but also for the introduction of utterances of a dialogue (dividing an occurseme into parts), as well as for the introduction of separate points in various enumerations.

In the third place, the paragraph in a monologue speech can contain more than one dicteme. For instance, the following paragraph is divided into three parts, the first formed by a separate sentence (i.e. by a sentence-dicteme), the second and third ones presenting cumulemes. For the sake of clarity, we mark the borders between the parts by double strokes:

When he had left the house Victorina stood quite still, with hands pressed against her chest. // She had slept less than he. Still as a mouse, she had turned the thought: "Did I take him in? Did I?" And if not – what? // She took out the notes which had bought – or sold – their happiness, and counted them once more. And the sense of injustice burned within her (J. Galsworthy).

The shown division is sustained by the succession of the forms of the verbs, namely, the past indefinite and past perfect, precisely marking out the events described.

On the other hand, the dicteme cannot commonly be prolonged beyond the limits of the paragraph, since the paragraphal border-marks are the same as those of the dicteme, i.e. a characteristic finalizing tone, a pause of two and a half moras. Besides, we must bear in mind that both multidicteme paragraphs and one-sentence paragraphs are stylistically marked features of the monologue text. Thus, we return to our initial thesis that the paragraph, although it is a literary-compositional, not a purely syntactic unit of text, still as a rule represents a dicteme; the two units, if not identical, are closely correlative.

§ 7. The introduction of the notions of dicteme and cumuleme in linguistics helps specify and explain the two peculiar and rather important border-line phenomena between the sentence and the sentential sequence.

The first of these is known under the heading of "parcellation". The parcellated construction ("parcellatum") presents two or more collocations ("parcellas") separated by a sentence tone but related to one another as parts of one and the same sentence. In writing the parts, i.e., respectively, the "leading parcella" and "sequential parcella", are delimited by a full stop (finality mark). *E.g.*:

There was a sort of community pride attached to it now. *Or shame at its unavoidability* (E. Stephens). Why be so insistent, Jim? *If he doesn't want to tell you* (J. O'Hara). ...I realized I didn't feel one way or another about him. *Then.* I do now (J. O'Hara).

Having recourse to the idea of transposition, we see that the parcellated construction is produced as a result of transposing a sentence into a cumuleme. This kind of transposition adds topical significance to the sequential parcella. The emphasizing function of parcellation is well exposed by the transformation of de-transposition. This transformation clearly deprives the sequential parcella of its position of topical significance, changing it into an ordinary sentence-part. *Cf.*:

... → There was a sort of community pride attached to it now *or shame at its unavoidability.* ... → Why be so insistent, Jim, *if he doesn't want to tell you?* ... → I didn't feel one way or another about him *then.*

With some authors parcellation as the transposition of a sentence into a cumuleme can take the form of forced paragraph division, i.e. the change of a sentence into a supra-cumuleme. *E.g.*:

...It was she who seemed adolescent and overly concerned, while he sat there smiling fondly at her, quite self-possessed, even self-assured, and adult.
*And naked.* His nakedness became more intrusive by the second, until she half arose and said with urgency, "You have to go and right now, young man" (E. Stephens).

The second of the border-line phenomena in question is the opposite of parcellation, it consists in forcing two different sentences into one, i.e. in transposing a cumuleme into a sentence. The cumuleme-sentence construction is characteristic of uncareful and familiar speech; in a literary text it is used for the sake of giving a vivid verbal characteristic to a personage. *E.g.*:

I'm not going to disturb her *and that's flat, miss* (A. Christie). The air-hostess came down the aisle then to warn passengers they were about to land *and please would everyone fasten their safety belts* (B. Hedworth).

The transposition of a cumuleme into a sentence occurs also in literary passages dealing with reasoning and mental perceptions. *E.g.*:

If there were moments when Soames felt cordial, they were such as these. He had nothing against the young man; *indeed*, he rather liked the look of him; *but* to see the last of almost anybody was in a sense a relief; *besides*, there was this question of what he had overheard, and to have him about the place without knowing would be a continual temptation to compromise with one's dignity and ask him what it was (J. Galsworthy).

As is seen from the example, one of the means of transposing a cumuleme into a sentence in literary speech is the use of half-finality punctuation marks (here, a semicolon).

§ 8. Neither dictemes-cumulemes, nor paragraphs form the upper limit of textual units of speech. Paragraphs are connected within the framework of larger elements of texts making up different paragraph groupings. Thus, above the process of cumulation as syntactic connection of separate sentences, supra-cumulation should be discriminated as connection of dictemes-cumulemes and paragraphs into larger textual unities of the correspondingly higher subtopical status. *Cf.*:

... That first slip with my surname was just like him; and afterwards, particularly when he was annoyed, apprehensive, or guilty because of me, he frequently called me Ellis.
*So*, in the smell of Getliffe's tobacco, I listened to him as he produced case after case, sometimes incomprehensibly, because of his allusive slang, often inaccurately. He loved the law (C.P. Snow).

In the given example, the sentence beginning the second paragraph is cumulated (i.e. supra-cumulated) to the previous paragraph, thus making the two of them into a paragraph grouping.

Moreover, even larger stretches of text than primary paragraph groupings can be supra-cumulated to one another in the syntactic sense, such as chapters and other compositional divisions. For instance, compare the end of Chapter XXIII and the beginning of Chapter XXIV of J. Galsworthy's "Over the River":

Chapter XXIII. ... She went back to Condaford with her father by the morning train, repeating to her Aunt the formula: "I'm not going to be ill."
Chapter XXIV. *But* she was ill, and for a month in her conventional room at Condaford often wished she were dead and done with. She might, indeed, quite easily have died...

Can, however, these phenomena signify that the sentence is simply a sub-unit in language system, and that "real" syntactic elements of this system are not sentences, but various types of dictemes or supra-dictemes? – In no wise.

Supra-sentential connections cannot be demonstrative of the would-be "secondary", "sub-level" role of the sentence as an element of syntax by the mere fact that all the cumulative and occursive relations in speech, as we have seen from the above analysis, are effected by no other unit than the sentence, and by no other structure than the inner structure of the sentence; the sentence remains the central structural-syntactic element in all the formations of topical significance. Thus, even in the course of a detailed study of various types of supra-sentential constructions, the linguist comes to the confirmation of the classical truth that the two basic units of language are the word and the sentence: the word as a unit of nomination, the sentence as a unit of predication. And it is through combining different sentence-predications that topical reflections of reality are achieved in all the numerous forms of lingual communication.

# A LIST OF SELECTED BIBLIOGRAPHY

*Александрова О.В.* Проблемы экспрессивного синтаксиса.- М., 1984.

*Андреева К.А.* Функционально-семантические типы текста.- Тюмень, 1989.

*Арутюнова Н.Д.* Предложение и его смысл: логико-семантические проблемы.- М., 1969.

*Ахманова О.С., Микаэлян Г.Б.* Современные синтаксические теории.- М., 1963.

*Бархударов Л.С.* Структура простого предложения современного английского языка.- М., 1966.

*Бархударов Л.С.* Очерки по морфологии современного английского языка.- М., 1975.

*Бархударов Л.С., Штелинг Д.А.* Грамматика английского языка.- М., 1973.

*Блох М.Я.* Вопросы изучения грамматического строя языка.- М., 1976.

*Блох М.Я.* Теоретические основы грамматики.- М., 1999.

*Блох М.Я.* Диктемная теория текста и лингвистическая практика.//Научные труды МПГУ. Сер. Гуманитарные науки.- М., 1999.

*Блох М.Я., Поляков С.М.* Строй диалогической речи.- М., 1992.

*Блумфилд Л.* Язык.- М., 1968.

*Богданов В.В.* Семантико-синтаксическая организация предложения.- Л., 1977.

*Бондарко А.В.* Принципы функциональной грамматики и вопросы аспектологии.- Л., 1983.

*Бурлакова В.В.* Основы структуры словосочетания в современном английском языке.- Л., 1975.

*Бурлакова В.В.* Синтаксические структуры современного английского языка.- М., 1984.

*Вейхман Г.А.* Новое в английской грамматике.- М., 1990.

*Власова Ю.Н.* Синонимия синтаксических конструкций в современном английском языке.- Ростов-на-Дону, 1981.

364

**Вопросы оптимизации естественных коммуникативных систем.** Сб./Отв. ред. Ахманова О.С. – М., 1977.

*Воронцова Г.Н.* Очерки по грамматике английского языка. – М., 1960.

*Гальперин И.Р.* Текст как объект лингвистического исследования. – М., 1981.

*Гвишиани Н.Б.* Язык научного общения (Вопросы методологии). – М., 1986.

*Долгова О.В.* Синтаксис как наука о построении речи. – М., 1980.

*Жигадло В.В., Иванова И.П., Иофик Л.Л.* Современный английский язык. – М., 1956.

*Есперсен О.* Философия грамматики. – М., 1958.

*Звегинцев В.А.* Предложение и его отношение к языку и речи. – М., 1976.

*Золотова Г.А.* Коммуникативные аспекты русского синтаксиса. – М., 1982.

*Иванова И.П., Бурлакова В.В., Почепцов Г.Г.* Теоретическая грамматика современного английского языка. – М., 1981.

*Иофик Л.Л.* Сложное предложение в новоанглийском языке. – Л., 1968.

*Иртеньева Н.Ф.* Грамматика современного английского языка (Теоретический курс). – М., 1956.

*Кобрина Н.А., Корнеева Е.А., Оссовская М.И., Гузеева К.А.* Грамматика английского языка. Синтаксис. – М., 1986.

*Колшанский Г.В.* Коммуникативная функция и структура языка. – М., 1984.

*Корнеева Е.А., Кобрина Н.А., Гузеева К.А., Оссовская М.И.,* Пособие по морфологии современного английского языка. – М., 1974.

*Кубрякова Е.С.* Части речи в ономасиологическом освещении. – М., 1978.

*Кубрякова Е.С.* Коммуникативный аспект речевой деятельности. – М., 1986.

*Кухаренко В.А.* Интерпретация текста. – М., 1988.

*Лайонз Дж.* Введение в теоретическую лингвистику. – М., 1978.

*Мороховская Э.Я.* Основы теоретической грамматики английского языка. – Киев, 1984.

*Москальская О.И.* Грамматика текста. – М., 1981.

*Мухин А.М.* Синтаксемный анализ и проблема уровней языка. – Л., 1980.

*Мухин А.М.* Системные отношения переходных глагольных лексем. – Л., 1987.

*Падучева Е.В.* Высказывание и его соотнесенность с действительностью. – М., 1985.

*Пешковский А.М.* Русский синтаксис в научном освещении. – М., 1938.

*Плоткин В.Я.* Грамматические системы в английском языке. – Кишинев, 1975.

*Плоткин В.Я.* Строй английского языка. – М., 1989.

*Почепцов Г.Г.* Конструктивный анализ структуры предложения. – Киев, 1971.

*Почепцов Г.Г.* Синтагматика английского слова. – Киев, 1976.

*Скребнев Ю.М.* Введение в коллоквиалистику. – Саратов, 1985.

*Слюсарева Н.А.* Проблемы функционального синтаксиса современного английского языка. – М., 1981.

*Слюсарева Н.А.* Проблемы функциональной морфологии современного английского языка. – М., 1986.

*Смирницкий А.И.* Синтаксис английского языка. – М., 1957.

*Смирницкий А.И.* Морфология английского языка. – М., 1959.

Спорные вопросы английской грамматики. Сб./Отв. ред. Бурлакова В.В. – Л., 1988.

*Старикова Е.Н.* Имплицитная предикативность в современном английском языке. – Киев, 1974.

*Стеблин-Каменский М.И.* Спорное в языкознании. – Л., 1974.

Структурный синтаксис английского языка./Отв. ред. Иофик Л.Л. – Л., 1981.

*Телия В.Н.* Коннотативный аспект семантики номинативных единиц. – М., 1986.

Теоретическая грамматика английского языка./Отв. ред. Бурлакова В.В. – Л., 1983.

*Тер-Минасова С.Г.* Словосочетание в научно-лингвистическом и дидактическом аспектах. – М., 1981.

*Тер-Минасова С.Г.* Синтагматика функциональных стилей и оптимизация преподавания иностранных языков. – М., 1986.

*Трофимова Э.А.* Синтаксические конструкции английской разговорной речи. – Ростов-на-Дону, 1981.

*Тураева З.Я.* Лингвистика текста. – М., 1986.

*Тураева З.Я.* Категория времени. Время грамматическое и время художественное. – М., 1986.

*Уфимцева А.А.* Типы языковых значений. – М., 1986.

Функциональные аспекты слова и предложения. Сб./Отв. ред. Блох М.Я. – М., 1985.

Функциональная семантика синтаксических конструкций. Сб./Отв. ред. Блох М.Я. – М., 1986.

*Хлебникова И.Б.* Оппозиции в морфологии. – М., 1969.

*Хомский Н.* Синтаксические структуры//Новое в лингвистике. Вып. 2/Сост., ред. и вступ. ст. Звегинцев В.А. – М., 1962. – С. 412 – 527.

*Хэррис З.С.* Совместная встречаемость и трансформация в языковой структуре//Новое в лингвистике. Вып. 2/Сост., ред. и вступ. ст. Звегинцев В.А. – М., 1962. – С. 528 – 636.

*Чахоян Л.П.* Синтаксис диалогической речи современного английского языка. – М., 1979.

*Чейф У.Л.* Значение и структура языка. – М., 1975.

*Шевякова Е.Е.* Современный английский язык. – М., 1980.

*Щур Г.С.* Теории поля в лингвистике. – М., 1974.

Язык и наука конца XX века. Сб./Под ред. Ю.С. Степанова.- М., 1995.

*Akhmanova O. e.a.* Syntax: Theory and Method.- Moscow, 1972.

*Austin J.L.* How to Do Things with Words? - Oxf., 1962.

*Bach E.* Syntactic Theory.- N.Y., 1974.

*Barry A.K.* English Grammar. Language as Human Behavior.- Prentice Hall, New Jersey, 1998.

*Bolinger D.* Aspects of Language.- N.Y., 1968.

*Bolinger D.* Meaning and Form.- L.- N.Y., 1977.

*Chomsky N.* Aspects of the Theory of Syntax.- Cambr., Mass., 1965.

*Chomsky N.* Language and Mind.- N.Y., 1972.

*Close R.R.* A Reference Grammar for Students of English.- Moscow, 1979.

*Crystal D.* The Cambridge Encyclopedia of Language.- Cambr. e.a., 1988.

*Curme G.O.* English Grammar.- N.Y., 1966.

*Dik S.C.* Studies in Functional Grammar. – Ldn. e.a., 1980.

*Dijk T.A. van.* Text and Context. Explorations in the Semantics and Pragmatics of Discourse. – Ldn. – N.Y., 1980.

*Dressler W.* Einführung in die Textlinguistik. – Tübingen, 1973.

*Fries Ch.C.* The Structure of English. – N.Y., 1952.

*Ganshina M.A., Vasilevskaya N.M.* English Grammar. – Moscow, 1964.

*Gardiner A.H.* The Theory of Speech and Language. – Oxf., 1951.

*Gleason H.A.* An Introduction to Descriptive Linguistics. – N.Y., 1961.

*Halliday M.A.K.* An Introduction to Functional Grammar. – Ldn., 1985.

*Halliday M., Hasan R.* Cohesion in English. – Ldn., 1976.

*Harris Z.S.* String Analysis of Sentence Structure. – The Hague, 1962.

*Hill A.A.* Introduction to Linguistic Structures. – N.Y. – Burlingame, 1958.

*Ilyish B.A.* The Structure of Modern English. – Moscow – Leningrad, 1971.

*Iofik L.L., Chakhoyan L.P.* Readings in the Theory of English Grammar. – Leningrad, 1972.

*Irtenyeva N.F., Barsova O.M., Blokh M.Y., Shapkin A.P.* A Theoretical English Grammar. – Moscow, 1969.

*Jespersen O.* Essentials of English Grammar. – Ldn., 1946.

*Joos M.* The English Verb. Madison – Milwaukee, 1964.

*Khaimovich B.S., Rogovskaya B.I.* A Course in English Grammar. – Moscow, 1967.

*Katz J., Postal P.* An Integrated Theory of Linguistic Descriptions. – Cambr., Mass., 1964.

*Khlebnikova I.B.* Essentials of English Morphology. – Moscow, 1994.

*Kobrina N.A., Korneyeva E.A.* An Outline of Modern English Syntax. – Moscow, 1965.

*Koshevaya I.G.* The Theory of English Grammar. – Moscow, 1982.

*Kruisinga E.A.* A Handbook of Present-Day English. – Groningen, 1932.

*Leech G., Svartvik J.* A Communicative Grammar of English. – Moscow, 1983.

*Lees R.* The Grammar of English Nominalizations. – Indiana, 1963.

*Lyons J.* Language, Meaning and Context. – Bungay, 1981.

*Matthews P.H.* Syntax. – Cambr., 1981.

*Nida E.* Morphology. – Ann Arbor, 1965.

*Palmer F.R.* A Linguistic Study of the English Verb. – Ldn., 1965.

*Palmer F.R.* Semantics. A New Outline. – Moscow, 1982.

*Palombara L.E. Ia.* An Introduction to Grammar: Traditional, Structural, Transformational. – Cambr., Mass., 1976.

*Quirk R., Greenbaum S., Leech G., Svartvik J.* A Comprehensive Grammar of the English Language. – Ldn. – N.Y., 1987.

*Rayevska N.N.* Modern English Grammar. – Kiev, 1967.

*Searle J.R.* Speech Acts (An Essay in the Philosophy of Language). – Cambr., 1969.

*Searle J.R.* Expression and Meaning. – Cambr., 1979.

*Strang B.* Modern English Structure. – Ldn., 1974.

*Sweet H.* A New English Grammar. Logical and Historical. – Oxf., 1900-1903.

*Tesnière L.* Eléments de syntaxe structurale. – Paris, 1959.

*Zandvoort R.W.* A Handbook of English Grammar. – N.Y., 1966.

classes of words: syntactic cl. of w. 41-44

clausalization 277-278

clause 282

cohesion of text 353

combinability: c. of noun 51; c. of verb 94-99; c. of infinitive 102; c. of gerund 105; c. of pres. participle 108; c. of past participle 109; c. of adjective 198; c. of adverb 215

communicative direction 353

communicative purpose 243

communicative sentence types 243-261; cardinal c. s. t. 243-244; intermediary c. s. t. 256-261

complement 95-96

complementive and supplementive verbs: *see* verb subclasses

completive connection: objective c. c. 226-227; qualifying c. c. 228

completivity 96-98

complex balance 306

complex object 103; 108; 110; 274; 334-335

complex sentence 295-323

complex subject 103; 108; 110; 332-333; 335

composite sentence 282-295; 295-351

compound sentence 323-330

concise composition 295

conditional mood: *see* subjunctive mood

conjugation 36-37

conjunction 39; 41; 46; 223; *see also* syndetic connection

conjunctive cumulation 356

connective 41

consecutive mood: *see* subjunctive mood

constant feature category 36; 57

constative 245

constituent parts of language 6

constructional system of syntactic paradigmatics 277-278

contact noun attribute: *see* attribute

continuous (verb-form) 151; 153-159

continuum 20; 115

conversion 85; 116-117; 206; 217

co-occurrence 23

coordinative connection of clauses 289-290; 323-330; marked, unmarked c. c. 327-328; open, closed c. c. 329

coordinative connection of sentence constituents 264; 342

coordinators 326

corpus 23

correlative cumulation 356

corteme 14

countable, uncountable nouns 57-60

cumulation 16; 224; 293-294; 354-362

cumuleme 354; 357; 361; cumuleme-sentence 361; factual, modal, mixed c. 358

## Dd

declarative sentence 243; 248

declension 36-37

deep case 234

deep structure 275; 331

degrees of comparison: of adjectives 207-213; of adverbs 220

deixis (deictic function) 38; 47; 125-126

deletion in transformations: *see* transformational procedures

denoteme 15; 17

derivation history 274

derivational perspective 45

descriptions of language 6

descriptive attribute: *see* attribute

determiner 72-73; 81-82; 83

371

development (category of) 104; 153-160; 170

diachrony: *see* synchrony and diachrony

dialogue speech 353-355

dicteme 17; 359; 360; 362

differential features 28-31

distributional analysis 23-24

distribution: complementary, contrastive, non-contrastive d. 24

*do*-auxiliary 159-160

domination (dominational connection) 225-229; reciprocal d. 225

double predicate 89; 333

### Ee

edited speech 284

elative superlative 209-211

elementary sentence 266-267

elliptical article construction 75

elliptical sentence 268-271

*eme*-term 23

environment 23-24

equipollent opposition 28; 30

equipotent connection 223-224

exclamatory sentence 248

exfixation 26

expanded and unexpanded sentence 267

extreme quality 213

### Ff

field 20

finitude (category of) 86; 101; 133

fluctuant conversive 217

*for-to* infinitive phrase 103

functional expansion in transformations: *see* transformational procedures

functional sentence perspective: *see* actual division of the sentence

functional words 39; 43-44; 46; 275

future tense 124; 138-150

futurity option (category of) 145

### Gg

gender 52-55; formal g. 55

genitive case 61-64; 64-66; 67-70; g. of adverbial 70; g. of agent 68-69; g. of author 69; g. of comparison 69-70; g. of destination 69; g. of dispensed qualification 69; g. of integer 68; g. of patient 69; g. of possessor 68; g. of quantity 70; g. of received qualification 68

gerund 105-107; 112-119; 169

gerundial participle 118

gradual opposition 29

grammatical category 27-31; 35-37; 151-153

grammatical form 27-31

grammatical idiomatism 34-35

grammatical meaning 27

grammatical morphemes 22

grammatical opposition 28; 29-32; 35

grammatical repetition 35

grammatical suffixation: *see* outer inflexion

### Hh

half-gerund 115-119.

head-word (kernel element) 224

hierarchy of levels 14
homonymy 10
hybrid categorial formation 36
hypotaxis 288-289

kernel element: *see* head-word
kernel sentence 274

immanent category 35-36
immediate constituents 264-265
imperative (verb-form) 182-185
imperative mood 182-185; 186
imperative sentence: *see* inducive sentence
imperfect (verb-form) 151-152; 160; 168
incorrect utterances 8-9
indefinite (verb-form) 151; 168; marked
   i. 160
inducive sentence 244; 250-252
inferiority degrees 212-213
infinitive 86; 101-105; 112-114; 156; 169;
   174; marked, unmarked i. 103-104
infixation 26; 32
inflexion 21; inner, outer i. 32-33
informative purpose 353
informative sentence perspective 236
*ing*-form problem 114
insert sentence 295; 332
interjection 39
intermediary phenomena 19; 47; 294
interrogative sentence 252-255
inter-sentential connection 351-353
intonational arrangement in transformations: *see* transformational procedures
inversive sentence 314

language: definition 6
language and speech 11-12
leading clause 326
leading sentence 357
*let* + Infinitive 184-185
letter 14
level of constructions 19
levels of language 14-17
lexemic level 14-15
lexical morphemes 21
lexical paradigm of nomination 44-46
lexicalization of plural 57
lexico-grammatical category 37
limited case 64
limiting attribute: *see* attribute
limitive and unlimitive verbs 93-94; 150;
   157-158; 168; 179
linear expansion 332
"linguistic sentence" 231
link-verb 88; 97
logical accent 242

junctional form 130

macrosystem (supersystem) 11
major syntax 15

objective connection: *see* completive connection

obligatory sentence parts 265-267

obligatory valency 95

oblique and direct mood meaning 180

occurseme 354

occursive connection 353-355

one-axis sentence 268-271

opposition 28-31; 52-53; 56; 78-80; 135-136; 139-140; 151-152; 153; 160-161; 172

oppositional reduction (substitution) 31-32; 58; 59; 60; 92-93; *see also* neutralization; transposition

optional sentence parts 265-267

optional valency 95

organizational function of verb 94

**Pp**

paradigm 13; 28; p. of nomination. 44-46

paradigmatic relations 13

paradigmatic syntax 46; 272-273

paragraph 285; 359-360

parataxis 287-289

parcellation 360-361

parenthesis 262

parenthetical clause 293-294; 319

parsing of sentence 263

participle past (participle II) 109-112; 174

participle present (participle I) 107-109; 114-119; 158; 169

particle 39; 66-67

particle case 67; 72

parts of speech 37-41; criteria of identification 37-38

parts of the sentence 262-265

passive (verb-form) 172-174; p. of action, of state 177-179

passivized and non-passivized verbs: *see* verb subclasses

past tense 135-138

peak of informative perspective 237

perfect (verb-form) 151; 160-170

perfect continuous (verb-form) 164-166; 166-168

performative 245-246

person (category of) 122-132

personal pronouns 70-72

phatic function 298

phoneme 14

phonemic distribution 23

phonemic interchange 26

phonemic level 14

phonological opposition 28-29

phrasalization 277

phrase: stable, free ph. 15; notional, formative ph. 222-223

phrase genitive 64-65

phrasemic level 15

plane of content 9-10; 29

plane of expression 9-10; 29

pleni- and semi-constructions 332

pleni-compounding: *see* semi-compounding

plural: absolute, common pl. 59-60; descriptive pl. 60; discrete pl., pl. of measure 56; multitude pl. 60; repetition pl. 60; set pl. 59

pluralia tantum 59

polar phenomena 19-20

polynomination 15

polypredication 282

polypredicative sentence 261; 282

polysemy 10

positional arrangement in transformations: *see* transformational procedures

positional case 62

positional classes 43

possessive postposition 64-65

segmental morpheme: *see* morpheme types

segmental units 14

segregative complex sentences: *see* monolythic and segregative complex sentences

selectional combinability 51

semantic role 234

seme (semantic feature) 30; 57

semi-bound morpheme 25

semi-clause 332

semi-complex sentence 330-341; identification 330-332

semi-composite sentence 262; 294-295; 330-351

semi-compound sentence 342-351; identification 342-343

semi-compounding: marked, unmarked s.-c. 344; homosyndetic, heterosyndetic s.-c. 348-349; *vs* pleni-compounding 350-351

semi-predication 101; 103; 106; 108-109; 110; 226

sentence (definition) 236

sentence length 283-284

sentence sequence 351-353

sequence of tenses 149-150

sequential clause 326

sequential sentence 357

set plural: *see* plural

sex indicators 54-55

*should* + Infinitive 184

sign 11; 12; 14

signeme 14

significative meaning 14

simple sentence 261-281; identification 261-262; parts of s. s. 262-267; structural types of s. s. 267-271; semantic types of s. s. 271-272

singular: absolute, common s. 57-59

singularia tantum 57

situation-determinant 215

specifiers of names 48

spective mood: *see* subjunctive mood

speech: *see* language and speech

speech acts 245

split infinitive 104

statal verbs: *see* verb subclasses

stative 40; 201-205

stem 22

stipulative mood: *see* subjunctive mood

structural meaning 43

subcategorization 39-40

subclass migration of verbs 99

sub-conjunctives 345

subject 49; 95; 128-132; 225-226; 262

subject clause 303-304

subject sharing 332-333

subjunctive mood (verb-form): spective m. 181-184; modal spective (considerative, desiderative, imperative) m. 184-187; conditional (stipulative, consective) m. 187-194

subordinate clauses 295; 299-323; cl. of classification 299-303; cl. of primary nominal positions 303-308; cl. of secondary nominal positions 308-312; cl. of adverbial positions 312-319

subordination: s. of sentence constituents 262-265; s. of clauses 289-290; obligatory, optional s. 319-322; parallel, consecutive s. 322-323

subordination perspective 323

subordination ranks 262-263

subordinators 301-303

substantivization 48; 205-207

substitute 47; 48; 71-72

substitution in transformations: *see* transformational procedures

substitution testing 43; 74.

substitutional correlation 356-357

substitutional function 46-47

# CONTENTS

*Учебное издание*

**Блох** Марк Яковлевич

**ТЕОРЕТИЧЕСКАЯ ГРАММАТИКА АНГЛИЙСКОГО ЯЗЫКА**

(на английском языке)

Зав. редакцией *Л.И. Кравцова*
Редактор *Л.И. Кравцова*
Художник *К.Э. Семенков*
Художественный редактор *Ю.Э. Иванова*
Технический редактор *Л.А. Овчинникова*
Корректор *З.Ф. Юрескул*

ЛР № 010146 от 25.12.96. Изд. № А-328. Сдано в набор и подп. в печать 27.09.99.
Формат 60x88$^1$/16. Бум. газетн. Гарнитура Таймс. Печать офсетная.
Объем 23,52 усл. печ. л. 23,52 усл. кр.-отт. 25,26 уч.-изд. л.
Тираж 6000 экз. **Заказ № 523**

ГУП издательство «Высшая школа», 101430, Москва, ГСП-4, Неглинная ул., д. 29/14.

Отпечатано в ОАО «Оригинал», 101898, Москва, Центр, Хохловский пер., 7.

ISBN 5-06-003669-3

**Блох М.Я.**
Б 70    Теоретическая грамматика английского языка: Учеб.— 3-е изд., испр.— М.: Высш. шк., 2000.— 381 с.

На перепл.: M.Y. Blokh. A Course in Theoretical English Grammar.

ISBN 5-06-003669-3

В учебнике рассматриваются важнейшие проблемы морфологии и синтаксиса английского языка в свете ведущих принципов современного системного языкознания. Введение в теоретические проблемы грамматики осуществляется на фоне обобщающего описания основ грамматического строя английского языка. Особое внимание уделяется специальным методам научного анализа грамматических явлений и демонстрации исследовательских приемов на конкретном текстовом материале.

Выходит в комплекте с учебником «Теоретические основы грамматики» того же автора.

В 3-м издании (2-е — 1994 г.) переработано «Предисловие» и обновлен «Список литературы».

УДК 802.0
ББК 81.2 Англ

ДЛЯ ЗАМЕТОК